Listen Closely

As Johnson County Speaks
Volume II

Compiled & Edited by
Nancy Tabb, Dolly Fraley and
Jonette Goraj

Listen Closely: As Johnson County Speaks - Volume II, compiled and edited by Nancy Tabb, Dolly Fraley and Jonette Goraj

Cover illustration and design by Steve Rzasa
Book layout by Steve Rzasa
Edited by Nancy Tabb, and Dolly Fraley, and Jonette Goraj

Excerpts from Oral History Interviews
Archived in Johnson County Library, Buffalo, Wyoming

Photos courtesy of the Johnson County Library unless otherwise noted
Front cover photo: Kaycee Mercantile in Kaycee, Wyoming, circa 1910
Back cover photo: Main Street, Buffalo, Wyoming

Page 103 photo: *Bison bison*, Jack Dykinga. This image was released by the Agricultural Research Service, the research agency of the United States Department of Agriculture, with the ID K5680-1.
Page 157 photo: John Fluevog Shoes Distillery Historic District, Toronto, ON. By tsaiproject. Creative Commons Attribution 2.0 Generic licensed.

Published by the Johnson County Library

International Standard Book Number: 979-8990768918

※※※※※※※※※※※※※※※※※※※※※※※

Dedicated to

Patty Myers

*who began our local history archival collection
and gathered many of these oral histories
for the Johnson County Library*

※※※※※※※※※※※※※※※※※※※※※

Table of Contents

Preface

Originally, we did not envision these sketches of long-ago everyday life in Johnson County, Wyoming, in book form. At the beginning, we three collaborators simply wished to create an easy-to-use research index for the more than 350 oral history manuscripts residing in the archives of the Johnson County Library. We recognized these stories as precious mementos of a more and more distant past. Once we dove into the project, we knew that these glimpses of the past are too beautiful to keep to ourselves. The difficult part was choosing which ones to include in these two volumes.

Dolly Fraley, a Johnson County native, originally transcribed most of these interview recordings. Nancy Tabb and Jonette Goraj, although not Johnson County natives, recognized how important the preservation of these entertaining and informative first-person accounts are for present and future generations. We learned so much about Johnson County and the people who have called this wonderful place home from these stories.

We began choosing the stories, verifying that facts are accurate, checking the spelling of names and places, and helping the stories flow. The storytellers became our friends as their voices lived with us through the past three years. It was our goal to make these stories more readable without changing the storyteller's character, the tone of the words, or speech patterns. Soon we became aware that it would not be easy to trim these stories down to just one book, so we are publishing Volumes I and II to include as many stories as possible.

Some of the memories go back to the early days of the Powder River Country. The people recorded on these pages treasured the fact that they were blessed to live at the foot of the Bighorn Mountains. They tell of arriving by wagon, stagecoach, or train and of homesteading, ranching, dry farming, cowboying, sheepherding, and tie hacking. They speak of good times and hard times, often describing the World Wars and the Depression. They tell of dances, brandings, and much needed social times. Their stories show how life was full of love and fear, birth and death, hard work, adventure, relationships, and celebrations.

A few of the people who graciously shared a peek at their personal lives and told of their ancestors are still among us and are valuable sources for local history research questions. They also have shared precious family photos when we could find none in the library collection.

The people who conducted and archived these interviews have indeed given Johnson County a treasure. We thank the interviewers and narrators for gathering these oral histories, and a special thank you to Nancy Jennings, who collected and protected them. Thank you to Sue Myers, Michael Marzec, Nancy Pedro, and Cynthia and Don Twing for a read-through of the manuscript. We also thank the Hoofprints of the Past

Museum, the Jim Gatchell Memorial Museum, the Johnson County Historical Society, and KBBS Radio for sharing manuscripts through the years. For their help in preserving these stories, we also thank the library directors, librarians, and library archive volunteers: Patty Myers, Barbara Fraley, Cynthia Twing, Steve Rzasa, Lindsey Belliveau, Nancy Jennings, Connie Norton, Deb Stoetzel, Megan Herold, Louise Joseph, Cheri Kelly, Denise Marton, and Peggy Skinner. Thank you to Bill Goraj, who image-edited the photos, and to Bob Perry, who answered questions about Kaycee.

Last but not least, to our husbands, who have been very patient and supportive throughout this process and have listened to the many great stories we've told them, probably more than once...Dozier Tabb, Dan Fraley and Bill Goraj...we thank you.

Nancy Tabb, Local History Librarian
Dolly Fraley, Library Archives Volunteer
Jonette Goraj, Library Archives Volunteer

Johnson County Library
Buffalo, Johnson County, Wyoming

Villa Moore Irvine

1896-1984
From an interview with Patty Myers
In 1982, when 86 years old

Ride to Douglas for Ice Cream

Dad [Lee Moore] bought a ranch out of Douglas, and I spent all my childhood on that ranch. We didn't have a school at the ranch, so I boarded 35 miles from the ranch at Douglas. I went to the Douglas School for 10 years. Then I went away to school–Christian College in Columbia, Missouri–in 1911. I didn't mind it at all. Once a week, I'd hire a horse from the livery stable and go for a ride. I stayed there a year, and then I thought I knew enough to get away from there and run a ranch.

I worked for my dad for eight years. I had my own string of horses, and they treated me just like a cowboy. We got along just fine. I helped my mother [Amanda Thomas Moore] a little, but if Mother needed something done, my brothers did it.

Dad started out in cattle way back before I was born. He run cattle out of Douglas. The men who worked for us slept outside on the ground. Later, we built a bunkhouse for them and had a grub house. We were 35 miles from town, and once a year, they brought the food from town that would last a year. Everything was canned then, you know. They bought enough canned goods to last us through the year. Dad would take the list down to the grocery store. He wanted cases and cases and cases.

Cowboys and cattlemen came. We didn't have many women. I never knew many women. There was one lady, a neighbor, Mrs. Wyker, she lived six miles from us. She was the only lady that I knew growing up. Every so often, Mother would dress me up real nice and curl my hair. The night before, Mother would put my hair up in curlers. You've seen those paper curlers? I had 12 curlers when I'd go see Mrs. Wyker. Dad and I would ride the six miles to see her. I was the only girl child in the country. Mrs. Wyker always had a can of soda in the well where she got water. She made root beer. When she knew I was coming, she always had a nice cold root beer for me. That was a great treat.

We never knew about ice cream until after I'd gone to school. Someone I went to school with and stayed all night with in winter–that's where I heard about ice cream and ice cream sundaes. When they first came out, they were quite the treat.

One day, Dad and I were riding, and I'd been talking all day about ice cream sundaes. As we were getting pretty close to home, he asked me, "How would you like to have an ice cream sundae?" I said, "Oh, boy, I sure would!" So he told me, "You catch you a fresh horse, and you go into Douglas and get yourself an ice cream cone. Don't you tell your mother because you'll have to stay all night." It was 35 miles to Douglas. I got me a fresh horse and went to the house and made a little package and put in a clean shirt and some underwear so I could take me a bath when I got to town. Dad told to

1

Mother, "I'm gonna send the kid off for the day, so she won't be back." Mother thought I'd gone to another ranch, but I'd gone to Douglas. I stayed all night and had my bath, got dressed up, and went to the picture show. Then I came home the next day. I was about 7 or 8 years old–wasn't anything to be scared of.

I rode every day with my dad. Early morning, we fixed a lunch to take with us. If Mother fixed a lunch, I always ate it just as I got over the hill. Right away, I got through with my lunch, and that was it. Dad and I would ride all day. Most of the days were a long, long, long day. He'd have me tie my horse up and say, "Now, I'm going on up to the top of the hill and meet Frank (that was my brother). I'll be back. You stay right here." Sometimes he'd be gone for three or four hours. I'd lie down and go to sleep. I'd sleep all that time right with the horse, and everything was fine.

The boys were much older than I was. I was their little sister, but they never called me "little sister" or made fun of me. I had my own string of eight horses. Nobody else rode them. I roped and saddled all my own horses. Nobody else touched them.

We were different from any other ranch that you'll probably ever hear about. My dad run it. He didn't want a foreman, a manager, or anybody. Dad was the boss. His sons worked for him. My mother was in the kitchen, and for years she never had any help at all. She did all the washing by hand. We lived in a log house that I thought was perfectly beautiful. I did just exactly what I wanted to do. I don't think Mother ever corrected me. I think she was the most perfect woman that ever lived.

We never moved the cattle to the mountains in that area. We never did use the mountains. Several years ago, my son, Billy, had a ranch out of Casper, and in the summertime, he had to move the cattle to the mountains. One day, I was helping him, and he said to me, "Boy, wasn't your dad smart not to ever have to do this." Dad just opened the gate–went to the summer pasture. That's all we had to do while here you have to move the cattle miles to get them to the mountains.

※※※※

Shirley Patch Jacob
1939-Present
From an interview with Nancy Tabb
In 2019,when 80 years old

Shirley Thinks Back

My name is Shirley June Patch Jacob. I was born June 30th very early in the morning in the Sheridan Hospital. My parents were living in Dayton, Wyoming, when my mom realized it was time to get to the hospital, so my parents left my older sister, Saralee, with neighbors and drove to Sheridan. The pains were so severe for my mom that she needed to get out and walk for a few minutes on the way to the hospital. Later, when I attended Sheridan College as a freshman, I had my English classes in the same room where I was born–the delivery room. The people of Sheridan wanted a community college, so they were able to convert the hospital into Sheridan College.

The Patch family came from England about 1640. They were very active as patriots–supporters of Independence. About the time of the Civil War, they began moving westward to Iowa and then Nebraska. My dad [Ellis George Patch] was born in 1898 near Broken Bow, Nebraska. His parents, Murray and Sarah Patch, were homesteaders there. The family lived in a sod house with a shingled roof–a step up from having a dirt roof. There was a really bad drought in the 1890s, so the family was having a tough time.

Dad grew up in a time when knowing how to work with horses was very important. But it was a time of change because before long there were automobiles and tractors. He was one the ranchers who learned how to do everything–be a good mechanic. He actually went to a school in Fremont, Nebraska, to learn how to work with motors. He lived long enough to know about people walking on the surface of the moon. He saw tremendous changes.

My mom [Nellie Cook Patch] was born in 1910 in Montana. Her parents were farmers. Clifford Cook was my grandfather, and his wife, Ora's, last name was Hill. I think both of those families came by steamboat up the Missouri and got off at Great Falls.

Mom was a very good student. She skipped a couple grades when she was in elementary school and graduated when she was only 16. The family had a tough time making a go of it in the dry years there in Montana.

In the early 1920s, Clifford Cook got a job helping build the railroad that went south from Buffalo to Casper, so he moved his family to Buffalo, but the railroad had gone broke. They got here and no job. My dad worked for a while at the Gammon TA Ranch for Clarence Gammon, and they became good friends.

I'm not sure of the sequence–whether they worked first for the Gammons or went first to the Veterans' Home. My grandfather was in charge of the dairy herds and the grounds at the Veterans' Home, and, Ora, who was a very good cook, cooked. My mother was paid a little bit for washing the dishes. She was 10 years old at that time, so that must have been 1920.

Anyway, Mom went to Buffalo High School and graduated at 16 and went to Normal School in Laramie for a short time. Then she began teaching out on Johnson Creek. Bob Twing was one of her pupils. Also, the Chesmore family sent their children to that school. Mom taught for about 10 years.

She was in Newcastle when she met my dad. He was working for the Forest Service as a supervisor of the CCC boys. They got married in Rapid City with Clifford and Ora Cook as their witnesses. They kept the marriage quiet because it was during the Depression and community feelings were such that most people thought that there should be only one government job per family.

When World War II happened, federal funding went for the war effort, and the CCC was closed down. That was the end of Dad's government salary. He had homesteaded on Muddy Creek south of Buffalo just as soon he was old enough and built a one-room cabin with logs. His uncle, Walter Patch, Sr., had a saw mill, so Dad helped cut the logs and built his homestead cabin and a granary.

While Dad was working for the CCC, his younger brother, Murray Patch, Jr. lived on Dad's homestead. When Dad's job ended, it meant he needed to go back to the homestead and try farming. Farm and ranch prices were pretty good there, so they moved back. This meant that Uncle Murray and his wife needed to move.

When Dad and Mom moved to the ranch, they built on a fourth room, and that made a rectangle. Then in 1949, when they had five little girls–Saralee, me, Sally, Sherrie, and Kathleen–they raised the roof and added three bedrooms upstairs.

We were good workers. We were a very efficient hay crew. Saralee drove some kind of old vehicle that had a buck rake on its back end. I drove a tractor with a buck rake on the front end, so we would zip out into the hayfield where Dad had cut and raked the alfalfa. With our buck rakes we would scoop up a load of hay and zoom in and unload it on the stacker teeth. We were using an overthrow. They were pulled by our work-horses–Bugs and Baldy.

When I was very small, I drove the team. The horses were well-trained. They knew to walk forward just a certain way and then stop and then back up, so I did nothing but keep the reins from dragging on the ground. Anyway, we girls did what Dad told us, and we did it well. I did like riding with Dad. We had a happy life. We were very shy and had a very sheltered life.

My first year in elementary school Saralee and I had to come to town to a school that has been torn down. For second grade another family moved to the 41 Ranch, so there were enough children to have a school. Then Saralee and I rode horseback four miles each way. You know, that was a great experience.

Oh, Mom was a very good cook. She'd learned from Grandma Cook. She made wonderful bread. We simply didn't have the money to go to town and buy prepared foods. After Grandfather Patch came to live with us, he did a lot of the gardening. A large garden was important. We grew our own beef, and, of course, Dad hunted venison. We always had meat to eat. We had vegetables in the cellar, and we had milk cows for fresh milk. We didn't have refrigeration until 1949. It gave my dad great satisfaction to be able to say, "We've got food to eat."

When we were little, we had bum lambs for 4-H projects. I can remember Mom standing at the sink and filling bottles with nipples with warm milk and calling us girls, "Now, get out there and feed those bum lambs so we can sell them in the fall and have money to go to college."

We had good neighbors. I'll give you the names of some of them. Over on Billy

4

Creek there was a family named Taylor. The dad was Burt Taylor–known as Cac–because he had such a scratchy beard like a cactus. He was a good cowboy. His wife was Effie, and they had three children. The Taylors were good friends. We trusted them, and they trusted us. Cac would kill one of his steers and bring us half. Dad would hang it in sacks from a ridgepole on the house so that no animals could get into it. It would generally freeze pretty solid in the winter. Mom could go out there and cut off some frozen meat for supper. Also, she would can meat in quart jars. That was another way of preserving it. When that meat was used up, Dad would kill one of his animals and share it with the Taylors.

Other neighbors were the Elsom family–Dave and Lila Elsom. Lila and my dad were brother and sister. Also, there was Marshall Herman and his wife, Arta. Up Muddy Creek was Robert Patch. He was my dad's cousin.

I think there was a slight difference based on economics. The 41 Ranch and the TA Ranch and other larger ranchers had a few more resources than we had. I guess you could call my family and the Taylors and the Hermans yeoman ranchers because they were so very self-sufficient and somewhat free of the market economy. Anyway, my dad made a point of never being in debt.

When Murray and Sarah Patch lived here, they attended the Union Congregational Church. I think Dad just thought we couldn't afford to come to town to go to church–that we had to conserve gasoline–but Mom wanted us to understand the basics of the Christian faith, so she contacted a Baptist missionary who had been to Africa and South America. He would come out and visit and bring Sunday school materials that Mom and Effie Taylor used. We had Sunday school in the Billy Creek schoolhouse.

I do remember an unpleasant situation when the minister's wife wanted to come out and do a revival. They arranged it in the evening at this little house. My dad and Cac Taylor and other friends were there, and we girls were there. That lady just preached and raved and shouted, and we all just sat there glued to our benches. None of us came forward to confess or weep at the altar rail–not that there was one at all. It was just totally embarrassing. She got kind of huffy when no one came forward, and I don't think anybody offered any money.

I met my husband at Littleton High School in Colorado where we were teaching. I married Bob Jacob [Robert Jacob] in 1966. He was the son of a man from Lebanon who immigrated to Nebraska. When he turned 18 years old, his parents sent him to the United States. When he immigrated, he was given the last name Jacob. If he had lived, we would've been married 50 years in 2016. He passed away in 2008. We adopted our son, Ryan, when he was 6 weeks old and our daughter, Elaine, when she was 9 weeks old. Now there are lots of grandchildren. Four of the grandchildren are adopted as well.

We had a piano. It was one of my mom's expectations that we all learn to play the piano. Grandfather Murray Patch was a violinist and played for country dances. That was one way of campaigning. You would go to country dances and during a break in fiddling, he'd have a chance to talk to people and ask them for their vote. He was one of two democrats–Grandfather and William Holland–who were elected during the Roosevelt landslide. I don't know if there's been any democrats elected to the state legislature since then. Grandfather was elected as county assessor too.

I have had some interesting turning points in my life. One of those was working at Eatons' Dude Ranch. I think my mom worried that her daughter's horizons were not wide enough, so she encouraged me to apply. She had a friend who worked at the guest ranch. Oh, it was just significant for me. I worked there five summers and got to meet people who were from very, very wealthy families. There was Ruth Pepperell of the Pepperell Sheet Company and Mr. and Mrs. Daniels from U.S. Steel. There were people from the East Coast whose families were extremely wealthy. Almost everybody was just wonderful and polite.

🌿🌿🌿🌿

Beth Brown James
1920-2000
From an interview with Marcy Elton for Hoofprints of the Past Museum*

A Simple Happy Life

We had a very happy life. It was very simple. We made our own enjoyments–our own pleasures, such as riding stick horses for miles and miles and miles and sliding down snowbanks with a scoop shovel because we didn't have a sled. A lot of times in the evenings we would gather around the table with a coal oil lamp, and someone in the family would read to everybody else.

We were very poor. Well, for a long time it seemed like there wasn't any changes during the Depression because we fought desperately to keep ourselves in a good state of mind even though we were going through the Depression and there was a lot of bad things. Still, we had togetherness in the family although my brother and I fought like cats and dogs all the time.

In the evenings, like I said, we would read, and we had an old cast iron Victrola that we wound up. The main spring in it was broke, so you would have to wind it up and then ease the handle back on a cinnamon can to keep the spring wound up. We had records to play, and we would dance together. We really enjoyed that. Sometimes my mother would play the guitar, and I chorded on the organ, and the rest of them would dance. We had to provide all of our own entertainment.

As far as cars were concerned, we had a couple old Model Ts that you could crank all day, and maybe they would start. If they didn't start and you really wanted to go somewhere, you started running the horses to get them in the corrals so you could go in the wagon.

We had no electricity. We had no radios, no telephone. Just visualize yourself living way out in the country with no electricity, no telephone, no TV.

Well, I think probably the biggest change happened when I left home at the age of 13 to go to high school. I worked for my room and board to stay with a family so that I could go to high school. My room and board was all I did get out of it. I took care of children, I done the housework, I done the washing, and I done the ironing. All but one meal, I done the cooking, so I just done all of the work in the house.

*Supported in part by an award from the Wyoming State Historical Records Advisory Board through funding from the National Historical Publications and Records Commission (NHPRC), National Archives and Records Administration. Original recording provided by the Hoofprints of the Past Museum in Kaycee, Wyoming.

❦❦❦❦❦

Millicent "Millie" Grigg James
1891-1986
From an interview with Patty Myers
In 1983, when 91 years old

Millie Tends the Bar

Interviewer Patty Myers: Millie, we've talked a little bit about your original family–the Grigg family. Tell me when they first came to Johnson County.

Well, they come here in 1884 from London, England, right after they were married. They were Alfred and Sarah Jones Grigg. I think my father studied to be a lawyer. I don't know how he come out to this country. He had traveled all over Canada and the United States and everyplace for about eight or nine years. Then he went back and married my mother and brought her over here. They never got back to England. My mother never got back to see any of her folks.

There wasn't hardly anybody around here then. They knowed that the nearest ranch was the Bar C. The Frewens had left there by that time, and there wasn't anybody around hardly.

Where did Alfred Grigg settle?

Do you know where Art Haines' place is now? That's the original homestead that he took up on Middle Fork of Powder River. Mile wide and an inch deep–yeah, that's the Powder River.

My dad, he used to go out and cook on roundups. One time that my dad was away on the roundup, these Indians come in and scared my mother to death. She had my baby brother. He was about 9 months old. She had him sitting in a chair, and an Indian started to pick him up. Mother was scared to death that they'd pick him up and take off with him, so she picked a pan of hot water off the stove and started after him and told him to get out of there. They finally got out, but she was pretty scared.

After they moved to the ranch, Dad built a little cabin, but it didn't have a door on it–just a skin hung up for a door. My dad was away, and he come home, and there was nobody around–bear tracks all around the house, and stuff scattered all over. He was just sure that the bears had got away with Mother. The Bar C was the nearest place, and she was up there. They'd come down and got her and took her up there–her and the children. She stayed up there a few days.

Did your family stay on this homestead all the years that you were growing up?

Yeah. We had a schoolhouse right across our hill from our ranch. We had to walk most of the time, but sometimes Mother or Dad would hitch up the team and take us.

I wore long skirts–great big, three or four petticoats with ruffles on them. They had to be hemstitched. My mother was a wonderful seamstress. I think she was in a seamstress store before she come out here. She made all of our clothes when we were little. Our shoes were heavy ones. I can remember my dad went to Omaha once and brought all of us kids some shoes. Of course, we had to wear them whether they fit or not. We hobbled around in them shoes.

What made your dad give up his homestead and have the Grigg Hotel?

He bought it from a Mrs. Ghant. It was a two-story frame building with 14 or 15 rooms upstairs. They were there for years. They didn't have a high school here then, and they wouldn't let me go away to school. They needed my help in the hotel. Mother did the cooking part of the time. When we could get help, we did, but us girls used to do a lot of it too. We had to work.

They had a post office up at the ranch for quite a while–the Grigg Post Office. Dad brought that down. I don't know why he ever bought the hotel.

When did you get married?

In November 1908. He [William "Bill" James] boarded at the hotel. I was 16 and going with Alec Cunningham, but my dad wouldn't let me go with him because he drank quite a bit, so I started going with Bill. They liked him, so when he told them we were going to get married, Dad said to me, "Now, I'm certain you're too young to get married, but I can't very well do anything about it. But I want you to know you're just jumping out of the frying pan and into the fire." Bill was about 18 years older than I was.

Bill had a little cabin on the alley out in the back of the Capitol Bar that he owned–what they call the goat house now. That's the first house that we had after we was married. I expect it's one of the oldest buildings in Kaycee. There wasn't any buildings out that way at all. Bill had the saloon until Prohibition.

He had sheep before he had the saloon. He had a 160 acres out there on Wall Creek. That hard winter, everybody lost pretty near all their sheep, and he lost about all of them. That was the year my first baby was born. He didn't want me to stay here by myself, so he took me to Buffalo. They didn't have no hospital up there then, but they took in patients. He got the doctor and nurse, and said they'd look after me.

Did you stay at somebody's house?

Yes, Johnny Jones' home. The doctor told me if I started having pains to call somebody, but I didn't. I laid there all night and thought I had a stomachache. In the morning, it was too late to do anything. The baby was turned the wrong way, so the doctor had to take it with his instruments. Of course, nowadays they'd probably perform a Cesarean operation. The baby lived only a month.

After about two months, I was able to return to Kaycee. I was crippled up. The doctor told Bill I'd never walk again. Well, I was paralyzed on the whole side of my face clear down. Well, I made up my mind that I wasn't going to lay in that bed the rest of my life. I'd keep a-trying and trying and trying to get up. My mother and sister would come and help me. I'd finally get up and take a few steps. I was in a wheelchair quite a while. Finally, I got over it though. This sciatic nerve still bothers me.

The hardware store burned down–about 1937 I think it was. Then Bill went back into the bar after they'd done away with Prohibition. We run both the hardware store and the bar for a longtime. But after Bill started losing his health I–this is funny–I wanted to help him out. I told him, "Why don't you let me come over and help you?" Before, he never let me in the bar or anything. So one day, he said, "If you want to tend bar, come in here, and you're going to tend bar," and he just walked out. He never told me anything. I didn't know the prices. I didn't know what there was or nothing.

Well, he was just playing a joke on me! He was always playing jokes on me. He went around town and told everybody to go in the bar and order all the fancy drinks that they could think of. So there was a couple of strangers that were in there. I think they was drinking beer, and they walked out. Bill was standing outside listening to it all. One of these guys said, "That's the damnedest Manhattan that I ever saw."

There was a dance at the bar one night, and we were awful busy. A young fellow came running through there, and he says, "Millie, fix me up a screwdriver." Well, I never thought about what a screwdriver was, and I went and hunted him up a screwdriver, like you'd find in a hardware store. I didn't know it's a drink. They like to laughed their heads off.

Let me tell you about when I got a new Studebaker. Bill, he'd been to Buffalo, but I never thought about getting a car. I never asked for one or nothing. These two guys from Buffalo–one was Reddy White–drove up to the door here one day. "Millie, come out here. We got something to show you." So I went out there, and they told me, "Get in this car. We want you to take a ride." I said, "I can't do it. I've got the kids here, and I can't go and leave them." "Well, bring them along. We'll take them too." So they put them kids in the car, and we started out. They got up here about six miles, and Reddy White stopped the car and said to me, "Now, you get over here and drive this car." I

9

told him, "Well, I'm not going to drive this car. I never drove a car in my life." Well, he told me, "I'll tell you how. You come over here and drive it." I said, "Well, you're taking your life in your own hands. I've never drove a car in my life."

Well, I finally let them talk me into it. I got behind the wheel of the car to drive it. But, you know, those Studebakers–they go awful fast. He told me how to press down on the pedals and make it go. I was going so fast I must have been going about 100 miles per hour, and he told me, "Hey, lift your foot up! Lift your foot up!" I finally got back around the house here, and I said, "How do you stop it?" because I didn't know how to stop the car. Well, he stopped it for me. Then he said, "Well, here's the keys. It's your car." Oh, I like to fell over! I didn't know Bill was even thinking about getting me a car. You know, Bill never did drive a car. I drove it all the time.

Another question I want to ask you is about people's feelings over the Cattle War–the Invasion. You said your father was really lucky not to be involved in the Invasion. When you were growing up, can you remember any angers flaring up because of the Cattle War?

Well, I have heard them talking about this war. And they come and give Bill Deane a warning that if he didn't get out of the country, they were going to kill him. But he says, "I'll be right here." He wouldn't leave. He stayed right there.

It was several years after that, that I was old enough to remember about it. Bill Deane was a United States deputy or something. He was sent in there to get some of these outlaws. These Curry boys said they were going to kill him. Well, this Bill Deane stayed at our place quite a bit.

One day, my mother looked out and saw coming across the plains out there two guys coming up to the house. She seen who it was, so she made us kids go down into the cellar and stay there. She knew there'd probably be some shooting. We could see the window over the top of the cellar door, so we looked in there. They called these guys the Curry boys. One of them went to the front door, and the other came to the kitchen door in the back, and he just raised his gun to shoot. My mother grabbed his gun, and the shot went wild. By that time, my dad and this Bill Deane got their guns– they always kept them handy–and made them get out of there. So after this happened, this Bill Deane said he wouldn't stay there and put our lives in danger anymore. He'd leave.

But, you know, that night they killed him up here above the old Kaltenbach place. They laid for him and killed him. The Curry boys belonged to that outlaw gang–the Hole-in-the-Wall gang. They were very hardened criminals.

A lot of this happened before I was old enough to remember very much, but I can remember Tom Horn. He used to come up to our place and stay quite a bit. He was awfully nice to us kids and my folks. He was just as nice as he could be. Tom Horn was supposed to have killed this boy, you know.

Was that the crime that Tom Horn was caught for?

But everybody says he didn't do that. I remember him. Us kids used to be crazy about him. He'd bring us candy and stuff, and he played with us kids when we were young.

❦❦❦❦❦

Charles H. "Harold" Jarrard
1919-2018
From an interview with Sandy Dixon for Hoofprints of the Past Museum*
In 2000, when 81 years old

On the Way to a Dance

Henry Mayor was a good friend of mine. Anyway, I was in town, and he had an old Chevy car with a turtleback. The back come up so two or three people could ride back there. He said, "Let's go to Sussex to the dance." That was when this road was first built and was just a dirt road. I got in with him, and we headed for the dance.It was dark, and he's going along about 50 miles an hour down there, and there were a bunch of horses right in the middle of the road. There was no way to miss them, and he just hit this big horse. It was about a 3-year-old workhorse colt and weighed between 1,500 to 1,600 pounds. We hit it, and it went right up over the top of the car and lit in the turtleback. This car, it just went plumb to the ground and couldn't stop. It just bounced along like that, and I thought we was killed. Anyway, we finally got stopped, and Henry said, "This horse is deader than a hammer." It never hit the front end of the car. There wasn't a light knocked out or nothing. The windshield–the horse never touched it. He went right on over it. If he had lit on it, he would have come right through the windshield.

Anyway, he's lying in there with his back down and all four feet sticking up, and his head was laying over to the side. He never ever kicked. We got out, and no prob-lem–we will just tip him out of here. We got up over him and couldn't even lift one leg let alone get him out of there. He kept settling down in that turtleback. So Henry said, "Now what are we going to do?"

"Well," I said, "Ed Beebe–I know he's not home, and he's got a chain hoist hanging in a tree down there. If we can haul this animal down there, we will just hoist him up." So we finally get down there, and we hooked the chain hoist on one front leg and pulled him up out of there. He's up there, and we just went to the dance.

Next morning Ed was home. He looked out and sees this horse hanging on his tree. There is enough Indian in Ed that he is just running up and down the road, looking for tracks in a little skiff of snow. I never did tell him. I don't know whose horse it was.

*Supported in part by an award from the Wyoming State Historical Records Advisory Board through funding from the National Historical Publications and Records Commission (NHPRC), National Archives and Records Administration. Original recording provided by the Hoofprints of the Past Museum in Kaycee, Wyoming.

✿✿✿✿

Mary Elgin Jarrard
1892-1957
From an interview with Mary Van Auken

Country School Life

My father, Walter Elgin, built the first schoolhouse and furnished the heat and water and lights–kerosene lamps. The school board hired the teacher. She came and stayed in the schoolhouse and taught in that same room. She didn't get along very well with my older brothers. I don't know why, but, anyhow, she finally left. I was 10 years old the fall when I started, so that made me pretty old to be starting school. However, I started to read in the third grade reader.

The next school I went to was at Klondike. The building was a frame building. We had a big potbellied stove in one corner that furnished the heat and burned wood and coal. It was a big one-room building. We had wooden desks and outside toilets. It was lighted by kerosene lamps. Mrs. Bessie Bullis was my teacher there. I really believe she was the most wonderful teacher. She would not let us come to the stove to get warm because that made your feet and hands too tender. When you came in, you could stomp around or do anything you wanted to but not go to the stove. She seemed to always have time for anything you wanted. You joined any class that you were capable of keeping up with. She made history live, especially the Revolutionary War. She started this school each day with a prayer. I don't remember that we had any flag ceremony. She was interested in every youngster, and she gave us real pep talks about keeping our honor bright, and I think it had a big effect on the children that went to school to her. Well, she would have us learn those poems, like "Paul Revere's Ride," and, you know, you just took that ride yourself when she talked about it–all of that early history. Her English class, or what we called grammar then–you pretty near lived those stories that we read and studied.

Mrs. Bullis took pretty good care of discipline. She did whip some children. When she whipped them, they knew that they had been whipped, but it didn't happen often. She talked to us enough that we felt like we knew what was wrong and what was right, and I think it did a lot for us. The teacher was the boss. There was no argument at all there. What she said was law. Nobody thought of treating it any other way.

The students came horseback or walked. Most of them came, oh, at least two and a half or three miles. There was one family that lived right close to the schoolhouse.

There was 36 of us scholars went to that school. They were partly girls who were reviewing so they could pass the teacher's examination. At that time, if you passed the teacher's examination, you could teach. I think you were supposed to be 18 years old although some of them weren't. All you needed was an eighth grade education if you could pass the examination. And those girls, of course, helped a great deal with the younger children.

We organized our own games. I don't think the schoolyard was supervised much by the teacher. She trusted us to have our fun. Of course, there were some fights, and if we got rough enough, she came out and refereed. Otherwise, we played. We played some baseball. We played run-sheep-run and fox and goose when the snow was on.

As a rule, the teacher did the cleaning, but some of the teachers lived so far away that they would hire some of the students to do that. One year, my brother and I batched at the schoolhouse most of the week and went home weekends. I remember it was a very cold building. We never let the heating stove go out, so we were always able to get up and fix breakfast on the heating stove. We mopped the floor once a week and swept and dusted and cleaned the blackboard and carried out the ashes and carried in the coal and wood. We built fires in the morning and carried the water from the creek which wasn't very far off.

The schoolhouse was not only the center of education, but it was the center of all social activities. We had a literary society for one or two years that met at least once a month. Everybody who came would contribute to the program. We had music. People who could sing would sing. It was a big event for us. We all enjoyed it. Dances—I can remember them the best. From the time I was 11 years old on I think we all went to the dances.

High school was harder for me coming in from a country school. For one thing, I was so bashful I was almost afraid to ask a question. Now I had these strangers around me. They weren't the youngsters that I had gone to country school with. And I needed more social life. Oh, I was just miserable the first day. In fact, I don't know whether I would have gone at all if my sister hadn't made arrangements for two other youngsters to come and get me and take me to high school.

I will always be glad that I had the privilege of going to a country school. I think the teacher, of course, had a lot to do with whether the school was good or bad. But I got a lot that I don't believe I would have gotten had I gone to a town school.

I know that high school was harder for me coming in from a country school. For one thing, I was so bashful I was almost afraid to ask a question. But I'm still thankful for my country school education.

Patricia "Pat" Murphy Jarrard
1930-2010
From a Hoofprints of the Past Museum presentation with Sandy Dixon*

Old Time Stories

Interviewer Sandy Dixon: Pat's family, on both sides, was one of the first families that settled in this area. Her grandfather on her mom's side was Hard Winter Davis, Henry Winter Davis. He homesteaded in the Sussex area in 1881.

Hard Winter Davis, Sr. was born in 1857 in Delaware. In April 1883, he married Annie Paynter Marshall, my grandmother. She was born in 1858 in Delaware. Her mother died when she was young, so she was raised by a Negro nanny. I imagine ranch life was quite a contrast to what she was used to in the East. They came to Wyoming and took up residence on the ranch and made their home there for 43 years. Grandfather was a prime mover in the building of the Sahara Ditch, one of the largest irrigation projects in this country at that time. He also served in the first legislature established when Wyoming became a state.

Where was the house?

It was across the river from where it is now. Mom [Madeline Davis Murphy] used to tell about when they would ride horseback to the dances at Sussex or Kaycee. She said in the spring when the river was flooding, it was pretty scary getting back across that river. The river finally washed under the corner of the house, so they had to move it. They moved it on the ice with a team of mules–skidded it across the ice.

How many kids did they have?

They had seven–Henry Winter "Winn," Frances Analena "Dolly," William Everett, Mark Jay, Dorothy Belle, Madeline Marshall, and Frank Robbins.

Aunt Dolly married Mart Tisdale in 1917. He was Johnson County sheriff for 16 years. One time, he was taking a prisoner to Rawlins, and he didn't have to have a guard with him. Things were different then. The roads were real bad. It was real icy down around Teapot Dome. He rolled the car, and it broke Uncle Mart's neck. The prisoner wasn't hurt and got help.

Before Mother was married, she and Aunt Dorothy and Aunt Dolly had a dude lodge up on Baby Wagon. They called it Maybelle Lodge. I'm not sure what a money-making enterprise it was, but it was a good excuse for them to spend the summers on the mountain. She said they would stay every year into the fall until they couldn't keep the horses up there anymore. The horses knew whether a storm was coming, and they wanted to come off. They had one big cabin. They used to fish up above timberline. They would ride up there. Before we moved to California, Mother wouldn't leave without going back up to see that. I remember I thought it was an awful long walk in there just to see that log cabin. The Forest Service burned it down. After they leave it for so many years, then they burn it.

What part did Hard Winter Davis play in the Johnson County Cattle War?

Spectacle Ranch House
Hard Winter Davis' Home

Well, I think he started out with the ranchers, but after they killed John Tisdale, he didn't think there needed to be any bloodshed, and he, as I understand it, quit them at the TTT Ranch. He didn't approve of them shipping the Invaders in either, and they were after him. I was always told that there was a noose hung in the tree in front of the house to warn him. He left the country and was gone for a year. My grandmother went back to Milford, Delaware, to her family. Anyway, he didn't think they needed to kill anybody.

When your Aunt Dolly married Mart Tisdale, was there much of a tiff over that?

Yeah, they threatened to disown her.

Your dad was Waugh Murphy.

The Murphys were living in Chicago at the time of the Chicago fire in 1871, and, I suppose, were burned out. They left there right after that fire and went to Nebraska and took up a homestead. When they came to Wyoming, my granddad brought an old Norwegian with him. My dad told me that he built the log cabin on his homestead. When I came back to Wyoming and worked out at the TTT for Uncle Mart, Mrs. King told me that the house had been two separate houses. The big house on the TTT–they took those logs from my grandfather's cabin and connected the two houses. She said that the builder that did it for him told him those were the most beautifully hewn logs that he had ever seen. They made a great huge living room that connected the other two parts of the house. She had no electricity.

Frank Hinckley tape recorded Pat's dad. Pat will read some of the stories that her dad told. One of the stories was about Hard Winter Davis when he first came into this country.

Dad said that the 76 Ranch had a cow-calf operation down where the old Spectacle Ranch was right down by that big bend in the river. I'm quoting Dad. He said, "Hesse told me about the first four-horse team he ever drove. Fort Reno was still in existence down there, and they didn't know that Hard Winter had set up camp up where he was. He had some red underwear. I suppose he got lousy. Everybody else did. Anyway, he was going to wash his underwear. He washed them and hung them out on the willows to dry. One of the 76 Ranch cowboys saw them, and he thought, 'Well, the Indians used to camp there quite a lot.' He thought the Indians were going on the war path. He galloped down there to the 76 camp. I don't know who the boss was, but he told Hesse to drive the team, and Hesse said he had never driven a four-horse team–didn't know a thing in the world about it. He said there was a man alongside each horse just a-whipping the heck out of them, and he was sitting up there just holding the lines. He said they never paid any attention to sagebrush, washes, or anything else. He said that was the wildest ride that anybody ever took, and he remembered that the only thing they got to the fort with in that wagon was down under the box. Well, they got down there, and whoever's command it was, he sent out a detachment of soldiers to meet these Indians. They said they rode clear up there, and everything was quiet and nice where this red underwear was hanging."

Did your dad ever tell any stories about when he was a boy in Nebraska?

Yeah, about the fire. That was a great place for prairie fires. The railroad company fired with coal then. I don't suppose they had spark arresters in those days. He said those sparks would fly out there and set that big old bushy grass afire, and the wind blew like a hurricane all the time. They had a colt barn. It would have held 25 or 30 colts. There was a stack of hay the length of that barn. It was just a single barn, just one stall right after the other. He told us, "Charlie Ford's family was staying with us. We knew there was a prairie fire in the country. We had smelled smoke for several days, but we couldn't tell where it was. The air was just full of smoke. On the 7th of April it was the Ford kids, six of us, and my mother. My mother wanted Charlie Ford to go down and get two teams. She said she knew the fire must be getting close. I remember we had the two-story house, and we were all in the upstairs of that house, looking out the window to the west. My mother tried to get Charlie Ford and my brother to go hitch up two teams, and Charlie Ford told her, 'Naw, we aren't going to have any fire in here.' I can remember it just as well as if it was yesterday. My mother told my brother, 'You go down and hitch up the team anyway.' He got the team hitched up and brought them to the house and tied them to the hitching post and came running in and said, 'The haystack behind the coal barn is on fire.' He and Charlie rushed down and hitched up another team. Well, my mother had taken a lot of the furniture–we had a pretty big garden–she took a lot of bedding, lots of furniture, and stuff and dug a hole down in this garden and buried the stuff. They had done that early in the morning. Everybody had a lot of buffalo robes in those days. I remember they put us kids in those two buggies and turned those buffalo robes upside down with the hair side next to us, and we made a run through that fire and run into the outhouse. It was made out of brick. My father was away. He heard that there was fire, so he came home. I remember we had a wood windmill, and there was just one leg of that windmill tower left. That's the only damn thing left standing on the place after that fire. All we had left was what was buried out in the garden. By god, they went back and built right there again."

Tell about your dad working on the railroad.

About 1904 when he was about 17 or 18, he lied about his age and got a job working on the Union Pacific Railroad. His dad hears about him working on the railroad, and he told them Dad wasn't 21 years old, so the railroad kicked him off. Dad went back to Nebraska. Fred W. Hesse, who was F.G.S. Hesse's son, was going to school in Nebraska. Dad said, "Fred got to lying about this country up here, so I decided to come." He came out in March and worked for F.G.S. Hesse that summer and fall. Dad said, "Then F.G.S. loaned me out to "Daddy" Burnett for the winter."

Dad gathered up 100 head of cattle and 30 or 40 horses and went in with Smith in 1919. The country was in bad shape. It wasn't a profitable venture. Probably nothing at that time was profitable. Finally, in October of 1922, Dad walked out of the outfit with 35¢ in his pocket. He worked in the oilfield for a while for Henry Forker, and then Mart begged him for those ewes, and he made money on them. With the money from those sheep and the money he borrowed, he bought some more of the old ewes from Jim Shepperson. They wintered good and had good lambs and got a good price for the wool and sold those ewes for $2 more than he gave for them.

In 1924, he and Mom were married, and they bought the place from Metcalf. Orange Taylor was there when we were there. Browns lived down there. I'd run away every chance that I got. There was six kids down there, and it was a lot more interesting than it was at home, but Mom had a green willow switch and whipped me on my bare legs all the way home. I wonder how far it was. It was a long way coming back. One of the last times I saw Helen Brown, she was talking about when I ran away once and had told her I could stay all night, so she made us a bed down on the floor for Ruby and I. About that time here came Mom after me. I got whipped a lot of times.

I have to tell one on my dad. During the Depression with the drought and all in the early '30s, one day this woman wanting to sell salvation material came. The Brown kids were all at our house. They always had my cousins in the summertime. All the kids are out in the yard playing, and it was hot and dry with the wind blowing. Dad met this woman at the gate. Of course, we didn't have any money to buy anything anyway. Finally, to get rid of her (she was pretty persistent), he said, "No, I don't believe in God." Then she told him, "You know, Mr. Murphy, with the drought and this Depression and all those children you have, I don't blame you."

*Supported in part by an award from the Wyoming State Historical Records Advisory Board through funding from the National Historical Publications and Records Commission (NHPRC), National Archives and Records Administration. Original recording provided by the Hoofprints of the Past Museum in Kaycee, Wyoming.

Ralph W. Johnson
1933-Present
From an interview with Nancy Tabb
In 2017, when 84 years old

Uncle Norris Shot a Man

I was born on March 14, 1933, at 592 High Street in Buffalo, Wyoming. That was the community hospital–a two-story frame house. I was delivered by Dr. W.J. Knebel. That's where I started. My dad's name was Harry Johnson. Later in life, they added an "M" to his name because there was a Harry Johnson that worked on the locomotive railroad. They traded at the same store, so they put "L" for locomotive and "M" for mechanic. My mom was Nettie Potts–pioneer family who homesteaded in 1894. She came from a big family and was born a mile and a half east of Kaycee.

My dad had no family. His mother died when he was a year old, and he stayed with his dad until he was 10. Evidently, his dad was a tramp coal miner from West Virginia 'cause he tramped a lot of mines. In the 1910 census, my dad was 10 years old, and he was with his dad at Dietz outside of Sheridan, Wyoming. He never seen his dad after he was 10 years old.

The Potts men was blacksmiths. They cut the first logs to build the first building in Kaycee. They had a sawmill and got the logs off EK Mountain. As they wanted to build a blacksmith shop, a man came along and bought the logs and built the first saloon. These are documented–not hand-me-down stories.

Then they came to Buffalo. My grandfather ran a livery stable right straight across from the Occidental Hotel. It was called the Tin Roof Livery Stable. Uncle Jesse [Potts] was a blacksmith. He was across the creek and was washed out in the flood of 1912. That was a bad flood for them days.

Mother was a homemaker until World War II came along. At that time, the laundry at the bridge–that was a laundry and a dry cleaning shop. That was one of four businesses there along on that side. It was called Morrison's Laundry. Barrett had the wash side. Albert Morrison had the dry cleaning side. My mom was a good seamstress, and they had her sew up sheets and pillowcases and mend socks, so she had a pretty good job there. I don't know how much it paid, but it was a job and stayed in operation. What was unique about that was that it had a whistle. Eight o'clock in the morning everybody went to work. Twelve o'clock was dinnertime. One o'clock you're back to work, and 5:00 you go home. The whole town could hear the whistle all the way south.

In 1939, George Howarth ran a wool warehouse, and the railroad was running there. Up on the hill where the houses are, that was a huge B. Gross and Company salvage yard. During the war, they really boomed because scrap iron was $35 or $38 a ton. The railroad would always have a car sitting there for scrap iron 'cause it was the war effort, and everybody was contributing.

The railroad had a coal chute probably down about where the walking path is now. The bridge used to be a swinging bridge. At the coal chute when the coal would spill, we would all go down there and pick up the coal and take it to some widow women. We were all kids, but it was income. The hobos had planted a lot of turnips along the railroad bed.

When the hobos came into my dad's pasture, they didn't know the railroad ended here. Here they are, and there was no place to go. During the war, the gypsies came in two or three times. They just traveled like the hobos. Of course, my mom would say, "Stay away from down there," so that is where I went immediately. They was from Romania. They sang and danced–really happy people. I had never heard castanets before. The women all wore long dresses. Everybody said that if you want to steal anything, wait until the gypsies get here, and you can blame it on them. That was 1942, '43, '44.

One thing I remember that I was really proud of is when I was 14. I killed 654 magpies. We was having a magpie killing contest in the county. I forget how long it took. It was a specified time–probably a month or two. I'd go down the creek. Up in there, there was tons of them. I won a .22 single shot Remington gun that is still in the family.

The 1948 and '49 storm–anybody my age will tell you about both the snow and the wind, but, you know, we never shut the high school down. It was the only time the kids could carry their lunch to school if you was a city kid. Sometimes they let school out to dig sheep out of snowdrifts. We used to have some terrific winters here. I mean cold winters.

My claim to fame is my Uncle Norris Potts shot a man in Kaycee. I know a lot about it because we went to Cheyenne, doing family research, and they brought up his prison record from Rawlins. He is registered in 1902. At that time, Wyoming had two prisons, the state prison and the territorial prison, and they put him in the state prison. The reason they did that was the territorial prison was before Wyoming became a state, and they had wrote no Wyoming state law, so they was pardoning all of those coming out of the territorial one because they had no state laws. They hadn't been judged nor juried, see, so that is why Norris ended up where he did. He was my grandfather's brother. He was a doctor. He doctored in Missoura, and in the early 1900s he came out to doctor my grandmother. He ended up shooting Boxcar Jackson down in Kaycee– love triangle according to the court proceedings. The judge dismissed everybody in the courtroom other than the defendant and prosecution and witness because it was a love triangle, and it was too mean to talk about in the public. Never heard my family talk about it. Course, that side of the family was pretty closed lip about what they talked about.

When we moved to 47 N. Lobban, I was 6 years old. That was my grandparents' house from 1903, but there was so many building liens they couldn't take possession till 1905. They say it was started in 1899, and then the building liens held it up.

That neighborhood–the businesses were on the east side of the street, and all the widow women lived on the west side. The first family that I remember were called Turleys. They were out playing guns, and they had a real one. The gun went off and killed this Turley girl. Then the family moved, and the next one was a German lady by the name of Mrs. Myers. The German lady was really nice. My mom taught German, Latin, and French. When Mrs. Myers got mail that she couldn't read, she would bring it over to Mom, and Mom would read it to her. The next one was a widow woman by the name of Mrs. Eaton, and the next widow was Mrs. West.

My mom was very musical. She played the accordion, the piano, the mandolin, the banjo, the guitar, most of the string instruments. She taught many, many Basco kids how to play the accordion. She had an old quilting frame. She quilted a quilt for every governor who came into office–Republican or Democrat–and she made quilts for all of her grandchildren. We still got them. Nothing came out of my mother's oven that you couldn't eat. Now, there was certain things I didn't like, but you didn't say you don't like it. You ate them anyway. She was a good cook. I'd go down on the creek and kill ducks, and she would roast duck. I mean they would just melt in your mouth.

I met Janet Sackett in first grade the first day of school. We have been married 63 years–June 27, 1954, First Baptist Church. I just got out of the Navy, and she was working for P.G. McCrady at the Big Horn Feed and Seed right next door to my mom. They sort've had a conversation, you know. One day, I walked out, and she was coming out of the store, and I said to her, "Do you want to go to the dance tonight?" We didn't date during high school. That's how I met her. She made me go to Dr. John Knebel's office there on South Main, where her mother was the receptionist, and get on my knee and ask Fannie Sackett if I could marry her daughter, and Fannie said, "Yes."

I was in the Navy a year. My dad was on the draft board, and I got a notice really early. I had just got out of high school. I graduated in 1952. I went and asked the clerk why was I getting a notice so quick, and he said, "You will have to go talk with your dad," so I went and asked my dad, and he said, "I'll tell you why. I am a business man in this town, and nobody is going to say that I kept you out of the service because I was on the draft board." At that time, if you volunteered for the draft, you didn't have to go full-term, but you didn't know what branch you was going to go into. Everybody was getting drafted into the Army, and I got drafted into the Navy. I served in the Gulf of Mexico on an aircraft carrier. I was stationed, basically, in Pensacola, Florida. I didn't see anything good about it. When I wasn't at sea, I was at the Naval Air Station. That was pretty good duty, but it was just duty.

We spent 23 years in Riverton, Wyoming. We moved down there because there was nothing here in Buffalo to support a family of five. I was working for an outfit out of Linch–Stafford Well Service. They moved to Riverton, and I went with them. Then they went back to Linch, and I just stayed in Riverton. Got all my kids through school there.

Then in 1983, I had been up in North Dakota all winter, and I got back to Riverton, and my boss told me he was going to send me back to North Dakota, but I told him I was going to quit. He said, "You can't quit," but I said, "I ain't going to North Dakota," so he said, "Well, we can send you to New Mexico, but you won't like it." I asked, "Why?" He said, "You will die of heatstroke." I said, "I want to try some of that heatstroke," so I stayed down there 30 years. It wasn't that hot there. Where we were at Farmington is in the northwest corner right up in the four corners and close to the mountains. Then it was time to come home.

I always had a job. When we got out of school for the summer, you could go find a job 'cause the ranchers needed help. We picked potatoes and topped beets. We went out to the sheep pens and worked.

The teachers we had was all coming back from World War II. All were officers, and they was strict. Our moms and dads had taught us respect, and they honed it. We really benefited because they took no bluff. Mr. John Driskill, he was a veteran. Then we had Dan Ahern–he was in the Army. We had Mr. George Grace come back. Mr. Grace–we know a lot about him because he was very open to us. He was at the University of Wyoming, and he went into the Air Force and flew B-17s.

I wasn't a renegade, but I was well-known to the city marshal. I was the kid at the end of the tracks, so when they said it was the kid at the end of the tracks, then they knew where to go. Just a typical kid–we never got bored. Oh, no.

My dad used to walk to the post office when I was a kid. They had these great big mailboxes at the bottom. One time, I asked my dad, "What are them for?" and he says, "For old fat men." About that time, Mr. Jim Gatchell walked in, and I thought, "My dad is the smartest man in the world."

I went to the old Carnegie Library. You always took your hat off 'cause the librarian looked right down on you. You come up that step, and when you come in that door, that hat better be off. Absolutely no visiting–never. I mean shhh, you know.

I don't remember Prohibition, but I seen some of the bootleggers later in life. There was a lot of bootleggers in Buffalo. Seems like bootlegging was the way to go. Living next door to the feed store, I had a first cousin that ranched. He had a World War I homestead out south, and every now and then he would come to the feed store and get a sack of corn, and my mom would say, "Look at that. He don't even have a chicken."

You see, we grew up at the best time. We had good teachers. We had the swimming pool–dirt bottom come out of the creek–no filters. Sometimes the fish would come in– sometimes the frogs. We'd spend all summer trying to catch them. There was a muskrat one summer, and every time we got close, he would go back up the culvert so we couldn't get him. I remember Madeline Iberlin, she was a lifeguard. It was 18 feet deep in the deep end, and they had a 20 foot tower. One board was at 11 feet. You'd get up on 18 feet, and the railing was 2 feet high. We'd get up on that railing and cannonball off.

Sometimes you'd get a firecracker under somebody's foot, especially at the Busy Bee Cafe because at the original Busy Bee they had stools. Them people would hook their heels on the rim, and you could sneak in there and get one. It wasn't no little dinky one.

My job at the Occidental Hotel was to empty the spittoons. When they filled up, I would go empty them in the creek. They had all these brass spittoons in front of every room and in the lobby. I couldn't get the ones in the bar, but they would set them outside for me. Well, when it come time to wash them, you just took them down to the creek and dumped it in and sloshed it about.

We had three clothing stores. We had New York Store. We had Penney's across from the New York Store. Right next door to it that was Van Dyke's Clothing. Boy, if you bought a suit from him, you was buying the best. I mean ohhh, yeah! We had five car dealerships. Three funeral homes, so funeral homes had competition, you know. They had salesmen and all. We had three hardware stores. As you go south down South Main Street just before you get to the bridge, there is a street that turns to the left–that was Jess Tullar's Bar. He had bootleg downstairs. The German lady that I was telling you about, she would send me up there every Friday for a pitcher of beer. The pitcher was 10¢. She gave me 12¢ and told me to keep the two pennies.

I remember the depot. You see, the depot was two-story. Today you walk in the door from ground level, so they had to fill that in there. Larry Gray and I used to go upstairs and steal the pigeons. Then we would go down to the creek and cook pigeons. There ain't much to them.

I worked at Skipton and Flynn for Mr. Charles Lawrence. He took a silver dollar and braised a nail. Then he pounded it down into the concrete in a crack in the sidewalk in front of his store. Folks would try to pick it up.

The Johnson County Cattle War caused problems for my uncle, Joe Potts, but it didn't bother us. It was a big thing. The two statues near the First Northern Bank on Main Street tells the whole story. You are either for the brand, or you're living on the edge. That little teeny plaque is all the history you need.

The one that impacted my life is when I was told I better quit drinking. That was good advice, and I have fulfilled that. You know, my dad gave me some advice. He would say, "Never take flowers home to your wife except on her birthday 'cause any other time you take flowers home, she is going to think something is up." He also said, "Never buy her a gift that you plug into the wall or you push on the floor."

We had five children. I think we got 15 grandchildren, 19 great-grandchildren, and we've got three great-great-grandchildren. If asked, "How come so many?" I offhanded just say, "Well, we plowed shallow and planted early, I guess."

🌿🌿🌿🌿🌿

Thomas I. "Tom" Jones
1934-2024
From an interview with Margaret Smith
In 2021, when 87 years old

Life with Horses

Interviewer Margaret Smith: I remember when I was growing up as a little kid going to the rodeos, you guys always had a lot of horses.

Well, we had good horses for a long time and run them right along with the cows. We had three stallions at one time–a buckskin stallion and a paint stallion and a palomino stallion. One spring after we had lived here for a few years, I gathered the horses. I gathered 102 and was two short. I had about 38 Shetlands at that time too.

What did you do with the Shetlands? Did you raise those for ponies for other families?

Yes, I raised them and sold them to other people for their kids, and they got along good with them. But we always told them to handle the Shetlands just like you handle a big horse–don't let him get away with nothing, and it worked out good all except one.

I sold one to–lived right north of Buffalo–and had two little girls. He wouldn't let the little girls in the pen with the Shetland, so they got sticks and started poking him. It finally got so he couldn't even get in the pen with him because he would kick, so he sold that pony to somebody else. I found out about it, so I took him back and gave them another one. They kept that pony for 30 years. If you treat them just like a big horse, you don't have much trouble with them.

What kind of horses did you run? Were they a mix of quarter horse and something else, or did you have purebred quarter horses or thoroughbreds?

We never had many purebred horses. They were all cross–thoroughbreds and quarter horse. Chris Jensen had about 60 mares and brought them down here. Then him and Dad was in partnership with the colts until the drought run us out.

Were you the one that did most of the horse breaking, or did your dad do it?

To start with, Dad done it, and then as I got older, I done it. I don't know how many horses I broke to ride but a lot of them.

Did you have a round corral someplace here that you worked them, or did you have someplace else you worked your horses?

I had a round corral right out here. We worked them there. Round corral was all there was. There wasn't no square corral.

Did you do most of the work by yourself, or did you have hired hands?

I done most of it by myself, but once in a while, I would get somebody to help me, like George Strausser. I guess he was about the only one.

Was all the groundwork done by you, and then somebody else rode them out, or did you do pretty much most of the riding?

Well, I done most of the riding, but after I would get them going good, then George would take them, and he would ride them. He worked here for quite a while.

Do you have any one particular remembrance of any of those horses that you broke that was either hard or just really a lot of fun?

Well, I had a paint gelding, and he was 4 years old. I started riding him in the corral and started up the creek with him. I don't know–something buggered him, and he started bucking, and he bucked the same way we was going. Pretty quick George says, "Hell, you can ride him. You ride him, and I'll do the whipping." That's the way we done things–with a bullwhip. You could hear that bullwhip popping behind me.

🌿🌿🌿🌿

William H. "Bill" Jones, Jr.
1924-2012
From a Hoofprints of the Past Museum presentation*
In 2001, when 77 years old

Shot Down

Presentation Host: Tonight's speaker is Bill Jones. I'm not sure what subject he is going to cover, but he's covered a lot of ground.

First, I'm going to tell you a little about my grandparents on both my parents' sides and a little bit about me. On one side of the family Albert and Julia Brock came out from Versailles, Missouri. My grandfather left there on the 7th of July 1884. He and his brother-in-law came out to Cheyenne by train. They bought horses, bedding, utensils, saddles and rode up to Buffalo and fooled around there and finally staked a homestead south of Buffalo on Kelly Creek. Then they rode back to Cheyenne, where their wives and children were waiting.

Grandfather had a 2-year-old son, who was Elmer Brock. They had a four-horse team, and they went up to the Trabing post east of Buffalo. It took them 10 days to get there from Cheyenne by horse and wagon. They stayed the night there. The man that ran that place was George Harris. He was married to a Cheyenne lady, and they had some half-breed children. My grandmother knew him and just threw this little boy out in the mix with all these other kids. When they got ready to leave, why, she just grabbed the first one she could catch and threw him in the wagon and away they went to Buffalo, so nobody was ever too sure about Elmer after that.

Anyway, they eventually had eight children. My mother was the second from the last of those eight. Grandfather had a tough winter. That first year they slept in a tent on Kelly Creek, and then they finally got the place behind EK Mountain. They went into the cow business and eventually moved over to Mayoworth, where the Brock Livestock Company is now.

During the Johnson County Cattle War, Elmer was out with a little bunch of sheep. He couldn't have been too old. Anyway, they sent his younger sister out to herd the sheep, and the Invaders were there. She gave him the news that these Invaders were in the area, and they were going to go out and shoot or hang every settler in the country, so they hurried back to the house. Elmer was thinking about this and expected to see his dad hanging from the tree, you know. He got back to the house and looked, and he didn't see anything. He was just about halfway disappointed. That's right from the horse's mouth.

Bill Jones & Friends

My dad, William Henry Jones, finished high school in Buffalo. Then he worked around and finally got a job with the Wyoming Railroad–Duffy's Bluff. He worked on that railroad as a fireman and engineer. One of his jobs was to open the gates. The engineer would slow the train down. He would jump out and run ahead and open the gate. Then the train would go through, and he would close the gate and run and catch the train. That was one of his jobs.

When World War I came along, he was the first man in Buffalo to enter the service from here, and he was the last one to get home. The war ended in November in 1918, and he got home on December 5th of 1919. After that, he had a job as the county treasurer. After an agonizing, long range courtship with my mother, Esther Brock, they finally got married. After that, he got a job with the First National Bank, where he worked until the day he died.

My mother, she was always busy. She eventually had five children. I'm the oldest. She was interested in church and music club and played the violin and the choir and Eastern Star and lots of other things. She never had a dull moment in her life. She did learn to drive when she was over 40, but you didn't need to when you lived in Buffalo.

Were you in the service?

I joined the service when I was 18 in 1943 and went to basic training in Texas. I went to aerial gunnery school, and then they sent us up to Pueblo, Colorado, where we joined a B-24 bomber crew. There were 10 of us on that. We trained there. Then they shipped us over to Italy, and that's where the stuff hit the fan, let me tell you. The war was very much on then. I was a ball turret guy. In one of those, there isn't room for a parachute, so you are outside the aircraft. You talk about isolation–times are pretty rough. Sometimes they hit one of those, and they would bring them back to the airport.

I remember one case where they had to wash a guy out with a firehose. So that is what that duty was like. I had 27 missions on that bomber which is quite a few. Then we got shot down over Vienna. I bailed out and was captured and was a prisoner of war for five months.

Were you shot down by ground fire or air fire?

Flak–anti-aircraft. They were running out of fuel. They didn't have many fighters at that time. A couple of our guys got shot down from the same area. We were lucky, but every time they captured a town, they would move more guns to the next target, so the flak was really heavy. That last day I looked up–in fact, that's what saved me. I was in that ball turret underneath, and I looked up ahead. I could see you could walk on that stuff. I thought it was actually another formation of bombers, and they said, "No, that's flak." I'm going to open the door and get that helmet and a parachute. I opened the door and got hit, and the hydraulics went out on that turret. Almost got my foot stuck, but I crawled up and reached for the chute pack.

Did they all get out of the airplane?

All 10 of us did. I had to push one guy out. He was the broom hand and didn't know what was going on, I guess. I put my foot in his back to get him out of there so I could go.

When you got on the ground, did you try to evade them or were they waiting for you?

Oh, yeah, that was standard procedure. I had a map. I have $15 in American currency, and in my escape kit I had dry socks and a locator. I was well-equipped, but we happened to have bad luck. We lit right in an area where there was a training camp for the Luftwaffe. There were soldiers all over the place. They captured all but one of us within 24 hours. The other guy stayed out about three days. Fortunately, nobody got hurt bailing out of there.

Did they take your money and your dry socks?

You bet. I even had a–every soldier had one of these little Bibles to carry in your shirt pocket. When they captured me, there were a lot of civilians. They started searching me, and they pulled that Bible out. That made them mad for some reason. They threw it on the ground, and I got mad. I went over and picked it up and put it back in my pocket. I don't know why it made them so mad.

Were you in a prisoner of war camp in Germany?

Yeah, the camp was in Pomerania, way, way up by the Polish border and Baltic Sea. I don't know why they shipped us up there from Austria, but they did. We took trains, of course. Then for three months we walked all over the stinking thing because the Russians were moving across Poland, and they didn't know what to do with us. Nobody had enough to eat. Everybody had dysentery and lice. The worst, coldest winter they had in Germany in 30 years. We had all that.

What did you do for food?

We didn't. I mean we had maybe a potato a day–a slice of bread. You got in the habit when mealtime came, you would get hungry, and after mealtime you weren't hungry until the next mealtime. You did get yourself used to that. But a bunch of young guys standing around talking at that age–they are usually talking about, guess what? We talked about food. I remember one time this rabbit ran through our little bivouac, and he didn't get very far and also a dog. In another camp, a couple of cats got in the barracks. They didn't last very long, and they were skinny cats. They used to feed us hog scraps. Put it in a big cauldron–that's what they fed us. If they didn't clean it, you were so darn hungry you ate it anyway.

How cold would it get?

It seemed like the sun would never come out. It was just depressing the whole time. When they first captured us, the Red Cross got a package in for everybody–came to us at the interrogation center. I'm not sure they had a full uniform, but they did have overcoats and little wool caps. That's what we had and our uniform. We had GI shoes. There was a lot of frostbite. A lot of people lost their limbs.

You just slept in barns?

Yeah, in straw. With everybody having diarrhea, you can imagine what that was like. You can't explain. It's impossible to explain it unless it was somebody that was with you right there.

Did any of the guys that were on the plane with you end up staying in camp with you?

I wasn't with any of them. Some of them were in the same camps but different compounds. Three of us got together later on during our little hike. We walked, someone was telling me, about 500 miles. We slept in barns. That was the only place they had for us.

Did you have communication with anybody?

Off and on we had a radio. We took it apart during the day. One guy would have a piece and another guy a piece and another guy a piece. We put it together, you know, at a certain time. We had a shortwave radio was how we got the news from BBC.

Did your family know where you were?

They didn't know for three months that I was dead or alive. You couldn't call them. You know when you are all right, but they don't know. That would be pretty hard to take. Well, you can't believe how many of us got shot down. They had camps all over that country. There was 6,000 in camp, and I was the youngest one at 19. I don't know how many got shot down. Our outfit, 15th Air Force, had over 100 some casualties, counting wounded and dead in my own detachment.

Were they pretty mean to you in the prison camp?

Well, yes. When you're confined, the whole thing is really kind of, you know… I saw one guy get roughed up earlier on. It was getting toward the end of the war. They could see the handwriting, so they kind of eased back. In the camp, they had to try to tend to obey the rules of the Geneva Convention, but they didn't pay much attention to that until real late in the war.

Did you know President Roosevelt had died?

Oh, yeah. One of the guards came up and said, "Roosevelt kaput," and I said to him, "So?" I knew he was going to die pretty soon anyway. That was the least of my worries. I didn't give a damn one way or another. The guard, he thought he was going to get my goat.

Did they all come out of the prison camps well and alive?

There was only five of us left that I know of out of 10.

How did you get released?

On the 26th of April about two weeks before the war ended. Our troops had stopped at the Elbe River, so we just walked that river. You could hear the small arms fire, so we just walked through the weeds.

Did the Germans try to stop you?

No, they went with us. They did not want those Russians. They knew they would get something to eat.

After you got out of the prison camp, were you still in the service after the war?

Not very long. I got home in June. They didn't need any of us. The war was over right after D-Day [June 6, 1944]. It took me until October to get out of it.

*Supported in part by an award from the Wyoming State Historical Records Advisory Board through funding from the National Historical Publications and Records Commission (NHPRC), National Archives and Records Administration. Original recording provided by the Hoofprints of the Past Museum in Kaycee, Wyoming.

🌿🌿🌿🌿🌿

Zola Evans Keith
1894-1995
From an interview with Patty Myers
In 1982, when 98 years old

From Oil Wells to Ranching

I'm a native of Illinois. My parents [Bruce and Louella Green Evans] both came from farm families. I worked outside a lot helping my dad a great deal. He was not only a farmer, he was a schoolteacher. He must have taught school for 20 years. I had four sisters and four brothers. We were a close, happy family. I have pleasant memories of my childhood. I just went as far as the junior year in school. Then I took the teacher's examination and got a teacher's certificate. I taught school for a time in Illinois.

Elden Keith and I were married on the 10th of March in 1920. His parents lived about three miles to the west of us. He went to school to my father when my father was teaching at what they called the Number 6 School. That's when I met him. He was a graduate of the Eastern Illinois College and taught school for about five years. He had quit teaching and gone into oilfield work in Kansas for a few years. Then he went to Texas. When we were married, he was working in the oilfield in Desdemona, Texas. We lived there for seven years. That was a booming field, but he was always hoping that he could get into a lease that would provide a lot of oil.

He and an Englishman by the name of Todd had a lease near Easton, Texas. They drilled on this leased land and had two producing wells, but Eldon and Todd didn't get along very well, so he sold his interest to Bill Zindel. Zindel owned a building here where the New York Store is now. I think that was in 1924. Since production was going down on the well, Eldon came to Wyoming to look the situation over and saw that he liked the looks of the country and decided to sell his lease, so we came to Wyoming. He paid so much cash and had a mortgage on this 480 acres.

He knew it was a small ranch. Well, you don't make it on a small ranch in Wyoming. You need farm land and pasture land, and there wasn't too much of either on the 480 acres that he bought.

Since we lived in Texas for seven years, I had made good friends there. I cried when we left. It was just real hard to leave for an unknown part of the country. I really didn't know what to expect. We arrived at the ranch on the 11th of May, 1927. The roads across the country were not paved at that time, so we traveled on dirt roads. I think the first paved road we ran into was from Casper to Midwest.

Oh, we ran into a terrible snowstorm in the western part of Nebraska. The oil companies had put in a one-lane pavement road to haul material for the oil people. The next day after the snowstorm ended we drove as far as Douglas. There were seven or eight cars going to Douglas. We all traveled together and made it through to Douglas. Then next day we came on to Kaycee. The snow, of course, had melted. Travel was pretty slow and muddy. We got as far as Jackrabbit Draw east of Kaycee and got stuck. That was the last straw. I didn't even want to see the ranch. But we heard a motor running off to the west of us. Elden went over there and found a man in a truck on his way to Kaycee, so he took us on into Kaycee, and we spent the night at the Parker Hotel. Eldon went to Diers Garage the next morning, and they pulled the car out–a four-passenger Dodge Sedan. It was a long trip.

The next morning we looked for groceries to take out to the ranch. Sam Gibson had a general merchandise and grocery store. We bought our groceries there. Mr. and Mrs. Gibson had just moved from Casper, and we were their first customers. We bought their first dollar of goods and became good friends.

Then we took off to the ranch in the mud and gumbo. It was a four-bedroom house with a large living room, dining room and kitchen and a porch on the back. It was wood frame, and there was an unfinished basement built of rocks with a dirt floor. Oh, we had lots of storage. It was really lots of room, and I learned to love that house. We were west of Kaycee near Powder River. The river was not further than a quarter of a mile from the house. We used that water when we first came there. We had to haul water in barrels. It just looked like a river of mud flowing. That was my first experience with water pollution! We had to let it settle before we could use it. I just supposed we'd all die from that pollution, but we seem to be a pretty healthy family.

The place had been neglected. I don't know if it had ever been painted. It was covered with a brick tin and was very rustic. First thing, Elden had it painted, which improved it a great deal. The yard was Russian thistles. I couldn't even go out to the clothesline, so we got a lawnmower, and I tried to keep the thistles down. There wasn't much you could do about a yard because we didn't have irrigation that we could turn onto the lawn every time we wanted to water it. There were no trees around the place, but Elden had the men put trees all around the house, and our boys, Lee and Leon, and I hauled water with the barrels on a little sled and kept the trees watered and growing.

Elden had to buy all the machinery and the horses to farm with. He also bought about 60 steers that first spring and leased the pasture to run them on. We were short of range land too. The first year we were there, we had a big rain one day, and the ditch for irrigation washed out, so we had to rebuild it. I cannot remember too well what kind of crops we had that first year, but I know we came out pretty well on the cattle.

We had hired men all the time. There was no bunkhouse on the place, so the men had to sleep in the attic. From the time that we moved to the ranch, oh, I know it was for years we never sat down to the table by ourselves. In all that time, I needed to cook for–it wasn't for just a few. Even in wintertime, there would be two or three men there. One summer, we had 20 people for the duration of the first cutting of hay. I did have a girl helping me, and my brother and his wife came and she helped me. That was the time I cut the tip of my finger off. I almost had blood poisoning. Old Dr. [W.J.] Knebel took care of that. I had to turn the cooking over to my sister-in-law. It seems like when I look back, the most I can remember is all that work. I wasn't used to cooking for so many people, you know.

I think it was about three years after we moved there that we bought the Bob Taylor Ranch–320 acres with a school section and more grazing land. We did get a good alfalfa seed crop that helped us out a lot. The next place we bought was the Bill Embrey place. That was more pasture land.

We had to send the boys to Kaycee for school. They stayed with George and Jennie Fischer the first year they went to school and stayed with Horace Cash one year. After about three years, Elden bought a small building for a school in Midwest, and we established a school out there on the ranch. The teachers boarded with me.

I had a big garden and did a lot of canning. We had a big icebox that we put ice in the top, and it stayed pretty cold. We had to cut our ice and had our own ice house. We kept ice all summer. I made my own butter and bread. I never made bread in my life until I was on the ranch, but I did make good bread.

We were not comfortable during the Depression. We were afraid we were going to lose the ranch. We had purchased more land by that time–the Kirtley Ranch, the Burnell pasture, and two sections from Bill Taylor, the Timmerman Ranch. With our leased land and the school land and all, we had about 13,000 acres. The old ranch was paid off. We didn't owe a cent on it when we left.

I wish I could find some of those sales slips that we had. The cattle were selling for 7¢ or 8¢ a pound. Nobody wanted them. Sheep were being killed. We didn't have sheep, but we had neighbors that did, and they sold them to the government, and the government had them killed.

Naturally, in acquiring the farms around there, we did go into debt, so when the Depression hit, we were just like everybody else. It was hard to get money. We had a federal loan on the old place. They even came out to look the place over, contemplating taking it over. Elden had an insurance policy that he could cash in, so he got the cash from that, and that's what saved our ranch. It was a pretty grim time.

Our sons both liked the ranch. When things were so hard during the war years and their dad and I both had to work so hard–I worked in the hay field too–Elden had written Lee that he thought he'd sell. It was just too much for us, but Lee wrote to us that if we could just hold on, that he and Leon would take it over and run it for us, and that's what they did. I'm very much at home in Wyoming now. We had a happy family life. Elden was a fine man. He was a good father to the children. We were happy.

🌿🌿🌿🌿🌿

Charles H. Kershner
1912-1983
From an interview with Patty Myers
In 1981, when 69 years old

He Worked for Wages

My dad, Harold Kershner, came from Missouri in the 1880s and worked for Cullen Watt. Then he moved to Basin at the Pitchfork Ranch and broke horses. He and some other cowpunchers from Missouri went back to Missouri in a wagon. That's when he married my mother, Ruby, from Illinois. Then he came back out here. She came out later by the train and stagecoach. My dad leased a place from Charlie Canterbury.

I was born there on Bull Creek and have one brother and four sisters. We went to country school–Redmond School for several years. Then we moved to Buffalo and went to high school. Only thing I went to high school for was to play football. Then when I finished football, I stayed to play basketball. Summer I had to work for a living. I couldn't fool around in the summertime.

I just worked for wages all my life. Even after Shirley [Shirley Branaman Kershner] and I were married, I worked for wages. I just paid for what I bought and never bought nothin' unless we could pay for it. I got the logs for the house from Tom Barker. He was going to burn a house down, and I asked him if I could have the logs out of it.

When I was a kid, I was an ice boy. All I did was lead that horse up and back, up and back, unloading those wagons of ice. They got the ice from the ice pond. The ice pond was just south of where the city shop is now. At the time, I think Guy Eschrich and Cleve Beam owned it. They had a big ice house there, and I delivered ice all around town.

Adams and Young had a butcher shop, produce, and everything in their grocery store. They had those big old-time iceboxes. That's where they kept things cold. Adams and Young were two brothers–John Adams and Billy Adams. Ole Billy ran the grocery store, and Ole John Adams hauled coal from the Munkres and Mather Mine. He was pretty hard of hearing. Mr. Richard Young was an early time sheep man. He was with the Scotch Outfit, but he wasn't an active partner. He just had money in it. Them days most of those outfits just settled up once a year. They did a big credit business. I know my dad would get supplies in spring and fall. He'd usually settle up in the fall. When Dad paid up his grocery bill, Ole Billy Adams put in a big sack of candy for us kids. If we ever went to town and went into that store, by gosh, they'd give you a sack of candy. Oh, I can still see them. Billy Adams was a real pleasant kind of man. As I remember, he was heavy set. They done a big business.

The Eschrichs had a butcher shop with an ice house across the alley. That was the old Co-op building. That all used to be corrals and a livery barn. I can't think now who operated that livery barn. Eschrich had clear to the other street.

Oh, I worked for Clifford Cook, and I worked for Old "Daddy" Burnett for about seven years. He owned the 41 Ranch–started that ranch Old "Daddy" did. At one time, he used to run lots of cattle here. He was a fine ole man. I broke horses around the country for different outfits. That's when they used horses. I worked for Otto Jones. I was on the Works Ranch out there for four to five years. Then I worked for Dave Whaley. World War II came along, and I was in the Army. After that, I worked for Artie Morehead for a while. Shirley and I got married while I worked for Artie. Then I went to South Dakota and worked for Ole John Lenahan down on the Pine Ridge Indian Reservation for several years. Then we came back here. Well, I skidded ties up at the mountain lumber camps and sawed logs for the Sourdough Timber Company. It was just another job. If a feller had to just turn back to that way of living tomorrow, it'd be rough because now people don't know how to live like that.

I know there were a lot of stills during Prohibition in Johnson County. Well, it was the only way some folks had to make a living. All those dry farmers down there on Powder River. Bootleg made out of corn. They bought the corn and sugar for the shine. It was the only way they had of making a living. They couldn't raise nothing. Some of them made pretty good moonshine. Some of it wasn't fit to drink. Old Dutch Zortman and Charlie Swan–there had to be a saloon. Harry Austin was a bootlegger. He lived over southwest of the high school–had a place there. He was easy to get hold of because every once in a while he'd show up in jail.

In them days, they used to cook there in the jail too, you know. They were allowed, I think, $1 a day for food. If there was four, five or six of them in there, they'd pool their money. One of them would be the cook. They'd make their grocery list, and the deputy would go to the store and get what they wanted. They worked, by gosh–whatever there was to do–shoveling snow or moving them rocks. They put those guys down there in that creek laying up rocks. I do know the prisoners were down in there laying them.

Mart Tisdale was sheriff in Prohibition days. Old John Stevenson, he was also. Mose Woodside was sheriff too. I think Mart Tisdale took Mose's place. John Stevenson wasn't very well thought of, you know. After he got to be sheriff, he kind of pulled his rank on a lot of people. Mose was a good sheriff. He didn't bother people. Mart Tisdale was a good, fair sheriff. Charlie Market was one of the policemen during Prohibition. I remember that Bill Potts was a policeman part of the time. He made a little moonshine in his day. There were quite a few of them guys they had in the klink there.

The Old Munkres and Mather Mine east of town was the main mine in town for years and years. They hauled it with teams. Rancher and town and all got coal at the mine. Munkres and Mather were early day freighters too, and Old Munkres set up a hardware store.

Buffalo Manufacturing Company–old H.P. Rothwell run that outfit. They had a big generator and made electricity before they went up the creek and put that in. They had a big generator plant up the mountain canyon on Clear Creek with a big water wheel. They generated electricity up there. They had another plant behind the grade school right on the creek bank. They didn't have a paddlewheel in there. They had generators. Well, they had a gasoline or steam motor or something in there that generated the power–wasn't much electricity. I don't know if it was a supplement to the one up the creek or whether it was for emergency or what, but that was their next place of operation. Then they done away with the one up the creek. They just quit using it. Modern times started taking over.

Buffalo was pretty much up town. Used to be wooden sidewalks and steps. Steps would go down, then kinda level off, then there'd be more steps. I can remember when there wasn't any filling stations. Old Jim Lowe used to sell gas, kerosene, oil and fix tires along where the First National Bank is now. He used to have a gas and tire shop in there. He had 50-gallon barrels with pumps for gas and kerosene out there on the sidewalk. That was the first gas station here in town. Then service stations started to spring up. I remember one of the first like they are today was right there on the northwest corner of Fort and Main Streets. I don't know who started it. It had a ramp you drove up on to change oil. There was a trough for wheels to go on–didn't have no pit. You drove up on the thing. That's the first service station I can remember in town.

🌿🌿🌿🌿

Irma Haskell Kirkland
1890-1989
From an interview with Clare Johnson

Looking Back

Interviewer Clare Johnson: Tell me some of your experiences as a homesteader out on Crazy Woman, where you homesteaded.

Well, my husband [Rollie Kirkland] came out here first. He would go down to the hotel and talk to the man down there and visit around. Edwin Burritt was a lawyer, and he told my husband he could locate him on a good piece of ground. It was right in Fred Hesse's pasture. My husband had always wanted to homestead. They put out literature, you know. They want you to buy a lot. There were several people who decided that they'd come out. Some of them proved up and then left. I said that I'd spend four years out there. I wasn't going to sell mine for nothing. You could only get $1 an acre at that time, so I said, "I'm going to keep it," and I've still got it.

The cowpunchers would go through there–maybe have a cup of coffee. Mrs. Canogla lived a mile east. Another couple came out here and homesteaded about half a mile from us, but they'd go back to Nebraska after their seven months were up, but I stayed there four years. I never did leave it.

Buffalo Baseball team

Describe the homestead cabin.

Well, it was one big room with a little kitchen and bedroom sort of together and a pantry on that. Three hundred twenty acres–that's the original. The addition was across the highway. That was 380 over there.

Well, my husband played ball. He'd been a professional ballplayer in Nebraska and Kansas City. He was with the major league teams. Of course, he was a person who had a wonderful personality and made friends easily, so, they gave him the lumber to build our house, and he played ball.

34

What was your means of transportation?

We didn't have any. I got to town on the Fourth of July if some of the neighbors took me in. That's the only time I got to town–once a year.

Did you raise crops?

We didn't have anything. We had good potatoes one year, but that's about all we had. We had chickens–depended on the eggs.

What are some interesting experiences that you had as a homesteader?

Well, the worst thing was when I first come out here. I came out here in January, and the snow was clear up to the horse's stomach. We had an old lumber wagon and had to go clear across country down by the Lott Ranch. That's as far as the train came. When we got here, it was dark, and we went across country to this little homestead shack. It wasn't ours, but that's where my husband was staying. The snow was so high you could just barely see the windows. If there had been a train back, I'd have gone back right then. I never would have stayed out there, I don't think.

In the beginning, I was so homesick my husband sent me to my parents in Nebraska. I went back there, and it was cold. The youngsters had colds all the time we were there. My husband came back in May and asked me, "Well, what's it going to be? Are we going to live in Wyoming, or do you want to stay here? I've got a good job offered me there." George Adams' father had a grocery store there, so I said, "I'm ready to go back!"

How did the prices compare then with today? Can you give an example–maybe the price of flour?

Well, coffee was 50¢ a pound, I think. The thing that I missed the most was fruit. That was hard to get, and, of course, you didn't get to town very often. But flour was quite a lot cheaper than it is now, but I don't remember how much flour was. We had to live on cornmeal because we didn't have potatoes. That's what we lived on and rice.

Can you think of any other experiences as a homesteader that you'd like to tell about?

Well, there is one thing–I went visiting my neighbors, and there was cows in the pastures. My neighbors were scared to death of the cows and rattlesnakes. I wasn't a bit afraid. I would go through them and over them.

The water was so hard I couldn't get used to that. I'd always lived where we had good water. I'd have to wash dishes in the same water two or three times, and we had to put alum in the water to clarify it to drink it.

Sagebrush–you could go out and pick those pieces up, and they just burn like that, you know. Those little old stoves burn everything.

One night there was the worst storm out there I ever saw. I sat right in the middle of the dining room table and held onto the lamp with both hands and had the youngsters in my arms. I was scared to death the shack was going to blow over. I'd never experienced anything like that.

You can look back and just think of the things you went through. It was a wonderful experience in a way. You can see what a woman can do if she makes up her mind–to come out and live in a place like that after you had always lived in the city all your life.

☙☙☙☙

Dr. John A. Knebel
1919-2004
From an interview with Robert J. Springer
In 1994, when 75 years old

Having Fun Making Memories

Interviewer Robert J. Springer: Describe your family when you were growing up.

Well, I come from a family that originally moved out here from Iowa. My father was a physician. He graduated from the University of Iowa in about 1913. After his graduation he moved to a little town called Struble, Iowa, where he practiced medicine for two or three years. He met my mother, Regina Brandt, and they were married within a year or two. He decided he would like to come to Wyoming to obtain some land and a homestead grant. My father and Al Brandt, my grandfather, and my uncles, Henry and Charles Brandt, all came out in an open car and established a homestead 28 miles south of Buffalo, Wyoming. My parents lived on the homestead until obligations were completed. After that, he moved to Buffalo to continue practicing medicine. Grandmother and Grandfather Brandt lived at the homestead for a few years, but as the times were–I mean no one was able to make a living on a homestead–so they all moved to Buffalo.

I had one sister, Phyllis, who was 2 years older. My mother was pregnant at the time they were homesteading. Several years later my mother was pregnant with me. I was delivered March 23, 1919, on the homestead by my father and a nurse who lived over in Nine Mile. My father rode horseback over to get her–Nora Freeman. She came to our homestead house and took care of my mother and I. It was a tar paper shack which was two rooms and was probably about 20 foot long and about 12 foot wide. This was the first home that my mom and dad had in Wyoming–no indoor facilities whatsoever. I can recall my father saying there was hardly enough water to take a bath once a week.

My folks left the homestead when I was about 2 years and moved to Buffalo. He bought a house at 266 E. Bennett St. from Martin Pelloux. It was a small home, but my uncle and grandfather rebuilt the house–made a two-story house out of it–a beautiful place, a big lawn, lots of trees. We lived in that home until we all got our education and moved away. After that, of course, my habitats were various apartments until I built my own home at 171 N. Wyoming Ave., which is about three blocks north of my parents' previous home. Donald and Harold, my brothers, and Joan, my sister, were all born in Buffalo in our original home.

Do you have a favorite memory of a particular place where you lived?

With all my brothers and sisters and parents it was always a very happy and busy home. It was a place where it was a home and not just a house. Everybody's friends could come and stay all night and stay for meals. Everybody was always welcome. Maybe they'd sleep on the couch at night if it got too late after listening to the radio. My mom and dad never objected to the number of kids that were in our house. They always had enough food to give them a good meal and send them on their way the next day. We had a beautiful home surrounded with large cottonwood trees. I was the care-taker of the yard, being the oldest boy. My home life was a very happy life.

What kind of responsibilities did you have as a child?

My primary obligation was to take care of the yard and flowers and trees–get every-thing groomed in perfect condition. As a child, I liked birds–chickens, ducks, pigeons. When I was about 10 years, my father built a real nice chicken house and a big pigeon pen so that I could keep my white king pigeons in there. Those are pigeons that we brought back in a little box when we were visiting our grandparents in Iowa. They mul-tiplied, of course, and I had quite a pigeon collection. Later on, I had a lot of chickens that I raised and sold to the grocery stores when they were spring fryers. Those were my duties primarily. I always took great pride in that because I had a lot of interest in the home and our yard and garden. I don't recall having ever received any pay for my work around the house. It seemed like whenever we needed some money, why, it was always available. My father was always very lenient that way. He'd say, "I think he has earned it," so he would give us our 50¢ to spend on Saturdays to go to the movies or whatever. It seemed like we were never really short of money. I think what is probably most important was the fact that work was always appreciated by my mother and father.

What kinds of pets did you have when you were a child?

When I was quite small, I always had a very favorite dog. It seemed like the dogs lasted about two to three years, and they'd either get run over by a car or get poisoned, and I'd always get another one. As I got a little bit older, it seemed like every spring, why, we always had a bum lamb or two in the yard that were orphaned lambs that was given to us by some of the farmers and ranchers or sheepmen. I always raised those all summer long. I don't recall ever eating them for food. I think we always gave them away at the end of fall. I also had a small pet bald eagle that was given to me. I kept it in a pen at home until it got big enough. It got kinda mean, so I turned that one loose.

One spring, I got a skunk out at the Springer Ranch. It was a baby one about as big as your fist. I found about three or four of those in a den and dug them out–dragged them by their tails so they wouldn't bite–and I carried them all to Buffalo. I begged my father to have one of them operated on so I could keep it as a pet. Well, he refused that vehemently. He made me take the skunks and turn the them loose at the edge of town, but I managed to make arrangements with a boy named Lionel. I left the skunks down at his place in a box 'cause I thought, "I'm gonna come back. I'm gonna get one of those sometime." In the meantime, I went back home and told my father that I had disposed of the skunks, but I still wanted one of them. After haggling and begging for about three or four days, why, he said, "Okay, if you get one of those skunks, I'll have Mike Hakert operate on it and remove the scent bags," so I went back and got the skunk. We took it down to Mike Hakert, and he operated on it with my father. I was down there watching. My father, being a physician, tended to know pretty much how to do that, but he ruptured one of the little scent bags during the procedure. Of course, he had the skunk odor all over him, which created a considerable amount of animosity for about a week between my father and I because he didn't like to have his patients ask him, "Oh, have you been out skunk hunting?" I had that skunk for about two years. It was an ideal pet. It was probably the most impressive pet that I ever had. It lived in the house with us and slept with me. It was just as clean as any house cat. One spring, I presume that nature's call drew the skunk away, and it disappeared. I never was able to find it. That was my most favorite pet.

I had a pair of badgers that Freddie [Fred W.] Hesse gave me. I kept those during one season until they dug up my family's backyard. I also had a baby coyote that one of the ranchers gave me. That didn't last very long. I had some owls and some hawks. One time, I had a goat that I found in town. That didn't last very long 'cause it was too foul smelling. It seemed my father disposed of that.

Who did you play with?

My closest friend was Bill Long. He lived about two blocks over the hill toward the Congregational Church from my home. We became friends as little children. We used to live together about half of the time. We'd trap and hunt together. We went all through grade school and high school together and remained friends until his death several years ago. Incidentally, I delivered all of his children.

Do you remember a particular incident of being punished or rewarded?

Well, I recall one time when we were playing out in the yard, my little brother, Harold, was always teasing us. We were always having fun and fighting. He came running around the back of the house one day, and we decided that we were going to catch him. I had a bicycle tire, and as he came around the house, why, I threw that bicycle tire, and it wrung around his neck like a hoop. It kinda knocked him out. Of course, that really scared everybody. We ran into the house, and Dad come out. By that time, Harold was kinda coming out of it. It sure as hell knocked him out. We did get the razor strap for that incident and a very good lecture about the dangers of that kind of playing.

Where did you go to school?

I went to grade school and high school in Buffalo. My grade school years started out in the old white school building in downtown Buffalo, which has since been destroyed. I went to Creighton University Medical School–pre-med. I was not a very good student nor a very good learner. I didn't take too much interest in school because I was always too busy fighting with my classmates on the playground or playing football. I recall my mother saying, "They just didn't think my dear son, John, was school material." I recall a teacher at the grade school who taught a Manual Training course. I loved woodwork. He had me teaching him how to teach the other kids how to do woodwork. During my practice of medicine when I was taking care of him, he said many times, "Well, John, all the woodwork that I learned for Manual Training I learned from you."

Do you remember any especially unusual or funny occurrences at school?

When I was in the fifth grade, we had a new teacher come to town. Her name was Vee Cooper. I was in her first class. I used to tease her an awful lot, and many times I would be sent to what we call the cloakroom. It seemed like it was about three to four times a week. She'd get her little paddle out and send me out of the room for teasing some of the kids–give me a good spanking on my hand. Sometimes she would even go to the point to where she would send me home with a note saying, "Johnny was obstructing the classes."

What kind of outdoor activities did you enjoy as a child?

I always liked to go fishing. My grandpa, my dad, and I would go fishing a lot. Probably, the most significant outdoor activity was hunting–always had a bug for hunting. When we were children, we would always walk out after school to the Springer Ranch or the Works Ranch and hunt and trap muskrats and skunks. Once in a while, we'd catch a mink. We always had a gun along so that we could bring back a duck or two.

What kind of social activities were there?

We had a real nice big skating rink down at the present ballpark which was flooded and covered about a half a block. In the winter, we went skating with our parents. Every Saturday it was just full of people. There were house parties. My mother used to have Altar Society meetings in our house. I always liked to come home early from school because everybody brought their special desserts and cakes and pies and donuts, which we indulged in very heavily.

Do you have any memories of storms or cold or other unusual weather during your childhood?

Well, one time when we were in grade school, it must have been one of those abundant amounts of snow. On the hill right above our house was an open lot, and there was always great big drifts. We could dig caves back in that snow. We'd have a cave that could be 6 feet tall and back as far as we wanted to dig in that huge snowbank.

I definitely remember the years of drought. That was a horrendous thing along with the Depression. One time, we were going back to Iowa during the drought season. Going through South Dakota, there was absolutely nothing growing as far as grass–very little living on the trees. The dust was so bad it had stacked up against the fences on the highway. There was no place for miles and miles that you couldn't just get out and walk right over the fence on the dirt. There was an abundant amount of grasshoppers and Mormon crickets. They just actually covered the road. As you'd drive down the road, there was a crackling sound when you run over them. It would sound like you're running over peanut shells.

Did you have special or secret places?

There was always some vacant houses around town that we had an idea might be haunted. We would have club meetings in these houses that were theoretically haunted. We'd wander through them and try to spook each other. We always had to have a little hideout. Those hideouts consisted mainly of digging caves in the hills above my folks' house up by the Congregational Church. We would always have one or two of those until one time we were back in the cave, and it caved in on us. It just about suffocated my brother, so we kinda put a stop to the cave business. We had treehouses that we always had as our fort.

Dr. W.J. Knebel

What experience or moment in your childhood had the most impact on you as an adult?

My association with my father, who was a physician. I always liked to go with my dad, and he always kinda liked to have me go with him when we'd make a house call–particularly when we'd make calls out in the country. I was old enough at that time to be quite impressed with his medical practice and his rapport with people–the things that he was doing to help save lives and relieve pain. I used to travel with him an awful lot. It was kinda almost my personal duty to go with him at night if he had to go to Kaycee or Sussex or Barnum. My primary purpose, according to my mother, was to talk to my dad and keep him awake when he'd be driving because he was always pretty tired. He worked pretty much day and night all the time.

Think of the place where you grew up and tell me why is it special.

Well, as I was growing up, I always kinda liked woodworking. There were a couple attic rooms, which were tall enough to stand in and about probably 10x12 foot in dimension. About the fifth grade is when I first got a jigsaw, so I decided I had to have a place to put that. I kind of renovated that attic. My dad put a floor in the attic, and I had my little workshop way off from our bedroom. That was kinda my haven.

When I started doing some taxidermy work about the seventh or eighth grade, I used my mother's fruit room down in the basement to tan my hides and mount my birds and fish. This lasted about three or four years until the folks said my hides were stinking too much, and I had to eliminate that hobby.

Those are the rooms that I specifically remember. Our bedrooms were rooms of activity for all of us boys. That's where we did a lot of our playing. We made little electric chairs which we would activate by an old generator or things out of a telephone. We pounded nails to the seat. We'd invite our friends up and have them sit on the chair. This generator–when they sat down, one of us would start turning the crank on that thing. Of course, that created a lot of fist fights.

🌿🌿🌿🌿🌿

Eva Kaltenbach Knepper
1887-1992
From an interview with Patty Myers
In 1982, when 95 years old

A Life Well Lived

For our move from Missouri to Wyoming we had a big sale–sold everything. My father [John Kaltenbach] sold the cattle and things like that, and he sold the farm. We came to Wyoming by train and stopped in Clearmont the first night. Then we went by a wagon with straw in the bottom of it because it was bitter cold in March. Snow was so deep you couldn't even see a fence post or the road. You hardly knew where you were going. We had four horses on. We came to the Peter Watt place and had dinner there. We stayed the first night in a rock house at a stage stop. I was never so cold in all my life. There was just the bare stone walls covered with a sheeting like they put on log cabins years ago. We slept upstairs, and there was no sign of any heat up there.

We got into Buffalo on the 13th of March 1899. The snow was so deep my uncle, my father's brother George, didn't get in from the ranch that he leased. He came out here in the 1890s sometime and lived down at Kaycee, where he herded sheep. My father was a camp tender for my uncle–gone sometimes longer than a week. He made $45 a month. We stayed in town in this little house on the north of the Occidental Hotel. It belonged to the hotel for a family, so we stayed there and ate at the hotel. We stayed there a whole week before we got out to the country.

Mother [Christina Kaltenbach] was very thrifty. She made every nickel count. She made all of our clothes. Of course, we had a garden in the summertime. She was alone with us quite a long time. I was 11 and helped some, but there isn't an awful lot to do in a little four-room house. We had to get out from under my mother in order for her to work. I took care of the younger children so she could do the cooking. I don't think we were much of a demanding family. We could get along pretty well without having a lot of quarrels. The boys used to get into it once in a while, and Mother would get after them. The boys chopped wood and brought in coal and carried out the ashes. We made our own cottage cheese and butter. We had our own chickens. Mother always took butter and eggs to town every Saturday. We had to buy beef. Although we had some beef, we didn't kill any. Mostly chicken and pigs. I was sewing when I was 5 years old, I think. I remember when Mother would be out, she wouldn't know that I used her sewing machine when I wasn't supposed to. Mother knitted stockings and mittens and things like that. We had a cow and sold milk–5¢ a quart–and delivered it. Mother did the milking because the cow wouldn't tolerate a man coming around her. I don't know if Dad even knew how to milk. I doubt that he could, but Mother was raised on a farm, you see, so she had done all those things. I remember one time when Mother and Dad went away, they had to have somebody milk the cow. Well, George Webber lived next door to us. We knew that he couldn't get in there with the cow without a dress, so he put on one of Mother's skirts so he could go in and milk that cow.

There were absolutely no houses on the outskirts of Buffalo. It was all just hillside. In winter, we used to go in the sleigh all around because the snow was deep. In the summertime, we used to go fishing down the creek because we lived there. There were no sidewalks of any kind except wood walks on Main Street. There were a few stores, but there were always plenty of saloons. They had a hotel building. Pap Myers ran that. We weren't allowed to date until after we were 16, so my father took us to the dances and taught us to waltz and two-step. Then we'd go over to Pap Myers' hotel for our meal at midnight before we went home. Marvelous meals–the most delicious chicken salad and things like that.

When Dad was undersheriff, my sister and I cooked for the prisoners. I often wondered how they thought the fare was because you can imagine two girls of 17 and 15 cooking the meals. Well, somebody had to do it. We were paid for the meals, so that was a way we had a little bit of money but not much because we got maybe only 50¢ or 60¢ a meal. It would be just an ordinary meal–nothing fancy. We could bake biscuits though, and we could bake pies and cakes. We learned to do all those things. Just follow a recipe, and we could make it. Mother taught us a lot of those things.

One time, I rode horseback up to the mountains clear to Onion Gulch. We stopped half way someplace and had dinner at some camp. Then we went down to Mayoworth to a dance at Lou Webb's. Long white dresses, embroidered petticoats, walking around in that red dirt. We used to go to Mayoworth every Fourth of July. We didn't always go horseback. Sometimes we used a buggy. They used to have a whole tub full of fish and a barbecued beef. Everybody brought in cakes and salads and things like that. It was an all-day and all-night affair.

I worked in a dry goods store in Buffalo–The Beehive–beautiful Haviland china and crystal, also some dry goods and dress patterns.

I can't remember exactly when I met my husband [John Knepper]. I think I first met him at a dance here in town. However, I was going with somebody else. Then we started going together, but I was dating him and another fellow at the same time. Of course, I'd date one and then the other. Finally, John said to me one day, "Well, who are you going with?" I told him, "I'll go with the first one to ask me," so he wanted to know if I wanted to go steady, and I told him I didn't mind. I was almost 21, I guess, when I started going steady with John. I was going on 23 when we got married. Maybe we went steady about a year. We married in January of 1910, and Dorothea was born in July 1911. George was born five and half years later.

I never wanted to go anyplace else than Buffalo. We took lots of trips, and I've been lots of places, but I'm always glad to come back here. I never gave happiness a thought. If something had to be done, why worry about it? I've enjoyed my family. They turned out fine. I really don't have anything to complain about.

❧❧❧❧❧

Marguerite "Maggie" Smith Knudson
1908-2003
From a Johnson County Historical Society presentation
Written by Maggie Knudson

Life Along Clear Creek & Powder River

My grandparents were John and Nora Slattery and John and Mary Smith. On my mother's side they emigrated from Ireland. Grandfather Smith was Irish but was born in the United States near Holbrook in Iowa. He had a land grant near Holbrook. This was land that wasn't cleared yet. The government was trying to get the land settled up. There were lots of walnut and oak trees in Iowa then. He was cutting trees for building when one fell on him and killed him.

My father [John Smith] was about 6 months old at the time his father was killed, and he inherited the farm. My dad's mother lived there until she died. This is where all of our family of 10 children was born. I am third from the youngest.

My mother [Honora Smith] was a beautiful seamstress and made all our clothes by hand, some out of flour sacks and made-over clothes that came from Grandma. She

"Victoria Station"
Copps' Clear Creek Ranch House

made many beautiful gowns all by hand, as there were very few sewing machines then. For a little extra money, she kept house for the priest in Holbrook. She sang in the church choir, where she met my father, who also sang in the church choir.

We lived in Iowa until 1915 when my folks bought the Copps Ranch at Charger [now Ucross, Wyoming]. They sold our place in Iowa and came to Wyoming. Dad and brother, Tom, had come in the fall in an emigrant car with my folks' cattle, horses, machinery, furniture, and Model T Ford. In the spring of 1916, Mother and all the rest of us children arrived in Clearmont on the Burlington Wyoming Railway, known locally as Duffy's Bluff. It was built from Clearmont as far as the double crossing but soon went as far as Charger and later was finished to Buffalo. Tom got a job as brakeman. Duffy's would stop at our gate to take on a can of cream and let off or take on passengers.

My dad grew some beautiful crops on the Copps Ranch–mostly wheat, oats, barley, and alfalfa, a big garden and fruit trees and sugar beets. I can remember my dad took loads of wheat to the Kearney Mill to be ground into flour. We stored our year's supply of flour in sacks in an upstairs bedroom of the house to keep it dry and the mice out of it.

Since my brothers, Tom and John, were the oldest in the family, they were grown up and gone from home. Both were in the Army during World War I. That left us eight girls at home. We helped with the work indoors and outdoors. We learned to milk cows, weed the garden, cook, and keep house. I drove a team on a buck rake every summer to put up hay. I especially disliked weeding onions. My mother raised a lot of onions from seed and sold them by the 100-pound sack to Skipton and Flynn Grocery Store in Buffalo. Our chores were to keep all the coal pails and wood boxes filled.

Mother learned to make cheese from a neighboring homesteader, George Maxwell, who had worked in a cheese factory in New York. It was brick cheese and very good. He was very particular about his cheese. He would whitewash the walls and ceiling of the room and had us kids catch some toads to put on the floor to catch any insects. He made frames about 2 or 3 feet off the floor to put the cheese on. He had us kids get wheat straws to lay on the frames to drain the whey off the cheese. He would walk to Buffalo about 18 miles, leading his horse, which we thought was a little bit strange!

I went to school through the ninth grade at Ucross and later finished high school in Buffalo. We had an apartment in the Reamer House on Carrington right behind where

I live now. We used to walk home for lunch, cook it, and walk back in an hour. There was a footbridge across Clear Creek where the Carrington Street bridge is now. Our older sister Nora stayed with me. We baked our own bread. Mother sent in eggs, butter, meat, and so on. On Fridays, we went back home on Duffy's. They would stop and let us off at the gate.

After the hard winter of 1919, we lost the Copps Ranch. During that winter, the cattle died from lack of food and the terrible cold. We shipped in hay from Nebraska, but it was slew grass and had no strength, so the cattle died anyhow.

We bought the 3U Ranch on Powder River from L.F. Johnston. That place had a log house with a dirt roof and was located at the mouth of Kinney Draw. People had found out that hardpan would shed the water, and they used it on the roofs. It turns out that it is really bentonite. Mother wasn't used to dirt roofs and dirt sifting down, so she put up sheets on the ceiling and whitewashed the sheets and log walls to keep out insects. At that time, Powder River had grassy banks, and the buildings were right down on the banks of Powder River.

In 1923, there was a terrible flood on Powder River that washed away most of the buildings–the barn, the shop and pigs and chickens. The jars of canned goods, which were in the cellar, went floating down the river. The folks piled everything on top of the tables that they couldn't take and loaded everything they could in the wagon and went to a neighboring homestead called the Gossick place on higher ground. I was going to high school in Buffalo at the time. Mary was going to school in Buffalo too and borrowed a horse and rode down to see whether the folks were all right. The water got about 3 feet high in the house, and they had to shovel the mud out of the house and clean up the mess.

Several years later, that house finally did cave off into the river, and my folks built another house of cottonwood logs set back about a quarter mile from Powder River. It had a sod roof too. That house was built on the ground–no foundation–and it was pretty hard to keep critters out. One morning when we got up, there was a rattlesnake stretched out on a log behind the kitchen stove where it was nice and warm. Another time I saw a snake crawling over the doorsill into the house.

My senior year of high school I took Normal Training to prepare to teach. Miss Mildred Beck was the instructor. Classes were held at the Occidental Hotel. By going to summer school, I would be qualified to teach that fall, and I got a school on Powder River called the Hollcroft School. This school was located on the east side of the river near where the Lee Hollcroft Ranch is today. The pupils were Delbert, Leo, and Ruby Hollcroft and Bill, Lenore, and Marie Donnafield. There hadn't been school held in that schoolhouse for eight years. The windows were broken out, and it was full of bird nests and dirt. There were no books. There were not enough desks–mostly just chairs. On the first day of school the kids volunteered to go home and get mops and brooms and water and help clean up the school.

The county superintendent was Margaret L. Smith. I got word to her about the books or rather the lack of them, and she sent some down. When she came to visit school, she borrowed a horse at the Crazy Woman Ranch and got one of the cowboys to show her where the river crossing was. It didn't take too many books because all the kids were in the sixth grade except Lenore, who was in the fourth grade. Before I started to teach that school, the Hollcroft kids had crossed the river every day with a boat to go to school at the Crazy Woman Ranch.

I was 16 years old, and I boarded and roomed at Frank and Deena Moore's, going home on Friday nights. There was a man named Brownie Crawford that stayed at Moore's that winter, who was very talented with machinery and electronics. He had read about radios and said he could make one. There were no radios in the country at that time. He did make one that was a piece of wood with tubes and wire. We would sit around the table in the evening–each with one earphone to listen to it. Mostly, we listened to the *Arizona Wranglers*. Ross Whitmire, who had been a Spear Ranch cowboy, would always sing "Strawberry Roan."

Community social life seemed to revolve around the school. The teacher had school programs and usually a dance. Sometimes there were dances in homes where there was a large enough room. Jess Schoonover used to have a dance every now and then at his place on Pumpkin Creek about 40 miles south. Jess was the only one who sent a car so there would be girls at the dance. This car was basically a pickup with the back covered and no endgate, so we were all sick from the exhaust when we got there. We rode horseback to the other dances. We girls were about the only girls in the country. We would start the day before and dance all night. A man by the name of Harv Mooney was a fiddler and would play all night for the collection. Sometimes he would only get $5. We would take a cake or sandwiches to eat at midnight. If there was any left, we'd eat again before we started home at daylight.

One time, there was a dance at the Nourse place on Crazy Woman. A bunch of us rode through the hills to get there. When we got there, the ice was going out of Crazy Woman. The ice was swelled up way high. Everybody crossed ahead of me, and a large chunk broke loose and tipped up with me on it. My horse slid off it and went down. Somebody hollered to stay on my horse, which I did. The horse finally scrambled out, but we both had a real cold bath. One of the men had my dress and the cake tied on behind his saddle, so I had dry clothes to wear when I got to the dance. My pants and coat had all night to dry before we started home in the morning. The next morning we couldn't even cross the creek because the ice was going out. We had to ride down to the Crazy Woman bridge to get home about three times further and took all day.

Some dances were held in neighborhood barn lofts. Mike Streeter and Bob and Fred Barton were the square dance callers. Occasionally, there was a program and dance at the Barber post office. The DeBarthe family lived there. Don DeBarthe was postmaster. Mrs. DeBarthe was the teacher. Other locations were Henry Baumgartner's homestead house, the Wolf hall, the Barber Creek schoolhouse, Redman schoolhouse, Enoch's barn, Double V school, Al Schoonover's house. One night we danced at Henry Baumgartner's homestead. He had made many loaves of sourdough bread for sandwiches. His sourdough bread was delicious!

People arrived by horseback or buggy or sled. In the wintertime, people traveled Powder River on the ice, so there were no hills. Model T cars had to be pushed up nearly every hill! In those days, the roads were all dirt–some barely more than trails. The road up Powder River was not much more than a trail, and the road up Dry Creek to Buffalo went up around the heads of all the draws.

One winter, Henry Baumgartner and Dick Mills started up Dry Creek to Buffalo in an old truck. That was before the days of Prestone antifreeze, and the water froze up in the truck. Henry knew of a homestead near the Ralph Hepp place, so they walked to it. When they arrived, there were about 10 other people who were stranded there as well, and the lady of the house, Mrs. Timar, had a brand-new baby, so Henry and Dick took some quilts, went to one of the sheds, built a fire, and stayed plenty warm.

In 1926, Dad was over at Dutchy Smith's on Crazy Woman. They started to brand a bull that Dad bought from Dutchy. The bull got mad and took Dad when he was on the ground, tossed him up over his back, and broke his hip. I went over to Dutchy's to see about getting Dad a doctor. Dutchy was a bachelor and very hospitable. He decided to fix dinner, so he went out and shot the head off a chicken, got it ready, and put it on to cook and then decided to make biscuits. He made a little hole in the flour in the top of the flour sack and poured in the sourdough and stirred it up and made biscuits out of it. They were the worst sourdough biscuits I ever ate!

Papa was in the hospital in Sheridan for some time with his hip, and my sister, Inez, and I were home. We milked 15 cows morning and night, separated the milk, took care of the cream, gave the pigs the skim milk, and kept house. When he came home, Dad walked with a crutch for a long time. Mother had been in the hospital when Dad broke his hip and died in 1926, so I kept house for my dad and taught school at the Redman School.

A government trapper named Charlie Vest always stayed at our place when he was in our part of the country. He poisoned coyotes with 1080 [sodium fluoroacetate poison] and eventually died from it because there was no antidote for it at that time. He would bring a new bunch of library books out from the Johnson County Library when he came and would take the ones we'd read back. He played the guitar, and my dad played the fiddle. After supper we would have music till bedtime. I remember him playing the Spanish fandango.

It was about this time that a young boy came riding into our place one evening. He was leading a horse and asked to stay all night. We fixed a bed in the bunkhouse, and the next morning he asked for a job. My dad told him he couldn't hire him, but if he wanted to stay until he found something, he was welcome. We thought he had probably run away from home, but we never asked him anything about himself. Because he talked so slowly, we thought he was Swedish, so we called him Ole. He stayed several years, and before he left told us his name was Arthur Wasnuk. He was Russian. He was a good boy and knew how to do ranch work. When my dad died in 1936, Ole stayed on to help with the livestock.

That year was the midst of the Depression. It was a very dry year. Things were very bad. There wasn't any grass for the cattle to eat. You couldn't sell cattle, and you couldn't winter them either. Franklin Delano Roosevelt was President then and started the New Deal to try to bring the country out of the Depression. One of the programs was that of buying the cattle and then shooting them because they thought there was an over-production of beef. They paid $4 for a calf and about $14 for a bull and $10 for a cow. The thing that impressed us the most was the fact that they shot the bull in the corral along the road and just left him lay. Ole hooked onto him and drug him up a draw and covered him up with dirt. The government allowed you to take whatever meat you wanted. I remember getting calves at different ranches and canning the meat. We could only do them one at a time because this all happened in the middle of summer, and it was awfully hot, and that's all the meat we could handle at a time.

I taught the Enochs school in their bunkhouse. Murel Enochs, Johnny Nourse, and Mildred Garretson were the pupils. I boarded and roomed at Enochs' during the week and went home on Friday. I always stayed at home as long as I could. One Monday morning, my dad woke me up early to ride over to the Enochs place to go to school. Nobody looked at the clock. It was 35 degrees below, and I got to Enochs' in time for breakfast. I found out afterwards that he had set the clock to 2:30 a.m.!

While teaching the Redman School, the families all moved away about Thanksgiving time. The Roebling School north of Arvada was available because the teacher, Mrs. Esther Rowley, wished to resign. I applied and got that school. I taught one year there. Then it was closed and consolidated with Arvada. I was transferred to the Arvada school, where I taught grades one, two, and three. There were about 30 pupils in all three grades.

While in that locality, I became acquainted with Carl Knudson, who was a cowboy on Senator Kendrick's OW Ranch. We were married in 1939 and went to live on the Crazy Woman Ranch. We leased it from J.R. Porter Kennedy. In a few years, we bought the place. He took our steers as a down payment. I don't remember signing a contract. His word was the same as a contract.

I had a homestead on Kenney Draw and sold it for $3.50 per acre, and we bought the Tom and Josie Lorah homesteads joining what we had, as well as some land from Spike Haegler. Carl's homestead was part of the Kendrick's LX Bar Ranch. He had taken a team of horses, harness, and a couple of saddle horses as payment for his homestead. He had worked the team, Nig and Rastus, at the K Ranch.

They were really an honest team. The neighborhood got coal a couple miles up and across the river. Carl would go to get coal with the team and wagon and take his saddle horse along. After he loaded the wagon, he headed Nig and Rastus home and trotted on home on his saddle horse to do chores. Nig and Rastus would bring home the load of coal across Powder River, cross the Crazy Woman bridge, and turn into the gate into the meadow–the short way home–and stop at the house. Carl would have the chores all done by then, and he would go unload his coal. Lots of times Nig and Rastus would get home after dark. They were always dependable–almost like having a hired man.

We drilled an artesian well that was really a good well. It furnished water for the house, two stock tanks, and the yard and garden. However, even after lots of watering, things in the yard and the garden died. The water had too much soda in it, so it killed all the plants. Carl drilled a shallow well for the yard and garden. We raised most of our food from the huge garden, our own meat, the chickens, and milk cows. We ran the light plant which generated our own electricity and heated the house with the gas from the artesian well. Carl brought the pipes from the well up inside an old carbide tank and trapped the gas inside the bell. He piled rocks on top of the bell to create 8 pounds of pressure to force the gas through the pipes into the house for heat.

Carl was a stockman and very good with animals. He particularly liked horses and enjoyed breaking and training them. He usually broke young horses in the winter and spring when he was checking the beaver traps and calving. He loved to rodeo. That was our main entertainment for many years.

A couple of storms come in mid-1946 and in 1949. In the spring of '49, there was a terrible blizzard that lasted about three days. Several people were stranded at our place. There was plenty of food, but the electricity was off, and cooking became a challenge. We set up a two-burner camp stove. I cooked stew on one burner and coffee on the other. The men helped Carl feed the cattle, but the storm was so bad that they would quickly get wet to the skin and have to come inside to dry out. One day, the visibility was so bad that they got lost in the meadow and finally managed to follow the fence into the buildings. The wind blew so hard that it blew away the hay before the cattle could eat it. It snowed everything under and buried livestock in big drifts. Our winter pasture has good protection along the river bottom, but we lost calves anyway.

Another story comes to mind–the ranch was about a day's cattle drive from the railroad in Arvada, so we had many shippers stop overnight. One time, it rained–the roads were still dirt–and we had 13 extra people who were stuck in the mud. As I remember, we had ham for supper, and the kids slept on the floor and loved it. In the morning, Carl took Nig and Rastus and pulled them all out, and they all went on their way.

We raised a family of three children–two boys and a girl. We sold the ranch to the boys in 1974. We live in Buffalo now although both of us would be happier if we were living on the ranch.

※※※※

Charles C. "Charlie" Lawrence
1888-1979
From an interview with Clare Johnson
In 1971, when 83 years old

The Horse Named Diamond–Priceless

One day Dad [John C. Lawrence] and I were in Buffalo. We met Billy Sayles, who was running the 41 Ranch wagon, and he told Dad he had four of Dad's big steers in the roundup at the mouth of Crazy Woman along Powder River and asked Dad, "What do you want to do with them? Shall I bring them up with the 41 cattle or what?" Dad said no, that he'd send the kid down–that's what he called me. I was 11 years old. The next morning, I saddled up old Burt and put my bedroll and lead on Diamond, took Ranger along, and started out. I had never been on the Crazy Woman of the Powder River, but Dad said, "You just follow that long draw up, cross over the divide, follow the other draw down until you come to Crazy Woman Creek, then follow it on down to Powder River. That's where you'll find the roundup."

First thing I came to when I hit Crazy Woman was a dugout where Ransome Babcock lived. He came out and said, "Hello there, boy. Where are you going?" I said I was going down by the Powder River, and he said, "You had better come in and have a bite to eat. What are you going down to the roundup for?" I told him I was going down there to get some cattle. It was about noon, and I was hungry, and he said I'd better come in anyway, but I said, "No, I think I'd better go on down. It's getting late."

I went on down the creek a ways until I came to the next ranch. That's where Eat-um-up-Jake or Ed Tway lives. They called him Eat-um-up-Jake. I went down along there. He came out, walked around the horses, and saw what my brand was. He knew who I was and said, "Well, boy, you had better put your horse in the barn and let him have some hay. After dinner I think I'll go down to the roundup with you." I found out afterwards that all he wanted to go down the creek for was because the creek had been up and washed out some of the crossing and he thought maybe I might not find them.

After we ate our lunch, I saddled up the horses, and down the creek we went. When we got down to the north of the Crazy Woman to the roundup, the first wagon we ran into, why, it was the 41 wagon, and I met Billy Sayles there. He tells me, "I'm sure glad that you brought Diamond along." I wanted to know why. He told me there was a 4-J steer in the outfit–an outlawed steer in the herd that no one could cut out. But he knew that Diamond could cut it out. He asked me if I could ride Diamond when he was cutting out a steer. I told him I could, and he said, "What do you do?" I said, "Well, I just tie my reins together, turn Diamond loose, and hang on to the saddle horn with both hands."

That night I turned my horses loose in the cavy–all but Diamond. Billy asked me to keep him up. After supper, Billy and I rode down to the 4-J wagon, and Billy asked them, "Did you get the outlawed steer out?" and the 4-J boss said, "No, there is not a horse in the outfit that can cut out that son-of-a-bitch." Billy said, "Well, I'll tell you. I'll bet you a month's wages that this boy on that little ole brown pony can do it." The 4-J boss called his bluff immediately.

On the way back up to the 41 wagon, Billy said, "If you cut that steer, I'll give you half the money." Next morning bright and early, we went down to the 4-J wagon. During the night, word got passed around that some little old kid on a little old brown pony was going to try to cut out that outlawed steer. Course, almost all the cowhands that he could spare were there to watch.

It was the largest herd of cattle I have ever seen. It was about a mile across in any direction. I afterward learned that they estimated that there was 10,000 head of cattle there. Well, we went into the herd. It wasn't hard to spot that steer because he stood about a foot taller than the rest of the cattle and had horns about 6 feet across. He was a big dun-colored bull steer.

I asked the 4-J boss where he wanted him cut out, and he said, "Down the river. That is where the rest of our cut is." The steer was in about the middle of the herd. As soon as we rode around the steer, old Diamond had him spotted. I tied my reins together and turned Diamond loose. Around and around they went. First, all the way around some cows, but Diamond was always there at the turn-in. We worked the steer closer to the outside of the herd. He was getting pretty hot. When we were within 100 yards of the edge of the herd, the steer turned around right facing Diamond. The hair on his neck stood straight out, and his eyes were as red as fire. He was blowing snot out of his nose. Gee, I never saw anything like this, and I didn't know what Diamond would do, but he laid back his ears and lowered his head and started right for the steer. That was where the steer had always gotten away from whoever was trying to cut him out. Within about 6 feet of the steer, he broke, but Diamond was right around there and turned the steer in the opposite direction. Again, Diamond beat him to the turn. Diamond run so close that one of those big long horns laid right across the top of Diamond's neck in front on my saddle because he was taller than Diamond. I was really scared! By this time, the steer had made a few quick turns, and he was almost to the edge of the herd. Then Diamond crowded in so close that he didn't have time to turn, and the steer was out of the herd before he knew it. About that time, a dozen cowboys rushed in with a war hoop. They tied that steer, and he was on his way down the river.

The 41 boss ran up to me and said, "I'd like to buy that horse. I'll give you whatever you want for him." I told him he did not have enough money to buy Diamond. He said, "I've seen a lot of horses work but nothing like that show Diamond put on. I bet Billy a month's wages that you could not do it. I'm not going to give Billy the money." He reached in his pocket and said, "Here it is. It's yours." Well, I never saw so much money in my life. Boy, it sure looked good to me!

Well, I cut out. I went down there and cut my four steers. Eat-um-up-Jake cut out a few, and we left Crazy Woman together. I stayed up to his place that night, and the next morning I took my four steers out of the little pasture he had where he kept his saddle horses along with my saddle horses. After we wrangled my horses, I saddled up, put my bed on Diamond, turned he and Ranger up the creek along with the steers, and headed up toward the ranch. Jake helped me up the Crazy Woman about two miles, and then he went back. The cattle went along fine from there, and it wasn't long before I got home.

It was many years after that when I was in Buffalo that I went to "Daddy" Burnett's. He lived in Buffalo at that time. "Daddy" Burnett was writing a letter, and I asked, "What are you doing, Daddy?" and he said, "Oh, I'm writing a letter to cattlemen, describing the biggest herd of cattle I ever saw." I said, "Where were they?" and he said, "Oh, it was on the mouth of the Crazy Woman on the Powder River. You know, there was something that always bothered me, and I could never find out. When I was there, there was a little old boy came up on a little brown pony and cut out an outlawed steer. I've often wondered who that boy was." "Well," I said, "just turn around, Daddy, and look at me." He turned around, and I said, "I'm that boy," and he said, "Well, I'll be darned. I've often wondered. We estimated that there were 10,000 head of cattle in that herd. That's the largest bunch of cattle I ever saw in one herd."

Diamond was the one that taught me how to work cattle. It was early in the spring of 1898. There were five head of cattle down in the field there at the ranch. Dad told me, "Take Diamond out there and put those cattle out through the gate," so I took Diamond, went out, and started to drive those five cattle out, but they went in five different ways. I had an awful time. I couldn't get them out. I finally rode back to Dad and said, "I can't get those cattle out. They are going in all directions." He said, "Well, I'll tell you what you do. You get on down there and open that north gate and ride on through it a ways and then come back to the cattle and just turn Diamond loose." I did, and old Diamond cut out one cow and took it out and put it through the gate and run up the gulch about 100 yards and come back and got another one. He did that until he got all five of them out. That kind of give me an idea how to handle cattle.

One day, the old milk cow–we was milking. We always kept the calf in the yard. Then we would turn her out that big broad gate. There was open range in there. Our cattle would always run over to Box Elder, and every so often she'd get it into her head to go over and join them. She didn't come home one evening, and Dad said the next morning, "You better go over there and get the old milk cow. You'll find her right there on Box Elder." Sure enough, when I got over there, there was the old milk cow. We started up the draw and got part of the ways. She was kind of ornery about going– wanted to go back all the time. Up the draw a ways there was a box elder tree, and the old cow went right under the tree. I went around the tree and on down the gulch about 300 or 400 yards and back up the width again. Again, she went around under the tree, and I'd always go around and have to bring her back. Well, she did this about three or four times, and old Diamond was getting tired of it, I guess, so the next time she started around this tree, why, Diamond, he started right in ahead of her under this tree and turned the old cow on up the draw, but he left me hanging on a limb of that tree because he went under this limb. It was too low for me. I caught it and was hanging there. I dropped to the ground. Diamond was standing up on the bank there, and he kind of looked around as if to say, "Come on and get on and let's go home." That was another experience I had on Diamond.

Dad bought Diamond at Upland, Texas–and Ranger and Roany. Diamond was a cattle-cutting horse. I never had a horse as good as Diamond since then. I've had one or two awfully good horses, but about the time I had a good horse broke–we had a lot of horses–about the time I got a good horse broke, someone would come along and want him, and Dad would sell him. That has been my experience ever since.

Well, Diamond was worth–he'd be worth anything you wanted to ask for him. I suppose I could have got several thousand dollars for him if I'd have asked it for him–if I knew anybody who had that kind of money–because he was just priceless. Well, Dad–I don't think he paid over $50 down in Texas for him because he was just a green horse then. Dad broke him on the way up. Diamond was just a natural born pony. That's all.

❦❦❦❦❦

Edward A. *"Allen"* Leath
1930-2018
From an interview with Nancy Tabb
In 2017, when 87 years old

Bronc Buster

While in high school I went to work for this old bachelor–1,000 head of horses–breaking horses and stuff like that. Then this neighbor kept after me. Bill Brown had a calf company with an outfit over by Clearmont. He kept after me to come work for him, and he paid me, I think, $125 a month instead of the $75 that I was making. Anyway, I went to work for him. It was going to last only through the summer because I had told him, "I got to go to school," you know. He tells me, "Yeah, we know that." Well, it come school time, and he said, "We'll take you to Sheridan, and you can finish up your sophomore year." Well, I never got there. I wanted to go to school to learn because I knew that a guy without any high school wasn't good, but I just got too busy to go to school.

From the time I was, let's say 5 years old, I can remember wrangling horses and Shetland ponies and then going right on up and breaking my own horses when I was 8 years old. Then I went to work for Henry Housetop. When I was 10 years old, he come and got me, and I went to breaking horses and picketing. You know what picketing is? Have five of them tied up on long ropes and training them. So my young history was nothing but breaking horses. He had 156 head of buckin' horses that old guys spoiled before I got there. I got them in and rode them all. It didn't bother me to get on a horse that would blow up and buck. It probably bothered my mom more than it would me cuz she was always afraid I was going to get killed.

I could get on anything and ride it, you know. It's like one day this guy said to me, "I want to buy your horse." Beautiful sorrel horse–socking-legged, big bald face. I told him, "Well, he's not broke. I'm riding him, but not everybody can ride anything I can." I took him down in this big corral, and I caught–Pilot was his name. I called him and caught him and saddled him up. Pilot knew me and bucked with me. He had spur tracks on him where I spurred him. So this guy got on him, and I mean this horse blowed up and went to bucking, so this guy said, "I don't believe I want that horse."

I took a lot of horses. Bought a lot of horses that was bucking and wasn't mean, but I broke 'em and got 'em over it. Pie was a bald-faced, beautiful roan with big white streaks down his legs. I went for colored stuff and classy looking stuff. Everybody always said, "Allen, he rides the classiest looking horses in the country."

One time–I always remember this one–I was riding bareback a Shetland pony, and he fell with me. Muddy and rainy weather, and my Shetland fell with me, and my ankle turned around and busted. There I was. I can remember hanging onto my horse, and my leg was hurting, and I was bawling to beat the band. Finally, I got on my pony and rode home to the house and told my mom through my blubbers that I'd broke my leg or something. She got me off and wrapped my ankle and foot with some plastic cloth. The anklebone was broke. She finally got me a pair of crutches. I must have been 8 years old.

❦❦❦❦

Lena Davis Leath
1901-1992
From an interview with Patty Myers

No Diploma

I finished the eighth grade and quit school two weeks before I got my diploma and went to work in the telephone office. I'd love to have a diploma, but I thought I'd rather go to work than to go to school. I drove to town with the buggy three miles and brought my brothers and sisters to school each day. Then I would go to work until school was out. Then I'd take them home. My folks didn't know I had quit school for about two weeks until the teacher called and asked, "Where is Lena?" They had a big joke about that because I was working in the telephone office instead of going to school.

I worked nights. We had a string that we tied around our finger for the night bell. It rang so terrible it would scare you half to death. We could lay down and go to sleep on the couch, but we had to tie that to our finger so we could jerk it off if it rang. One night, I turned over in my sleep, and the night bell didn't ring, and they needed an emergency call. Boy, they were knocking on my door! I tell you I came awake in a hurry. They asked me, "What happened?" and I told them, "Well, the night bell must have stuck because I had the string tied to my hand." But they said, "Maybe you jerked it off." Anyways, they got the doctor, and he got to the emergency whatever it was. But it made it a little bad, you know. I was a scared too. I worked there a year.

In 1917, I married Jim Leath and moved to Powder River. For five years, I helped him trap coyotes and break horses until the twins were born. In the flood on Powder River in 1923, water was 4 feet deep in our house. Nobody had cars in those days. The twins were a year old, so they were packed out in slings. Dave Muir had one in a blanket around his neck, and the other one was in a blanket around Al Smith's neck. Jim was on the roundup. We waded the five miles to the Bugher place in water up to our knees. My sister was pregnant at the time, so her husband and I had all we could do to help her get through the mud and water. We lived with the Bugher family for two weeks. There was about 36 of us that got flooded out. We lived on beef and gravy because they ran out of all the groceries there was that they had. You couldn't get to town because it was too muddy and wet. After that, we moved up to the Alexander place on Indian Creek for the rest of that winter. In the spring, we bought the Hamlin place.

🌿🌿🌿🌿

Robert L. "Bob" Lepper
1910-2003
From a Johnson County Historical Society presentation
In 1985, when 75 years old

Friends & Neighbors

I guess if I needed a title for this little talk like any accomplished public speaker, it would be "Friends and Neighbors." I've always had a kind of a slogan: Friends are a person's biggest asset. If you have a million dollars and no friends, it's a pretty empty world.

I was 75 on the 12th of December, being born December 12, 1910, in a little town of Flores, Iowa. The best birthday gift or pre-birthday gift that I ever received was on December 11, 1962, when Eva [Phillips] and I were married. We were married in Pacific Grove, California, by the Justice of the Peace with the Clerk of Court and his wife as witnesses. She has been my best friend and supporter for 23 years.

How did I happen to come to Buffalo? In 1943, I was enroute to Yellowstone Park.

The Pines in the Bighorn Mountains

Incidentally, I was using gas stamps provided by a friendly rancher because gas was rationed in those days during World War II. We visited two or three resorts around Yellowstone just kind of getting the feel of the country. I had never been out here before, having been born in Iowa. On the way back we stopped at The Pines and liked it very well. Worth Butler was managing it at the time. We had good food and stayed overnight.

I went back to Rapid City, South Dakota, where I was operating a little cafe, and came back later that summer and bought The Pines from Otto P. Carr. He was an old fellow from California–very tight-fisted. I paid him $6,000 with $1,000 down. At that time, Bill Holland handled the legal end of the sale.

In all the time I was there, there was a cabin just off the road as you drove in that we called the winter cabin. There was a root cellar underneath the kitchen. Since then it has been torn down. Old Man Holland stayed there in the winters. The only running water when I went there was in the Middle Fork of Clear Creek. The lights were coal oil and some gas pressure lamps. The only hot water was in a 50-gallon steel oil drum fastened to the end of the cookstove. If you had the stove going, you had hot water, and if you didn't, you didn't have any hot water. Later on, we made a few improvements.

To begin with, it was really–as far as my operation–a one-horse operation. I bought the horse from Chuck Barrett. He was a good old horse. I used him about five years. By borrowing or renting horses from Chuck or from Skip and Bob Hancock or Golden Jolley, who used to run the Red Owl Store, we made it through the first fall and hunting season. The first morning of that first hunting season we saddled up 10 or 12 saddle horses and four or five pack horses for hunters and guides. We had a real good hunting season because the whole area around The Pines on both sides of the road with the exception of the Cross H cow camp back over two or three canyons was open that year, so we had a good area all the way around.

After moving the family over from Rapid City and getting the hunting season underway, Ben Klinkhammer hired me as the night bartender at the old Occidental Bar. I went to work at 5:00 in the afternoon and worked until closing time. One winter, I got up at 7:00 in the morning and went to work at the creamery for John Polson and worked there until 4:00 in the afternoon.

The first fall and winter, I met Andy Hanson at his mill on Little Sourdough. I bought firewood from Andy. He gave me all the slab I wanted just to haul it away. We bought all of our logs from Andy from that old burned off timber up behind South Fork.

He would unload those logs and toss them on the ground. They were just as hard as a rock and did a great job. We built onto the old lodge and made the bigger dining room.

Andy was quite a Swede and a great worker. I tried to keep up with him one winter. He said, "Why don't you come up and cut corral poles with me?" Well, I would take about 10 swipes at the corral pole, and Andy would whack them down in two, so that didn't last long. I couldn't keep up with him.

That happened to also be the place where I shot a beautiful big buck deer for camp meat out of season. I had an old truck that I had bought over in Rapid City that used to haul CCC workers. It was enclosed all but the back, and I had a bunch of slab on. I threw this buck deer on the back of the slab and covered it up with a tarp. I had just pulled in back of The Pines, and here come Jack Odie, the game warden. He said, "Let's get him dressed out because I might want a steak." So fine–later on he had the steak and a couple of drinks to go with it.

One of the best friends that I had all around was Herb Post, the forest ranger. Herb was firm, but he was fair. I failed to present the plans for the building of the new lodge before we added it on. We were pouring the foundation, and here came Herb just boiling. I hadn't turned in any plans, which was one of their specifications. After we got the builder's plans in his file and took his instructions and followed them very closely on the septic tanks and the laterals for the sewer system and the water system, he was okay.

Going back to that first summer I was there–my first pack trip was three Kaplan brothers, who had Kaplan Wholesale Grocery in Sioux Falls, South Dakota. They had been recommended to come to The Pines by another friend of mine I had worked with. That was my first experience of packing, and I worried quite a bit about that because I didn't know the first thing about tying a diamond hitch, but I had a lot of tie rope, so I just wrapped and wrapped what you might call a squaw hitch and got along very well. Sure enough, everything went fine. The same group came back the next year. They were good customers. The year after that, I bought George Gardner's outfit. He had a pack string and used to do camp cooking at shearing camps. There were 10 or 12 horses and tepees and tarps and pack saddles and all the gear that you needed to do a good job in taking care of the tourists and the dudes.

One day at work, we weren't very busy, and I took some sheets and just jotted down a list of friends who have meant so much to me and have given me many favors. I have so many fond memories of people I considered and was happy to call friends that are gone. It is surprising in that number of years how many there are. I got down here in the list Bob Hancock. Of course, Jim Dillinger was in the store probably at the time that he let me charge my first pair of cowboy boots, and I later paid him. Later on, I needed a pair of dancing shoes, and Bob sold them to me for $8 and put that on the tab. I went to a dance over to the Elks with Sis and George McCrea.

These are not in any particular order. It is just people that I thought of. Henry Gill, a trucker, he hauled many loads of slab and firewood for me when he would be on the mountain with another job. He would haul it back—never charged me a thing. He was a good old bowling buddy.

Bud Mead, the barber, he found out after I had been in the barber shop a few times that I was a Blue Lodge Mason, and he wanted to see my card. I was back three of four years because I had traveled around a lot and didn't have any money to pay my dues. Probably six or eight months after that, I went in one day, and Bud said, "Here's your card." It was a paid up Blue Lodge Masonic card. He had written Sioux City, Iowa, where I became a Mason back in 1936, and got all the dope and sent them a check and paid my dues and handed me this card. I said, "Bud, what do I owe you?" and he said, "That's okay."

I've got Frank Lawrence. Frank showed me how to tie the real diamond hitch. He was up the mountains one day and stopped in. He gave me a lot of pointers about how to handle the hunters and what to tell them. Once in a while, he used to visit me down at the Occidental.

Marvin Shelton, the sheriff, he used to come into the Occidental quite regularly. He used to come into the bar and check every day. He never took a drink on duty, but he would always come in.

Then Safford Fairlie and Harold Kaltenbach. Of course, Harold is still living. They kept my vehicles running and gave me credit when I needed it. Harold happened to be the potentate when I went into the Shrine in 1953.

Louie Falxa and his uncle, Albert. Louie did me many favors and loaned me money one time. His uncle stayed up at The Pines one fall when they were finishing the cabin that Louie built up Middle Fork of Clear Creek. He was a good cook. They had quite a bit of mutton stew.

John Watt, the banker. Dear Old John, he loaned me small amounts of money in those days—$100 at a time. When I went over to the Sheridan Inn, I didn't have much money and come to get ready to open up, they asked, "Where is the change?" I said, "Oh my gosh, no change!" I was down to my last dollar. I called John—I still had a Wyoming Bank and Trust check—I called John and said, "I wrote a check for $100. Would you hold it until I get money from these receipts?" He said, "Sure, I'll hold it until you let me know." That's how I got my $100 worth of change from the Bank of Commerce. You talk about friends.

Jean Van Dyke, the clothier, sold me a suit on credit one time. Later, we bowled together against a team from Casper and Sheridan, and he complained about putting up the $10 that we put up for a jackpot. I think it finally ended up that Seney and I put it up. On that team there was Russia [John] Milnichak, Fred and Frank Seney, Jean Van Dyke, and myself. We had a lot of fun.

Louis Brock, he gave me reasonable pasture for my horses one winter when I didn't have anyplace else to go and never pressed me for any money. In his later years, he was a darn good customer.

Coni O'Leary–everybody knew Coni. Some of the stories that you heard you didn't know whether to believe or not–there was a lot of them. He added lots of color to tending bar at the Occidental. He would come in and try to con somebody into buying a beer for him.

There are so many with whom I got acquainted when I was tending bar. Fred Goin at the Idlewild Hotel–every evening, Fred would come down and bring a couple of pieces of fried chicken and have a glass of wine. He was a grand old guy.

John Camino–I got acquainted with him although John didn't do much imbibing at the bar. He took me a couple of times with him over to Sheridan when he picked up some of the boys–two or three of the old-timers that came over from Europe.

🌿🌿🌿🌿

Billie May Little
1936-Present
From an interview with Nancy Tabb
In 2019, when 83 years old

Buffalo High School PE Teacher

After I graduated from college, I applied to teach Physical Education in several towns, including Buffalo, Wyoming. The first call I got was from Mr. Merida Maggard in Buffalo. Would I come up for an interview? So I got on the bus, and the angels were with me. An old man sat next to me. I knew all the gossip about everybody in Buffalo by the time I got here because he was a Buffaloite and told me all about Buffalo. We were just yapping, you know.

When I got to town, I went to get a room, and the lady wouldn't rent me a room because I was a single woman. I got pretty haughty about that and said, "I'm here for a teaching interview." "Oh, okay," so she rented me a room. It was right down the street. The next morning, I got up real early and started for my interview and here came the superintendent, Mr. Maggard, down the roadway to meet me. He took me up and gave me a tour.

He and I just got along. You know, you can tell. Mr. Maggard gave me a tour of the school and showed me where my girls would be. We talked about discipline, and I told him that I was very strict, and he told me, "Oh, good." We went to the office, and when we went in–I don't know if you remember the gossip about Louise Mueller, the secretary–she was pretty tough. Anyway, he went by her and asked, "Well, Louise, shall we hire her?" Louise looked me over and said, "Well, I guess so." I thought, "Oh, boy, Billie, cool it with her!" She turned out to be a really good friend, but she was pretty strict.

I lucked out with everything. I signed the contract. Mom and Dad had purchased me a car for graduation. I told them, "Goodbye, I'm doing this on my own. I don't want you to help me." I drove up to Buffalo and went downtown to the Busy Bee of all places. I asked, "Where can I find an apartment near the high school?" Sara Roberts, who was cooking, said, "Well, I have some apartments. It's unlocked. Go look at it." She told me where it was, so I drove over there and unlocked the door. I'm standing there looking in, deciding what I have to do. It was nice and clean. It was a little three-room–a bedroom and a bath and a kitchen and a little living room. It was a series of four apartments on Western Avenue. I just had a block to walk to school. It couldn't have been nicer.

I taught with Miss Marian Lester and Miss Jane Lutzke. I was Miss May. The kids referred to us as the old maids. Mr. Maggard's son had an old car with a rumble seat. He would pick us up after school, and we three old maids would sit in the back and give our queen waves down Main Street. The kids would say, "There go the old maids." Well, we were to them.

One of the teachers who I just adored was Joe Motica. I stood 5 feet 10 inches easy, and Joe probably stood 5 feet 5 or 6 inches. When I taught health classes, we had rooms next to each other. One day, I sent him a note. He taught Spanish, and they were singing in Spanish, so I sent a note, "You are disturbing me." He sent back an old plastic rose with a note that said, "I'm sorry." I put the rose in a vase and had a kid take it back to him. Then he put a note on the vase that said, "I'm so sorry," and sent it back to me. I sent the kid down to get water in the vase for the plastic flower and sent it back. We got a lot done that day. Of course, the kids were in hysterics. Joe and I would stand in the hallway because we all stood as the kids moved from room to room. Joe would stand with his arm around my waist, and I had my arm across his shoulder, and the kids would giggle. You could do things like that then.

George Grace taught there with me. He didn't want me to have a new dressing room because he wanted to save it for the visiting team officials. I asked Mr. Maggard about it, and he said, "Well, yeah, I thought you were already in there," so I just moved my girls in. Oh, George and I just locked horns steady, but we were good friends.

We got our first trampoline. I had read the instructions, so I'm showing George and another fella what to do, and I did a front drop. Well, all my blouse buttons went through the holes on the trampoline, and my blouse and I landed down. The other guy–not George–he clapped his hands and said, "Let's see it again, Billie!" I could have killed them!

I have to tell you a funny–one day I walked into Health class, and all the girls were really being nice. I thought, "Okay. What are they up to?" There was a pillow on my chair. Well, for some reason I didn't sit all the way down on the pillow. I stood up and picked up the pillow, and there was one of those snotty things underneath, so I just put it in a drawer and didn't say a word and went on with class. After class here came the girl who had put it under the pillow. She asked me, "May I have that back?" I said, "No, it's mine. You gave it to me. It was on my chair," but she said, "But I paid 25¢ for it." Finally, I gave it back to her and said, "Don't you dare do this to another teacher." She did it to Mrs. Helen Meldrum, and she came over to my room in tears. So I caught the girl after school, and we went to the gym, and she ran and ran.

You know, it was just that type of relationship at the school. There was nothing naughty about it. We enjoyed each other. I had a lot of fun. I can't think of a teacher that I just didn't really enjoy. I was there 10 years.

☙☙☙☙☙

Virgil B. "Babe" Lund
1923-1993
From an interview with Patty Myers
In 1992, when 69 years old

Kaycee, Wyoming Grocery Merchant

Interviewer Patty Myers: What year were you born?

I was born in 1923. I was the youngest. They kind of babied me. Well, they still do. Evory [Hanson], my sister, still spoils me. She does all my laundry and cleans my house. Course, now she's living half the time in Arizona, so she doesn't wash my clothes only twice a year.

I don't believe this mountain of laundry that you save for her.

Well, you have to have a dozen or 20 pairs of pants and all the rest of things and maybe send some of the stuff to the laundry in between times until she gets back here. Then she does it all the time. I never say a word to her–never ask her to do it or anything else. She just does it. She spoils me. I do her favors too.

Tell me about the first people in your family who came to Johnson County.

We come to Johnson County in May of 1926 from North Dakota. My folks was farmers there, and it was hard times. There was a Danish settlement in Buffalo. We come to Buffalo, and then in three months we come to Kaycee.

You come from a Danish family. Did you grow up speaking Danish?

Well, we used to speak some. I didn't have no accent. I spoke English. My mother self-educated herself in English, but when she first come over here, she didn't speak English. She never communicated too much with other people because they would all make her say the bad things, so she kept her mouth shut. She was an intelligent woman. They had a Danish community and lots of ranching. They had a Danish Lutheran Church started at that time. Services was most of it in Dane. It changed later. Course, us kids could understand Danish. Our family spoke mostly English, but they'd speak

Dane when the kids would come around and there was something they didn't want them to hear.

Do you remember how you traveled?

We come to Wyoming in a Model T truck and a Model T passenger car with all our belongings. It took five days. We camped along the way. I was only 3 years old.

Did you come in the spring?

Uh-huh. We got to Buffalo in May. We lived in Buffalo for a while. There was a brick house by the Catholic Church. We lived in there for two or three months until we come to Kaycee. There was a creamery next to where the old grange hall is on the north side. They tore it off. It's where the museum is now. We lived there for almost five years. Then we moved to where we are here now. The First State Bank of Kaycee had the building here. They went under, and we bought the building and moved it to live in behind the store. It has a vault just like it was, you know. We built on a little since then.

When your dad moved you into the creamery building, was he running a store at that time?

We put in a meat market. We butchered and sold a little meat is all. Then we put in a few canned goods and expanded.

Would all your childhood memories have been as a town child in Kaycee?

Um-hmm. Two people that I went to school with all through the years was Willis Tilton and Shirley Jarrard. We were in the same grade and went through all the years at Kaycee and through the first four-year high school in Kaycee. Of course, it was different then. Kaycee high school district was the smallest school district in the United States population-wise. There wasn't much financing, but there was a lot of communication between the students and teachers and school board. The school board had quite a bit to say about what was going on and the last say.

Did you go into the military?

Yes, I went into the military in July of 1943 and got out in December of 1945. I was in there two and one half years. I was over in the Hawaiian Islands for two years–easy duty. They had it so easy at Hilo, Hawaii, at the air base there. I was in the Navy–the Seabees. There was several of them around here from the Seabees. One of them is Culbertson Brock. At Camp Parks, California, they just got back from the Aleutian Islands–I never did know Cub until that time, but I really got acquainted with him there. I see him quite a bit.

The Seabees was the most liked outfit in the service, especially with the Marines. They had a better grub allowance than the rest of them, so the mess hall was always visited by the Marines or the Army or the Navy. We had it better than the regular Navy. The regular Navy had a better allotment than the Army, and the Army had a better allotment than the Marines, so they liked to visit our chow hall. The Seabees was mostly a construction battalion. They did underwater stuff and anything that was connected with the Marine Corps. Of course, the Marine Corps at that time was the first invasion of any of the islands. The Seabees were with them.

When I went into the Navy, you have to learn to swim. I thought everybody knew how to swim because we swam here all our lives down here in Powder River. We'd go swimming in Powder River as soon as the ice went out and ice still on the banks. It'd be the first of April or May, and we went swimming. You went swimming all summer because that was what you had to do. There was always two or three different big holes. Got in the service, and there was only about 30 percent of them who knew how to swim.

Was it hard for you to make the transition from Kaycee to California to Hawaii?

Not anymore than anyone else. In fact, it was easier. And the eats–hell, I ate better than I did at home. A lot of people didn't adjust to it that way. We did physical exercise all the time. I was in pretty good condition even though I was a fat boy. Go fishing and hunting and a lot of walking and work, but some of the kids who went in at the same age, they weren't used to that.

Did you work in your dad's store when you were growing up?

Yeah, in the early days we put up ice. We refrigerated with ice since I was 10 years old until we got refrigeration. That was probably about 1940. All those years, I got ice out of the ice house every day. I'd be 10 and worked until I was 17. I took out a lot of ice. We'd use ourselves probably 1,000 pounds of ice–get out about that much. We'd sell some.

We cut it in the wintertime. They'd have ice crews put it up. When it would get colder and get a little ice in the creek, we'd get some hauled up and stored just outside until they started cutting. You couldn't tell when you was going to cut until the ice got ready enough to cut. Some years the ice wouldn't be that thick. Some years it would be 24 inches. They had machines to cut the ice with. It would be a motor with a blade on it that would cut 20 inches. They'd cut it two different ways, and then they'd chip them off. Of course, if the ice was thicker than 20 inches, you'd have a lot of chipping to do because it would just cut about 20 inches thick is all. Usually, when you put up ice, it'd be nice days. You wouldn't be putting it up when it was a blizzard. You like to have it much above freezing, and you like to have the ice as dry as you can. We packed it in sawdust on the outside–never put no sawdust between the ice–just on the outside and on top was sawdust. We had one big ice house and two or three small ones. When we used up all our ice, we would get ice out of Casper. There was Kaycee Transportation, owned by Howard Thompson. They went to Casper once a week. We'd get back three 300-pound cakes. Well, that's just 900 pounds.

It was Depression years, and that was work for them. Everybody would be working, you know, hauling or putting ice up–a good day's wages. All the ranchers put up ice.

After your dad's death, did one of your brothers or you go into the store?

I went to the service, and my sister run the store–Evory and Clifford Hanson. Then Cliff went into the service, so Evory run the store for two years. She lived in this building here. She is a very capable person. When I got out, she worked for me for six months or so. Then I had different hired hands since then.

Did you inherit your mother's share of the store?

Yes, I inherited it. We were in partnership until she died. There was just barely a living here to get by. I just inherited the business. I probably would have done something else if I hadn't. All of us worked. My brother, he helped me here after he got out of the service some, but he went into the motel business.

How much competition did your dad have in the grocery store business?

Babe Lund with Penny, the Dog

Well, there was always competition. You was in the business just to make a living. We worked harder and never spent no money–the only reason why you could stay in the business. Kaycee used to have five grocery stores at one time. None of them made any money.

I believed that anyone that wanted something to eat should have something to eat. You never turned anyone down that wanted a handout. You fix them up something and give it to them and never say nothing. If they didn't want what you give them, well, they wasn't hungry. I'd eat it myself. Anyone that needed something to eat–I saw that they got it unless they tried to cheat you, you know. You still get hooked by drifters, but we always give them a chance. If someone needed something to eat, I never did ask them to do nothing. I never give them cash. Kay, the station next door–they'd come hit him up for cash for a meal. Whenever they did that and I was there, I would say, "Come with me. I'll get you something to eat." I'd go out the door, and I'd go towards the store. About half the time, the guy would go the other direction. He didn't want a handout. He'd want 50¢ or $1 to buy a jug of wine, so we limited that. If he wanted something to eat, he could get it.

We're sitting in the storage room part of your grocery store on bags of cat and dog food. This looks to me like a big supply of cat and dog food for a town the size of Kaycee, so I'm assuming this is one of your big sellers.

I sell lots of cat and dog food, and I sell it reasonable. Every rancher has three or four dogs. The dogs do all the work. If they didn't have a dog, they'd have to do a lot of the work, so they feed them good.

I can remember a basketball game in the 1950s over at the Kaycee Community Hall and the dust rising from the floor.

Yeah, it wasn't that clean a building. You didn't have any janitors to do it. The town cop kept it swept out. Old J.F. Skiles and Harv Turk, they got $25 a month for all their services. That was the cop services, and they cleaned it up. Course, that was back when $25 would be like $250.

You only had five or six kids in one team, so we would all go in one car. Harv Turk, he was an elderly man, and he couldn't drive very good. We would get some blankets, and it would be 20 degrees below zero, and the roads were slick, but no one ever worried about it. We always got back at 2:00 or 3:00 in the morning. Whether it was to Big Horn, Clearmont, Dayton, or Ranchester, we wouldn't have no problem–loaded up and went. The parents didn't worry. We had some blankets with us to keep warm, and he'd drive slow 'cause the outfit wouldn't go over 40 miles an hour.

Kaycee has lived through a lot of changes. It has had a number of fires in this community. Do you remember any of the buildings?

All of them. Probably the biggest fire–well, I wouldn't say the biggest–James' hardware store burnt down. It joined to Diers garage. It caught fire, and Diers Garage burnt down with it. It was an awful hot fire. The next one was the Kaycee Hotel burned down. It was a real cold night it burnt down–20 degrees below zero. It was a hot fire, but they had a little bit more water then than they did at the Diers fire. The Diers fire was all bucket brigade.

Some of them was set. We had a lot of small fires. They finally caught him. His name was Clyde DeBotkin. He probably set 25 fires. He was a firebug. He set the bridge on fire twice and just about burnt it down twice too, but they put it out. Luckily, they had water pretty close. Most all the fires was about 1:00 at night.

We haven't had many fires much lately until this week. Charlie Graves' garage burned down. It was caused by a butane tank leak. It caught fire and blew up. There wasn't anything you could do about it. There was five minutes before they could get there. Well, that propane was 500 feet in the air.

Did electricity start in the early 1940s?

Chet Hall had bought Diers Garage that had been burnt out, but the rock structure was there. He rebuilt it and put in living quarters. He had a filling station and bulk station and the telephone exchange there. His wife's uncle's brother, they applied for application for electricity and got a permit. That was the first electricity. They serviced everybody in Kaycee. Then the Johnson County REA come in and bought them out. They had to have so many people so that they could come in for the rural electrification. That was the beginning of all the electricity here. Diers Garage years ago serviced a couple of business in Kaycee with electricity–Kaycee Trading Company and the Telephone Store across the street. Just before that, Mart House put a plant that serviced several people in Kaycee. It wasn't that efficient. There was some businesses earlier that had little plants. Some ranchers did too.

What about telephone service? Has that ever been a local service?

Well, see, all the services out of here to Barnum and Mayoworth, Sussex–everything went through in town. You had a battery with your phone exchange here at Kaycee and for local phones. It was connected to a central station. Halls, they run it. Before that, Mart House for years run the telephone exchange. You had to have someone on the switchboard all the time. At night you had to have someone get out of bed and answer the exchange so they could put in a long distance call.

Do you remember any Indians traveling through Kaycee during your childhood?

Oh, yeah, Indians traveled through. Some of them might have camped overnight. A lot of times they'd camp at Buffalo. They were just like they are now except they'd been on the reservation just a short time. Some of them couldn't talk English. The younger ones would do their things. They'd buy things, but they'd only buy one thing at a time. Then they'd buy something else. They never bought two or three things at a time. Now they have a generation of being on the reservation. They're more Americanized.

We had gypsies too. When the gypsies come to town, they usually camped down here by the creek. If they knew gypsies was in town, they would close up their front doors. Sometimes you didn't, but then you'd have to watch them.

What is the best thing about living in Kaycee, Wyoming, most of your life?

Probably the lack of people. I wouldn't want to live in a big city. Then there is a lot of hunting and fishing.

Are there any drawbacks?

Well, yeah, if you want them to be drawbacks–I mean you don't have a lot of social activities that you would in a town. For some people that is good. A lot of women don't like the isolation. Then there is a lot of hunting and fishing and so forth. But a lot of women don't like that.

Harold Madsen
1914-1996
From an interview with Janice Moore
In 1987, when 73 years old

Harold's Hobbies

Interviewer Janice Moore: We are in your little museum here, and there are, I would say, thousands of arrowheads.

There is. I don't know how many, but there is a lot of them. Actually, they are from 1970. That was the first summer I started artifacting. That was just on the spur of the moment. We was up there on a picnic one day, and we just all decided we would see if we could find an arrowhead. Well, I did find one. It was the only one that was found that summer.

You have a hobby of collecting artifacts, but do you have other hobbies?

Well, yeah, I've got a few old clunkers–a 1919 Model T Roadster and a 1929 two-door Model A Ford.

How many years have you driven your 1919?

The first year I drove that was in 1958 or 1959 when I had it put together. It took me about three years to find pieces enough to put it together. Anymore it's really hard to find original parts. Not only that, but they are expensive if you do find them. Well, what took me the longest was the Roadster had a little turtle on the back end. That's what they called them. The turtle has a lid that opens up so you have room for one little suitcase or something small in there, and that's it. I didn't have a rumble seat. That was the last thing that I found that I was looking for, and it had taken me pretty near three years before I found that alongside the road in a barrow pit out here on the county road. It had been there all that time, and nobody had picked it up. It was just what I was looking for.

The seventy-fifth doings here was the first year that I had it in the parade. All except one year I was in the parade. I don't remember what the deal was that year, but I was told to go down on such and such side street and stay there until they called me. Well, nobody ever called me, so I turned about and went back home. I didn't get in the parade that year. They had a different kind of a set up that year. The parade was all gone, and I never heard nothing from them.

You have one other hobby. Do you know what year it was when you took an art class at Buffalo High School?

Well, I drew those pictures in 1953–just something to do in the wintertime. I had some friends that decided they was going too.

Tell us about your photography darkroom.

Well, I had a room down in the basement on the ranch that was my darkroom. It was just primitive equipment. I used the same cameras that I got today–an old Argus C3 camera with a 35 millimeter lens. I have an enlarger. Black and white was the only thing I worked with. I kind of joined a photography club. That was just taking pictures mostly. Then they got to where some would go to developing and enlarging, and I was one of them that did.

Tell us a little bit about this teddy bear.

Well, that was my teddy bear when I was only a couple years old. The inside of it is straw. He is in kind of sad shape now.

What is in the milk jars? They look like little tubes.

Oh, those are cartridges–empty shells. These first five jars here is cartridges and slugs that I picked up here on the post flat. When this fort up here–Fort McKinney–was going, these were out on their rifle range. Of course, I got an old metal detector. That's how I found them. I just found them in the last three or four years. They got the dates on the cartridges. They date back to 1881–the oldest I've seen in there. That one pint jar there–that's all lead slugs I found up there.

What is this?

All right, you've heard about this bomber that crashed up on Bomber Mountain back in 1943? It wasn't until 1946 that they found it. It was a sheepherder that saw something shiny up there. That's when they got to investigating, and there was this bomber that had crashed.

Well, it was cloudy and miserable weather, and they had gotten off course in June of 1943. Later in 1946 after all the officials had been up there, why, then three of us went up there on a pack trip to see this bomber that crashed. In climbing the mountain, the first thing that we saw was one of the landing wheels, which was laying there on one of the parts that's on the east side. There was also one of the motors. Those two objects were big enough that we could see them before we got right up to it. There was very little pieces of any size up there. There was a little part of the fuselage. It was probably the biggest piece there was. The rest of it was just all small pieces just scattered over the mountaintop there in amongst the boulders.

Of course, there was all this stuff laying around. This was one of the tail guns. There was two tail guns, and they were fastened together. Well, I unfastened them and packed this tail gun off of the mountain. Really heavy–I have all I can do to lift the thing now. Of course, I can't lift anything as I used to either–out of practice.

❦❦❦❦❦

Charlotte Baker Maggard
1904-1992
From an interview with Patty Myers
In 1983, when 79 years old

From Forts to Buffalo, Wyoming

Grandfather Charles Hogerson was born in Stockholm, Sweden, and Grandmother Sarah Hogerson was born in Norway. They came to Wisconsin. He was a wheelwright. In fact, Louise Mueller told me the other day that when Grandfather Hogerson had a shop. They did their horseshoeing. Louise Mueller's father came through, and he needed a wheel fixed, so he went to Grandfather Hogerson, who encouraged him to stay in Buffalo, which he did. At the time, the town was very small.

They were at Fort McKinney before they came to Buffalo, but my mother and her twin sister, Lulu, were born at Fort Fetterman in 1877. He was in the Army at Fort Fetterman. There also was a son, Carl, now deceased, who was born late, and one child that died real early. They were down at Fort Fetterman, then Fort McKinney, and then they moved to Buffalo in 1888. The Hogerson house is still standing next to the big old Rothwell house that Maxwells have now. I don't know when that house was built on South Main Street.

Father and Billy Graham had a blacksmith shop and did a little bit of everything. It was here on South Main. I remember it was hot. They made their own shoes to fit the horse, you know. He did a lot for the community. The community couldn't understand Grandfather Hogerson–why he was sending his daughters to college. Women didn't need an education, but he thought they did.

My Grandfather Hogerson planted the trees at Willow Grove Cemetery and named it. Oh, mercy, they are old–nearly 80 years old. I think it's beautiful now. The caretakers they have out there are doing a bang up job.

My father, Charles Selah Baker, came from Galesburg, Illinois. He met my mother there when she was in college. He decided he'd come to the West. They were married on the old Hogerson property.

I was born in 1904 in October across the street from this house where Pearl Isenberger is now [224 S. Lobban Ave.]. We lived there, and then the Gammons bought the house. My grandmother built this house [207 S. Lobban Ave.]. We've made it over several times. Merida [Charlotte's husband, Merida Maggard] and I were talking the other day about how old this house is. Merida thinks it was built in 1911. Mr. June owned this land and sold it. I tell you, it was just a prairie.

I attended the little white school, and I taught in the little white one, too, when I first taught. It was dismantled. I finished high school in Chambersburg, Pennsylvania, because the Langworthy girls were going there. The Langworthys had the cabin up there next to ours. Supposedly, it was a finishing school. That's where I went to get finished.

We rode on a stagecoach, and when we crossed Powder River, the water was running through the stagecoach. It took us four days on the train to get to Chambersburg. Of course, we'd stop in Omaha and Chicago to see friends. That's why it took us four days.

While in college in Nebraska, I came in and out of Buffalo on Duffy's Bluff railroad. I can remember there was a big bunch of us that went to Nebraska. Al Smith from Buffalo went there–Sam Adams and a bunch of them. Well, there were so many of us. The train was late, and we were going to be late getting into Clearmont. I told them, "Now, just let me handle this." So I said to the conductor, "Now, there are at least eight of us that have to go to Buffalo. If Duffy pulls out of here, here we are in Clearmont," but Duffy was waiting for us. All the time I was on it, they were stopping and letting people off at their ranches. Sometimes we'd get off the train and run a while and come back and catch it. You know, it was kid stuff. Merida came on Duffy's Bluff when he came from Kentucky. That was kind of a shock for him.

Back to Carl Hogerson–he and I went to college together. He was in World War I and had one year more to become a lawyer. He lived here with us. He had decided he wasn't going to go back to college, and my mother said, "Oh, yes, you are," so he was a senior at Nebraska, and I was a freshman. No one could understand how an uncle and a niece could have so much fun. He had no girlfriend, so he'd invite me to all the fancy balls. We had the best time dancing.

St. Luke's Episcopal Church

Mother's [Lillian Hogerson Baker] whole life was the Episcopal Church. Of course, she was involved in a lot of community things–history and art and a lot of clubs. At her fiftieth year–she played the organ for 50 years–the church people put a window in the church for her. The bishop came, and I played the violin and gave her a cross. I said to her, "Now, Mother, you've got to be strong. The bishop is going to be here to present you with a window," and she said, "I'll not cry." Guess who cried! As I was sawing away, I got through, but there were a lot of tears on the violin. She played the organ longer than 50 years. She learned to play when she went away to school.

In her will she left money for an electric organ because she knew no one would know how to pump that pump organ. The new electric organ in the Episcopal Church is dedicated to her, and they gave us the old pump organ. We have it at our cabin. Our son, Phil, who was an accomplished musician, did a lot of writing on that old organ in the summertime.

Dad did most everything that had to be done at the Episcopal Church just like my husband. He was civic-minded. He was on the city council seven years and 13 years as mayor.

I learned to play the violin when I went to the University of Nebraska. I played a great deal. After the university, I had a big class of violin students. Some were Sam Adams and Lloyd DeVoss and Margery Laing–I'm going back to the old-timers, you see–the Todds.

I majored in French in college, but I minored in music–the violin. I played in the church, and our son Phil played all through high school before he went to college. I have played violin solos for the CCC up there in the mountains. John Flint, who was involved in civil service in Buffalo, used to say, "Get your fiddle out. We're going up to the CCC camp, and you're going to play a violin solo." Sometimes I was the extent of the program. My only recollection is of them working in the mountain, clearing the forest–cleaning it up.

Our home was Catherine Marton's first home when she came to Buffalo. She couldn't speak a word of English. She'd been raised in a French convent, so she spoke beautiful French. My mother, my brother, and myself, we could all speak French, so we'd speak English, and she'd speak French. She helped us with our French pronunciation. She always went to the cabin with us. I remember one day we had an old coal stove, and she was shaking it. She was just furious, and she came out and said, "Mrs. Baker, damn fool stove won't burn," and I said, "Katie is beginning to learn English."

I met Merida when I was teaching in Buffalo. He had intended to go back and study law, but he liked the West so well that he stayed. He came in 1929. At that time, he was principal of junior high, and I was teaching third grade. We could look at each other across–you know, I don't think we did a lot of teaching! After we met, I don't think there was a night we didn't have a date–just sit around and talk and take walks. We were married in 1930.

Our interests were with nature. It always has been. Until Merida had a heart attack, we had horses and went horseback riding. We had so many horses. They had nice big pastures. We always did a lot of hunting after we were at Camp Comfort and our cabin. We hunted elk, deer. We could hardly wait to move to the cabin.

You can't drink the water up there we'd been told. Dr. John [Knebel] told us that when he goes to his cabin, he always takes water from town, and we've read lots of articles saying not to drink the water. The creek that runs by our cabin is the full creek. North Fork and South Fork come in way up, but they say not to drink the water. I don't know what's in the water. Whatever is in there won't purify itself [giardia]. Nan Bejino gave us a lot of plastic bottles because they buy milk in those big containers. We always pack up our water. We have running water in our cabin, but we use it just to scrub. It upsets me just terribly, you know, because the water is on the back porch, and you're almost afraid to brush your teeth in that water.

Dr. John was my third grade student, so you know how I love him. In fact, that chair in there in our dining room is one that old W.J. [Dr. John Knebel's father, Dr. W.J. Knebel] gave my mother. Mother was in the hospital for something when W.J. had the hospital. Mother mentioned to him, "W.J., don't ever throw that chair away. It's an antique," and one day it arrived at the house for my mother. Of course, Merida had Dr. John in junior high. I asked him one day—I was over at the hospital for something—and I asked him, "Dr. John, will you be one of my pallbearers?" and he said, "I sure will, Charlotte, but don't make it my day off!"

I made homemade ice cream in the mountains when we took care of Camp Comfort for 13 years for Mrs. Thom when she was so old she felt she couldn't come down there and look after it. She had an ice cream freezer, so we made ice cream. People loaned us a cow because they wanted that cow on that good grass. Seems to me we made ice cream every day, and the kids would just pour out of those hills. We stayed there, and my mother stayed at our cabin. It's only just a quarter of a mile from Camp Comfort.

Most of my friends were my mother's friends—the older people. In fact, my mother and Mrs. Laing and Merida and I used to play bridge several times a week. When Mrs. Laing died, Merida said, "Now, that ends the bridge playing as far as I'm concerned. Nobody can take Flora's place." I don't think he's ever played a game of bridge since. I've done a lot of bridge playing, but recently I've quit too. I tell you we played bridge. We really played it and by the rules. We had a lot of fun.

You see, I was teaching when we were married. I could finish out my contract. That was it. In the meantime, I raised three boys. They called me back because they needed a teacher badly. One member of the board was against married teachers, so that took care of that, but pretty soon they needed the married teachers, so I taught the first four grades. I started with the first grade and moved up. I taught through my child bearing years. Every so often they would call me back for two or three months. Fortunately, I could get an awfully good woman—Mrs. Grayce Provence. She was in Buffalo, putting her children through high school. She would take care of the children. Then I'd be back again—housewife. Then pretty soon I'd be called back to teach. I taught 31 years all told.

Jack was the oldest, and he's dead. Then Charles. Jack was born in '31 and Chuck in '34. Phil, well, they were five years apart. One was in '40. But we never had a girl.

Charles—we call him Chuck—is with Standard Oil of Indiana, Amoco, in Tulsa, Oklahoma.

Phil is dead. He was killed in an airplane crash while in the Peace Corp in the Philippines. He was only 22. We made a trip down there to see where he taught. He didn't know anything about Boy Scouting but had a Boy Scout troop there—a little bit of everything. A doctor in Billings told us we shouldn't go. We took about a thousand pills with us and shots before we went. It was clear down at the end of the Philippines 15 miles from the headhunters and the humidity. It was beautiful country. It really was because we could visualize what he was doing. He loved what he was doing. It was his choice.

Phil did a lot of composing. That's his piano there. He did a lot of composing on it. We went to Sheridan on his birthday to get him a sports coat, and we missed him. Pretty soon he caught up with us and said, "I want you to come down to the music store and see this beautiful piano. I've been down there playing." Well, you know what we came home with. We got the sports coat, but we came home with the piano. Maxine Hammond taught him to play. He played carillons when he went to college at the University of the South at Swanee, Tennessee. He was invited to have a concert at Carnegie Hall in New York City.

Phil and Chuckie Kaltenbach were great friends, and the Falxa boys were great friends of our sons too. Well, I think we mothers all knew where they were. I can remember the Falxas and Phil–we had a shed out here instead of the garage. They were having some kind of religious service. Oh, they had curtains at the windows and candles burning. It was a real religious service. We looked, and the place was on fire. They'd gone down the alley. They'd found something else to do. They had a religious service after that with a paddle! They never were in anything very bad. Since this had started with a religious service, what could you say?

We have a granddaughter, our son Jack's daughter, that we almost think of as a daughter. We have other grandchildren, but somehow Cindy [Maggard Fulton]–it's awful to say–she's a bit of a favorite. You see, she lives in Powell, so we get to see her more often, and she calls and writes a lot. When her daddy died, we wanted to adopt her in the worse way and send her to college and have her make her home with us. She was going to be a doctor and was accepted to Creighton University but fell in love with a farmer. All her plans–she's a wonderful farmer's wife. I talked to Dr. John about that, and he said, "I'm for her marrying this farmer if she's in love with him. If she goes to medical school, she'll be spending 10 years of her life learning to be a doctor when she could be married and having babies." She hasn't been unhappy, and she didn't know beans about being a farmer's wife. She does now–bakes her own bread. Big family of Fultons over there near Heart Mountain.

How well I remember Jim Gatchell. My mother took me to Sheridan on a little trip. I was 2½ years old–just toddling around. We were visiting, and I was told not to go in the third yard, but I went to the third yard and burned my feet bad and had to have skin grafting. I walked through some hot ashes, and my dress caught on the box–you know, wire–and I couldn't get out. It almost cooked my feet and almost burned a toe off. Well, my mother gave me first aid, and we rushed home on terrible old roads. The doctor said, "All I can do is cut her feet off," but my father said, "Couldn't you do some skin grafting?" and he said, "I've never done it, but I'll try." My dad and Jim Gatchell and the doctor all rolled up their sleeves. They took a razor blade and took skin off my father to put on my feet. Of course, my father's skin was the only skin that would take. So you know to me Jim Gatchell was quite a hero. I don't remember the doctor so well. Now,

I not only have a bad back, but I have to baby my feet! But I can walk.

I certainly remember the old Indian that camped up the creek. He had a tepee. He'd come into Jim Gatchell's drug store, and they'd talk Indian. Jim could talk Indian. I remember, as kids, oh, it was great fun to run up there and see his tepee and not get scalped. There was an Indian cemetery back over in that area. Of course, the Indians were buried high in the trees. I've heard my mother say that she and her twin sister would take sticks, hit the trees, and beads would fall off the corpses. They'd use those beads for their doll clothes.

We did everything with our children. I've heard the boys say, "Well, I hope if I ever have any children, we can raise them like we were raised." Of course, they were thinking more about pack trips and horses.

Johnson County High School

Merida worked in the schools from the 1930s clear through the '70s. I found this thing–"The Bulletin Salutes a Valuable Citizen" [*Buffalo Bulletin* February 9, 1956]. It tells about him teaching one year in grade school. Then he became principal, and for a year he was the coach at the high school. He was quite a basketball player himself. Then he became superintendent. He spent 39 years in Buffalo in the school business. He did about everything there was in the Episcopal Church–lay reader, taught Sunday school. He was a Boy Scout leader. He gave a lot of himself to the community.

We decided together to retire at 68. Then he had his heart attack. They wanted him to stay on for a year to coach the new man, but he had his heart attack, and that took care of that–also the horses. We got rid of the horses.

We go to Tucson, Arizona, for six months. We fly. We leave a little car down there. We call for help when we get off the plane, and they have wheelchairs there for us to get us around to the next concourse. We've learned that. Of course, we always have to have a friend take us to Casper to get Frontier Airlines. That's the only inconvenience. We hate to bother our friends to take us down and come get us.

༺༺༺༺༺

J. Merida Maggard
1904-1990
From an interview with Patty Myers
In 1987, when 83 Years Old

Forest Fire Timekeeper

I was the first one at the Duck Creek Burn fire scene with Ranger Herb Post except the Pierson boys–Milo and Charles. They had the sawmill up there and were in there with saws working on the fire. That was a Saturday morning around noon, and we were the only ones in there until about midnight. Then they got firefighters locally that began to come in, and we had a little rain shower on Sunday morning. If they had had a big crew, they probably would have stopped it, but it got hot and, of course, the fire broke out.

The supervisor, Conner out of Sheridan, started getting a lot of firefighters in, and they fixed a tent down on Little Sourdough. Conner asked me to keep tab of the firefighter's hours they worked. Then I moved to South Fork Inn and stayed there 23 days before I got back home. My job was to organize the firefighters into groups. They were groups of eight with one person in charge. That way we had order. It was a night and day business.

They started building fire lines. They would move back so far and get a fire line built with the hope it would control the fire. It would last until the sun got good and hot the next day, and then it would jump the fire line. I remember Dave Whaley had saddle horses and was packing things in. Conner kept begging them to move the line back further so that they could hold it, but they didn't want to give up more ground or timber than they had to. They wound up losing most of all of it in that area. One time fire came right down close to South Fork Inn. They had trucks backed up to move everything out of there if necessary.

So it was quite an experience. I didn't have to do actual firefighting except that first night and part of the next day. I was stuck there at South Fork Inn. When it was over, just as I was leaving, Conner told me, "Tomorrow Dave Whaley is going in to pack out some of the pumps and horses and things that was caught in the fire. I want you to go in so you can see the result of the fire."

It was awful. We went in through Long Lake and Feather Lake and Sherd. It was burned all around. The hoses there were all burned, but the pump was saved because it was in the lake. The amazing thing to me with all the people fighting on that fire, there wasn't a single accident. Buffalo sooted nearly black. There was soot everywhere, and it was strong smelling. At nighttime, the whole town could see a glow on the mountains. There were ashes as far away as Casper.

🌿🌿🌿🌿🌿

Charles B. Marton

1924-2004
From an interview with Sheila Francis
In 1994, when 70 years old

A Simple Life

I was born, let's see, November 21, 1924, in Buffalo at the Irigaray house. My family was from the old country–the Basque Pyrenees. My dad [Bernard Marton] was a sheep rancher. Him and Simon Harriet were partners for 40 years. At one time, they had over 20,000 sheep. I don't remember how many acres of land, but they had quite large holdings.

I did, well, whatever I was told to do, principally–shearing, lambing, trailing. You name it, we did it. When we weren't in school, we were out with the livestock. Every summer we'd go to the mountains. Mostly, all I did was fish, hunt, trap, play just like any other youngster.

Irigaray Family Members

We were disciplined by my mother who was very gentle but strict. She was pretty strict about us going to church. I was an altar boy from probably sixth grade clear through high school. We celebrated our holidays as a family–not only our family but all the relatives. For instance, we'd have Christmas at the Irigaray house. Then the next celebration–Easter or whatever–would be at our house. We were a very close-knit family–no question about that.

Every stray dog, every stray cat I brought home, my mother let me keep. I had a dog named Rascal. Him and I were pretty darn close. In fact, he used to sleep on the foot of my bed. He was my protector.

I remember one summer or maybe two in a row, I can't remember for sure, but all our range was inundated, deluged with grasshoppers. The whole country was totally bare. There was absolutely nothing left except cactus. The hoppers, I guess, couldn't eat the cactus. About all the sheep had left to eat was cactus. They were so thick it was unreal. In fact, I think they took sheep clear over into Campbell County to lease pasture, and they had to supplement the livestock with a lot of grain. It was just unreal.

After I graduated from high school, I herded sheep for about a year and then was drafted into the service. They gave me a choice of which service, so I picked the Navy. I was a second class petty officer and served on a PT boat in the South Pacific for about 18 months. It's a lot of water–thousands of miles of nothing but water. I never got home for two years. What a welcome sight! People don't realize what us young people went through back in those days going overseas. We were on a ship for 23 days–never saw land for 23 solid days. There were 3,000 of us on that troop ship. It was hot, and we took baths in salt water. The food was horrible. By the time we got to New Guinea, we were eating soda crackers and dried up salami. That's what we had for lunch. I don't remember what we had for dinner, but it wasn't much. Time went pretty slow. The day I got out of the Navy was the fondest day of my life. Almost three years–33 months.

Once I got out of the Navy I went out to the lambing camp–back to the old grind, which suited me just fine. I was married in 1950. My first child was born in 1951–seven children. Been living here ever since. I'm a semi-retired rancher.

🌿🌿🌿🌿

Helen Kaltenbach Marton & Patricia Ripley Marton
Helen 1927-2021 & Patricia 1926-2018
From an interview with Nancy Tabb
In 2017, when Helen was 90 years old & Patricia was 91

Two Sisters-in-law

Interviewer Nancy Tabb: First of all, tell me what brought your family to Buffalo

Helen: I was born in Lavoye, Wyoming, May, 1927. There isn't such a place anymore. My mother passed away when I was born, and my aunt and uncle, Eva and John Knepper, raised me out around Midwest. I came here to teach school in Buffalo about 1949.

Pat: I was born in Sheridan. I lived there until I was 5 years old when my folks moved to Hulett, Wyoming. My dad bought a Conoco Station there. Well, first my dad died when I was in the eighth grade, and my mother remarried Harold Dillon, so we moved to Chicago. Every summer I came back here because I had a lot of relatives.

Tell me the names of your parents.

Helen: My dad was Carl Kaltenbach, and my mother was Florence. My dad was from Midwest. He worked in the oil fields. My mother worked in the commissary there.

Pat: My parents were George and Bertha Ripley. Mother was from Hulett, Wyoming.

Do you have any family heirlooms that you're really proud to own that have been in your family for a while?

Helen: Well, see that platter over there. Ninety years ago that was on the porch when I came to that home. One of my daughters said to me, "That's got to go." I told her, "That's not going anywhere." I have early pictures from my aunt and uncle, and that platter is on the porch, so it just means something to me. It's not going to go!

Pat, do you have anything that's just really precious to you?
Pat: Most of my house is antiques from somewhere along the line, and I have pictures.

Were you only children?
Helen: Yes, later my dad remarried when I was about 9 years old, and they had three boys. My dad came up to Buffalo and was city clerk here. Then he was commandant at the Veterans' Home for 13 years. Later, he went back to City Hall. He passed away in 1975.

Pat, did you have brothers or sisters?
Pat: No I didn't.

Pat, when did you get married?
Pat: In 1950, he [Charles Bernard Marton] asked me to marry him on the third date. It was a blind date. Helen and John were standing across the street to see who that girl was. That was my first date with Charles, and they were down there watching to see what the blind date looked like. And we got married in April.

What places did you live in Buffalo?
Pat: We lived in that Munkres' apartment. Then we moved to those big white apartments on Main Street–the Hersey Apartments. Anyway, in 1951, we built a house and moved in across from the Catholic Church. We lived there for 11 years, and then we traded. The Catholic Church wanted our house for a rectory, so we got that "big mausoleum" on the hill and lived there about 20 years. It's a gorgeous house.
Helen: My family built it–the Rothwells. My dad's sister married Paul Rothwell, and they built that house. My dad sold it to the Thorne-Riders. The Thorne-Riders got angry because they wanted to be buried behind the altar of the Church, Father Grannan said "no." So they left the house to the Church with the stipulation that the Church could not sell it until they passed away. They moved to Sheridan and built that big Thorne-Rider stadium there.
Pat: Gave Sheridan all their money.
Helen: So when this other priest came in, they wanted to trade houses so that's how Pat and Charles got the house. Because at that point the Thorne-Riders had passed away, so they could do away with the house. When I got married to John [John Peter Marton] in 1948, we lived where Tracy Jelly has his office. We were upstairs in that apartment. Lola and Ed Pheasant were on the other side, and we shared a bath. We lived there for a year. Then we moved up to what they called the Munkres' apartments. It's up on the hill on Wyoming Avenue. We built up on Williams Street and lived there for 50 years and then sold that to my grandson.

The house that they traded for that you built, is it the one that they still have as the parish house?

Helen: Yes, Father lives in there.

Helen, did you have a happy childhood with your aunt and uncle?

Helen: Yes, I had a wonderful childhood.

What were some of the things you did for fun when you were young?

Helen: Swimming in the pool. That's where we lived all summer.

Pat: I don't really remember, but I was perfectly happy all the time. In the summer, I was always back here from Hulett.

Helen, tell me how you met your husband.

Helen: Well, we just grew up together. I don't remember being proposed to. We went together for eight years. We just had an understanding. We were married in 1948 at the Knepper home.

What work did your husband do?

Helen: John had so many jobs I'm not even going to mention them all. His last one was the ASCS [Agricultural Stabilization and Conservation Service] office. Then his brother died, and John inherited part of the ranch with Charles so that is what we did from then on. The ranch was from out here to Gillette almost to the Powder River.

Did you help on the ranch?

Helen: Oh, we did a lot of cooking.

Pat: We had to cook for shearers and do things like that.

Helen: Docking and all that. John was in the Wyoming Legislature for 18 years and went out as Speaker. That was wonderful.

Tell me about your children.

Pat: I have seven without trying–Chuck, Jack, Denise, Tim, Jane, Kate, and Lisa. Think what we could have done if we'd been trying. Chuck and Tim and Jack live around here. Denise is here. Jane lives in Sheridan. Kate lives here. And Lisa lives in Sheridan.

Helen: Sheila, Randy, Phil, and Ann. Ann lives in Baggs. Phil moved to Oregon. Randy is on the ranch out of Casper. And Sheila lives here.

What kind of jobs did you have?

Pat: I taught school until we got married–then no more. Well, I got in the art business. In the 1950-60s, we had the Painting Place downtown–me and Dollie Iberlin. We sold art and gave workshops.

Do you still paint?

Helen: She paints pots.

Pat: Two or three years ago I ended up in the emergency room from the turpentine. Well, just one day suddenly I was covered head to foot with a rash. I was perfectly happy painting out on my deck. Then I was in the ER. It finally caught up with me, so I haven't painted much. Now I paint these pots. They're fun. I have a painting in the White House in Washington, DC. Not everyone can say that. It was when Gerry Ford was President. A Wyoming congressman was a good friend of his. Gerry Ford had a house in Fort Collins, and he'd seen this painting in the Wyoming Governor's Capitol Art Exhibition in Cheyenne, and he wanted it. I was going to ship it to him, but he said, "Why don't you deliver it?" So Mary Lawrence and I went to Washington. That was great fun!

What about you Helen?
Helen: I went to college for two years in Hastings, Nebraska, then came home and went to work in the bank for two years.

Tell me something in your life that you are passionate about. Pat, yours is probably painting.
Helen: No, my passion died.
Pat: You read all the time.
Helen: Yes, I'm a three B-girl–books, bingo, and bridge.

Tell me about some of the most unusual weather that you've experienced. You were here right after the big winter of 1949.
Pat: I was up in a second floor room at the Black Hills Teachers College dorm in Spearfish, South Dakota. I went to bed that Sunday night, and it started snowing. It was 28 days before I got out of the front door of that dormitory–before they got a snowplow to get us out. There were 30 of us that couldn't get out. We did very well for about the first week. Then it turned into potato soup a couple of times a day, and then we were down to oranges. You had to go up on the second floor to see out of a window. You couldn't see a car. The cars were just humps. Fortunately, we didn't lose the electricity.
Helen: You know, I don't remember the winter of 1949. I was working at the bank and probably walked to work. I don't remember it being that bad.
Pat: It didn't hit here. It hit South Dakota right straight down the Nebraska line.
Helen: But I remember 1984 here. That was awful. We could not get out of the house up there on the hill. It was terrible.

Do you remember any advice somebody gave you that really made an impact on your life?
Pat: I can answer that one. I went from school in Hulett, Wyoming, with two people in the eighth grade class into a freshman class in Maywood, Illinois, with 1,400 students and did not know even one person. I bawled every night for Wyoming. My dad had just died, and I was homesick. I had a homeroom teacher–Mr. Kant, who taught

math. He looked exactly like a math teacher should look–a little man with the glasses. He told me, "Come see me after school. I want to talk to you," so all day long I worried what I'd done. I went in, and he said to me, "I'm going to tell you what to do. I know your problem. You're just overwhelmed with all this. Just tell yourself, 'I can do this,' and eventually you'll be able to. You won't have to keep saying it." Well, it has worked for me in my life. He saved my life. It worked then, and it's worked another time or two. But it does not work for labor pains.

Have you ever met a famous person?

Helen: Debbie Reynolds–my husband met her over in Worland. We gave some land up on the mountain to the Girl Scouts, so they had this big party over there. Oh, this is a terrible story! But I have to tell it because of Jim Hicks, who is still alive. Jim Hicks and John went over to Worland. They were party boys and were late–strange as it seems–to get to the banquet. So they weren't going to let them in, but Jim says, "Look, I'm the press. We have to get in," because he had the newspaper then. So they let them go in. Different people were being introduced, and Jim said something like, "Well, I'm sitting next to the Mayor of Buffalo." The funny thing of it was the Mayor of Buffalo, Sam Rosenthal, was also sitting in that crowd. Jim went up to Debbie and said, "I want you to meet the Mayor of Buffalo." And Debbie said, "Oh, I'm so glad to meet you." I've got a picture of her shaking John's hand. So she said, "I just met the Mayor of Buffalo. Will you stand up please?" John said to Jim, "What am I going to do?" and Jim told him, "Just stand up," so he did. I guess they looked over at Sam Rosenthal, and he had a funny look on his face–like, "What are those two up to now?" Anyway, that Christmas as a joke Jim Hicks put a present under the tree "To John from Debbie." John didn't think that was funny at all.

🌿🌿🌿🌿🌿

John P. Marton
1926-2010
From an interview with Robert J. Springer
In 1976, when 50 years old

Modern Sheepherding

We don't get Basque herders from the French side anymore–just the Spanish. They herd sheep. Camp tenders take the food to them. They will come in once every three months now. Of course, they used to come in once a year. They stay out with the sheep. Well, we have sheep wagons. They are only in the mountains in the summer, not in the winter. They took the sheep to the mountains in the spring of the year and brought them off in the fall, but they stayed down in what we call the flats all winter long. It's flat country off the mountains where the grazing areas are. Now everything is fenced off. We turn our sheep loose, and we don't need the sheepherders like we used to. Also, we can't get them. Years ago, none of it was fenced, and all the sheep had to be herded. Now it's all in pasture. We only use one herder now where we used to use six. It's a family operation now. Our sons do it. We truck two bunches to the mountains every year where we used to trail them. We take a band of 1,200 to 1,300 ewes and their lambs. It takes, oh, seven to eight trucks, depending upon the size of the band of sheep. Everything is mechanized now. They drive around in pickups and use horse trailers. Before, everything was done horseback, and teams pulled the sheep wagon.

We sell the wool. As a rule, it goes to Burlington Mills. This old herder that we have out there–he still cooks a lot of Basque, and he bakes bread occasionally. Lucien out in his sheep camp–well, we have the sheep wagons, but he didn't like them, so we bought him a trailer. It's got the propane stove rather than the old wood stove. Whenever you go visit with him, he's got a big mutton stew and homemade bread. You never go to his wagon that he hasn't got something prepared. He's 50 years old, and he's been here for years and years. He's from the French side. He just speaks French and Basque.

The Basque just don't get together anymore. When the priest is here, we have the Mass. That's about the extent of it–maybe once a year. It's a small community. Everybody sees everybody and talks, but as far as having a get-together–not anymore. We don't have the 15th of August celebration in the mountains anymore. It's being held down in the Catholic recreation hall. They still have one up on the mountain, but it is very small now. It's up at Pierre Iriberry's camp. The priest goes up there and says a Mass. All the people that are in the mountains are invited–you know, the Basque people that tend the sheep. No dancing–not like they used to. We have a Basque program on the radio every Sunday. At the Fair this year they put on a little dance, and at our Rodeo they put on a dance. The women had a Basque skirt and a top, and the guys wore a beret and a scarf tied around their waist and then just the Levis and shirts. They did this dance because of the Bicentennial.

We used to have a handball court back of John Esponda's house. Years ago when all the Basque were here, every Sunday they had handball games, and we all got together. All the Basque would go down there. We had regular seats where you sat and watched. They had a concrete floor and walls.

Some nights you get both fish and a meat at the table. One night we had this great big platter of French fries with everything else. I don't remember salad. For dessert this bowl of apples and oranges and then cheese and a few nuts in that bowl. Sometimes a custard. I don't know how it's done but a souffle. It's in a brown crock about that high, and it comes up over the top.

※※※※

Clyde F. May
1914-1989
From an interview with Patty Myers
In 1988, when 74 years old

Civilian Conservation Corps Cook

In 1935, I helped set up the camp at Wapiti near Cody, Wyoming. I had been working in the timber in the Black Hills, and the railroad quit taking ties, so we were out of work. I started looking for something to do, and what I come up with was to come into the CCCs–$30 a month. I got $5 a month for camp, and $25 went home. You could advance up to $35, and if you were capable, why, you could move up to $45 a month, which was top pay. Of course, at that time, if you got $40 a month, that was a lot of money really. That's what you had to work toward.

I was in just a short time, digging the ditch to lay out the sewer, when they came out and wanted to know if there was somebody who would go into the storeroom and kind of look after things in there, so I got out of the ditch and went into the storeroom. I worked in that for about two months.

Then I went into the kitchen and started cooking. I think one of the reasons was they had sent our truck to Casper to get supplies, and they got snowed out from our camp. We didn't have anything to eat except 1,000 pounds of black-eyed peas, and they didn't know what to do with them, so I cooked them. I got sent up as second cook. Then I was sent up to first cook until I got out in 1936.

The camp was set up on army regulations. They had reveille every morning, and we saluted our flag. We had breakfast set up on army regulations. Everybody had the same opportunity. Didn't make any difference if you was black, red, or white.

I remember, particularly, the last bunch of fellows that was in our recruits. They came in from Oklahoma and Arkansas to Cody on the train. We picked them up with trucks and then hauled them 40 miles out in the country in forest service trucks with this canopy on the back. Those poor guys were froze to death when they got to camp. We had orders to have a meal ready and feed them when they come in. I was in the kitchen, and when those fellows came in, they wasn't interested in eating. They wanted to get warm.

I was in the CCCs about seven months. Then I got married, and married men couldn't stay in.

We were completely away from the city. Well, we had chances for education. In camp it was offered to us. We had an educational advisor, and we had a doctor in all this. It was in camp, though. I'd really be in favor of having it again.

❦❦❦❦

Robert W. McBride
1918-2006
From an interview with Patty Myers
In 1982, when 64 years old

His Love of Horses

My grandfather, Wilson McBride, came here in 1892. He was superintendent of schools. They had had a lot of trouble in the schools the previous year. This is a story that he told me directly. It was the time of the Johnson County Invasion, and the kids played on opposite sides of the school ground at recess time and threw rocks at each other. It was a real division of the school. Of course, a lot of the kids were real old even though they were in grade school because a lot of times they only went to school short times, so they were pretty big kids. They'd run the other principal out. The first day my grandfather was there–of course, he taught classes as well as being principal at that time–some kid challenged him. He went over and pulled him out of the desk and pulled the desk right up out of the floor. From then on he was in command.

My father, Sam K. McBride, was born that summer. He and his mother came out that fall and got off the train at Suggs, Wyoming–which is Arvada now–and from there on the stage. In 1902, he bought the homestead where the present ranch is. My dad lived out here 69 years when he died, which was in 1971. My mother, Nercilla, lived there 54 years, which is the number of years they had been married when he died.

They bought part of it and homesteaded part of it. Part of it they bought from a man named Spiering, who had the original 160 acres where the house is. The bunkhouse at the ranch that we had for all those years was his home. My grandfather had moved it over to its present location. It's a clapboard garage. I thought it was interesting that they numbered all the logs with an ax so they could put it right back up.

My dad was born in Dorchester, Nebraska, and came here when he was 3½ months old. My mother always said he was not a native. She was a native because she was born in 1895 out on Shell Creek.

My mother's family name was Fullerton. They came here earlier than that–about 1887. Granddad Fullerton ranched. In the time that I knew him, he ran a livery barn up on North Main Street and had teams that he had for hire. I have a sign, "The Red Front Livery, Feed and Stables, Fullerton Prop., Best of Rigs and Stock, Driver That Knows the Roads, Phone 55." That was in the lobby of the Occidental Hotel at one time.

I can remember when I first started school because I was a ranch boy, I went up at noon and had my lunch with my aunt, Nettie Owen, who was a sister of my mother. My granddad lived with that family because his wife had died when my mother was in high school. I can remember drivers that worked for Granddad Fullerton coming there and eating the noon meal.

My granddad was a real horse lover–had running [racing] horses at Big Horn Basin.

I had a running horse here a few years ago. I love horses and have a few, but I don't do much. I go on the trail ride once a year, but that's about all I do. I justified the running horse because it was in my blood from Granddad Fullerton.

I think it's rather interesting that you see teams of workhorses today that are generally very well matched. Granddad Fullerton usually had good matched teams. I remember teams that we had. We had them because they were about the same size or had about the same speed but weren't matched.

Robert McBride

Oh, I cherish that memory of having lived in a time when I harnessed horses and drove teams. I drove a team during the Fair parade this year with Hank Barlow. That's the first time I have driven a team, I would guess, since maybe when I came home during the war. We still had a team or two then. Once you learn to swim or milk a cow or drive a team, generally, it's something you don't lose. It's kind of like going on the trail ride every year. People ask me, "Don't you get all bunged up?" I really don't. I might get sore or stiff being my age. The people who really get buggered up are people who have never ridden horses much. A lot of times on the trail ride you have people there who have never really done much riding. There are some awful sore people.

My dad had a homestead on Bald Mountain and built a cabin up there. When they first married, they moved up to that cabin Dad had built. Mom is Nercilla. They were married on the 4th of April, 1917. That first night they went up there, three fellows from Buffalo walked all the way up there and shivareed them. Can you imagine that–seven or eight miles!

It was probably early 1920s they bought another ranch that my grandfather and grandmother moved onto. They lived on that, and my folks stayed on the home ranch. During the Depression years, they lost the extra place, and my dad sold off the land on Bald Mountain just to save the ranch south of town. That's just the facts of life.

Back in those days, we probably always were milking anywhere from 10 to 15 milk cows. I don't know if it was a moneymaker, but it was probably the only cash that was a lot of times developed as far as taking cream into town and selling it. You know, back in those days it amazes me how little cash people actually had. You lived on a ranch and had everything you actually needed.

My dad kept a diary every day for about three months, and it is a real prize. He was a real character. He never had a pickup. We only had the family car, and he used that for everything. Of course, around the ranch we used teams. It wasn't until I was in high school, oh, early 1930s before we had a Model T Ford. We always had at least three or four teams all the time and probably four or five saddle horses.

We weren't big cattle growers. As a matter of fact, when they had the Bald Mountain land, my folks ran sheep more than they ever ran cattle. Cattle were more of the milk cow type thing. My dad sold a lot of hay.

My brother and I had sheep starting when we were in 4-H. We each bought a pure-bred Hampshire from the Moncreiffe Ranch over at Big Horn, which is where the Bradford Brinton Museum is today. They raised registered Hampshire. By the time I went to university, we had 40 or 50 head of registered Hampshire ewes. They're beautiful. We took first prize here in the county, state, and Billings and thoroughly loved it. I wouldn't mind whenever I quit at the bank, getting a little bunch of sheep.

Kelly, my brother, and I still own the ranch. We lease it to Jim Guyton. The ranch is just exactly a mile and a half south of town. It's on the second hill as you go south on Highway 87. The ranch buildings are on the west side of the road. It's easily recognized by the big grove of trees that's around it. That grove was put in by Grandfather and my dad. They took a wagon and went down on Powder River. Those shoots just grow up in that sand, you know. They took a shovel and just brought them up. My grandfather just plowed a furrow with a one-blade plow, and my dad came along and dropped those trees in there. They covered them up and started irrigating. That's one of the first shelter belts, I bet, in the country. Living out there on that ranch on that south slope with the shelter belt–until you got past the trees, you wouldn't realize how cold it was or how hard the wind was blowing.

We always had running water. However, we didn't have hot water in the house except from a copper boiler that was attached to the coal stove. Later years, they put a hot water tank right beside the coal stove, and the pipes circulated through the stove. I remember leaning against that tank if you came in cold. It was just one of those old galvanized tanks. Before we got that tank, we used to have a copper boiler and would go over with a dipper and dip hot water into a washbasin. Of course, we didn't have an inside bathroom for many, many years. When we did get one, my mother was about the only one allowed to use it.

Our water in the wintertime came from a cistern that we filled out of the ditch. It held 500 barrels. It's still there. Now, we have a well. In the summer, of course, we could use all the water we wanted, but when they finally had to shut the ditch off, they'd wait just as long as they could to fill up the cistern. It was just up at the top of the hill.

We rode the school bus for many, many years. It was always put out for hire to some person who had a car. They'd be the ones who had the bus. Generally speaking, there would be seven or eight of us who would be riding in a car. The cars were so rugged. They were iron. Fancy upholstery and all those things didn't play any part in those days. The roads must have been gravel. I don't remember when the road was paved. One of the persons who had the bus for many years was Mr. Huston. He came out from town. I suppose they put it up for bid. The school didn't own any buses at all. Whenever the athletic teams went anyplace, all the dads furnished the transportation.

One of things I enjoy telling about is when I first went to university, I had to take freshman English. Second quarter was English poets and that type of thing. I remember the teacher saying that one thing we'd be required to do would be to learn part of Chaucer's tales, so I raised my hand and asked, "Can I say mine now?" She was amazed. In school Mrs. Bess Muir insisted that we had to know that. When my kids came along, I forced each one of them to learn it, but they don't remember it now.

Back in those days you provided so much of your own fun. We did a lot of riding, of course. After we were up to about age 8 or 9 years old, we had Shetland ponies and rode all over the country. My brother, Sam, and I were particularly close. There were just two years between us. Kelly came along, and he was about six years younger than I. Every year just around Fair time we'd really get with it as far as our interest in roping. Of course, we hunted quite a bit too–rabbits, anything. We had BB guns and in later years .22s. Generally, my dad made us go by ourselves. He didn't like the idea of two kids out hunting together.

When we were putting up hay in the summertime, my dad would be in the field by 6:30 haying. Usually by 2:30 or 3:00, he'd say, "Well, I think we ought to go swimming," and we'd all pile in the car and come to town. I bet I spent as many afternoons in the pool as a lot of the city kids just because my dad loved it and figured that life wasn't all that important. I remember most other people were usually an hour and a half later than my dad was getting out there. My dad was a fast mower. He'd have his hay up by the time most of them were getting started. Being on the ranch was never a hardship as far as my memories are concerned. It was a beautiful experience. My mother was a great cook too.

I went to work at the bank on October 8, 1946. This October 8th I will finish 36 years of banking. When I went to university, I didn't take Ag. It was almost as bad then as it is now to be in the ranching business. I had hay fever bad, so it was kind of always understood I probably wouldn't do something like that. I don't have hay fever now, but if I was out mowing hay, I'm sure I'd find out I still had it.

Harry Gallup was at the First National Bank. Harry and his wife [Helen Ramer Gallup] were great friends of my folks. They were quite a bit younger, but they were great friends. At that time, they needed somebody to come into the bank. Bob Holt started in May of 1946, and I started in October. Bob and I have always been close friends. Of course, Mr. Holt was the president, but he didn't work. He had retired. He came down every afternoon. There was Harry Gallup, George Darling, Opal Beatty, Max Hughes, and Bob Holt and I. There were six of us. Bob Holt and I did all the posting. We were the two bookkeepers and posted for eight years. Back in those days you had to work all the way up through because you had to know everything. The last two or three years we alternated–one on the teller line. They had hired another bookkeeper, and we'd take a month at a time out front and in back.

❦❦❦❦

Samuel K. "Sam" McBride

1892-1971
From an interview with Stuart Frazier
In 1964, when 72 years old

A Torn City

My father [Wilson McBride] came out here in mid-August to find a place to live and get lined up for the work ahead in the school. He was to be the sole teacher in the high school of about 35 students and superintendent over the whole system. However, there were only 11 grades in school, and the prior superintendent had been egged and run out by five or six over-aged hoodlums during the spring of 1892.

Buffalo was a torn city as far as feelings go about the Johnson County Invasion that took place that spring in April. The residents had naturally taken sides, and the students followed in their parents' footsteps.

He came by four-horse stage from Suggs, Wyoming, which is where Arvada is now. Jimmy Childs, who was the stage driver, tipped them over at Double Crossing–this side of Clearmont about four miles. He got the 13 on the Concord and their luggage all wet. They stayed all night at old Doc Frederick Huson's. That's about three miles west of Clearmont where the stone house is that Tex Ellis now lives in. It was a halfway house between Suggs and Buffalo.

Doc Huson is a Civil War veteran and a very colorful storyteller. He entertained his guests after supper with stories of the old West. One of the young ladies who was on the stage asked Doc, "Mr. Huson, did you ever fight Indians?" "Well, did I ever fight Indians?" he said, "Why, we used to fight them every fall here when we would go up hunting deer. One time, we went up back of Big Horn hunting deer. We looked back, and here come a whole bunch of Indians with war paint on following us up this canyon. So we thought we would go right up the canyon and then go out on top and get away from the Indians. We got up to the top of the canyon. It was a straight up and down wall about 300 feet high, and we couldn't do a thing. We had to stop right there." Old Doc kind of stopped and didn't say anything for a few minutes. A schoolteacher said, "Well, Dr. Huson, what happened?" Doc replied, "They killed every damn one of us."

My father arrived in town that evening, and before he had a chance to eat, two members of the three-man board asked him how he stood on the question of the cattlemen and the settlers. The board was divided three to two on the situation. My father told them he would have nothing to do with it. He knew nothing of the background, and it was all over as far as he was concerned. And he knew nothing of the merits of either side and would only try to see that the students would become reconciled so they could go to school peacefully and learn their lessons.

Kids fought with their fists and with rocks, and it was three or four months before they got a semblance of order on the grounds. The five or six hoodlums–the cause of the former principal not showing up for his fall term–didn't come to challenge my father.

He was a strong disciplinarian at home and in school. He was fair in his dealings in the family, and his students have told me that he was fair in school, but I'll say what we call nowadays, tough.

He taught all five subjects in the high school grades–English, Algebra, Geometry, Latin, and History. After he taught six years, he retired to a small place south of Buffalo and in 1899 bought the ranch where we now live. I have lived there for 65 years and my wife for 47 years of our married life.

For years, my hobby has been interviewing old-timers who were here and took part in the Invasion or the Indian wars. I feel very fortunate to have known several of those prominent men of that day who had an active part in those events. The main source of my material comes from my old friend and neighbor, Dave Cummings. He lived there from 1898 to 1934 when both he and Mrs. [Mary] Cummings passed on.

Uncle Dave–as we called him–came west from Virginia, where he was born in 1856, to Virginia City, Montana, with his parents and an uncle. His parents both died there of some disease like smallpox or typhoid fever. This little mining town was the scene of some real important early Montana history. Their sheriff, Captain Plummer, helped road agents rob Wells Fargo Express coaches that carried gold dust in the mail. This became so flagrant the citizens formed a vigilante committee and took the law in their own hands and hung Captain Plummer, Cripple Foot George, and four or five others. Uncle Dave, as a 6 year old boy, saw these hangings, and, of course, it made a deep impression on him.

Uncle Dave grew to manhood in and around the central area of Montana and later wandered into the western part of the Dakotas. He was in the Custer Campaign as a bullwhacker, driving a team of oxen hauling supplies for the government. Later, he hunted buffalo for their hides in eastern Montana for the government. Hunting buffalo for their hides would probably bring $1.50 or $2.00, and in a few years' time, the buffalo were decimated. In the 1870s, Uncle Dave worked for Joe Carey down on the Platte River at the Carey Ranch, where he met I.J. Phillips, a nephew of Portugee Phillips. His uncle was the man who made the ride from Fort Phil Kearny after the Fetterman Massacre there.

Of course, Uncle Dave had nothing to do with that because it was before his time. In 1933, we were down at a Masonic meeting in Rawlins, and I met William Daley, Sr. He was a Civil War veteran, and he told me that he had been at Fort Phil Kearny at the time of the massacre. He was a civilian employee and had built the flagpole.

In 1916–an anniversary of the battle of the Fort Phil Kearny massacre–I rode out from Buffalo with some boys for a celebration at the Fort. At that time, Colonel Henry B. Carrington was still living in Boston and came out here. He was in command at the

Fort when the massacre occurred. It was very interesting to hear him tell about the battle.

One of the most colorful characters in the early days in Buffalo was Wildcat Sam [Sam Abernathy]. He called his wife Pussycat Annie. Sam was a trapper and hunter, and he couldn't read or write. He had a cabin about a half a mile above town. He was quite a colorful character. He never shaved and used to hunt muskrat out near our place.

This is a muskrat story. One day, I wanted to go see him down at his camp. He had a tepee down there. He always wanted me to stay and eat dinner with him. My mother told me, "Well, Sam, if you want to, you can." So I went down, and Sam had a kettle boiling on the stove at his camp, and there was a tail hanging over the edge. I asked Sam, "What are you boiling up, Sam?" "Oh," he said, "this is a muskrat. Haven't you ever eaten one?" I said, "No." "Well," he said, "they are sure good." So I asked, "Why didn't you cut the tail off?" His reply was, "You leave the tail on so you can turn it." I went home without eating, and my mother said, "I thought you were going to stay for lunch." I told her, "Well, I changed my mind."

The Invasion–now, I feel that that was always kind of a question that people didn't talk much about all through my early years. Since I am getting well along in years, and there aren't very many people that took part in the Invasion living here now–just second generation–I feel it isn't too bad to make a few remarks along that line.

What was the cause of the Invasion? Now, both sides were in error–there is no doubt. Men I have talked to on both sides–Mr. Hesse and Mr. Cummings and Mr. Brock and Mr. Mather–they all admit after a good many years that it was rather a sorry state and should never have happened, but it did.

In those days, the big outfits had all the creek fenced up, and most of the outfits were owned by people back East. Some of them–the 76 Ranch was owned by Englishmen. Cowboys worked for these men through the spring and summer. Then in the fall, they helped gather the beef. After that, their job was through, so the cowboys would stay with some of the ranchers that lived along the mountains and hunt deer and fish and try to pay their way by chopping wood and earning their keep through the winter. In the spring, they would return to the ranch where they had worked.

Dave Cummings told me the cowboys would stay all winter with Lou Webb. He had the Hat Ranch. As they rode east towards Nebraska, they used to go over to the edge of the Dakotas and Nebraska to start work because cowboy work started up earlier in the season in that area before it would start here. As they would go along if they saw a maverick, why, they would put Lou Webb's brand on it or Tom Gardner's or some other ranch that they had spent the winter with.

Now, a maverick is a calf that has no brand on it, and it was okay to brand a maverick. These big outfits would give their cowboys $5.00 a head to brand these mavericks for them.

Well, it got so the cowboys thought, "Why not get a brand of my own and brand these for myself?" So gradually the homestead law came in along in the late 1880s or the early 1890s. They would take up a homestead on these creeks and gradually fence up the creeks and have enough room there to own a few saddle horses and a few cows. And they began to brand the slicks for themselves.

However, it just went from bad to worse. Finally, they found where fellows had been so anxious to brand a slick that they even dry-gulched–as they called it–killed a cow maybe to make a maverick out of a calf. That happened until the cattlemen finally decided they would bring in these men from Texas to clean up the situation.

But Mr. Hesse told me, "Sam, it was more of a settler's war than anything else. The outfits could see there were no springs, no reservoirs, no wells. Once the settlers began to fence up these creeks, we were done." The big outfits were done. They just had to quit because they had no place to water their stock.

We are happy now that everybody has practically forgotten all about it–even to the second and third generations–and we are all living peacefully here in our Johnson County that we all love so much.

❦❦❦❦

Lottie Potts McCoubrey
1889-1976
From an interview with Elogene Robinson

Early Days in Johnson County

We started from Missouri in 1896. It was in the springtime, and there had been lots of rain. We drove teams. My father had some horses he was very proud of, and there was no sale for them. It was very, very hard times. Everybody was poor. Just no money. Why, if we had a nickel, it would look as big as a silver dollar would now. So we decided to drive the teams out. We had two wagons–one with a heavier team and one with a lighter team. My uncle drove the lighter team on a spring wagon. It had a cover over it. My father drove the heavier team with a heaver wagon. My father, all four of us kids and my mother rode in this. It was great sport for us kids. Of course, we got tired. When we got too bored in the one wagon, we'd go to the other. I remember my uncle was a great hand to tell stories and keep us kind of perked up. I know my mother got awfully tired. At that time, she was very thin, but she never batted an eye at anything.

We encountered quite a few difficulties. One horse kicked the other, and we had to layover for several days until it was able to travel. Then it rained so that we couldn't travel because the mud would get too deep. So it was 52 days from Missouri to Johnson County, Wyoming, south where Kaycee is now. All the way we would keep sending letters saying when we might be here to my uncle here, who was expecting us. Well, I expect they got pretty tired of waiting for us to come. I was only 6 years old, I believe.

I was next to the oldest. I had this one sister older, and then I had two little brothers. I was born in 1889.

My father, Jess Potts, was a blacksmith. Being a blacksmith, there was lots of horses needing shoes, and there were other things too. He repaired wagons and all kinds of things like that–farming machinery. There wasn't a lot of farming like there is now though. My father could work a whole week and hardly get 50¢ a day.

We were one of the first two families to live in Kaycee. We had some exciting times then and a little bit of blood and thunder. Well, Billy Deane was killed there in the early days. He was a police officer, and he was going to get some of the cattle thieves. He'd come down to arrest them. My father told him not to go out facing them, but he did. He walked right out in the open. The outlaws hid in the rocks. So he walked right down through where these outlaws were hidden. Course they just shot him. They made a stretcher and carried him up to the house and left him in the granary all night. It was a little spooky for us kids. This was 1897, I think.

George Peterson came in there about the same time and started a hotel. I think they had four rooms to let. A hotel and a store and a blacksmith shop–that was Kaycee. I think it must have been A.D. Metcalf, who sent a man down there to start the grocery store. There was a mighty little bit of everything, but we didn't need much. There was so little money that you couldn't buy anything.

Oh, we went to country school. We'd have three months in the summer and three months in the fall–always to some vacated homestead house to have school in. It was a long time before we had a schoolhouse. Even Kaycee didn't have a schoolhouse there. We usually had a young teacher from town, and God pity her, you know. We didn't have grades. We had readers. We went by the readers–first, second and third, fourth, and so on. Well, I don't believe we even got through one reader in the length of time because it was a very short period. You weren't compelled to go any length of time, but we went till we were grown. Just imagine taking that long to get a little smattering of this and that. Eventually, we did come to high school in Buffalo. Sometimes Father would take us to school with the team if it was bad and get us at night. We didn't have any light vehicles then because the roads were not very good. Sometimes a big blizzard would come up in the middle of the day. If a big blizzard came up, he'd walk to the schoolhouse and bring extra coats and things for us to wrap up in because, you know, you can't tell about the weather.

The houses were well-built and warm. They were all made of logs with a cover of boards over the roof so the dirt couldn't seep through. Then they put dirt up on top of the boards to keep the rain out and to make the house warm. It was kind of a sticky– what you call gumbo. When it got wet, the cracks would fill in, and it wouldn't leak. Not only that, but it helped to keep the house warm. We were here a long time before we ever saw a frame house like most houses are now. Once in a while, you'd see a house with just a dirt floor. It was surprising to see that when they swept the floor, it was quite packed. That floor would be pretty clean. The reason they didn't have board floors was there wasn't too much money then. If a kid had a nickel, he thought he was rich. We had enough plain food to eat. If we had a nickel's worth of candy, we had quite a treat.

We didn't have near neighbors then. You see, you had to hook up a team to go anyplace if you went very far. If you had a neighbor that you could walk to their house, that was wonderful. I mean, that was in the country where they were homesteading, and the homesteads were quite far apart. If anyone got sick, they would go for a neighbor. They couldn't go for a doctor because it was so far. You had to do everything yourself. Buffalo was 50 miles away, and we didn't make trips to town. A freighter or somebody would bring our supplies.

There was very little to break the monotony. We played games, and my mother read to us, but we were happy. I think it probably brought the family closer together than if we had been going hither and yon. We really have a lot here to be thankful for, don't we? It's funny how you can be happy without having everything.

🌿🌿🌿🌿🌿

Elise Mayor McKenna
1905-2004
From a Hoofprints of the Past Museum presentation*
In 1990, when 85 years old

Weather Reporting During World War II

It was 1940 when we decided to contact the U.S. Weather Bureau and see if we could get a Cooperative Weather Station. Dan Koch, they had one, and we thought Kaycee didn't have anything weatherwise, so we decided to contact the bureau, and it wasn't very long until they built the equipment we needed. In 1943 during the war, because we had this Cooperative Station and knew a little bit about the weather, the Casper Air Base contacted us and asked us if we would be willing to report the weather for the airbase in Casper, and we would be paid. Now, this cooperative business–it's all free. You don't get any pay at all. It's all in a day's work.

We decided that would be okay because we got paid. It was at the end of the Depression and the beginning of the war, and, believe me, the going was tough. By the way, I had been offered a school on Nine Mile, so we went out there and told them that I couldn't teach because a job had come for us right here at home, which was really a godsend at that time.

There were three of us. Pinky Brown took one of the shifts, and our relief observer was Roy Fauber. We were given a crash course–what I call it anyway–of two weeks of study. They gave us books and things to study concerning the weather and everything that goes with it. At the end of the two weeks, we took a civil service test, which we had to pass before we could go on. We had to get our work certificates. This was wartime, remember. I didn't think I would ever get one but finally did, and after two weeks of training, you might say, we were weather observers and more or less qualified because we had taken the test and passed.

There were three shifts of eight hours each. We reported the weather on the hour, every hour, 24 hours a day. We rotated eight-hour shifts and sometimes more often if there was a storm or something like that.

We had no days off for a year. This was during World War II. They made us get away for two weeks at the end of a year, and now I can see why. Let me tell you, at times the government was really rough–especially the nightshift, which I didn't like. We were sworn in just like a soldier. That's what they told us, "You go. Only if your life is in danger, you might not send in your report."

At night we had to go from the station here. There was a switchboard, and we had to take our report down to the old Red Horse Station and put in our own call. There were times that I was almost frightened to go out at night at 3:00 in the morning down the street to the telephone office and put in my call, but I kept thinking, "You're under oath. You have to go." Nothing ever happened that was bad although some very funny things happened.

No matter what shift I had, I could stay home, and before the hour when my report was due, I could go to the station and make my observation and call it in. That wasn't bad at all, but that nightshift was the one that was bad. I had it when it was fairly cold. I have done it in a snowsuit. I must have looked like a teddy bear.

Anyway, we did it. By the end of the 30 days, I tell you, you could just fall asleep almost anywhere. You didn't dare go to sleep during the night. It wasn't so bad for Ross [Elise's husband, Ross McKenna], but for me I had two kids in school. I had the meals to get and everything else to do, so it got so it was pretty rough. I served for a year and a half until the war ended. Ross kept on after that.

We were supposed to have just a few minutes to get our observations and make these calculations. If the report was late, boy oh boy, they would say, "Why was that report late?"

We got $110 month, and whoever had the nightshift got $30 more to go and phone in. The phone expenses were all taken care of. If the war had continued, they told us they would have given us a telephone.

At first, we thought, "Why are we here? Why are we doing this?" They really instilled in us as time went on that this station was important, and it took us quite a while to realize that it was important. After the war was over, different ones would stop in and tell us how they depended on what the Kaycee station sent.

The worst thing for me was to figure out the altimeter setting for the airplanes and keep in mind that the boys depended on what we sent. I tell you, many times I prayed that I would give the right facts. You had to read the mercurial barometer to the thousandth of an inch, take the reading, and then figure out the altimeter setting and a few other things you had to do.

The balloons were made out of some kind of rubber. We filled them with helium and then had to stopwatch it. We released them only if we couldn't determine or guess, you might say, how high the clouds were at night. In the daytime, we used the balloons. At night, we used the 1,200 watt lamp that we turned on. It made a spot on a cloud at night. Then you had to go down about 500 feet with our instrument—our clinometer—and take the angles of that to figure the approximate height of the clouds. We just had so long to get our report, make our observations, everything. It wasn't over five minutes, and you were done. We called in every hour.

Of course, as time went on, it became more and more easy for us. We understood things better. We were to report different things that we saw or heard that weren't right or maybe if we heard a different plane flying. We got so we had to be able to tell the planes just by their sound.

I remember one time during the afternoon I noticed two planes south of here flying back and forth. There was a thunderstorm to the southeast and one to the southwest, and I thought, "Okay, they are afraid to go through," so I reported it. They asked me a few questions. Then I went outside to see, and sure enough those planes were going where they were told after my report went in. I thought, "Well, I've done my good deed for the day."

They discovered from the reports of the station that our worst storms originate in the Bighorn Mountains. We would report snow or rain or a blizzard or wind blowing. We had to measure the wind too. Casper didn't and neither did Sheridan, so that's when they decided there was something that went on through here that they didn't know anything about. It was that this place was situated just right for the air currents. Buffalo didn't get that, and neither did Casper nor Sheridan. It seemed to be in this area here that there were storms, and the air pressure was different. The altimeter setting would be different.

I never knew just what to expect. A woman alone at 3:00 in the morning going down the street–there wasn't much traffic then, but there were times that I just didn't feel very safe, and yet I had to go–like the time when the bar down here–the Invasion Bar–was broken into. As I went down the street, I went way on the other side past the present-day Hoofprints of the Past Museum. I crossed the street where the lights were on in the saloon and loud voices. They were singing. They were having a good time in there.

One day, there was a couple of truck drivers. I used to go down by that big light pole by Babe's store [Lund's Meat Market & Grocery Store] and lean against it so I could get a better measurement because a clinometer–it's about that long and tapers like this, and there is crosshairs on top of it so that you can tip it and get the crosshairs on that spot and then just set it and dash back to the station and do your figuring to see how high the clouds are. Anyway, these truck drivers were down right in my place, so I had to go out in the middle of the street. I sort of braced myself because this clinometer had to be rather steady. I could hear them giggling out there. Well, these fellas used to stop at the station, and Ross knew them. They told him what they had noticed one night–you know, seeing a woman on the street. "Oh," Ross said, "that was my wife. She was on duty for the government trying to get a measurement of the clouds, and you guys had her place down there by that pole." Oh, they apologized. Anyway, things like that went on that weren't very pleasant when you find yourself all alone on the street at 3:00 in the morning.

Then came the time they asked us if we would notice and pay special attention and watch–observe I should say–the mercurial barometer to see if there was anything different. When the time came, we just watched the thing. It didn't move or anything happen. Later after the war was over, some fellow came and told us that day was when they detonated the first atomic bomb in Arizona, and they wanted to know if that thing that far away made a difference, which it hadn't, but we didn't know what that was for at the time.

Of course, during blackouts we used a candle at the station to see. We had to have some light. Once, there was a plane that crashed down by Casper somewhere. It flew low. Evidently, there must have been one light somewhere, and I often wondered if it could have been our light that they saw–seeing a light when flying very low.

Another time I was on duty during the afternoon. Of course, we were to keep our eyes open–eyes to the skies–to see if we could locate anything, and I located this thing. It was a Japanese balloon. It looked yellow. I watched the thing for a long time and reported it. It came down in Shirley Basin, where they found it. I thought afterwards, "Well, here for all we know there was a bomb up there."

Nothing serious really happened. I always locked the door behind me and then would go to the telephone. One time, there was this fellow pounding on the door, and I wasn't going to open it. Pretty soon, I recognized him. It was Ed Beebe, so I let him in. He wanted me to put a call through. That's another thing–people found out we were down there on the hour and could operate the switchboard, so they would stop in at that time and ask us if we would put a call through. I put Ed's call through.

To begin with, we had quite a time after having such a short course in meteorology. So much of it was foreign to us that we were constantly making errors, and the error would come back such and such a mistake. Finally, the day came when the paper came back "no errors." I know more than once I prayed I wouldn't make a mistake. It wasn't especially difficult to figure out what the altimeter setting was, but you had to read that mercurial barometer to the thousandth of an inch.

Ross reported for the Weather Service 45 years for which he didn't get any pay. It was all volunteer at that time. He did receive a citation for dependability, and I don't know what all. He loved it.

Of course, they wanted me to continue, but I didn't want to. I did stay and kept it going until I got a replacement. The Kaycee weather station was 51 years old last year.

*Supported in part by an award from the Wyoming State Historical Records Advisory Board through funding from the National Historical Publications and Records Commission (NHPRC), National Archives and Records Administration. Original recording provided by the Hoofprints of the Past Museum in Kaycee, Wyoming.

⸙⸙⸙⸙⸙

Peter A.L. "Pete" & Naomi Streeter Meike
Peter 1901-1985 & Naomi 1906-1999
From an interview with Patty Myers
In 1983, when Peter was 82 years old & Naomi was 77

They Came from Ranching Families

Interviewer Patty Myers: We are going to talk about when Peter and Naomi Meike grew up in southern Johnson County and the things they remember. Both came from ranching families that settled here. Naomi, do you want to start?

Naomi: My parents came to Wyoming in 1890 but not to Johnson County until 1900. They settled on the homestead this side of Kaycee about eight miles east of Kaycee. Mother and Dad, David and Anna Streeter, they had seven boys when they arrived in Johnson County, but Johnson County put a stop to that. They had four girls after that. The last two were twins. Of course, they tried to make a living off the land, and it was pretty hard in those days because there'd been no improvements–no ditches in the country like there is now to irrigate the ground. It had to be just dry farm and a few stock, but they seemed to manage to keep us off the county welfare rolls. Mother was a practical nurse. She was just forced into that vocation. She took care of practically all the kids that were born probably from 1900 until she passed away. If anybody got sick in the community, why, she did for them. She had up-to-date medical things. She brought me through tick fever when the doctors couldn't diagnose and treat it.

Peter, what about you? Were you born here? Who were your parents?

Peter: Emil and Emma Meike. I was born in Colorado in 1901. I'm not sure of the month, but we came here in early 1903 or 1904.

Naomi said that her mom did doctoring. I read that your mother, Emma, did midwifing in this area too.

Peter: Mom went out quite a few times as a midwife. There were only three or four families lived out here when Dad came to file on the homestead in 1902–Hard Winter Davis and a couple of Halls. That was about it. This was Indian territory that was hard to get control of. The Bozeman Trail came through about a mile up the creek. I have heard Dad mention the fact that when he came in, he came down at Salt Creek from

Casper with a team and wagon. He got to the river and met Mr. Davis and asked him about possible homesteads this way. Mr. Davis told him that there was lots of open land around, but all the river land was taken and no river water, but it didn't prove that way. Hardly any of it that was taken. It was just being used. Dad had been in the cattle business in Chadron, Nebraska. Homesteaders started coming in there thick fall of 1901. Summer of 1901, he went to northeastern Colorado. He was going to set up there, but that winter the sandhills grass didn't keep the cows alive. He lost most of his cattle. What he had left he got rid of. I better mention he had been a cowboy for Keeline. He had been rounding up cattle around Chadron, Nebraska, and had been told about this big river–Powder River. That's where he got the idea. After getting winterkill, he decided if he did get another home, it was gonna be one he could grow some winter feed. Really, it was his desire to get a year-round, manageable place for livestock. He was looking for a place near here. When he came in, he came down Salt Creek, camped the night on Shannon Creek, and thought he found what he was looking for. He circled the map with the native grass meadows there with a creek running through it. He thought maybe that was where he'd make his home. A creek and a little water in it–he thought maybe he could do some irrigation. When he tried that water, its name was "Can't Drink It"–rancid with alkali–so he decided he wanted sweeter water than that. Either 1903 or '04, we had a log house–huge logs. It was cottonwood logs and dirt roof and floor, but it was a snug little house. I can remember being there when a pretty heavy rain hit. The water came in through the door on the dirt floor, which made quite a mess. Mother had quite a time with that water.

Did the Indians ever go by that cabin that you can remember?

Naomi: The only thing we ever had were gypsies. I certainly remember lots of them coming through. I remember one ole gal–a neighbor of ours was just getting breakfast fixed. She was frying bacon, and this gypsy came in and wanted something to eat, so she gave this gal some hot bacon. She handed it to her, and she grabbed it and ran–hot grease and all. Beggars–she must have been pretty hungry. I can't remember any coming through after I was in high school.

Peter: Yes, they traveled through to Phoenix. They were horse traders. You'd want to watch them pretty sharp because they'd get somebody's old crippled horse and heal it up. They were masters at keeping a horse doing good and looking good and trading horses all the time. A good-looking horse would break down. They migrated with the weather. They had a get-together down in the southern part of the country. This is where they kept the horses. Entertainers, singers, dancers. I'd say they went out maybe in the late teens.

Do you remember Mr. Davis, Henry Winter Davis, as a child?

Peter: Oh, yes, he was a typical Englishman, like Edward Burnett, who used to run the 41 Ranch. They both had little white beards and mustaches. He was very well-educated and very well-read. He was a master in mathematics and a believer of things and making a go of it. He was ready to take the plunge and make it work.

What happened to Mr. Davis?

Peter: That spring of 1929 after the hard winter, prices had been pretty good. Costs had been so he could keep livestock buying. He got through all right for some reason until the later part of April when we got a blizzard. It wiped out the balance of the country. It wiped out better than half of the herds of Davis' sheep. Also, terrible losses with the cattle, and they never did come back.

Naomi, when did you and Peter start seeing each other?

Naomi: Well, I guess probably…

Peter: When the roads got good enough.

Naomi: Yes, when the roads got good enough to go to Kaycee from Sussex. I was going away to school in Buffalo, and he was going away to school at Billings Polytechnic in Montana, so it was after I was teaching. We had a car when I was in high school, but we didn't head out in wintertime because it wasn't as easy. I boarded one year, and then my sisters and I shared a cottage. I took Normal Training. They gave it in Buffalo in 1926. For quite a while, the people around here who taught and are still teaching started out that way. I taught the Holmes School one year, then the Christensen School one year. Oh, Pete even came in sometimes when it was freezing weather. Mostly, he'd just come and take you to a dance. We got married in June 1928.

Did you have a lot of chores when you were children growing up?

Naomi: There was always wood and water to get and the cows to milk and a few little sheep that we used to take turns watching in the summertime so the coyotes wouldn't get them. There was plenty to do. There wasn't much time to idle, but I don't ever remember feeling sorry for myself. We kept ourselves busy and contented.

Peter: My chores were very easy. There was always hired men or winter feeders–men who would come in and chore for board and room. They took care of all the heavy chores.

When did your family move from the homestead location up to here?

Peter: We moved here in 1935.

Naomi: We lived on my homestead on the other side of Pine Ridge on Meadow Creek. We lived there until our oldest boy was old enough for school. Then we had to come closer to school. Now there is a school right underfoot.

Do you still have your homestead land?

Naomi: Well, yes and no. When we split up our ranch after Pete's mother died and the boys and girls each took a share, why, it was easier for me to turn my place to one of the others in the family and get all of our land connected. That's what I did.

Did Emma take over the ranch after Emil died?

Peter: Yes. All the boys, of course, were all heirs. Dad planned this and kind of separated us and got us out of each other's hair. He could see the future of sheep. He thought better than most of the boys around here, and he decided he wanted to be a sheepman. Well, I was a hand. I worked on this place as a boy. The next boy, he got management of the farms. And the third one, Harold, he give him the cows, and he went into the cattle business. The oldest boy was a jack-of-all-trades. He broke and trained horses. It's more of a sheep country than it is a cow country. It's a short grass country. With a combination of sheep and cattle together, you get a pretty good harvest. With either one of them alone, it's not near as satisfactory. Well-balanced proportionately– not too many cows or too few sheep and vice versa. The sheep for the short grass and the cattle for the long, and there's a chance of breaking even each year.

Naomi: Vivienne Hesse expressed it pretty good. They asked her what her business was. She says, "We raise cows for respectability and sheep to make a living."

Do you remember the Scotch Outfit down here?

Peter: Oh, yes, they were a big outfit. They bought all of Dad's hay for the first five years that it had started to grow. It broke up the sagebrush and grass from the 1800s. They were pretty much free range. Everybody was. Up until 1916, there were a few homesteads and quite a few desert claims here. They would file on water, stone and timber or desert just to get control of the grazing by owning the water. That was the rancher's policy. Then in 1916, they passed the 640 homestead act [Stock-Raising Homestead Act]. That was a bonus for the GIs. They could come in. I believe the requirements were that they had to prove up on a section of land which without any improvements amounted to $1.25 an acre on the land, not counting the house and even residency. They could go there and live on it for seven months and build a corral or two and a reservoir. They could prove up on it then. It didn't cost too much, so that's what brought the homesteaders. Then the squeeze came on. Pretty soon they got to fencing. Why, then there wasn't grass enough left. They had to start leasing homesteads and had problems with cost production. The ranchers didn't believe that the homesteaders would ever stay. I was foreman up in the mountains. We leased a camp from the Scotch Outfit that they had up there after being sold out spring of 1920. They leased their mountain land to different people to use then. Homesteaders started coming in up there. Richie Young came up to survey their water up there. They got most of that water up there on desert claims–just straight 40s without the creek. A person was allowed four 40s of desert claims–the top limit that you could get.

Where did your family get supplies when you first came here? Kaycee wasn't much.

Naomi: It meant a freight trip three or four times a year–usually to Buffalo. Some went to Gillette. You could get a few things in Kaycee. Casper you could, but most of us went to Buffalo.

Peter: There wasn't any road through to Casper here until the oilfield.

Peter, did you and your boys build up this area around your house? I can't get over all your sheds. Is that all for lambing?

Peter: Yeah, that's Peter Meike and Sons turnout now–even these cottonwood trees that we planted here in the spring of 1935.

Naomi: The last bit that was here–well, this middle room was here when we came. We had a shed which burned down last year. That was the last of the original land grant.

Peter: We've still got the hole in the ground out there–the cellar. I'm kinda proud of that. There was one of those board 'n room types that wintered with Johnnie Graham. He stayed here and wanted something to do. I told him, "We need a root cellar here if you want to dig a cellar." Marked it out and gave him a shovel. He came back that night, and, by god, he had it dug. What is it–12x14? It is pretty good size, and he dug that all out by hand. Johnnie just couldn't get over that. After you get down about 14 inches here, you hit sand. He dug that with a scoop shovel. He really dug it out of here.

One of the reasons I came down this week is I know that by next week everybody will be too busy to talk to me with hunters coming in.

Naomi: Well, really these three days are about the busiest. I don't know how many we signed up today.

Peter: They're exceptionally careful, these people who come in here. A couple of days ago, I was going over the calendar of last year's hunters, and we had 272 head of them last year.

Naomi: They're people just like most of us are. They're not rolling in money.

Peter: These guys that won't let a hunter go out without a guide–they don't make enough money to pay for their time and management as far as that goes. Rancher spending his time riding herd on hunters isn't making any money, that's for sure. We show 'em what we got, show 'em where the roads are, turn 'em loose. We don't charge anything.

Naomi: Well, no income–we don't get anything out of it, unless you'd say, just now a fellow came in and brought me 20 pounds of cheese and another brought us some salmon and another brought us some apples. We have less trouble with the out-of-state hunters than the, well, the people from Casper. They kind of like to tell you what to do, but we don't have that trouble with the out-of-staters.

Peter: Well, the BLM is to blame for that. They put out their maps of federal land. You get east of the Missoura River, the Mississippi, and those people consider that these empty acres out here are unowned acres, you see. Just, "We're entitled to go on that anytime, anyplace because it doesn't belong to some person." You get further west where there are ranchers and stockmen, why, it's different. But the guys come out with those maps. I have to swallow once in a while when those guys come.

Naomi, I want to ask you about raising a family out here.

Naomi: Well, I guess maybe you'd say we were progressive. My husband and brother built us a wind charger, so I had electricity probably longer than anybody else in this end of the county. We were the first ones to get in bottled gas, so I had gas to burn since, oh, I don't know how long but a long, long time. Really, we started several phases here in the community. I guess we had the first indoor plumbing, and it didn't come easy. I raised turkeys for a while. That did our bathroom and kitchen. Oh, that was probably between 1935 and '40.

Peter: Yeah, turkeys were profitable when we came to this turkey raising question before the coons got to them. Coons and foxes have moved in since we came here. They just like the country and decide to stay once they come.

Naomi: And skunks! Pete went out a couple of nights ago to see if a cow was calving that he was keeping his eye on. He said there were five of 'em went out of the barn.

Peter: The mice are coming in the buildings now. The skunks are following them. They're mousers–part of the cycle.

Naomi: I suggested he take a gun and eliminate them, but he said, "No, they'll kill the mice." I wasn't happy though when I went out the other morning. I had just planted my tulip bulbs, and the skunks came here in the yard and dug up quite a few of them. They didn't seem to hurt the bulbs. They just dig it up and leave it laying there. It must have a smell to it. I don't know how else they knew it was down there.

Have you retired, Pete?

Peter: Ah, yes, retired. I've taken my itchy fingers, thumbs out of all the business, so it's the two boys managing, planning, doing it. Their mother still cooks for them, but that's about the only tie we've got. They're living here yet.

Naomi: We have traveled quite a bit in the past. I don't know if we'll do much more in the future. Pete's health isn't that good anymore. He brought me some travel literature the other day. I would sure like to say "yes," but we gotta think about it for a while. I don't want to go away from home and have him get sick. We've done that a couple of times. We do like to travel. We like to see the places we've read about.

Peter: Not too long bus trips. I'd go maybe three, four, or five days.

Naomi: We've been too busy to take a trip this summer.

Peter: I like a place to flop down and turn everything loose and go to sleep if you feel like it. You don't find that everywhere.

Naomi: About the only way we'd go is on a plane. We made one trip to the east coast in the car, and that's all we want of that. That was just too much!

James A. Miller
1850-1936
From an interview with Lester E. Ollis
In 1936, when 86 years old

The Last Buffalo

Buffalo were not hard to hunt in those days. We would go to their watering places on the river and conceal ourselves in their wallows. Wherever buffalo water, they fight and dig holes. They paw and throw dirt just like domestic cattle only more so. They get wet and wallow in the sand, and those great shagged beasts can carry a load of sand in their hair. They would usually come to water at 10:00 or 11:00 in the morning just like a bunch of cattle do. When they come, they string out in long lines, put their heads way down low so their noses are just a little from touching the ground and walk. A buffalo cannot see directly in front of him because of the heavy mop of hair on the forehead, so it looks off to either side as it walks. If anything was in front of a herd of buffalo, it just got walked over. In any buffalo country you could find long, deeply worn trails.

When the buffalo got in the right position to suit us, we would shoot one. Instead of the rest of the herd running away, they would gather around the one we had shot, and we could kill all we wanted. At that time, we could get a $1.50 for a buffalo hide, 75¢ for the tongue, and $1.00 for the hump. The hump is a delicious piece of steak that sits right on top of the shoulder. It is separated from the rest of the animal by a tissue. You can peel the hump right off the body. An average size hump weighs about 20 pounds. The flesh of the buffalo was left to rot and the bones to bleach on the sand.

The last wild buffalo I ever saw was an old bull that we killed here in 1884 at Fort McKinney on the post flats between the Soldiers' Home and French Creek. I think that was the last buffalo killed around here. Church Cook, Willie O'Neal and I were together at the time. I think Church Cook fired the shot that killed it, and we all three took part in butchering it. If there was one killed here at a later date, I never heard of it.

The United States' National Animal

John L. Miller
1938-2022
From a conversation with Nancy Tabb
In 2022 when 84 years old

Sisters Reunited

Mom [Eva Miller] told me that when she came to Buffalo, she needed a job, so she went to the Lariat Cafe, which was located where the First Interstate Bank is now, and applied for a job. The owner told her to show up the next morning at 6:00 to go to work. When she arrived the next morning to go to work, she was surprised to find her sister, Lillian, was working at the cafe. They were from the East coast and had lost track of each other. Both of them were single moms and both had a baby. They moved in together and got different shifts so one of them could stay at home and take care of the children. They lived in a house on Main Street south of the Meldrum home.

✺✺✺✺

Loren O. "Owen" Miller
1907-2000
Written by Owen Miller
In 1988, when 81 years old

The Civilian Conservation Corps Was a Good Thing

One morning in the early 1930s a truckload of Buffalo boys took off for Jackson Hole. This CCC camp was governed by the military. They had charge of the camp itself. It was made up of boys and men from Sheridan, Buffalo, Rock Springs–to name a few of the towns in Wyoming. New York, Philadelphia, and some Eastern cities had boys there. We were all throwed together in this camp.

It was pretty primitive, but for most of us it was like a big picnic or a paid vacation. I know it was for me because I'd been used to hard work. I think most of the boys that were there had been because I didn't see any of them that had been born with a silver spoon in their

Civilian Conservation Corps Camp

mouth. If they had, they had lost it a long time ago. Most of them had to work in order to eat, and they felt they were pretty lucky to be there.

We were issued hand tools–mostly axes, picks, shovels, and saws. We were supposed to work on a road. It was pretty much hand work. A lot of it was physical work. It was kind of frustrating because it just seemed like they were trying to make coolies out of us. We felt we could do a lot more if we had more mechanized equipment. About all we had where I was working was some horses. They had some horses on a road grader and a few things like that, but when you have to dig out stumps and chop off trees and shovel dirt all day long, it gets pretty monotonous. A lot of the boys, well, they complained quite a bit.

In the early days there on Taylor Creek at Jackson Hole, things were pretty disorganized to begin with. The boys, as I say, they came from all walks of life. Even those hand tools–there was a lot of them that never had them in their hands or anything like it before. An axe, no matter how sharp it is, after you bang it on a granite rock a few times, it really isn't much good. Things like that happened. They soon found out you couldn't use a shovel for a crowbar because the handle would break off it. In sawing with a two-man crosscut saw, unless you had somebody on the other end of the saw that knew what he was doing, why, you worked against yourself. It turned into a lot of work, and you didn't get much done. Things were pretty well disorganized for the first few days until they got things straightened out.

To start with we had our tools checked out, and we would check them back in, but they got to where they weren't doing much of that. Some of the boys, they got to where instead of gathering them up and putting them in the vehicle that they hauled the tools in, they would cache them in a brush pile. I remember one time they had cached quite a few tools in one of the brush piles. Our boss, he didn't know they were there, so he went out early in the morning and torched these brush piles and burned the tools. When we got there, we were short a lot of tools. The boss, when he found out what happened, he was furious. He jumped up and down and lined us out and dressed us down pretty good, and he wasn't very pleasant about it at all.

After that, things began to change a little bit. All the tools were checked in, as well as checked out, and the guys were supervised a little closer on using the tools. After a week or so, why, everything smoothed out, and those boys, no matter if they was from town or mines or ranches or anyplace, they started getting in the groove and getting something done with the kind of tools they furnished us.

Even as inexperienced as the crew was, we didn't have any accidents. The ones we had weren't serious. During pole climbing practice, there were a few bumps, and once the crew pulled a pole over on a boss and broke his pelvis. He claimed it was a murder attempt, but I don't think it was.

We had a camp newspaper. Some of the boys that had been used to that kind of work ran the outfit. While they was having all this trouble about not getting along and quarreling about the food and different things, why, I thought to myself, "I'll just send an article to this paper–let the editors have this article." I thought at the time when they got ahold of it that, they would probably kick me out of camp along with the rest of them that they had kicked out because it wasn't very flattering. But it kind of explained things the way I seen it. It was kind of a ballad that I penned and had them put in this paper. Well, they didn't kick me out of camp. It was kind of like the old Archie Bunker TV show–if you insult everybody and everything, why, you can get away with it if you don't just pick out somebody special. The military that run the camp, they thought it was all right. They said that was the right spirit, and, by golly, it was okay, so I got away with that.

It wasn't long until I got off this road building job. They were putting in a telephone line from Moran clear to Wilson. It was a Forest Service line, and I got on there with a crew. I was climbing all the time, and it was really a good job. I learned quite a bit there–how to splice the wires and how to make the ties on the insulators and how to get the tension right on the wires to take care of the slack during cold weather and other things. It was something I liked. I stayed on it for quite a while. It was better than I had been doing.

I'll mention a few names here that was with me. Pete Balden, he was there with me and Harold Kester and Eddie Gibson. That's four of us. We knew each other quite well. We worked there until it began to cool off and get cold, so they decided they was going to break up the camp and ship them out of there. I and Eddie Gibson, well, we stuck together. They shipped us down to Eggers, Colorado up in the mountains up working on a road. I run a compressor jackhammer up there on the night crew. It was very interesting. I got quite a bit of instructions on the use of dynamite and powder and got to where I wasn't afraid of it. I could handle it myself. Eddie–I think he worked in the first aid tent quite a bit. We were just in a tent camp up there at Eggers. It's up in these mountains quite a ways. We stayed up there until it started getting real cold.

We moved down to Boulder, Colorado, into barracks. They had made them out of wood. It was kind of like coming home when we got down there. The food was just perfect, and everything was just a change completely. We worked on trails back up there in the mountains–mostly handwork.

In those days in the 1930s, there wasn't such a thing as unemployment or relief like you get now. About your only hopes–well, most of us ranch hands, anyway, we could always find work through the summer, but there was long winters. Then it was get out in a trapper's cabin someplace or just go without any kind of work at all, so this CCC work came in awful handy. It was really a winter's job, and that's what a lot of us were looking for. Pert near everybody that I knew of that was there was there temporarily because they knew what it was, and they used it that way. It was just kind of a leg up– kinda of a stopover until they found something better to do.

Eddie and I, we went to night school there at the university while we was in Boulder. We took Public Speaking, and we got in an outfit that was putting on plays and things like that. We also got in an orchestra. We really enjoyed it. We had a lot of things you could do in your spare time if you wanted to do it. It didn't really cost you that much money. When we went to picture shows there in Boulder, the two of us could go for 15¢. That would be 7½¢ a piece. That way, why, we could afford to go to a show once in a while.

We did quite a bit of fishing while we was in Jackson Hole. The cooks, they were really good guys. A bunch of us would go fishing, and we would catch quite a few fish because fish was very plentiful over there in those days, and the cook would rustle enough gear so we could fry these fish up. We had some pretty good fish fries that way.

Around the camp, of course, we didn't have TV in them days. There might have been a radio or two, but we didn't have any in our tent. We had to depend on, you might say, home grown entertainment. There was musicians in camp. There were some people in there that could sing pretty good. They got together into quartets and different musical groups and used to put on programs. Sometimes they would put on a boxing match. Of course, in Jackson Hole there was a lot of dances on Saturday nights. This was dude country, and a lot of the boys went to those dances.

I didn't work there too long because I soon quit there. I had a partner back in Buffalo, and we were going to start ranching. He had found a ranch, so I quit the CCC while I was there at Boulder and came back and started ranching.

I think that the CCCs was a good thing because it got a lot of the boys out in the fresh air. The military had ahold of them, and they taught them quite a bit that later on came in awful handy when they were throwed into the military in the World War II. I know quite a few of the boys got tangled up with that. They had a little training, you might say, right there in the camp. The military having charge of the camp, they kept things kind of in line. I know I enjoyed myself while I was in the CCC. I never saw any brawling to speak of. The boys got along good with each other. I can honestly say I thought that they were a good bunch of boys and I liked every one of them.

❦❦❦❦❦

Virginia Sheridan Milnichak
1917-Present
From an interview with Nancy Tabb
In 2017, when 100 years old

The Lott Mansion & Early Memories

My dad [Walter K. Sheridan] must have come over here from Sheridan in 1918. I was born in 1917. It would have been before I was 3 years old. The only house that was available was the one down on Bozeman, and ours was the very last house down there.

I have memories of that house and living there. Then my father bought the house at 343 N. Main in 1920. Eventually, I fell heir to the house and continued to live there until 2004. That's a long time. It's the second building north of the Mansion House. When we lived there, the Mansion House was our neighbor, only it wasn't called the Mansion House at that time. It was owned by a little lady named Mrs. Ella Lott.

Mansion House

Mrs. Lott was a really interesting little lady–tiny little person. She had two grand-daughters, both older than me. The house sort of fell to one of her granddaughters, so I heard a lot of the history about Mrs. Lott. Sometimes I think it is too bad that all the little stories are lost about these different people.

Well, Mrs. Lott came here originally because she was a cousin of a lady who lived here. Her name was Addy Jones, and Addy asked her to move here. She was a widow and had one daughter. It was my understanding that she had lived in their house before she married Dr. [John Howard] Lott. Her daughter, eventually, married a rancher from down south. His name was Hibbard. They had three children, and as I say, the two girls was older than I was. The boy was younger, and it was my understanding that their mother had died. Mrs. Lott did have two sons by Dr. Lott–Howard and Warren.

When I knew her, she was always a little old lady, just working very hard and always took in roomers. At that time, there were no hotels around the place, so tourists would stop there for rooms in the summer. In the winter, she also had permanent residents. When they were rebuilding Main Street, she had a lot of boys who worked on that. She took in all those roomers and served meals.

It was a really nice old house. She had a grand piano and beautiful furniture in her living room, and her dining room was really nice. The kitchen was a real old-fashion little place. There were other small rooms in back, but in that whole house there was only one bathroom, and it was upstairs.

In 1935, about February when she died, they threw tons of stuff out of that attic through the attic window–hauled it away in trucks. I don't think she ever threw away a candy box or anything. Later in the spring, they asked my mother if she would like to rent the house and then rent it out to tourists like Mrs. Lott had, so we did. We moved over there in the spring of 1935. To me it was just really fun. I'm sure it was work for my mother, and my two sisters were here at the time.

We converted the attic into bedrooms for ourselves in the summer and rented all the rooms. The winter of 1935 and 1936 was the coldest winter that they had had on record for years. Actually, there was so much ice on the creek they had a hard time getting water for drinking water, and fish froze. It was so cold that you could see your breath in the hall upstairs. Two of the ladies that had been residents for years were still there, and they were really familiar with that little old coal furnace. If it hadn't been for them, we probably would have frozen to death. There was a fireplace in what was the dining room and also in the front hall, so we survived it, but I can remember going to bed and wearing a hood over my head. It was right after I graduated, and I had a job at a little dime store downtown. One day, I washed my hair and went to work at noon, and my hat froze to my head.

Anyway, we lived through that winter and stayed the next summer. The Lott brothers wanted my mother to buy the house–$2,900. This was my Mother's [Mabel Sheridan] exact words, "I wouldn't have this barn if you gave it to me," so we moved back home, but it was a fun experience for me. Everybody had their own little job to do. Of course, it was during the Depression, so everybody worked hard at everything they did.

You know, when we moved up to that house, as I say, I was very small, so I have lots of memories of living at that time. We lived there until I was through the first grade, and then there was plans to build a north and south railroad that would come from Casper through Buffalo and go to Sheridan, so we all moved to Casper for three years while that was in the works. But it failed, and we came back in 1927–moved back to our house.

Anyway, as far as Buffalo's concerned, Buffalo was always known for being such a beautiful treey little town. In past years, why, along Main Street there was an extra little area between the sidewalks and little parking area, and a lot of people had trees planted along there, so we had lots of green trees, and it was a beautiful little town. Then when they had to widen the street, they had to do away with those trees.

Another interesting thing about way back in those olden days–the streets were not paved, so in the fall when the leaves would fall, we'd rake them all up. We'd rake a big pile and put it out on the edge of the street and have bonfires and throw in a potato or an apple to roast. Course, you can imagine how they looked blackened and crusty. You'd eat them anyway, and they were delicious. We had lots of cotton that came off those cottonwood trees. I can remember when I was a kid, the cotton would be all over the ground. You'd light a match to it. I never heard of anybody's house being burned down, but I bet there were many times when kids were afraid it was going to happen.

I can remember all of the people who lived up and down that street. Jack Meldrum's mother lived at the end of the street, and the Martons lived on that block. There are a lot of different people who have come and gone in that area.

John Stevenson–if you're going north, his house would have been the second on the east side of the street. John Stevenson was a taxidermist. He had this stuffed mountain lion crawling up a tree. It was there for years and was quite an attraction for people. Another thing about John Stevenson–he owned a filling station right where the parking lot is on Fort and Main and had a jackalope hanging on his wall. It was called the

Grease Spot.

Kubes had the Golden Rule Store. In back of our house on that little street that goes east and west, the Joe Hakerts lived there. Mrs. [Aurelia] Hakert was a really good friend of my mother's–just run back and forth across the alley to visit.

Well, it was in the middle of the Depression, and in Buffalo I don't know whether anybody really suffered terribly here. I know we didn't. My mother was a really good seamstress. Sometime during that time, they asked her if she would have a sewing room and teach the people who were on welfare how to sew. They would make clothes for their children. During that time when things were hard, we probably would not have bought a lot of things that we actually ended up with. The government shipped in things like bananas and grapefruit and oranges for the people on welfare. Well, all these welfare ladies got so much they'd give some to my mother, so we never suffered from things like that.

When things were really hard, there were hobos that would go through. I can remember they would come to the back door and ask if there was some kind of work they could do for a sandwich or something to eat. My mother would tell them, "You can go out and pull a few weeds in the garden." Mainly, that was what they did so she would fix them food. They would come into the house–just open up. We had a little breakfast nook right by our back door, so they would come in and eat at the breakfast nook, and she would fix them meals.

Another thing that was interesting at that time–the Indians would come down from the reservations in Montana in the summertime and camp up on a hill. There was a fence along that area, and they'd set up their tepees there. There was always things hanging on the fence. Everybody said that was their meat curing. The ladies would come down to town and go up the alleys. If you had a garden, they would come in and ask if they could have some of the garden produce, so I think a lot of our garden produce went to them. One of the ladies most familiar to us–her name was Sally Look Behind–she would be trailing up the alley with a few of the other women and kids. It would be the Crows. I can't remember exactly when that all stopped because we also had gypsies sometimes that would come to town and would camp along Highway 16. You were always warned, "Don't you go down there. Those gypsies going to steal you kids."

I don't know whether anybody else has told you about the livery barn on Main Street. When I was probably in the first grade, the livery stable was a big long, red wooden building that reached from Main Street clear back to the alley. To a little tiny kid walking by, you know, you'd look back in there, and it smelled terrible–water troughs and the stalls for all the horses–so it was kind of an awesome thing for a little kid. The man who was the livery stable man always wore a dark brown jacket and dark brown chaps and a dark brown hat. I haven't a doubt but that he was slim. We were scared to death of him–Mr. George L. Zimmerman. We were just half a block away, but we had to walk back and forth by there unless we went on the other side of the street. Sometimes we'd be tempted to walk by just to see the horses, and he'd always say, "Okay, you boys, get licken' to school today." He always called us "boys"–Dorothy and I. He made a big impression on me, I'll tell you.

I would walk downtown with my mother when I was very little. At that time, there were residences clear down to where the Kum and Go is now, and across the street was a filling station that was owned by the Stevens brothers. The Stevenses lived where the little real estate office [Buffalo Realty–294 N. Main St.] is now. Their daughter was a really good friend of mine. We played together when we were little kids. Mrs. Stevens had made a really good friend of one of the Indian men–Weasel Bear. He used to stop and visit her all the time, and he gave her beautiful moccasins.

When I was small, there was a little store with a big long candy case. You could stand for about as many hours as the people there would put up with you–just trying to pick out penny candy. That was a wonderful place. The Fenusz family owned it.

Marguerite and Mable Perkins lived in a little house over there [Salon 202 & Day Spa–202 N. Main St.]. At one time, it was a chiropractor's office. Mrs. Clara Accola was a chiropractor and had her business there. Her husband and his brother owned the bakery downtown. Also, the Burgers lived there at one time. Mr. Otto Hart had a candy shop. At first, it was just kind of a little wooden trailer. Mr. Hart made taffy. Everybody loved it. He made this in some kind of big vat. Then he'd take this great big huge piece of sticky stuff and hang it on a hook and pull it that way. Later on, they put in a kind of nice little trailer thing. It had a glass front, and they had a candy shop there. It was fun just to watch him pull his candy.

Ed Chappell's Watch Shop

In the building where the spaghetti place [Pie Zanos–17 N. Main St.] is now–my earliest recollection of that building was that it was kind of divided. On the south side was a little shop where Ed Chappell mended watches. You could hardly see him working at his little desk right at the front window because the window was so dirty. His wife used to sit out in front on her little wooden chair and embroider pillowslips. Edith Chappell was her name–she was very intellectual. Her daughter Alice was a nurse for a long time. Next to that was the bakery that the Accolas had. Then there was the Skipton and Flynn Grocery Store.

The swimming pool was slimy and muddy. We had a wonderful time in the swimming pool. They had a really tall slide on the east side and a big raft. It was maybe 12 foot square. A whole bunch of us would get on the raft, and we'd all crowd over to one side until the raft would sink and go up this way in the air and then go that way. Then we'd chase the raft and do it all over again. When the WPA people were put to work, why, they put in the cement on the west side of the pool, changed the bathhouse, and changed it all.

CCC camps were the Civilian Conservation Corps. They had a camp that was located down by Crazy Woman Creek. The CCC boys started to rebuild that road. Since then, it's been rebuilt again, but they're the ones that built that road the first time. That was a wonderful program.

My brother, William Loren Sheridan, when he graduated from high school in Casper, he went to Lincoln, Nebraska, to work. He worked in a railroad yard, and every three weeks they would let everybody off for a week or so–probably ran out of money– and then they would go back. Working on the railroad, he would always come home and spend those extra weeks at our house. He was always a really hard worker–always doing something. He would go out in the country and walk along the fence lines. Where the sheep had gotten caught on the fence lines, there'd be little tufts of wool–pick off the wool and fill it in these bags and sell it. He also would rewind engines for people. Now, I don't know anything about rewinding an engine, but I can remember whatever it took, he had to heat it up in our oven sometimes, so lots of time in our oven at home instead of bread baking, it would be an engine that Bill was remodeling.

I worked in the high school office sometimes and in the library and loved to do that. Of course, that leads to another story. By that time, I would have graduated in 1935, and it was in the winter of 1938. My brother, Bill, was in Yellowstone Park. Bebe, his wife, had an appendectomy, so he asked if I would come up and take care of their little kids while he was working, so I went up in the middle of the winter–deep snow and nobody around. No tourists ever went through there at that time. Oh, but it was wonderful! I used to go hiking all around there–be so quiet. I was at Mammoth Hot Springs. Their first house was right by where those travertine things are. To walk down to the store we had to pass those travertine cones, and there were always at least eight elk around there. It was really an adventure for me, and I loved every second of it. When I was there, it's the only time I'd ever seen lightning in the midst of a snowstorm.

Anyway, after I got home that winter, I decided I would like to work at Yellowstone Park, so I wrote the lady who owned the store. She lived in Los Angeles at the time, and I got the nicest letter. It wasn't just, "Yes, you can have a job." It was a long letter. I got that job, and she always treated me like I was family. Her family had started that store way back in the late 1800s. Her brother was an ex-chief ranger, and his wife worked in the store where I did. I had four wonderful years up there. I just loved it.

The first year I stayed at my brother's house. By that time, they had had to tear down the house they had lived in because the travertine was building right up under the house. It was a duplex, and the lady next door opened up her pantry door one time, and floor was gone, and here's this bubbling water. Then they lived in one of the apartments in all the stone houses. I had to count every time I went up there to get the right house because they all looked alike. After that, I was up at the store because it had living quarters upstairs. We had a cook that was a wonderful cook. Her husband was the butcher. She treated me like I was one of her kids too. It was a wonderful time for me.

I was 18. At that time, the summer employees couldn't have their own cars, but the son of this lady I worked with had a car. He liked me, and I liked him all right. He always had a car at his disposal. It would be his mother's car, his dad's car, his aunt's car, or the grocery truck, so we could go anyplace we wanted on our day off.

When I used to walk home from the store after I got off at 7:00 in the evening, I could hear the bears going through the garbage cans in back of the hotel. Of course, they were in back of the apartment house, always tipping over the garbage cans. In the house next door there was a man in the downstairs apartment with five children. His wife had died, so my sister-in-law just mothered those kids. If you saw a bunch of kids on her front room floor, you couldn't tell whether they were Bebe's kids or the neighbor's. Anyway, a bear got into his apartment one time, and, of course, when they're in there, they're boss. You just walk away.

One time, later in the fall when the tourist season had thinned out a little bit and I was still working, they were doing some painting in our kitchen. Our curio store was in the front, and on one side was the kitchen and dining room and living room. The backdoor opened out into this little U in the back where there was a parking area. It was in the middle of the afternoon, and I heard this terrible noise. I went down the hall to see what was making all the noise in the kitchen, and a bear was in there. They'd left the door open because they'd been painting, and a black bear had gotten into the pantry and swished all the plates off the pantry shelf and then opened this great big refrigerator. There was a big round bowl of green Jell-O, and he was just slurping that up. We didn't have any grizzlies down in that area, but we had black bears all the time.

Actually, I met the man I married [John "Russia" Milnichak] up in Yellowstone Park. He worked as a blacksmith in a CCC camp. He was just the same age I was. He was really nice and had a charming smile. He was one of my brother's favorites, so he was at their house all the time, and that's why I met him. Russia started stopping at the store all the time. Eventually, he moved down to live in Buffalo before I got through working in Yellowstone Park.

When I came home to Buffalo, I had a job in the county agent's office. During those times, there weren't any people to work in the beet fields like there had been. Sometimes we girls would go out and work in the beet fields. Since we worked in the county agent's office, I imagine the county agent thought that would be a great thing. When Pete Jensen was county agent and I worked for him, the first thing I had to do in the winter was make up the Fair book and go around and get ads all over Buffalo and Sheridan to put in the book. Then I had to type the Fair book up and the superintendent's book. During the Fair, we'd go out early in the morning when they were judging things. I would sit there keeping track of everything. Then after the races, we'd go down to the courthouse and pay off the people who were in the races who had won. I'd write the checks for that, so we did everything. Oh, it was a lot of fun.

At that time, the County would not hire married women, so when Russia was called into service, we got married just before he left and didn't tell anybody except my mother. I think that was kind of a dumb law, but that was the law. They didn't hire married women in offices like that.

Russia was gone three years and never got home on a furlough. He was a NCO in Africa. He was in an ordnance unit, and because he had been a blacksmith, he was in a group that repaired trucks and guns. They were on their way to Japan to serve over there when the war ended. They were just getting ready to go through the Panama Canal, so they brought them back.

In the meantime, I had a friend who worked in the New York Store. Every night when I'd get off at 5:00, I would stop at the New York Store and putter around, and then I'd walk home with her.

I also had a job working the books for the man in the theater. I'd go down in the evening and do that. It was Mr. Tom Villnave. He said to me one day, "Why don't you start a dress shop? You really ought to do that. If you will, I'll back you." So this one day when I stopped to pick up Molly and we walked home, she'd had a terrible day. She'd been so mad at somebody in the store she was just fuming, so I said to her, "Why don't we start our own store?" So we did–the Suzanne Shop.

We went to the Denver wholesale mart. The war was still going on, so the salesmen asked, "What's the name of your store?" "We don't have a name yet. We just want to see if it was a possibility to get merchandise." Oh my, they were so nice to us. They were just really, really very helpful. One day, we went to a fixture store. They had mannequins and all kinds of stuff, so that night when I was lying in bed staring out the window of the hotel, I thought, "We need that mannequin, and we'll name the shop Suzanne Shop and do all our advertising around that." There now, we had a mannequin, and we had the store name.

It started in 1945 end of March. When Russia came home from the war, all he wanted was a little Suzanne under the Christmas tree, so in 1946 we had Suzanne. I didn't sell the store to my partner until 1952. Then after my kids, Bettina and Robin and Tim, were in school, I went back and worked there for a few years. In the meantime, I bought a fabric store. I was in the fabric store for 10 years and liked that okay. Russia worked for John Deere Implement Company for a long time, and then he worked at the Highway Department.

I loved being at the historical meetings in those days because when I went, there were still a lot of really old-timers there. One time, when we were talking about what was going on in the past, Old Dave Watt was there, and I said, "You know, I remember hearing sometime in the past that when the people went to one of the dances where they congregated in somebody's home at night and everybody came with their kids and stayed practically all night, when they got home, they discovered that somebody had switched the babies." Dave Watt began to laugh and said, "I remember when we did that," and I said to him, "You were part of that?" "Yeah," he said, "all the wives with their little babies would have their own distinctive blankets that they had their little child wrapped in. They would lay them someplace where it would be quiet. The boys went in and switched babies and blankets. You know, there were some of those babies that didn't get back to the right mommas for months because it was in the middle of winter." You know, no communication–if you're way out on this ranch and somebody's way out here, how are you going to get ahold of somebody?

It was really fun to be there when some of these old, old-timers were. They did a lot of talking about the redlight district. Howard Watt said, "At recess we'd go out and sit on the side of that hill where the creek is and could look directly at the redlight district and see who was coming and going." Vance Lucas, his father owned the *Buffalo Bulletin* newspaper at that time. The office was downtown. Vance's bedroom window looked right down on it, so he could sit there at night and see who was coming and going.

You know, telephone operators were wonderful. One time, I wanted to call the dentist's office, and Gladys Ross was at the telephone company right across the street from the post office. When Dr. [H.S.] Long didn't answer his phone, why, Gladys, who was the operator said, "Virginia, do you really need Dr. Long?" I said, "Yes, I was just going to call him and make an appointment." She said, "I met him on the post office steps this morning. He said he was going to Sheridan, and he'd be back by noon."

Of course, sometimes they listened in when they shouldn't have. Some of us girls in the evening–after I got through with doing my work at the theater, I'd meet somebody down at the Capitol Cafe, and we'd have a Coke or a cup of coffee. One of the ladies was a telephone operator, and she said, "I'm not supposed to hear this, but I just heard that Bob McBride was taken prisoner." That was during World War II.

Of course, I remember Vivienne Hesse. Vivienne was wonderful. Now, I never knew how old Vivienne was. You know, everybody was scared to death of her driving, but she'd always say, "Now, dear heart, you don't have to drive tonight. I'm going to come and pick you up." She'd pick up as many of us as she could. I had one friend that was frantically trying to get into her own car and make a getaway before Vivienne got there. That particular night we had to pick up somebody, and it was down there in the southwest part of town. You go up a little hill on Western Avenue, and there are houses up here, but down here is another little road. She drove right off backwards of that. We all survived it. I thought after that, "I'm not going to worry. God's taking care of Vivienne and all the rest of us." She was a great person. We really liked Vivienne. She was always one of the girls.

Mae Bateman Morgareidge

1871-1972
From an interview with Patty Myers
In 1972, when 101 years old

Country School Teacher

I came from Missouri to Wyoming in 1898 to visit relatives who had invited me for summer vacation. I did enjoy it. Missouri wasn't a very healthful state at that time. There were so many things like typhoid fever and consumption, and I found Wyoming more healthful and loved the pine breeze. I was 27.

The country schools were all grades together in one room. Sometimes there would be as many as 40 or more pupils in wintertime. First, I taught in Wyoming in what they called the Frewen Castle. They were just organizing a new school for the district. I had four pupils all near the same age–about 10 or 12 years old. They were two girls who stayed with their married sister to attend school. The other two lived in the neighborhood. I taught in one room of the Frewen Castle and lived there with the old lady and her family who were living in it at that time. The salary was better priced than in Missouri–$40 a month. I paid the old lady $10 for my board. I had the northwest room for a schoolroom–small but with only four pupils. They were anxious to learn. They just studied the elementary subjects–Writing, Arithmetic, a little Geography. At the Frewen Castle they just gathered up the books in the neighborhood that had been used by older brothers and sisters before coming there. The benches and seats were homemade. They recited in classes. A spelling class would stand up alongside of the room. The teacher pronounced the words of the lesson, and they would spell them. If one was missed, the other went ahead of them. The teacher gave headmarks for the ones that had the best lesson. There was a blackboard on the wall to jot their problems.

I taught there in the winter. Then the next summer, I just visited with my relatives, getting acquainted with people. The first of September I taught for my cousin as a substitute. It was a larger school. I think about 12 or 13. Some of them were beginners, and some were what would be part of an eighth grade now. No schools were graded then. Children were anxious for school and to learn. Six months I taught that term of school and lived in a home with a family who had four girls for school–the Judge Ritter Ranch on Powder River–and there were some neighbor children. A new, good-sized log building to be used for a school room joined onto the house that would be used as part of their home after the six-month school. Of course, the children walked to school from their homes.

At the Ritter School, I had attended the teacher's institute in Buffalo and gotten a good certificate. I introduced Mental Arithmetic in that school and some other classes that were new, and the children were interested in them. The county superintendent was Mrs. Cornelia Snider. She wasn't an educated woman. Her husband had died, leaving her with five little children, so the commissioners gave her the job to get that pay to raise her children. She visited my school and was rather surprised and pleased with the new subjects I had introduced in the school.

The last day of school Mr. L.R.A. Condit, a commissioner from the Barnum neighborhood, came and offered me the summer school of six months when there would be children who could walk the distance–another three miles. They could not attend the wintertime because of the distance and storms.

In that school, I had beginners and little folks mostly. The little folks were so anxious to learn they would take their books outside at noon and sit in the shade of the willows along Red Fork and study their spelling lessons. In the warm days, the two little beginners might lie down and take a little nap. They were nice little children. There were three from the Dennis Rinker home, three from the Johnny Jones home on Red Fork, and two from the George Fraker home on Middle Fork. They walked across the hills–some of them more than three miles–but they were there on time and ready for school.

I lived in a home with a family that had three children in school. We walked and crossed Red Fork on a bridge. The directors and parents built a new large building for school, but we still had homemade desks, and children brought their dinners from home and ate out in the shade. That would be the summer of 1900. They were six-month terms. That was all that could be afforded. It was a new school building that people interested in school had built. The floor had cracks in it where little green lizards came up and played around on the floor, but the children assured me that they were harmless. They never bit anybody. One day, a big bullsnake came in the open door and was crawling around the stove. The Fraker boy carried it outside. After work we found there was a nest of mice in the stove. That was what the snake was after, but they were harmless. They didn't bite anybody. That year the commissioners raised the salary to $50. They were so glad to begin getting teachers from the East. Teachers were scarce here, and they had to depend on them from other places.

When I got married, my father and mother visited at different times but thought the life and company too rough for old folks. There were many hardships caused by the weather. There were hailstorms in the summer destroying the gardens and crops, hard winters with severe cold and deep snows with blizzards causing loss of stock, and dirt roads to make travel difficult. But in time improvements came. There were cars, good water wells, highways, electricity. These were better improvements and an easier life. There were always good neighbors to help in sickness or need. I have many happy memories of my early-day experiences in Wyoming.

❦❦❦❦

Louise D. Mueller
1907-1994
From an interview with Patty Myers
In 1984, when 77 years old

Far From Town

I can remember my mother [Linna Froehner Mueller] saying that one time my dad [John A. Mueller] had gone across the creek. Usually, it was just a small stream, but there was one of those cloudbursts, and he had to stay on the other side. She was going to throw some food over to him in a flour sack, but the first time she missed, and it went down the creek, so she had to do it again and succeeded.

Quite frequently, she was out there by herself. My dad took the sheep up the mountains. One time, he was going up the mountains, and he met somebody who said the Indians were coming. Of course, he was concerned, so he went back home, but they never did see any Indians. One night, Mother was frightened because she heard the doorknob turn. She got up to find out what it was. The calf had gotten into the yard. One of the youngsters had left the gate open, and he was licking the doorknob.

Mother, she says she recalls coming to town and seeing the McBrides. They were grubbing out the cottonwoods and sagebrush there on that hill prior to building there. She told me she can remember the youngsters helping out there. She'd see them out there. I can't remember Mr. McBride's name, the old man.

Really, think how isolated they were. It took one day to come to town by wagon and then one day to go back. Of course, they would stock up on groceries for the winter pretty much. I think they came twice a year, but I don't know for sure. Mother always had a garden and had to pack water from the stream for the garden and what little they could raise that way. Mother told me one time she went to the chicken house to gather the eggs. She got in the chicken house, and when she went to come out, she saw a rattlesnake right there, so she jumped over it and ran and got a shovel and killed it. That was a hazard all the time when the youngsters were out playing—fear of the rattlers, you know. She was there a lot of times by herself. I just know I wouldn't be that brave to be out in the country like that.

My dad tells about one time during a bad winter how the sheep would bunch up along the fence and how he worked all night to keep them moving so they wouldn't smother in the snow against the fence. I tell you, it wasn't an easy life. When he was out north of town, he had cattle, and it was a diversified ranch or farm or whatever you call it. It was open—no fences. They could go a long ways to graze. I'm just sure cattle was all over those hills down in there. She was there a lot of times by herself.

❦❦❦❦

118

Sue Cash Myers
1937-Present
From an interview with Patty Myers
In 1994, when 57 years old

Free to Grow Up

I grew up on a family farm down towards Kaycee–the Mayoworth community. My parents were Harold and Lois Hendricks Cash. I had two sisters and a brother. Living on the Cash family ranch was great. We didn't know that there was any other way to live. It was a close neighborhood actually. It was the kind of neighborhood that if you went someplace to visit on a Sunday, you were automatically expected to stay for dinner. It was a small ranch. We didn't have a lot of acreage. My dad and his brother, Gene, were in partnership for quite a number of years, so we were quite close to their family. Dad's sister and her husband and family lived a couple of miles down the river from us, so we had relatives, as well as close friends.

They had an irrigated place and ran cows. My dad never ran sheep. He didn't like sheep. We had some horses to work with. They weren't to play with. They were cow horses and draft horses to pull the rakes and help with the haying. My mom worked with my dad. Both of them were qualified teachers, but after they were married, neither one of them taught. They just worked the ranch for most of the time. After us kids got older, then Mom got a job in Kaycee as postmistress.

It was a little log homestead house. It looked plenty big to me when I was growing up. I went back to it after I had grown up and couldn't imagine how we could have all lived there. When my brother, Jimmy, got older, he moved out into the bunkhouse where the hired men were. My sister, Jackie, had a little bedroom in the back, and we had a bedroom that Ginger and I shared next to that. The folks had the bigger bedroom off to one side with a door that went outside. It was five rooms. The living room was good-sized for a homestead. The back door was a cold room where the icebox and the separator were. We had an underground cellar outside for both canned goods and storage. The outhouse and the washhouse, where Mom did all the washing, were outside. We got our water from the river. We didn't have a well. We didn't have electricity. We had coal oil lamps and gas lanterns. My mom played the piano, and we used to have neighborhood dances–just moved the furniture back. Some of us danced in the kitchen.

It was 1949 or '50 that we moved into a new house we built. The REA was just coming up the river then. My dad was on the first REA board to get electricity into that community. My mom always said that it was the biggest thrill of her life to look out the window and watch the lights come on up the river as the REA line moved up. When we first moved into the new house, we used the light plant until the REA was activated. We never had plumbing in the homestead, yet we didn't miss it. We'd come to town where we had relatives, and they had a bathtub inside. We never felt sorry for ourselves because everybody in the neighborhood was the same way as we were.

We had lots of hired men. There was one that did become a part of the family. He worked for us for a long time. They all had some problem it seemed. This man got to drinking too much and then got involved with some woman and left for a while, but he came back. He always was in touch with the family. His name was Jimmy Johnson. In fact, my older brother was named after him. We had one that always sang "If I Had the Wings of an Angel" every morning and every night. Every time he was doing anything, we would hear him singing. We had one that was a Seventh Day Adventist, which was entirely new to us. We couldn't figure out why he kept telling us that we were supposed to go to church on Saturdays. We had one during World War II that would put at least a half a cup of sugar in his lemonade even though it was rationed. Those are the ones I remember. We just went through usually one or two hired hands a summer. They were just transients who would work long enough to get some money in their pockets and then move on.

Memories? It was home. The dances we had in the house. Ginger and I wrestling in the front room. Walking the corral poles. We made our own fun. Oh, a great big cottonwood tree out by the front door–you could climb up in that tree and scoot out on this great big, long, wide branch. After you got out so far, there was a curve with another branch above. You could sit on that branch, lean back against the other branch, and read your book. It was just great! It was probably my very favorite hideaway. We had a willow patch down below the house, and we always had our hideouts down in the willow bushes. We just had a good time wherever. Swimming in the creek. In the wintertime, we had ice skating on the creek. We would take all of Mom's old nightgowns and stuff and play dress-up up in the attic.

Oh, we all had chores–feed the chickens, slop the hogs, and when we got older, we helped milk the cows. We had to separate the milk. One of the things we hated–absolutely the worst was cleaning the separator. Every week we had to mop and wax the front room floor. The folks had a little carpet in their room, so we took a wet broom–that's how we cleaned their carpet.

I suppose we were disciplined. I remember the only time my dad spanked me because he never spanked us kids. I don't even remember what we did, but I remember he told us to go out–my sister Ginger and I–go out and get a willow tree branch. Instead we got leaves off the cottonwood. That was a mistake. We should have gotten the branch. I don't think he would have spanked us if we had gotten the branch like we were supposed to. I remember getting sent away from the table because we'd get the giggles. We'd go behind the woodstove in the front room and just keep on giggling. We'd try to go out and eat, and we'd get the giggles again. We spent several nights hungry because we couldn't quit giggling.

One other thing I might mention from my childhood is my sister, Ginger, had a language of her own. Nobody knew where it came from. I was the only one in the family who could understand what she said. For example, Jimmy was "Meela," and Kitty was "Leeka." That's the only two I remember right now. She'd go to tattle on me, and Mom wouldn't understand her, so she'd call me in to explain what Ginger was saying. Of course, I wouldn't tell her what Ginger was saying. I wasn't going to get myself in trouble. Ginger would just have a fit because she knew I wasn't saying what she wanted me to.

When we'd go to town, which was probably about once a month, we'd get to go to the show, and we'd get to buy some penny candy, which we would save, hoard and make last all month long if we possibly could. We did not share very much–not candy. As far as the incentive–"If you do this, I'll give you some candy, or I'll give you a dollar,"–no. The things that we did we were expected to do.

We'd go to Kaycee to the dances more than anything else. We did most of our shopping and our doctoring in Buffalo. There was no doctor in Kaycee then. I don't know why we went to Buffalo more than Kaycee. I think there was a grocery store in Kaycee, but I think at that time what they had was very limited. We used to get our groceries on the rural mail delivery. The mailman would bring it up to the ranch. We'd meet him at the mailbox.

My parents were very conscious of our grades and our grammar, especially. We were corrected if we didn't use the right grammar. We didn't resent it. That's just how it was. We had others in the family that were teachers, and we all were taught to speak correctly. We weren't taught our numbers or how to write our names by my parents. That was the school's job. That was part of the curriculum. We had a good library at school for the size of it. We read all those books, and the teacher always read to us. Oh, we read books avidly. We still are all big readers.

We played cards. Ginger and I played bridge before we went to school. That was one of our favorite types of entertainment. We had favorite radio programs. We always listened to *Queen for a Day* when we ate lunch. That was before we went to school.

Sue Myers & Family

We went to Mayoworth School. It was within walking distance. It would have been short if we could have gone across the fields, but we couldn't get across the river, so we always had a bus that picked us up. It was probably about three miles from the house. You could see it from the house. It was a two-room school, grades one through four in one room and grades five through eight in the other room. One year, we had four boys and four girls in the upper room, and we had a teacher that taught dancing, so we learned all sorts of dances that year. We square danced. There was just enough for a square. We always had good Art. We made all sorts of things for our parents for Christmas.

We did a lot of ornery things at school. We made our own entertainment. We liked to slide down the hill where it went down to the river in the wintertime. We'd pour water down there. That was where the teacher was supposed to go down and get water, so she had to make her own path because she couldn't get down there. It was a lot of fun though.

One year, we took the tin off coal sheds and put wire around the top of it. We went out in the schoolyard and across the road and up on the hills and tobogganed down. Nobody ever got hurt. I think about it now and just cringe–that ole rusty tin and the rocks and sagebrush. They finally put a stop to that. They told us we couldn't leave the schoolyard, so we didn't get to go down on the river where the ice was.

We had a big cave down there. We older kids always snuck around down there in the cave and smoked cigarettes. We'd swipe cigarettes and go down in the cave and smoke. Everybody expected you to smoke. We didn't smoke tobacco in front of our folks, but we smoked cornsilk in front of them, and that was fine. They were the ones who showed us how. They just figured, I guess, when you got old enough to buy your own cigarettes, you would smoke.

We had a big schoolyard, so it wasn't like we were confined in a small space. Sometimes we wouldn't come in when they rang the bell. I remember one teacher, Mary Jean Smith Christensen. We told her we weren't coming in–that we were going to play hooky the rest of the afternoon, so she said, "Wait a minute. Let me get my boots, and I'll go with you." It was an April day that was really nice. We spent the whole afternoon out wandering around in the hills, and she just went with us. That really impressed me. Kinda took the fun out of it though.

At that time, we were only 12 or 13 miles from Kaycee, but the way the school district was divided, we were in the Buffalo District. We would have had to pay tuition to go to school in Kaycee, so we boarded with families in town when we came to high school.

In the spring, we always had a big neighborhood picnic. Everybody brought food and played games, played baseball, went fishing. We had community brandings. It was a big thing. The women all brought iced fruit for the ice cream, baked beans, chicken, pies, rolls. I don't remember salads, but I suppose there probably was. During the branding, we would have fresh Rocky Mountain oysters cooked over the open branding fire. It was work, but it was also a social gathering. You didn't get in your cars and go someplace unless you went to your neighbor's because it was too expensive and took too long. The cars didn't move that fast.

There was a minister that came out and held Sunday school in the schoolhouse. I remember some Sunday school lessons and that type of thing, but he didn't make much of an impression on us kids. We went because, you know, we didn't have much of a chance to dress up. We always dressed up to go to Sunday school. We didn't say grace before dinner prayers, but we knew there is a God. My mother came from quite a religious family, and though we didn't do any Bible readings, she referred to her faith. We knew there was a God that took care of us. It was just another one of those things that was just the way it was.

We always celebrated birthdays but nothing in particular. We always had a cake and presents. I don't remember even any birthday parties where people would come. We had 4-H. That was one of the community activities that everybody got involved in. Christmas was always a big deal, and it still is in our family. I think most of our gifts were ordered out of the catalog. Then the folks had to find some place to hide them. Jimmy and Dad built things for Ginger and me. When Santa Claus came, somebody would take us out for a ride down to my aunt's, who lived down the river from us. When we'd come back, Santa had been there. I remember one year I really, really wanted a chemistry set, and I got one and was just absolutely delighted with it. It was something that was really a big surprise. As far as any special Christmases, that's the one I remember the most because that's the only time I think I got something I really, really wanted. Oh, I got dolls. We always wanted dolls.

We had pets. We always had cats. They were in the house or at the granary. We had one dog. His name was Bingo. He was a big part of our family. I don't even know where he came from except he looked like a coyote, and we were always worried he was going to get shot. He was just more or less a pet. A couple times he tried to work cattle, but Dad didn't have much patience with him. One year, we did get some lambs from Leroy Smith and raised them for 4-H projects. We had about 15 and were going to pick the best ones to take to the Fair. One day, they had gotten out into the alfalfa. They were all bloated and dead, so we didn't have any sheep that year. We'd have some bum lambs every now and then.

I hated chickens. They're dirty. We'd have to clean out the chicken house. They'd sit on their eggs and wouldn't get up. You'd have to try to get the eggs, and they'd peck you. We had turkeys. They were for eggs and for meat. The only thing fun about the chicken house was it had a gumbo roof. After it rained, it was fun to go up there and slide down. Mom didn't like us to do that because, gee, it was hard to get the dirt out of our clothes.

We had a pack rat one time that kept taking Ginger's and my barrettes. We found where his nest was, and we'd go back up there and get them. We never did have any squirrels out there. Raccoons–I don't even remember raccoons then. Skunks–we always had trouble with skunks. They'd get in and kill a bunch of the chickens.

You know, there was that winter–1949. They say it was 40 degrees below zero, but we never missed a day of school. The bus made it. It was that winter that everybody talks about how cold and snowy and everything it was. I just remember that everyone thought it was so marvelous that we never missed a day of school.

We all knew we didn't have much money. The only thing I really remember is one time I needed a pair of shoes. I had big holes in the bottom of my shoes, and Mom told me all the money they had was $5 and my shoes would just have to wait. That impressed me because I knew we didn't have much money, but I didn't know we were down that much. Later, Mom told me that they really, really didn't have any money at all because it all was part of the ranch. The only money they got was from selling eggs and milk and cream.

Telephones had their own ring. You had the wall telephone with the handle that rang two longs and a short or three shorts or a long and two shorts. Everybody had their own ring. It rang into every house, so you always knew when someone had a telephone call. If you didn't have anything better to do, you usually listened in. Us kids didn't, but our parents did. It was just obvious. If it was a long distance call, you would usually have to say, "Would you all hang up because it is draining the power, and I can't hear?" Most people would hang up, but some wouldn't. If there was any kind of emergency or any kind of trouble, they would ring, and then everybody would pick up. If there was a fire or an emergency, that's how they would let each other know.

The river was there. In the summertime, we'd bathe in the river, and Mom wouldn't have to heat up the coal stove to heat up some water for us to take baths. We had some high water, and it would flood down around the barns and came pretty close to the ice house one time but never anything that would cause any damage. The mountains were just so beautiful. We didn't get to go up there an awful lot because the folks were always so busy farming. When we did, we'd put an old car seat in the back of the truck, and we'd sit in the back so we could see the scenery as we went up the hill to the mesa or up Slip Road. It was just part of our lives–the mountains and the river. I couldn't live where there wasn't mountains and a river.

We had an old Model A. I don't remember what the other people on the river had, but a lot of times the Model A was the only one that could get to Kaycee in the wintertime or in the springtime when it was muddy, so we would go to Kaycee and haul groceries back. I remember one time that the mud just got bigger and bigger and bigger on the wheel. We made it as far as the Eychaner place. It was about 10:00 at night, and we had to leave the vehicle. We crawled across the fence and went across the field and spent the night at the Eychaner place.

My mom played the piano for dances in Kaycee, so we went to dances from the time we were old enough to walk. When we got tired, we'd crawl up on a pile of coats and go to sleep until the dance was over. There were some pretty wild dances. There were always two or three fights and somebody ending up in jail. We were always told we weren't to go outside and watch, but we always did. Dances at the schoolhouse–that was another big thing. People would come all the way from Buffalo to go to these dances at the little country school that probably wasn't as big as most people's front room.

We learned to dance at a real early age and to appreciate music. Mom and Dad sang a lot together just for fun. Dad would come in singing a song, and Mom would sing with him. They would harmonize. Mom played the piano, and we would all sing. That was an important part of growing up because we all still really love music and to dance. Mom gave us piano lessons, but you know how it is when your mother's going to teach you, you don't always pay too much attention. We did learn the basics, and I can play the piano, but she gave up on us. After she taught us the basics, we just wouldn't practice. Ginger and I sang at various functions. Grange was a big part of our life. We belonged to the juvenile grange, and the folks belonged to the regular grange. Grange meetings were in Kaycee, and Ginger and I would sing. Later, she played the harmonica, and I played the piano.

It's hard to make the decision to become a full-time town person–still is. After almost 40 years–that's counting when I went into high school–especially in the spring and the fall, I would give anything to be back on the ranch again. It's one of the things you accept because you can't change it. You can take the girl out of the country, but you can't take the country out of the girl.

I still have a very strong feeling for relatives and having people in for dinner because out in the country, you always fixed more. Especially on Sundays, you always planned for more people because usually somebody would be there. I still, I guess, have that in the back of my mind. My mom baked a lot. I still like to bake. I don't as much as I used to, but it was one of the things I did with my kids. That's what you did, you know. You just had to have homemade desserts and breads. I always used to bake on Fridays, and I always had company all day Friday. They said they could smell it when they walked in.

Maybe one of the most important things about the childhood that most of us had then was that we grew up with a sense of values because what we did didn't cost any money. We made our own entertainment. We found our own things to do. We found our own camaraderie in the neighborhood. Maybe that's it–just the sense of having a good childhood.

Sue Myers

When we got married [Arthur "Coog" Myers], we tried to instill in our kids–well, we made memories–that's what we called it. "Let's go make memories this weekend," and that's what we did. My folks didn't do that. They didn't have time, so the memories we made, we made for ourselves. Because we didn't raise our children in the country, we felt like we had to make those memories when we moved to town–memories that did not have a price tag.

Both my husband and I chose not to leave here because of the mountains and the fishing. Lots of times on Sunday afternoons or when we'd get through on a real nice day, I'd take a fishing pole and take my book and go up the creek and prop the fishing pole up on the bank. I wasn't much of a fisherman, but it was an excuse. I could read my book in peace and soak up the sun. If I caught a fish, that was great, but if I didn't, I really didn't care. I'd had a good afternoon anyway.

Wyoming is special. We were free to grow up. We didn't have a lot of restrictions. We didn't have a lot of people planning our lives, planning our day, planning our weekends, planning our evenings. We were free to be kids and grow up and find our way–find what we wanted to do. The closeness of the people–people really caring about each other. I felt from the time I was old enough to feel anything, that it was like one big extended family–the whole community. Everybody cared so deeply about everybody else. I still feel that way about the people that are still living that were out there when I was growing up. I still feel real close to them.

※※※※

Gertrude Parmelee
1900-1986
From an interview with Patty Myers
In 1980, when 80 years old

The Invasion

At the time of the Johnson County Invasion, my father [Judge Carroll Hathaway Parmelee] wrote to my mother–I've heard her tell it–"I don't own a single head of cattle. How could I get involved in this rustler business?" At the time of the battle at the TA Ranch, he foresaw that there was going to be bloodshed, and he thought that it should be prevented–that an open battle should be prevented. So Father telegraphed Governor Amos Barber, and Governor Barber contacted President Benjamin Harrison and got orders for the troops to be sent out from Fort McKinney to put an end to the fighting. My father rode down with the troops when they went down to accept the surrender of the Invaders, who said they would never surrender to the local forces.

The feeling was so intense that both sides really blamed my father for putting an end to their little private war. There was no possibility that anybody was neutral in that situation. You were either for us or against us. So the local rustlers–they weren't really rustlers–it included many people who were very honest and well-respected. As a matter of fact, Father was very much against any group taking justice into its own hands instead of applying the regular routine of the law to settle its disputes. I've heard Mother say that when they received the surrender, some of the men said to Father, "Well, what would you do if you were losing cattle and you couldn't get any conviction of cattle thieves?" My father's reply was, "I don't know what I'd do, but I can't imagine myself doing what you people have done."

For some time, there was a good deal of tense feeling in the community, but my

Gertrude Parmelee
Circa 1923

sister and I didn't hear much talk about that as we were growing up as small children. It was the thing that people didn't talk about. Nobody mentioned the Invasion or their feelings because their feelings were still too harsh. It was just a forbidden subject in any group of people, so we never heard very much talk about it.

I've heard Mrs. Margaret Bowman tell about seeing the bodies of Nate Champion and Nick Ray when they were brought into town and how the children were all excited about that. I've also heard Mrs. Annie Holloway tell how everybody was rushing into the Foote Store to get guns. She said her father went with the local posse when it went down to the TA Ranch. He said a lot of the people that went with the group were simply riffraff. They were simply taking what they wanted, and there was no point in the local people trying to support that because it wasn't a reasonable operation that was carried out. There was just a lot of riffraff that were taking advantage of the situation.

But there was such excitement in the community that nobody knew what was going to happen. There was a good deal of reason for that because it had been broadly advertised that the Invaders had a list of people that they were going to eliminate. Nobody knew who was on that list. Even many honest small ranchers felt that they were up for elimination. There was every reason for them to be excited and anxious to overcome the Invaders. Certainly, it was an unwarranted and illegal thing for them to come as a vigilante force simply to wipe out those people that they suspected.

🌿🌿🌿🌿

Ellis G. Patch
1898-1991
From an interview with Patty Myers
In 1980, when 82 years old

Remembering Old Times

Interviewer Patty Myers: Let's talk about the Patch family.

In 1895, Grandpa Patch came on up to Buffalo from Arvada and went to work at the Cross H Ranch. George Washbaugh homesteaded up the creek about a mile. He was one of the early settlers in Johnson County. He was the man that received a suit of clothes for driving his team of oxen down in front of J.H. Conrad's store in Buffalo. That's what made the curve in Main Street there. Then Grandpa went to work for Charlie Robbins right there at the edge of Buffalo which is at the intersection of Interstate

25 and the north edge of Buffalo. Uncle Walter Patch homesteaded about 1895. He took a 160 acres homestead. Then he fenced in a 640. It wasn't his, but he used it. Everybody did that. We lived there in 1902. We just had a board shack about as big as this bedroom in here.

When Dad and Mother came out here, they came around by old Fort Laramie in 1896 with a team and buggy. They worked down on Piney Creek. Dad told me the first job that he had when he come here that winter–see, he and Uncle Walter fenced the Klondike schoolhouse yard. They had to get pitch posts and this woven wire to fence the yard. There were poles at the bottom and poles at the top. They dug a cellar out there where the plum thicket is now. I was a little bit of a kid. The boards was put up, and Mother pasted paper over them with flour paste. They were digging this hole for the cellar, and they had some big boulders that they couldn't roll out of there. Here come three or four cowboys along. Glen and Clyde Wolcott–I remember these big fellows rolling them boulders out. I couldn't see out what they were doing good enough, so I poked my finger between the cracks behind that paper so I could see what was going on.

Who was Mr. Healy?

There was Patsy Healy. The Healy place was about five miles east of Buffalo on Clear Creek. They called it the Patterson-Healy Sheep Company. About 1911 and 1912, they had, oh, about 20 to 21 bands of sheep in the area of Crazy Woman and Powder River and all over the country. Charlie Pierson, he worked for them. He told me that 1911 and 1912 was terrible. He said that he was working for Patterson-Healy six miles below Buffalo, and old Patsy went back East and turned it over to the boys. But Patsy came out to the ranch on the train and got up there to the ranch. Men was sitting around the bunkhouse, doing nothing, and the sheep was starving to death. Old Patsy went to the bunkhouse, and he said, "Get your clothes. We are going to work." They told him, "You can't do anything out there," but he said, "You gather up this bunch of horses out there, and you drive this band of sheep to Rattlesnake Springs. You trail them sheep out here, and the sheep will follow the horses out because the horses will make the trail. Then get this band in there." They got busy, and they saved quite a lot of them, but they had terrible losses.

Tell me about Kingsbury-Todd.

It was around 1880 that Dave Kingsbury come here. He homesteaded about one mile south of Russell Stokey's homestead on Kelly Creek. Frank Washbaugh told me that Kingsbury was number six in the Crazy Woman drainage for Powder River. He homesteaded on Kelly Creek and brought the first band of sheep into Johnson County. Then he accumulated land. That's from about 1880, you see. In 1904 and 1905, he lived on what they called the Fairview. It was a very modern house for that time. They had a well and a wooden windmill. It was really one of the nicest country homes you would find anyplace. Kingsbury accumulated more land down the creek to Fairview, and he accumulated what they call Louise Richter's place now and everything clear down to the Kitchell place. Kingsbury bought the land a little bit at a time. Before he moved away from there, he had a contiguous piece of land running from over on Kelly Creek and the old Elgin place at Sisters Hill along the face of the mountain and to Bull Creek and then back down Bull Creek. They called that the Kingsbury and Todd big pasture, which is a quarter of mile that he fenced. That was his range. He had the land and controlled the water. Whoever controlled the water here controlled the grazing with it, so he had it. Kingsbury turned it over to Joe Todd, his stepson. Joe Todd was born in 1870. Kingsbury and Todd operated shearing pens on Bull Creek. They had a well up there and sheds.

By the way, Bull Creek got its name when the early freighters would freight into Buffalo from Rock Creek. That was the closest route in here. They'd stay in Buffalo quite a while. It was very sheltered up Bull Creek, so they would take their bulls up there when they weren't working and ride out and see about them every day or two. Bull Creek got its name because they turned the oxen and the bulls out in there while they were waiting to start back.

Right north of where Rogers lives now about a quarter of a mile right out to the north–the old road used to go out there. There is an old house there and a basement. I was riding by it with Frank Washbaugh. He used to take me around when I was a kid, and we gathered cattle together. Every place he went, he would tell me, "This is the old Albert Brock homestead." Well, Albert Brock was J. Elmer Brock's father. They became some of the prominent people in Johnson County. Anyway, Kingsbury was instrumental in getting the Brocks out here to begin with. Albert Brock, from what Frank told me, evidently homesteaded right there. Out there was a little dugout house back in that hill. He said, "That's Gary Gallup's homestead."

The Gallups were quite prominent here. Washbaugh says that Gary Gallup got the Kingsbury homestead and then the old Charlie Sisters place. Charlie Sisters homesteaded there and built Sisters Hill. It was a road to get on the mountain to haul poles off of. Sisters burned lime and taught Walter Elgin how to burn lime.

The Elgins came here in 1887. They thought they had TB. Merle Elgin told me they didn't, but the doctor told them to go west, so they got out in the fresh air. They came into Buffalo down by Trabing on Powder River someplace. One of their horses died, and they were working the milk cow with one horse. Albert Brock said, "Well, we remedied that. We had an old horse, and we give him another horse into Buffalo." He got there to Buffalo, and he immediately went up on the mountain. It's the west end of Elgin Park on the old road. That's where the Woodard's sawmill is.

How did Louise Richter get the Fairview?

Louise bought the Fairview. Dick Richter was one of the earliest settlers in here. He

Louise Richter

came in when the soldiers was here. He was a sawmill man and came in here with the soldiers. In 1876, he helped in the construction of Fort Reno, which was down east of Kaycee. He came in here and could have had any piece of land in Johnson County. Uncle Walter [Patch] told me, "He took that rock pile up there [Ritcher's Ridge]. He could have had his choice of any piece of land in Johnson County, but he was a sawmill man, and there was the timber."

Here's a story all by itself. When Johnson County first originated, it was Pease County–P-E-A-S-E–man by the name of Pease, and they named it that way. Okay, so when Johnson County was set up as a county in the territorial days, the western boundary was the Bighorn River on the west. The southern boundary was Natrona County on the south, and Montana was the northern boundary. It went nearly into the Belle Fourche River on the east. Well, with the county seat in Buffalo, which it was in 1884, and here is the people over there. They wondered what's going on, and here comes the land office in here. There was no roadway across. They could go down to Mayoworth and Kaycee and over the mountains to Thermopolis, but that took a long time. They had a mail route or two that went across the north end of the mountain, but the snow got so terribly deep–6 to 8 feet deep–that they just couldn't go. The people wanted a road, so the commissioners advertised for bid. They started in 1884. It went on for nearly two years, and then they let the contract to Jim Averell for something like $3,800. He built the road up the face of the mountain and got on top. There was timber to cut, but most of the work was getting up that first half mile. There was old cabins and homesteads in there years ago. Boy, it's steep going down and coming up, but that was the road when I was a little kid.

Can you remember "Daddy" Burnett?

Yeah, in 1913, he was on the school board. Come out with a team and wagon out there for graduation. He made the welcoming address. He talked rather high voiced. I knew him quite well. I never worked there for him at all, but I helped them brand.

One day he'd been over here, and somebody borrowed his crowbar. He said, "I was looking for a crowbar. There wasn't any at home. Ellis, you got a crowbar?" I said, "Yeah, I've got a crowbar," so he said, "I believe I'll go over and borrow it." He got my crowbar and never did bring it back. Old Fred Hesse was the same way. When they said something, you never forgot it. I can talk all day, and people forget what I said.

Were they quiet men who only spoke when things were important?

Yeah, they didn't do a lot of talking like I do. Dick Richter–I remember him. He liked to visit. He would take a plug of tobacco out of his pocket. He had a little old knife with a blade about so long and not much bigger–just a little bit of a thing. He'd pull out a plug of tobacco and shave a little bit off here and shave off of there, talking all the time. Then he'd reach in his pocket and get his old corncob pipe and take this plug of tobacco and light it. Then he would say, "Ellis, just wait till I light mine pipe." Spoke very broken German.

Another thing, when Teddy Roosevelt went across the mountains here, he just traveled horseback. He stopped and stayed all night with Dick Richter. In his history he records spending a night before crossing the Bighorns at the home of Richard Richter. Old Dick took an awful liking to him. He'd tell his neighbors, "By Joe, that's a mighty fine man. Someday he be president of the United States." That was Dick Richter's estimate of Teddy Roosevelt.

Can you remember the Billy Creek field?

Yeah, it roared. You couldn't hear. If we was talking here right now, you couldn't hear a thing we said. It roared continuous. I think it run two to three weeks. That winter I was up cutting logs at the HF Bar Ranch. I quit my job up there and come back here and hung onto my homestead. Horace Snider was there. He had two teams of horses in there, and one team was completely deaf, you know.

Another name for this area is the Buffalo Wallows.

Buffalo Wallows are over there east of the highway on Wallow Creek. The buffalo would get them potholes in there. They were just all over. They wallowed around in the bends of the creek where they would hold water. Those old wallows would be eight to 10 feet across. The buffalo to keep away from the flies would go down there and wallow around in those creek bends. That's the way it got its name. You can probably see them yet if you go down the creek.

What can you tell me about John Winchester?

I met him, but I can't tell you much. I was into his place and talked to him a few times. Him and his father and his brother–there was two or three–they homesteaded out in there. Nobody cared too much about him. He bought the Rubottom land which laid on the side of Sisters Hill Road. He closed up the road and wouldn't let them take cattle up there. He charged them a trespass fee which was exorbitant.

Dave Cummings?

Dave Cummings, he was one of the early settlers in the country. Fred Hesse told me that he loaded his beaver hides down on the Platte River and floated them down to the hide market. He lived just this side of the McBride place where Louie Brock lives now. He lived there for years and years. He's been dead a long time. He always wore a muskrat cap in the wintertime. Old Wilbur Williams was another one that always wore a muskrat cap. He was an old-timer around here. It took several of them muskrats to make one cap, but they were very, very warm, you know.

Bill Potts told the story about he wanted to go camping with Dave Cummings. Dave said, "Sure, we'll go some night." So he told him one day to come over and they would go. Bill said, "I wanted to find out what I needed." "Just go like you are," Dave said, "That's all you need." Bill had his .22 or something like that. He said, "We got to have something to eat," and Dave said, "You'll take it there." They went east over onto TW Creek and camped all night. There was wood there enough for fuel. Bill said he wondered what they was going to eat. He said that there was water and muskrats in there. Dave just rolled up his sleeve and reached in there and brought out about five or six of these young muskrats. He killed them, and that was their supper. Bill said, "It was really good. You just add a little bit of salt. That's the way we lived. We was gone three or four days. We didn't need anything–just a gun. That's all we needed." They didn't have a bed or anything.

When were you and Nellie [Nellie Cook Patch] married?

Ellis & Nellie Patch

I was working there on the CCC camp. That was in 1936. When we came back here, she was teaching school. She taught the Johnson Creek School. She finished the term teaching, and we rented a cabin on the mountain right close to where I was working. That fall we moved down to Dayton and finally ended by having a house there.

Sarahlee and Shirley and Sally were born before we came back here, and then Sherrie was born in 1942 and Kathleen in '45. Three of them was born while we lived in Sheridan and two of them after we came back to town here.

Was it hard raising five little girls out here?

Well, I don't know as it was. We didn't have a lot of money. We milked cows and sold hay and one thing and another. We got by. As soon as they was big enough, they helped. We had to work horses on the stacker. They would have to take turns. One would drive ten loads up. They would always quarrel about it and get mixed up on it. We used horses then. In about 1947 or 1948 we went to machinery.

The kids grew up. Kathleen graduated from Laramie in Secretarial Science. Sherry and Sally, they went to Michael Reese's Nursing School and graduated there. Shirley, she graduated from the University at Laramie and then went to Redlands, California, to a college out there for two or three semesters. And Sarahlee, she just got two years of college is all.

Rosemary Perkins
1926-2018
From an interview with Nancy Tabb
In 2017, when 91 years old

Rosemary's Secret

Interviewer Nancy Tabb: Did you know Joe LeFors?

Joe LeFors

Joe LeFors and we go way back. Joe LeFors was a very good railroad detective. Oh, I loved Joe. He was wonderful. I must have been 9 years old or less. On Saturdays–they were Seventh Day Adventists–he would come and get me, and we would walk to his house before dinner. He would wear a black suit. I was so proud. I'd be looking to see if anybody was looking at me. He taught me to shoot. We'd go out in the orchard. We would set up targets there, and he would bring out pistols. They had a big orchard, and Mrs. [Nettie] LeFors always had apple pie.

Rosemary, I've turned my recorder back on because you have one more thing to tell me. You said it's a secret.

Did you know my aunt was married to Butch Cassidy, but her parents had it annulled. She didn't want that secret out, but I want to share it with you. Well, I had a cousin named Margerite after my mother. She was beautiful and talented and was allowed out more than I was. She had been somewhere and ran into an old sheepherder, and he said, "I knew your mother's husband." Her mother's husband was Farley Driskill–very prominent family, the Driskills. Very handsome–he had gone to Yale. This man said, "No, she had another husband." So my cousin kept trying to argue, and this man said, "No, I knew him. You ask her." So Margerite went home and asked her mother, and her mother said, "I'll tell you once, and I never want it mentioned again." You know, in those days having that was a scandal. So Margerite immediately told me. I told my mother, who was a huge, big prude. Aristocrats! I asked my mother, and there was like a bolt. Mother told me, "I never want this mentioned again. Yes, she was married to a very unsuitable person."

Okay, so years go by, and I was working on some land for the ranch. I'd become involved in the Broken H Ranch, and I had to go to Cheyenne to look at some land deals. While there, I ran into Tommy Tisdale, so we had lunch and a visit–we were old friends. I'm ready to leave, and Tommy said,–I'm halfway up–"Rosemary, which one of your aunts was married to a man that lived on the Blue Creek Ranch?" I said, "Tommy, I only had one aunt. Why?" He said–get this–"It would appear she was married to Butch Cassidy, who lived on that ranch." But her parents had the marriage annulled. Apparently, the Blue Creek Ranch had been in her name. She was the most loving, wonderful, kind, gentle–she gave a lot to the poor. Anyway, I had to tell you that about my aunt.

❧❧❧❧

Grayce Bodell Provence
1909-1990
From a KBBS Radio program
In 1975, when 66 years old

Homesteading the Nine Mile Area

The Nine Mile Creek crossing was close to our place and nine miles from Fort Reno. That's how it got its name. In 1914, homesteading in Nine Mile country was being filed on before the Homestead Act ended in 1931. Then people began to leave because of the shortage of water, so there were many auction sales.

During the good years, there was lots of spring and fall rains and heavy winter snow, and crops were abundant. Corn, wheat, barley, and oats were the main grain crops. Wheat made 30 bushels an acre on the average. One year, some had wheat that made 50 bushels an acre. Many other crops and wonderful gardens were raised on nearly every ranch along with cattle and sheep. The country was full of wild horses too. Many of the ranchers had large herds of milk cows and separated and shipped cream. Grass was stirrup high, and blue stem hay was cut in most of the draws. Now, I've heard a lot of people say they never saw stirrup high grass. It wasn't every year, of course, but there were years. Most of the years back through the 1930s we did put up blue stem hay. Wildflowers, of course, of all kinds and colors covered the hills every spring. An aunt of mine had wondered why we lived in such a forsaken country because she had never been here anytime except in August. One year, she was here earlier in the spring, and she couldn't believe how beautiful the country really is. Of course, we had lots of antelope and deer. You could see them in large herds everywhere. We had lots of them on our place and hunted.

Our neighbors always worked hard and played hard. The schoolhouses were used on Saturdays for either literaries or dances. Hague Paxton and Jay Cristler were always ready and willing to furnish the music both being the best fiddlers in the country.

In the 1920s, the Nine Mile Community Bureau was formed and a community hall was built. Charlie Wells headed the bureau. Donations were asked to buy materials, and labor was donated by the ranchers. The completed hall was 30 feet by 60 feet. It was built on government land. Later, land was purchased for $1.25 an acre to move the building to its own land, but it didn't get moved because so many people were leaving. They finally just left it where it was and sold the piece of land that they bought. There was 40 acres in all–a piece of the Pearl Waggoner homestead.

Grayce Provence

Fairs were held each year that rivaled the present-day fairs with all the products from the Nine Mile Community. Hundreds of folks from all over the state attended. Contests of all kinds were held from races to catching greased pigs. Mr. Ralph Seney, Sr. brought his airplane out from town and sold rides–his airplane being the first in the county.

After the drought of the 1930s, folks left one by one until only a handful were left, so the community hall building was sold to Dan Koch for $200, and the 40 acres was sold to Bruce Pheasant for $900. The bureau held the oil rights. Mr. A.M. Kester headed the group to bring about a transfer of the oil rights to Johnson County Memorial Hospital. The hospital now has the oil rights leased to the oil company for $7 an acre.

In our district there were five schools in the early days. The buildings had to be furnished by the ranchers. The schools did the hiring of the teachers. Geraldine Davis–now Geraldine Kinzer–taught in one of the schools in about 1929. The school didn't furnish coal, so she chopped sagebrush to keep the school open so she wouldn't have to close it.

They used to send a visiting school nurse out to the country schools in those days. The nurse would come out, and she would feel so sorry for the poor, underprivileged ranch children. She would talk about their being hungry and one thing and another. There wasn't anybody better fed than a ranch kid.

The first post office was Peckville in about 1919. Then it was moved to the Kinzer place and was named Bonnidee. Bonnidee was the name of a cousin of the Kinzers. The mail days were Tuesdays and Fridays. The post office was later moved to the Willey Ranch, where it was until it was closed and a route maintained only on Fridays. The mailman hauled supplies, cream, eggs, and passengers. Sometimes the roads were so bad that it took several days to make the 90-mile round trip with car or horse and sometimes both. It would be time to start out again by the time they got back to town.

The community boasted a blacksmith shop. Hague Paxton was the best blacksmith in the state. Once, when an axle on the mailman's Dodge Commercial broke, Hague welded it together using a hand forge. It was so perfect it lasted the life of the car. If it was made of iron, he could make or mend it. I have a hand forged link chain he made.

We had church and Sunday school each Sunday for years at the community church, which the ranchers had built on a piece of ground donated by Henry Laurie. After they all left, we held Sunday school in the schoolhouse.

A store which carried most of the staple articles was run by J.R. Smith until it burned down about 1920. Eggs, chickens, turkeys, beef, mutton, and vegetables were hauled to the Midwest oilfield, where they found a ready sale.

Folks visited and helped each other in spite of the long distances, thinking nothing of going 10 miles with horse and wagon to visit neighbors for the day. Everybody got together putting up ice and thrashing and branding–things like that.

It was a three-day round trip to town by team, so it wasn't attempted very often. Folks put in their staple articles in the fall for the entire winter and usually made one trip a year to town to buy clothes and so forth. With their cellars full of vegetables and meat and their coal bins full of coal they were set for a hard winter.

Coal was dug by hand either from Crazy Woman Creek or Pine Ridge. The Crazy Woman coal was full of sulfur, so not as desirable as the Pine Ridge coal, which was the best coal that could be found anywhere. It would catch from an almost dead fire. Later, when oil was discovered in the Pine Ridge, we realized why it was such wonderful coal. Four-horse loads–two tons were hauled every fall until enough was put in to last a year. Some of the ranchers worked together to get out the coal as they did the ice.

Every rancher had an ice house and put up enough ice to last all summer. We usually waited until ice was 18 to 24 inches thick. It was cut from large reservoirs. Homemade ice cream was made all summer from this ice, as well as being used to keep food cool.

Some folks made their own hominy and canned as many as 1,000 jars of meat and vegetables a year. Bread was made from a yeast starter. Sometimes it would freeze, and you would then have to go to a neighbor and borrow a new starter. One woman roasted green coffee beans. Some of the women made their own soap. One in particular made snow white soap that would even float. A lot of ranchers took loads of wheat to Kearney to the flour mill every fall to exchange for a year's supply of flour. The flour mill was water powered.

Dr. W.J. Knebel was the doctor they could depend on to come to their aid. He traveled the roads regardless of mud, snow, or cold if he was needed to fight influenza or tick fever or to deliver babies. He even wrote instructions by mail when necessary. He doctored my daughter through scarlet fever and pneumonia with instructions by mail. I had a good faithful doctor book that really came in handy. I also had a very good veterinarian's book. We did our own veterinarian work, as there wasn't any veterinarian anywhere in those days.

During the 1940s, Nine Mile had a telephone line between the neighbors. In later years, the only phone went from the Douglas trail two miles to the Provence Ranch house, which proved handy for motorists in trouble or for neighbors to make a call for any reason.

There were many tragedies in that part of the country in the early days. Many humorous things happened too. Once, the family started to town in the spring, and the snow was real deep. They had a spring wagon which was equipped with runners instead of wheels. A chinook came up, so they had to come home in the mud and had a real terrible time making it.

We had lots of box socials and pie socials that were enjoyed by everyone throughout the country. There was always something going on. We would have a party at the drop of a hat. It just didn't take anything for everybody to get together and have a good time.

❦❦❦❦

Virginia Steffensen Purdy
1916-2012
From an interview with Patty Myers
In 1989, when 73 years old

Mayor & Councilwoman

Interviewer Patty Myers: Virginia, I want to start this morning by asking you how you ended up in Johnson County.

I had an uncle, Speck Peters, who homesteaded in this country in the early 1900s, and he had an interesting life. It was interesting for many points because, I'd say historically, he was one of the characters in the county. When he first came here, he was only 16 years old. He came out on a cattle train with Lee Moore. There were nine children in the family who came from Denmark and settled in the Omaha, Council Bluffs, Nebraska, area. Cities didn't mean anything to him, but he loved to sit and watch the cattle trains come in and the stock operation, so he thought, "Well, when I can get away from the city and all these kids..."

When he first came, he worked for the Moore outfit. Then he worked for Pumpkin Buttes Brown, who was a historical character. He worked for the Bud Ranch, and he worked down in the Salt Creek area. He was an awfully, awfully good cowboy. In fact, he had the reputation of being able to ride anything. He was small, and he was wiry. Villa Irvine said that when you saw Speck riding, you could see his form. There was not another cowboy that rode as he did with the balance and lightness in the saddle.

My mother and father [Walter H. and Clara Steffensen] were Danish. They were dairy people in Wisconsin. Daddy was a purebred breeder of Holstein cows, which he milked. So here I thought, "My father is tied to those milk cows every morning and every evening." I thought about my uncle who lived on a ranch in Wyoming and what a wonderful life. Just look at them in the spring. You brand them and you gather them and you ship them and that's it. Well, the summers between high school and college vacation, I thought, "I'm coming out to Wyoming."

I came out here the first time in 1939, so I've been here 50 years. I thought it was wonderful. I was here at the time the Hesses were running the 28 Ranch. At that time, my uncle worked for George Hesse, and I would stay down with Grace Hesse and the children. I spent my summers there. I would ride in the mountains when they moved cattle. It was great!

Uncle lived in this little old log cabin that he built. It was two rooms. In the summertime, he lived in the second room as a bedroom. In the wintertime, he bunked in the main part that just had his stove and a bunk bed and table and furniture. That was it. It was pretty rustic–pretty crude. There was a little patio, and in the morning you could hear the birds. I think there was a sod roof on it because one morning when I woke up, I heard something and thought, "What is that strange noise so early in the morning?" The prairie chickens had roosted on the roof that night.

I finished my years of college and married, and my husband [Fred Bailey] had died. Well, I was coming and going back and forth, but I always came back to Wyoming, so I came to stay.

When you came back and really lived here full-time, was that with Bob [Robert H. Purdy]?

No, I didn't come out here with Bob. I was not married to Bob until 1950. Bob and I had known each before. He was a neighbor. In fact, he used to ride my Shetland pony when he was five years old. He fell off of it, and he told me, "Well, your dad didn't cinch the saddle tight," and I told him, "Well, any dumb city kid who didn't know any better and would leave the saddle cinch loose and not be able to balance and put more weight on one side than the other, you ought to fall off."

I really didn't live out here in the wintertime until I was married and lived out here as a family. I have been a taxpayer since 1939 when I bought the Van Auken place. That was a dude ranch that joined Uncle's. Uncle would tell us when there was property adjoining the original homestead, and Mother and Daddy said, "Well, we can help him," so we did.

I would come out in the summer and work with the cattle. Then we would ship them, so we got some of the percentage of the livestock sales. It was under absentee ownership for some time. Later on, you think that was part of the way you got into this business. Unless you are in the country early on, you don't develop these things. I had about 7,500 acres when I married Bob. Then as some years went by, we bought the 28 Ranch, which was south of the original land and joined us. Then later on, we bought the Willow Glen. We sold the upper Willow Glen to John Gammon. Anyhow, you grow, and you change and move things.

What brought you into Buffalo politics? You were ranch people.

I think watching some of the things that were happening. If you've ever done anything with the public, you still feel like there is something that you can do with them and for them. I had a good education and had enough training in college to be able to. I was literary editor of our newspaper back in Wisconsin, and I was editor of the school yearbook. I was always interested in editorials in newspapers. I would take the time to answer newspaper editorials and write them. Little by little, people said, "I wonder what Virginia would say about this. I wonder what she would do about that." At that time, I thought there are things happening here that I would like to take part in.

We had a residence in town because my son was in school, and because I had a home in town, I qualified as a resident of the City. I am more or less a dual resident, and I have been on the County Planning Board. Of course, you become interested in what's happening in subdivision development and outlying areas to try to have something that's quality. I felt this community had so much to give, and it should not be cluttered up and messed up and just everything let go just any which way. Anyway, I was the first woman that got into the politics in the City Hall of Buffalo, which is no great kicks. It was a tough job, especially coming from my background. I had always been interested in more than just my own little front yard.

I found that I could not believe how comfortable it was. There was a great deal of respect. Instead of feeling antagonism that many times comes with new people on the block, I think there was a hesitancy to say anything because they didn't know just where to attack. It was, "Well, let's listen and see what this gal has to say."

The years that I served as mayor, I think we had a superb council. We had people like Safford Fairlie, who was so knowledgeable. He was a moving force in this community and a man whose knowledge and judgment was respected. We had Burley Johnson, who certainly knew the City. We had Al Kuhn, who was outspoken and came with a feeling of cooperation of the Basque community. At that time, why, we had Dick Condit, who was on the council. Dick knew everybody in town. The finances was checks and balances–Burley was great because he had a good knowledge and background in bookkeeping.

As the months phased on, and I was mayor, the council knew me, and we had good camaraderie. In fact, after meetings often the group of us would go out to the Crossroads and sit down over coffee–maybe somebody would have a beer. We would hash over things and what the next thing was we were going to do. We didn't just drop it as we walked out the door after the meeting. We carried on and thought about it.

There are so many things I addressed along with the City Council during my time as councilwoman and mayor. Just to name a few–we worked on a new waterline. We amended the electrical code. We enacted an ordinance making offenses of possession, transporting, and selling hallucinatory drugs. At that time, we had no city garbage collection, so we finally got mandatory trash pickup. We had streets that needed attention. The stinking, smoking city dump was above the golf course. That is such a beautiful area up there up on a hill. From there you could look down over the city and up into the mountain. Then you would see these piles of trash up there. So we closed the dump and created a park and recreation area. It still stands today as Country Club Park.

Well, let's see. We passed one very good resolution which authorized the mayor to be the official administrator of water and sewer projects. For its economy Buffalo decided it had better start charging for some of the city facilities. We created the cemetery district so we could put a mill levy on the tax structure. We created the City of Buffalo

Personnel Commission, establishing the length of terms. Another important thing was we filed an application for underground water rights for the City on 24 of its 40 acres of land that the City owns. We bought a garbage truck for the city–our first garbage truck–and we bought police cars. At this time, we were getting ready to do the Highway Department's new bridge over Clear Creek. We started that in November of 1974. We started the study for the Criminal Justice Facility, and we started a Housing Authority so we could share in federal money and funding to assist people on fixed low incomes. I think our wastewater treatment studies were going on too.

If you do things and keep them honorable and whistling clean, you have nothing to regret. It's a wonderful experience because you feel that you have done something–you aren't just here as a consumer. You are a producer. I have enjoyed working in this little community. It's very near and dear to my heart. I've spent a lot of the years of my life here. I've also helped the economy in this community because we have run a good operation, and we have given excellent housing and salaries to people in the work force. The worst thing is that I ran out of time. I would love to have had more time. It was the end of the year, and it was a cold night in December. I was sitting up there in my house on the hill and looked over Buffalo, and I thought, "I love this little community."

ﷺﷺﷺﷺﷺ

Joyce Graves Reculusa
1944-Present
From an interview with Diane Orme
In 1994, when 50 years old

Just a Kid

Because I didn't like to work in the house, I followed my dad or the hired men around. Whenever they were going riding, I tried to go with them. If they weren't doing anything, I would go out with a can of oats and catch my horse and go to the barn or the house and find someone tall enough to bridle my horse for me. Then there was always something I found that I needed to do really badly. From the time I was probably 4 or 5 years old, I'd go catch my horse and have to lead him to the barn to have somebody help me. I thought I had really accomplished a lot when I finally was big enough to climb up on something and bridle my horse by myself–I suppose by the time I was six or so. I rode bareback all the time because I couldn't put the saddle on.

When I was 7 years old, my grandparents were on the mountain herding sheep. My grandfather's horses were foot sore, and he needed a spare horse. Dad was busy. It was about eight miles up to sheep camp, so I rode my horse and lead the extra one up to my grandfather on the mountain. The first time I went up there by myself I was hoping that I remembered all the right places to turn because when we got fairly close, we left the road and took a shortcut to sheep camp. We grew up that way and never thought much about it.

Way, way earlier, there had been a few bears up there. I suppose that was in the 1940s, but there were no bears or mountain lions at all until after 1080 [compound 1080 poison used to control predators] was abolished in the 1970s.

They lived in a sheep wagon up there during the summertime. They usually had a tent that they set up wherever they had their permanent camp so that there was always room for anybody else to go up and help them when they worked sheep or just needed to spend the night on the mountain.

In the summertime, us kids helped with the haying down on the ranch. Of course, first we started raking. Probably my sister–because she was older–ran the buck rake most of the time. By the time I was a seventh or eighth grader, I started doing quite a bit of the mowing. But we were all in the hayfields. It kept us all busy and out of trouble.

✿✿✿✿

David R. "Dave" Redmond
1942-Present
From an interview with Nancy Tabb
In 2018, when 76 years old

We Eloped Twice

Interviewer Nancy Tabb: You just told me that you actually had two names in your lifetime.

Now it's David Ray Redmond. My birthname was Lawrence Wayne Warne. My parents went to Lansing, Michigan in 1942 and adopted me when I was one month old. They brought me back to Buffalo. It took three years back then for an adoption to be cleared. My birth mother was my adopted mother's sister. We were all taken away from our birth mother and adopted out.

Your parents had the Redmond Ranch.

I remember one winter my dad [Charles McKinley Redmond] went to town to do the shopping. Oh, he'd leave like in the morning to come in and buy supplies. Then he would go back out at Crazy Woman and spend the night. He would sleep under the wagon, and the next day he'd go on home. Well, once he did that in the wintertime, and when he woke up, he was snow blind. So Dad had to harness the horses by just feel, ya know. Yeah, he did that. He called his team Rex and Texie. He told them, "Head for home," and he just let them go. My mother [Eva Grant Redmond], she said it was about gettin' towards dark–of course, it gets dark early in the wintertime. She got on a saddle horse and headed out to find him. About a half mile from the house here he came. After that experience he had to have dark prescription glasses and had to wear them all the time. Ronna [Ronna Hubbell Redmond], my wife, was snow blind too. When she was a kid, her glasses had to be tinted. She couldn't take bright sunlight.

Tell me Ronna's story.

She was born in Gillette, but her parents came to Buffalo. Her dad worked in the oil fields. Well, we met, and her parents had no use for me. It was kinda odd how it all turned out. We dated but had to sneak around. Then Ronna said that that's no good, so she broke it off, and we just went our separate ways.

I went to Denver and lived there for a while. Then I went in the Army. They was going to send me to Korea, but I said, "No, if I want to go somewhere, I wanna go where I wanna go," and that was Germany. I had volunteered to draft. I went over in April 1961.

All of sudden, lo and behold, November of 1963, I got a letter from Ronna. I was kinda stunned, so I opened it. I thought that I should write back to her. So we started writing. I couldn't send letters to her parents' place, but I wrote Ronna at her girl-friend's P.O. Box number. When I got out in 1964, her folks was so mad they was gonna move to Clarkston, Washington. So Ronna said, "Let's get married," and we eloped–what we did. The thing about when we got married the first time–we tried to elope twice in one month. We went to South Dakota, and the cops stopped us over there and took her. Her parents had to go get her. I was over 21, but she was under age.

So I talked to a lawyer, and he said, "Don't worry." One night, I got home and was eating supper, and the phone rang. Mom said to me, "Phone's for you." I took the phone, and it was Ronna. She says, "I've run away again. I'm up at Keith and Nancy's house. You ready to go try it again?" I called my mom after I got up to their house, and I says, "Do you have $100 I can borrow?" So Keith and Nancy took us clear to Sundance. Ronna's aunt knew all about it and said we could use her car. Well, we got in to Sundance about 4:00 in the morning. Then we headed to Bismarck, North Dakota. We got there and found it was a three-day waiting period, and this was Friday of Memorial weekend. So we headed back to South Dakota and went to McIntosh. They got the county clerk out of bed to come over to the courthouse, and we got a marriage license there–no waiting period. The minister from a Baptist church performed the ceremony. We were married 51 years.

The biggest thing I learned when we got married was you make your decisions and only you. Also, I found it very important to say, "I'm sorry. Forgive me. I was wrong." You must do it before the night is over. I probably said that more times than I can count to Ronna. I think that as the years gone by you become more trusting in your spouse.

Dixie Lynne Reece
1938-2018
From an interview with Nancy Tabb
In 2017, when 81 years old

Dixie's Trick Horse

I had an old trick horse that I taught 28 different tricks. Dusty was my helper. He would help me pull the baby calves. He was just a super good horse. Oh, he did like pawing his age, you know, and saying "yes" and "no." I had a handkerchief or a big ole rag that I would tie on his back leg, and he would reach around and undo that. Daddy would tie my hands together behind my back, and Dusty would get me loose. I used to show him at rodeos.

How I knew I would be able to train him was when we went to the Sheridan Rodeo. George Rudolph picked up the cowboys off of the bucking horses. George knocked his hat off, and he just rode up and reached down and picked up his hat.

I thought, "Wouldn't that be neat?" so I tried it with my old Dusty horse, and he figured that out. He knew I was reaching much too far, so he reached around and picked my hat up and handed it back to me. I petted him and gave him a piece of cow cake that is a treat. Anyway, I put the hat back down, and Dusty did it again. We had the cutest tricks. I did rope tricks too. Daddy would put a rope into a hondo [knot]. I would put one end into Dusty's mouth. Then Daddy would get at the other end, and I'd jump rope. Old Dusty would get out of time swinging it by shaking his head and then go over to Dad and spit the rope out.

❧❧❧❧

Carl R. "Dick" Reimann, Jr.
1935-Present
From an interview with Nancy Tabb
In 2017, when 82 years old

Slee or Reimann?

Well, my name is legally Carl Richard Reimann, Jr. I had always gone by Richard. A little later on, I started being Dick, and that is where I am at this time. I was born in Buffalo April 24, 1935, at the Freeman Hospital.

My mother was Lorraine Sophie Buckingham Reimann, and my dad, Carl Reimann. My mother grew up in the Big Goose, Sheridan area and then lived in Story with her folks. She passed away two days after I was born. I think she was still in the hospital. Apparently, a very tough infection took her life. My dad was born in 1904 in Buffalo. He probably completed his education in the seventh grade.

Carl "Dick" Reimann

My dad's mother raised me. She was Ida Mae Reimann. As I understand it, she was raised in Boston, Massachusetts, and had a brother who lived in Buffalo. She came out here probably because of him and was here as a single lady for a while and then met Joseph Reimann, my grandfather.

He left home fairly early on in his life and ended up moving to the West, joined the Army, and was in the Army for several years. I believe it was in 1880 when he was discharged from the Army at Fort Laramie, Wyoming. Prior to that he had been in the Indian wars mostly in northern Colorado. He came to Buffalo in 1882 and lived the rest of his life here. I'm not sure when he and my grandmother were married.

In those days, a lot of the people that joined the Army would have two names. They would have their real name, and they would have an alias. We don't know the whole story. However, when my grandfather got out of the Army, his discharge papers say "Joseph Reimann, alias Samuel Slee." We really don't know whether we are Slee or Reimann. His discharge papers gave both names.

Those Depression days were tough days for most people. My grandfather did pretty much anything he could do to make a living. He delivered freight. He had an office downtown. He was justice of the peace for many years. I'm told that my grandfather hid out in that attic for quite a while during the Johnson County Cattle War. He tended to favor the homesteaders and the new people rather than the big companies. I'm sure he was on that list of who were to be killed by the Invaders.

I went to Clear Creek for elementary school. There was a swinging bridge across Clear Creek, so I walked from home across the creek on the swinging bridge. When I graduated from high school in 1953, I went to college at Denver University and studied Accounting. Starting in my junior year, I joined the Lambda Chi Alpha Fraternity. I worked as the treasurer of the fraternity for my room and board. The different fraternities and sororities would have socials. My wife, Kathy [Kathy Keaton Reimann], belonged to a sorority, Kappa Delta, that was on campus as well. I went to a dance at Kathy's sorority. That is where I met her. She was born and raised in Denver. She went to Denver University and worked at a Sears Store when she could.

On the 14th of June 1957, I graduated from the University of Denver, and on the 15th we got married. We had our sixtieth anniversary in June. After we got married, we rented a basement apartment for the summer. It wasn't very far from the Sears Store, where she worked. I rode the bus to downtown and worked for an oil company in Denver for the summer. I had joined an Army reserve unit earlier in January of that year, so in September she moved back in with her folks, and I went to Fort Leonard Wood, Missouri, for Army basic training. I was in a program for reserve units called the RFA [Reserve Forces Act]. The unit I joined was active out of Fitzsimons Hospital. I went there for weekly meetings from January until the fall when I went to basic training. After basic training, I was transferred to Maryland. The unit I joined in Denver was intelligence, so I spent the rest of my six months active duty in Baltimore. Kathy continued to stay with her parents, and she was with child–Carla.

Over the period that I was at Fort Leonard Wood, I corresponded some and ended up with a job in Casper, Wyoming, as an accountant for Pan American Petroleum Corp. We lived in Casper for over two years and had another child–Rick. Then we had Steve here and Karen–girl, boy, boy, girl.

I got to where I wasn't real excited about what I was doing and ended up making a deal with my dad. He had Reimann Oil Co. here in Buffalo, so we moved back here in 1960. When he bought into the company, it was Wilson Oil Company–Caryl Wilson and his wife, Mildred. It was a little station right on the corner.

My dad and Alabam Deloney–well, his real name was Ned–he and my dad had a business and partnership together. They had the service station and the bulk plant where they delivered out in the country, and they ran a school bus route down Clear Creek. They also had a taxi service. That was World War II times. Alabam sold out to my dad and went in the Seabees during the war. Then my dad made a deal with Caryl Wilson. I don't think he owned the property, but my dad moved in with Caryl Wilson. It was a fairly small service station–three pumps, one lube bay, and an old, old pitched roof. Anyway, as near as I can remember, my dad bought in with Caryl Wilson in 1949. I think it was probably 1954 that he bought out Wilson, and he operated it alone for a number of years.

At that time, there was a lady, Mrs. Della Stone, she ran a restaurant that was across the street where Kum and Go is now. It had a counter. In the summertime, when I was growing up, I would go down there and be with my dad while he was working and do whatever. We used to go over there and have coffee, and I got to know Mrs. Stone pretty well. She would always hand me a piece of pie.

Next door was a Chevrolet garage building–Waugh Chevrolet. Over a period of time, two men, Willard Dickey and Joe Felix, owned that Chevrolet agency. Then my dad and I made a deal with them to buy their building. That is how we ended up with that. Then they rented it back from us. What it amounted to is they were short of cash and needed the cash to operate. Well, Joe Felix bought out his partner, Will Dickey. Joe Felix decided he wanted his own building, so he bought a garage building that was in south Buffalo across the street from the Episcopal Church.

At that point in time, I was wanting to modernize and expand, and my dad and I worked things out. I remodeled the front of the building that had Reimann Oil Co. in it and put the angle on the front with the front door and built the lube bays and had a garage in back that we operated. My dad ended up pretty much retiring.

This was when you came and filled them up with gas and checked their oil–even at times swept out their car. We carried the whisk broom right in our pocket. It was all full service. Then self-service came along and really upset the apple cart.

One other thing I can mention–across the alley behind Reimann Oil for many years was the Huff Blacksmith Shop–Elmer Huff. He built wagons and did all sorts of black-smithing and horseshoes–all sorts of things like that. Later on, there was another small mechanic's shop in that same building. As I recall, Smitty was a single, young man that worked on cars. After that, when I was running Reimann Oil Co., I bought that building from Mrs. Vashti Huff. That building is gone, and there is a fairly new building in that spot.

There used to be two lumberyards. The one directly across from the old Reimann Oil Co. was W.F. Smith Lumber. To the south on the corner was the Pioneer Lumber Co. Both of those lumberyards went clear back over to Adams Street. They had their lumber storage behind the retail stores where Buffalo Federal and part of the library is. When the library was in the Carnegie Building, I was on the library board for a number of years, and we didn't have much room. Then the library built and moved over there and now has expanded on that.

As far as how things have changed, the industry that I worked in–the oil and gas and repair and tire field–has changed completely. You don't see a service station any-more. If you have a problem that needs help, then you have a problem because they are all separated. You don't have a whole lot of choice but to go to the dealership. We did all of that when we were in business. We sold tires, we did service work, and we did repair work. Now those are all separated. If you want gas, you go and pump it yourself, and you can use a credit card to pay for it.

ɬɬɬɬ

Wilbur P. Robbins
1917-1997
From an interview with Patty Myers
In 1989, when 72 years old

Johnson County Clerk

Interviewer Patty Myers: Wilbur, tell me a little personal background about why you are in Johnson County.

Well to begin with, I was raised in Johnson County. I'm third generation. My kids are fourth, and my grandkids are fifth generation, so we've been around a while. Actu-ally, I was born in the Basin country.

My dad [Perry Robbins] died of the flu during the1918 epidemic when I was 11 months old. My mother [Edna J. Robbins] came back to Buffalo after he died. She orig-inally came to Johnson County in a covered wagon from Kansas. My dad's folks originally were in the Barnum country and then moved up on French Creek. That's where my mother and father met. She was teaching school on Dad's place and stayed with Grandfather and Grandmother Robbins.

When did you decide to run for county office?

Well, I had an accident in the oilfield. I got blowed out of the header house and had a back problem. Anyway, I come over here on vacation, and Dick Hughes and I bought Nielsen's Furniture Store. That's how come I came back to Buffalo. Because of my back problem, I went to Casper for a spinal fusion, and I sold my interest in the store to Lester Nielsen. After I got out of that, why, George Knepper, Gene Cowan and Bill Kirven talked me into going back into a furniture store, and I had the Buffalo Furniture Mart.

But I got curvature of the spine in that fusion, and my doctor told me I had to quit laying floor covering. He told me that I would have to do nothing for 11 months. But I told him, "I can't stand that," and he said, "Well, you will have to anyway," which I did. When he said I'm going to have to change my occupation, I asked him, "But what am I going to do?" His answer, "Run for a county office." That's when I decided to run for county office. Fact of the matter is I'd never given anything like that a thought. I talked to Mr. C.C. Palmer one day, and he told me that he wasn't going to run, so I decided I'd run.

There was three of us that run that year, and I lucked out and won the election. I didn't win by no landslide by no means. I run against Art Greenleaf's wife [Gertrude Greenleaf]. She was deputy county clerk. I also run against Golden Jolley's son, Alan Jolley. Alan gave me a pretty close second, I'll tell you.

I took office in the fall of 1967 and served 16 years as county clerk. I think it is the best job in the courthouse, but there is a lot of work to it. If you will check a Wyoming Statute book, you'll see that for some reason the Legislature gives 90 percent of the new jobs to the county clerk. Now, if you could take the elections out of the county clerk's job, it would be the best job in Johnson County, but the elections are truly a headache, believe me.

I'll never forget the year I took office was the year we voted for a new courthouse. I had been in office less than six weeks when we had that bond election. I remember that morning at about 8:30 the phone rang. I think it was Helen Baxter on that board. She said, "We've got a problem. You'll have to come over." As I walked in the front door, Mr. Palmer was coming out, and he grabbed my hand and shook it and said, 'It makes me awful happy to see somebody else putting on an election." He was really tickled.

It was a very good job, and I had some very good help. Believe me, in that position you have to have good help. You have to have competent people, and I did. We sell the car titles, the marriage licenses. We went through the uranium boom and took thousands of uranium claims a day. I mean we worked day and night on those uranium claims. It was a godsend to Johnson County because those oil and gas leases and uranium leases puts a lot of money back into the county. I don't think a lot of people realize how much money. Of course, that's kind of in the past because there is not much activity in either uranium or oil today. At that time, we had three things in Johnson County–oil and gas and the stock industry.

Sometimes when I'd go to the Courthouse that whole backroom would be full of people.

We had them piled up. We almost had to issue chips to let them in to work on the books. That was one of the things we accomplished while I was county clerk. They built the new Criminal Justice Building, so they gave me the old sheriff's office, and we made the old jail into a vault for storage. We really were just completely out of space before that.

The amount of records that you keep is just astonishing.

Enormous. You have to have that storage. We done all our work the hard way–the indexing by hand and all the books. When you was indexing thousands of uranium claims a day, it was a lot of work, plus we had oil and gas claims at the same time–quite a lot of them–and lots of land checkers in and out. There was many days that we had 15-20 people, all trying to get a book to work with. When we got our first bunch of uranium claims, why, we hired our second girl. Then we hired our third girl. Then there were four of us. It worked out very well.

Mr. Palmer was very helpful when we had our first examiners. Of course, that's something that scares you to death because you think they are going to cut your throat. Our first examiners come in and said, "Well, you're off." I forget, but it was off $3 or $4. It was not a big amount, but we had to find it. Mr. Palmer came down and sat with us. We looked for that, I guess, for six weeks before we found it. When they set up the budget the year before is where the mistake was made. But we had to find that.

The first examiner that examined me after I'd been there a year examined Mr. Palmer's books, not mine. I'll never forget him. He came in, showed me his badge, and said, "I'm from the State Examiner's Office. Give me your cash drawer." Just like that. The first thing they do is take your cash drawer and check it. When he got all through, he said, "You owe the drawer $2. You missed a title on such and such a date." Sure enough we went back and checked it, and we were short $2 that day, so I gave him $2, and we balanced the books.

When he come in, he asked, "Have you got some place I can work?" I said, "You can work in my office." That is where they had always worked–in my office at the back end of the room. But he said, "I don't want to be in there. I want to be by myself," so he went across the hall. When he got through, he told me everything looked pretty good and we'd done a good job. I never saw the guy again for about four years. One day, I run into him. We visited a little bit, and I told him, "You know, you liked to scared me to death. You were the first examiner I'd ever had. I didn't know what to expect." And he replied, "I'll tell you a little secret. You were the first customer I ever had–the first time I ever went out on my own."

Have you ever figured out any rhyme or reason to the way Johnson County people vote?

Oh, yeah, I think you could pretty much see the handwriting on the wall. We had one fellow that could pretty much set an election for you. It was amazing. It's Bill Holland I'm talking about. Bill Holland told us just exactly how many votes would be in each precinct. He had it all figured out ahead of the election. I mean to tell you he was almost 100 percent right in what he had set out. He had every office set down who was going to get elected and by how many votes–the whole works. He was tremendous. He always told me what was going to happen.

What about coffee breaks and things like that?

Well, when I went in as county clerk, that was the first thing I done. There wasn't a coffee pot in the clerk's office, so I bought a coffee pot, and we made our own coffee. We never did go out for coffee breaks. If you wanted a cup of coffee, you went and got it and drank it. We always kept the coffee pot on. The land checkers were awful good. Charlie Porter with American Rissler Corporation–I don't think Charlie ever came into my office that he didn't bring a sack full of cookies for the office. The land checkers always threw some money in the pot so we could buy coffee. It worked pretty nice really.

I met a lot of awful nice people. The people that worked in the courthouse were just mighty fine people. It's work. I could have probably gone another term, but I was 65 and my wife [Caryl Robbins] wasn't well, so it was a good thing that I didn't try to run another term.

❦❦❦❦

Samuel J. "Sam" Rosenthal
1910-1995
From an interview with Patty Myers
In 1989, when 79 years old

Buffalo, Wyoming's Entrepreneur

Interviewer Patty Myers: Sam, why did you come to Buffalo?

I lived in Chicago for 25 years and then moved to Buffalo. My wife [Leona Kaja Rosenthal] and I used to vacation here. I had the misfortune of observing my father being murdered in Chicago and felt that I didn't want to raise a family there. I picked Buffalo, and I haven't regretted it–see, I've been here 49 years now.

Was it a mugging?

It was a hold up. My dad was deaf in one ear. He was talking on the telephone and didn't notice these two guys. His back was turned toward the rest of the room. He didn't hear what was going on behind him. They told him to shut up, and he kept on talking because he didn't hear him. They hit him with a gun, and he assumed that somebody accidentally hit him, and he kept on talking. When this fellow hit him the second time, he swung around on his chair, and when he swung around, the man pulled the trigger and killed him. It's a little difficult for a 17 year old to observe the murder of his father. It took me nine years to get out of Chicago. You don't simply just walk out. We had a family business–dry cleaning, where the six of us were involved–but I always had in mind that I wanted to get out of there. I've never regretted it.

When you came to Buffalo, did you have a little financial backing?

I had very little money to start with. The first business I went into was the bowling alley up at the old Ford garage. Frank Seney and I were partners. It was November of 1940 when we opened that bowling alley. It was a very fine establishment, you know. We had four regulation alleys, three duck pin alleys, pool tables, snooker tables, roller skating rink, a little snack bar, and a live shooting gallery.

Everything went along fine, but the war came along and took all the young people out of here, and I had to go back to Chicago in 1942 to run our dry cleaning plant because my brother-in-laws had to go to the Army. I went back there for two and a half years to run the plant until they came back out of the Army.

I came back here in April of 1945 and purchased the theater the first of May. In 1948, I purchased Keahey's Motel. In 1950, I built the drive-in theater. Then in 1951, I purchased the Buffalo Creamery. I can't remember the exact time when I got involved as a partner in KBBS Radio. Then I purchased the Dairy Queen and built the stockyards. In 1961, I started KROE Radio in Sheridan. That about completes the businesses that I was in.

I had no experience in any of them. Just picture yourself walking into a creamery and taking over. I had never been inside of one. Each one was a challenge, and it was rather interesting to take over some of these businesses that were in pretty bad shape, and I did very well in all of them. I had a good business background, you know, in Chicago. Basically, I think most businesses are the same. You got to take in more money than you pay out. I really enjoyed all the businesses that I had, particularly the theater, where you met young people who wanted to have a good time. When you are around young people all the time, it kind of has an effect on you. It makes you think young. I really enjoyed that business. Well, as long as the bank would give me credit and I made my payments, it worked out very well.

The partnership with Frank Seney–how did you fall into that?

They were the first people that we got acquainted with when we vacationed in

Buffalo. I think it was in 1934. After that, we came out almost every year and went fishing with them. We are very close friends.

You purchased the theater when you first came back after the war.

Yeah. When I took over, I put all new seats in and new equipment in the booth and a new marque up to dress it up a little bit. It was a good paying business. I enjoyed it most of all because it was cash. There were no accounts receivable. Everybody that walked in paid. The only other business that was a cash proposition was Keahey's Motel. The rest of them were a typical business where you are involved with credit. Of all of them, I liked the theater most.

John Keahey tried to sell the motel to me. I just didn't have the money to purchase it, and he sold it. I can't remember the man's name. When we bought it, we bought it of this fellow. My sister, Bess [Amundson], ran Keahey's Motel for 22 years. When we bought it, there were only 16 units, and it had a filling station. When we sold it, there were 40 units. We put additions onto it and built the second floor on there. When Bess and her husband left, Lil and I had to move down there for a while until we could find a manager to take over. I enjoyed the business. You met people from all over the world. I made a point of talking to them and getting acquainted and giving them Western hospitality.

When you moved into your house on Adams when you first came to Buffalo, was it already built?

It was almost finished. The garage hadn't been finished. They worked on it after we moved in. Aside from that period during the war, we've been there all this time. Art Dilts built it. He had two 50 foot lots. He put this building on one lot and left the other one to build another house. I think it was two or three years that I rented it, and then I wanted to buy it, but he wanted to keep that 50 foot lot and build a house for speculation. I told him if I couldn't have the lot, I wouldn't buy the house. I had a little tussle with him, but I won out. I like to have a little space and a few trees. I planted trees that are 45 years old now. I like to see something green in the wintertime.

How did you happen to fall into the Buffalo Creamery?

Ezra Jones was a good friend. My brother, Morris, used to come out each summer. We were sitting out in front of the gas station one evening, and Ezra started talking to us about the fact that the people involved in the creamery were having difficulties, and he thought it would be a good business to get into. At the time, I was running three businesses. He said, "You've got a son in college graduating this year. It would be a good business for him," and my brother said, "Why don't we take a look at it?" I said, "Shucks, I've got three now. I'm not really interested in it." "Well," he said, "let's take a look at it." We did, and we purchased three fourths of it. What did I know about cheese and butter and that sort of thing? There was a requirement. I wouldn't buy the thing unless John Paulson stayed, so John Paulson owned one fourth of it.

You said you built the stockyard.

Un-huh. My wife has a younger sister, Viola Williams, who lived back in Wisconsin. They were farmers and had turned their farm over to their son. My wife talked to me, "You know, I would like to have my sister come out here if we could find something for them." They came, and we talked about a stockyard. Jim Mader and Al Smith, they were interested, so we formed a corporation. I had three 40s out where the drive-in is, so I sold 40 of the acres to our corporation and separated that out. The stockyards was right across from the drive-in. We put in two large scales and corrals. It was well-built. The reason I got out of it is because my wife's sister and husband were here, I believe, only about a year and a half. Then they told us they were leaving.

🌿🌿🌿🌿

Fannie Firnekas Sackett
1903-2002
From an interview with Patty Myers
In 1986, when 83 years old

Dad the Beekeeper

My dad [Fred Firnekas] was 33 years old when he married my mother. She was only 14 when he married her. My mother's name was Maggie Jane Cook–her maiden name. There was seven children. I was born 2nd of November in a one-room log cabin out here on the edge of Johnson Creek. I was the fifth child.

It was a hard life. By the time Mother was 17, she had three children. I was six months old when they moved up to the head of Johnson Creek. Dad bought it from Bill Fisher–the two-room log house, and that's as much as we ever had. My dad walked from there to the Soldiers' Home and helped with the threshing crew and back every day. My father never had a threshing machine. Never! He did everything by hand. He was German. He flailed the wheat by hand. We stacked and shocked hay. Didn't have shoes–I can remember those stubbles. Dad would ride the hay rack, and we'd help pitch the hay up onto the hay rack. Yes, we worked.

Dad was also the water commissioner for 32 years. He had Clear Creek and Rock Creek and French Creek, Johnson Creek and the Piney Reservoir. He had to make the trips to regulate the headgates every year all on horseback. He never owned a car.

Folks called my dad the mathematical wizard, He could figure in his head. He could figure a haystack or a wagon box full of grain and take the measurements. He measured water that way. He was very good at math. Also, he liked good reading material. All his spare time he spent in reading. He kept up with all the world did in history. We had good reading material–newspapers and magazines. I don't know about the older three kids, but we younger three each had a magazine subscribed for our own. The boys had the *Outdoor Life* and the *Boy's Life*. Mine was *Needlecraft*.

My dad never owed anyone a single penny as long as he lived. We were brought up to know that if you cannot pay for this, you do without. We didn't charge anything or have anything unless we had the money

My dad was a beekeeper. He had 52 beehives . He had an extractor that he put the great big sections of honeycomb in. It was like a big cream separator that separated the wax from the honey. He also had the little square combs of honey that he just left as honeycomb. He sold the strained honey for $1 a gallon and 50¢ for a half gallon and hauled it 11 miles with the team and wagon to Buffalo about twice a week. The bees was just during the summer. We made candy out of honey and used honey to sweeten tea and coffee. My dad worked with the bees–brushed 'em off and never get stung. He wore a big hat with a veil tight around his neck that went over his face and head. He had a smoker that burned wood and you pumped by hand. He used that to drive the bees away from the hive. I had to watch where the swarms went. Then Dad would go and find the queen and bring her home for another hive. If I was stung, my eyes would be swelled shut. I was very allergic to bee stings, but we didn't pay any attention to those things, you know. You had to work.

My dad was no hand with livestock whatsoever, especially horses. He was afraid of them although he had workhorses and saddle horses, but he didn't handle horses well. That's all the transportation we had. We either walked or rode a horse, so we grew up on horses. He was very old-fashioned. He NEVER picked up with modern times at all. Anyway, he always drove a lumber wagon. He never owned a buggy or a light spring wagon. We never had a car. Dad always was real old-fashioned.

My dad carried our water from Johnson Creek. He went down the hill to the creek maybe a block to get the water. He always kept wood. Joe and Church, my brothers, would saw and split wood when they got older. Then Cap and Charlie when they got bigger did. I helped carry in wood, but Dad kept it sawed and split. Every fall he filled the coal house so we'd have coal through the winter. We didn't burn wood in the winter.

There was the kitchen range, of course. We just had two rooms. We slept in the living room on two double beds and put straw ticks on the floor to sleep at night. We'd put the ticks up on the beds in the daytime so there would be a little space for some chair if we had company. We used the kitchen as the dining room. See, we had to eat on a big table with benches on the sides. We used a big washtub for baths. Of course, all the water had to be carried and heated on the stove. We little ones were first to be bathed. Then my mother had the tub. Then it was emptied and my father's turn. That's the way we lived.

William A. "Bill" Sand, Sr.
1912-2017
From an interview with Nancy Tabb
In 2017, when 105 years old

105 Years Old & Counting

Interviewer Nancy Tabb: I take it you were born in 1912.

Yes, April 23, 1912. I was born in Geneseo, Illinois, at home. My dad is William Sand and my mother is Ada Sand. I'm William Arthur Sand, Sr. Dad, his folks came from Germany, and my mother's came from England. Dad was an auctioneer and a speculator. He'd buy anything that he'd think he'd make money on. I had, let's see, four brothers and two sisters.

How did your family wind up in Buffalo?

Well, Dad wanted to go to Colorado, but my sister had a boyfriend in the Dakotas, and she thought maybe he would come and see her if we'd go north. She had all of us hit the road to go north, so we did. We got into Buffalo on the 30th of August, 1926. We got to the tourist courts and pitched a tent and stayed there probably a week. School started the next day. Dad said, "We're all going to stay here and go to school. In the spring, we'll go on." He liked it so well in the spring he said he wanted to stay.

When you were growing up in Buffalo, who were some of your friends?

Terrance and Gilkey were the two closest friends. Fred Gray and most of the high school kids. I graduated in 1932.

What did your family do for fun when you were a little boy?

Dad hunted a lot. Dad, he was a hunter and fisherman, and he liked baseball too. He didn't play, but he watched it. Mother didn't do much of anything–only visited with other women. I hunted a lot.

Other than hunting, what kind of hobbies have you had?

Sports of all kinds. Well, I was athletic myself and played basketball and football and baseball. I suppose basketball was my favorite. I played about 17 years of basketball.

Were you involved in any organizations or clubs or church in Buffalo?

Well, the Boy Scouts–a member. The Methodist Church.

Do you remember any particularly bad weather that you've experienced?

Yes, in the 1930s it was 50 degrees below for two days and 20 degrees below for two weeks. The stock water froze up, and we had to pump water for them.

Do you remember Prohibition?

154

Yes, there was a lot going on that they didn't tell about. My dad never drank, and I never drank, so it didn't bother us. But they got it some way.

Tell me about serving in the military during World War II.

Well, first I was in the cavalry in Sheridan. Then we went on the West Coast and patrolled the Oregon coast. The Japanese had fishing nets for a quarter of a mile. They had floats to hold it up. As we were patrolling the coast, we would find those that cut loose. It took them a whole year to float over. They wanted us to make a reconnaissance outfit. We had Jeeps. Then they wanted to make a signal corps outfit. I didn't like the signal corps, so I transferred over to a truck company and went overseas in the Philippines with the truck company–drove and assigned trucks. After I told them where to go, I didn't have anything to do.

How did you get to the Philippines?

By boat. It was just an old Dutch ship, and it was slow. We got on that thing, and we got over to some of those little islands and pulled in, and they found out there was 6 foot of water in the bottom of this boat. All the vehicles were under water down in the hull, so they pumped it out. They welded up the crack, and we moved on. It was so slow, you could get up in the head of it and throw something in the water, and you could just walk along the side and keep up with it. It was that slow.

After you got out of the military and came back, what kind of jobs did you do?

Well, I hauled gasoline for a while. Then I worked for an electrician–Knepper Electric. When the highway first came in, I worked for the highway quite a few years. I worked for the laboratory. I tested for capacity. I did samples for the road–pack them down and compare them with what they got.

How did you meet your wife?

Thelma [Thelma Woolsey Sand]. I came back from the service, and I didn't know anybody. I was about 35 or 36 years old. I was hauling gasoline for Jack Meldrum. His wife taught school, so I asked her if she knew of any single girls. She said, "Yeah, a fourth grade teacher name Thelma," so I met her, and after a while, I married her. She taught fourth grade, but as soon as I married her, she quit.

How many children do you have?

Two sons, William and Rodney.

When did you lose your wife?

It was 2011. We were married about 1950, so a very long time.

When did you retire?

Let's see, about 1968. I was 65. With the highway it was mandatory. You had to quit, so I was off for two years. The highway repaired the road a bit, and they called me back. I went back to work for two more years, and I retired myself.

When did you move into this house? Do you know its history?

I bought this place [146 N. Burritt Ave.] in about 1950. When I moved here, there was one house on the next street. Two houses here. One of them was Bill James, and the rest of it was all blank. There was no church like there is today. There was a horse-shoe business. I don't know who built this house. It was old when I bought it. There's a picture up there of 1880, and it was built before that. There was no streets. It was just plain all over, so they built wherever they could. When they built the street, that put this house back up there.

Thinking about Buffalo through the years, can you tell me things that you thought were changes for the better?

Well, they made the roads a lot better. There used to be a U-turn on the bridge.

❦❦❦❦

Lucia "Lucy" Giaccino Sarantha
1904-1998
From an interview with Sue Myers

From Italy to Wyoming

Well, where I come from Alpette, Italy, we didn't have a farm. We had pieces of land scattered all over there. We kept a couple cows, and that's it. What we did at that time–everything had to be done by hand. We didn't have no ox or no nothing.

I went to work when I was 12 in a cotton factory. See, you make threads out of these cottons and make it into a big spool. Then they moved me to the bigger machinery, and we had the spool all lined up and weaved the thread into material. I stayed with the nuns because these buildings were run by nuns. That was only because I was Catholic. From home I would say it was about an hour and a half of walking distance.

Joe [Lucy's husband, Joe Sarantha] came to America when he was 18, and I was just born. I was just past 16 when he came to Italy for a visit in 1920, and I met him. I knew the family real well, of course, because we were just a little group of homes–maybe 40 or 50 people–a little place because Alpette is like Buffalo.

I came to America in 1921 myself. I left on my seventeenth birthday. I didn't get here until the 15th of June. I came to Sheridan because Joe lived in Sheridan. The boat took six and a half days across the water. You get seasick, but you get used to it.

I was so, what you call, so naive that you expect different things than what they really are, you know. Of course, I could not speak English, and everything was just sign language. I had a dictionary when I couldn't make out what they were asking me or what I wanted to say. Everything wasn't easy.

We were down by the bakery. When you first started up to the Main Street, that's where we had the shoe shop. We lived right back of the shoe repair. It was a rooming house. One side they had a pool room, and the other side we have the shoe shop, and we lived in back of that. Another really bad thing for me was just open country back to the mountains. It took quite a while to learn to cook.

Wooden Shoe Forms

Let's see, I came in June, and the following year the mine would go on strike, see. By the mining going on strike, the work at the shoe repair was very slack, so Joe sold the shoe repair, and he went to Illinois. Of course, there wasn't work for any of us. The most that Joe used to make every two weeks was $16, so you can imagine what we had to spend. So Joe decided to come back here. Again, he went to shoe repair. As a matter of fact, it was from the same fella we sold it to before.

We moved to Buffalo in 1926. We had an old shack, let me put it that way. Anyway, Joe bought that place. Joe pay $50 for that mansion, so we moved into that. Two rooms we had. Of course, Joe and I did the carpenter work.

The hardest part was not only financially, but we like the place. It was really, really hard. We could never have meat. Joe used to go down to the slaughter house from where we lived and pick up soup bones. I make soup and cut off if there was any meat. Most time you could get a little meat out of a soup bone. We had those two babies. I tell you there were many times I did not have a dime. We try everything. We try chicken. We even sold a little milk, and I kept two or three boarders. That's all there is to it, and it was hard.

The well was so bad that you have to let the water settle like you put clay in the water. Washing–I'd get up in the mornings between 4:00 and 4:30 in the morning. I'd light the fire outside to warm the water to wash. I got out before the children were up to do a little bit of washing. Well, I tell you, it was hard. I wasn't used to that. I wasn't made like that. If the ocean had a bridge, I would go back home.

We never had a couch. We never had a chair until the kids were in school–just a table–make the best. To begin with, I never knew what it was to owe anyone. There was the children, and they were very satisfied. There was never much complaining. We always tried very hard just to make a go of it.

Frank S. & Fred M. Seney
Frank 1911-1994 & Fred 1911-1991
From a Johnson County Historical Society presentation
In 1977, when 66 years old

The Seney Twins & Seney Drug Store

Frank: First, I want to thank the Historical Society and all its members for inviting the Seney twins to be here in front of you all. Well, I'm the oldest. I'm seven minutes older than this guy.

Fred: Well, our folks left Apple City, Iowa–that's Mary and Ralph Seney–and came to Sheridan, Wyoming, in 1910. They were visiting Sid Seney and Uncle Roy Seney, who owned the Brown Drug Company in Sheridan. They made plans, evidently, for our dad to come to Buffalo and open up a drug store. They came to Sheridan by train, and Mother Seney had her first auto ride, so they arrived in Buffalo and secured the Holt Drug Store.

Frank: Dad received his license here approximately two weeks ahead of our birth. You had to reside approximately six months, and he got it July 15th, so I imagine he was real happy having a drug store.

Fred: [showing a photograph of Seney Drug Store] In those days, it was all in mahogany. It was quite dark. It was the same store we're in now. You see, the center of the store then was plum full of tables. In those days, ice cream was real popular.

Frank: You didn't have anything on that edge of town. We didn't have enough merchandise. The store was only half as long because we had a garage in the back of it. We later opened it up, and now it's totally full.

I'll bet a lot of people here don't know this. Our dad always said when we were little, and I'm sure he was right, probably from the day we was, oh, maybe say 2 years old or maybe even less than that, we started eating ice cream. Dad always said we ate a gallon of ice cream every day. A lot of people tried to say, "Well, maybe," but Dad would say, "No, sir, those kids eat a gallon a day." We were swimming and running. We would walk to French Creek and go fishing. That's no fooling. A lot of people would. There wasn't any transportation around here.

Fred: One of the stunts that we pulled when we were pretty small is we started with a nice white roll of toilet paper at the Seney Drug Store. We were maybe 3 or 4 years old. We decided to go home and, evidently, grabbed a roll of toilet paper. We chased it all the way to our house, so we could find out where we'd been. We were a little bit hard to keep track of too.

Frank: Dad had a big radio at the drug store. Radio had just come out. I remember that it was about 10 feet long in three sections and sat on quite a large table. It was such a novelty that our dad wouldn't let anybody touch that radio until Willard Stevenson could come down at night. Everybody would come into the drug store at night, and

Willard would sit there turning all these dials until finally he would get a little trickle of noise from Chicago or somewhere. Many nights, I'm sure, he wouldn't get any. That thing must have cost $150.

Fred: Dad always kind of liked to be a prankster. In those days, you always had those old jars with candy and nuts, peanuts and different things, you know. It was kind of an oval jar with an opening in it. You could just shove your hand in it if you wanted to. Well, Dr. C.A. Conyers, who brought us into the world, come in one day, and Dad was busy. Dr. Conyers come along and shoved his hand in that jar, and, my god, he got it in a mousetrap. Dr. Conyers didn't come in there for days and days. He was so mad. Dad just tricked him on that deal.

❧❧❧❧

Elizabeth "Phyllis" Stanley Sims
1938-2015
From an interview with Ann Spomer
In 1994, when 56 years old

Phyllis' Pets

From the time I was born, I always had a dog. I grew up with a small terrier. Actually, on one of the family trips to California we were in the mountains, and he saved me from being bitten by a rattlesnake. Later on, I had a Boston bull terrier that lived until she was probably 13 years old. I got her when I was in third grade. I always had a dog. Also, we almost always had cats.

I tried to raise mice. I'd find baby mice. After a while my mother would decide it was time for me to visit a cousin out of town or something. When I came back, the mice were always gone. The same way with a bat I tried to have as a pet. I also had a hamster.

I had a horse, but the horse was sort of something I couldn't ride. Because I was never taught how to ride, I had to teach myself how, and it ended up being a sort of a sad disaster, so we eventually sold her.

As a younger child, I was a tomboy. I played with my uncles, and we made roads and played with trucks. We explored. When I got into junior high and high school, I participated in sports, went to ball games.

I was a student that wasn't known for getting into trouble. One day in our biology class the teacher came in, and one of the boys was playing at the teacher's desk. When he walked in, he said, "Babies must play," and before I even thought, I said, "And fools must watch." If I hadn't been such a good student, I'd a probably ended up in the principal's office.

❧❧❧❧

William "Bill" Skiles

1919-1994
From an interview with Patty Myers
In 1990, when 71 years old

Wyoming Brand Inspector

Interviewer Patty Myers: Why did the Skiles family come to Johnson County?

It was my father, James Frederick Skiles–J.F. Skiles. He came here from Missouri in 1916, but he didn't move the family out until a year or so later. Myself and a younger sister, Becky, are the only children out of 10 that were born in Wyoming. Dad was a carpenter in Buffalo and built a few houses and did work like that.

When were you born?

I was born in 1919 on the place that Dad had rented from Dr. Willard Hampton on Sand Creek north and west of Buffalo. We didn't live there too long. My folks went through that bad flu epidemic. The Whaley family helped my mother, and we had no deaths in our family. Then they moved down to the Brock place, and we lived there for relatively a short time–for two to three years. Then he homesteaded right directly south of there and moved onto that.

Dad did a lot of dry farming there and raised for a number of years terrific crops on the dry farm. He was used to planting row crops–corn and sorghum, cane and millet–all that kind of stuff that he had raised in the East he planted here, and the rains came to where we made a bumper crop on everything. Of course, that lasted until up in the 1930s when the drought hit and then nothing. They had a Fair at Bonnidee, and those homesteaders brought in their produce. They had gigantic pumpkins and garden produce and crops of one kind and another that were fantastic. It was a big, big Fair, and then the drought wiped that out. There was no need to plant anything after that. People depended on rain to grow a good crop.

We could survive. We had feed stacked behind the barn–rack after rack of good feed. I remember the first dry years when you could look out across that field where Dad had 100 acres plowed–real good land. He sold grains at one time–oats and barley. It would just get about 2 inches high and turn back into the ground. It was real depressing–that drought. It never really did come back to what it was when Dad was there. The only way to make a living was we milked a lot and sold cream. It was just range cows. Part of them was part Holstein and part Jersey and part white-face and everything else, but we milked quite a bunch of them–oh, 14 to 18. We would separate that cream and take it up to the mailbox. It would go out via the mail carrier up here to Buffalo. Then on back East someplace they would make butter out of it. It was a grocery buying thing.

Brother Fred did a pretty good job of trapping coyotes. That added to spending money for a kid. I'd pick wool off these barbed wire fences, get a few gunny sacks of that, sell it to Sam Ruben, and get a few pennies for my pocket for when we went to town. I think I was pretty small. You could pick off quite a little because those big herds of sheep, especially, when they would go scooting under. When a dog hit them, you know, they would go scooting under that wire, and the wire would just be full of wool. Of course, there was always dead ones, and you could get quite a little dead wool too.

Who was Sam Rubin that you sold it to?

He was a man that bought stuff all over the country–cowhides, coyote hides, old batteries, dead wool, horsehair. Anything you had to sell Sam Rubin would buy. He was an early-day junk man. I think he lived in Buffalo. Then we had a man from Kaycee, George Reece, he kind of took up where Sam Rubin left off. He was the same way. He lived in Kaycee and worked the country all the time. As I say, he would buy everything.

Did you help your dad with the farm chores? Was he using mechanical farming equipment or still using horses?

Strictly horses. He had 100 acres plowed up there–real good benchland. There was a lot of discing and harrowing and mowing and cultivating. It was all by teams. Dad was good with workhorses. A lot of times, he had two–sometimes three or four abreast–on harrows and discs. They were heavy. You take a disc–a 10 foot disc–that's quite a drag. That's too much for two horses. Pretty near all your farm equipment of that sort was fixed for four head of horses. You would drive, and they went round and round. That's about all they had to do. There is very little you had to do. Sometimes with a harrow you would straighten the teeth up, or sometimes with a disc you would toe it in a little bit. There is levers that you do that with. Mostly, it was just sit there and drive the team.

You sort of had a love affair with horses, didn't you?

Oh, yes, indeed. It meant quite a bit to me–horses have. I can remember some of those horses by name that I knew when I was 6 years old. I can see them just as plain as anything and remember their names. Nate and Nellie and Brownie and Spade and Spud–we had names for all of them, and they had personalities. One horse was old Pat– the best workhorse I ever saw. I can hardly believe some of the things he did. He was a miserable old horse around other horses. He would fight with the other horses real bad. In fact, he whipped every range stud that ever came close to the ranch, but he was just gentle and strong and pulled and did just anything you wanted to do. There was a lot of them like that that really stand out in my memory–good horses.

Dad was real good. He never had a horse that wouldn't pull his heart out. I wished I'd paid more attention because there is not everybody that could do that. That's the way it was because you didn't breed them. You functioned with what you got. I mean the horses we had are the horses we gathered or got ahold of by hook or by crook.

In those days, there was a lot of dirt work–a lot of Fresno work. That was usually with a four-horse Fresno. On the mouth of Soldier Creek there was a big gigantic earthen dam that they irrigated out of. That was an irrigated ranch–the Brock place was–but every once in a while, there would be a gopher hole through that dam, and the reservoir would go out. Then that was an all summer's job filling that back in, so there was a lot of dirt work. A Fresno was a scraper. There was a long handle that you'd trip it with to dump it. I've got one sitting here out back. I built most of this hill here, and I built this terrace and pared up this driveway with that Fresno that's out there and a team of mules–a two-horse Fresno, so I used two mules. It was pretty efficient because you put the dirt where you wanted it, and it usually packed in there. It was tamped with the horses just walking on it all the time. You could move a lot of dirt in a day. The government paid for reservoirs for a while to alleviate the poverty while the Country was in the Depression. They would pay you for putting in dirt dams. I worked for the U.S. government at the time, and we put in several dirt dams. Government reservoirs they called them. We did that with four-ups and Fresnos and moved a lot of dirt.

Where did you go to school?

To the Long School. It was the Long School because the Long family lived closer to it than anybody else. It was about two and a half miles from the homestead when I was a kid. We walked to school unless it was real, real bitter. Sometimes you rode horseback. Fred, my brother, took me on a sled behind a horse a time or two. If we got caught at school and it was real bad, why, a few times he would see to it that I got home. My sister, Margaret, and myself and towards the last Becky–the three of us at one time walked to school. That's quite a long walk. They did move the school closer in later years. I believe they moved it on wheels and a wagon. They were just little old buildings–didn't amount to anything much. I went two years to Midwest. My sister, Marcia, and her husband lived in Midwest, so I stayed with them and went to high school. Then I come up to Buffalo for a good bit of my senior year, but I never did graduate from high school. It was important, but it wasn't to me. Something I couldn't stand was school although I have some real pleasant memories of school.

What were some of the fun things you did?

They used to have dances there at Sussex and around. I was really too much of a kid to really take part in them, but I do remember them. A lot of people would entertain in their houses and have country dances. There was one family there–their name was Keeter–down on Nine Mile. I believe that the walls of their sod house are still standing there. They built it with that in mind–of having country dances–gigantic room and kitchen and bedrooms off it. The walls were 3 foot thick built out of sod. I can remember sleeping in those windows while they danced and played music all night long, and we'd go home at daylight. We had one or two dances at home. On Nine Mile, Hague Paxton, a well-to-do blacksmith and a good fiddler, and the Keeter family were all musicians. They square danced. The music–I can hear it yet. I've always been fond of good fiddlers and old-time music.

When did you start working away from the ranch?

Oh, about the earliest work I did was I used to go down to Meike's shearing pen and wrangle and tie wool for the sheep shearing groups. It was kind of a kid's job, but it paid. Gee whiz, I couldn't believe the money I was getting–2½¢ a fleece or something like that. You could tie close to 3,000 fleeces in a day, so I was making all kinds of money. I worked there quite a bit. Then I was in the CCCs. I tried that for a while. I was up here at Dayton for about a year. Ellis Patch was up there. He worked for the Forest Service. He was the foreman. Joe Felix was up there when I was there and Emil Christensen. We were real good buddies. We went up together and joined together and worked together and were very best of friends. That was an experience too. It was a great thing. It was one of the greatest things that Old Roosevelt ever did. I think that was good. There was drawbacks to it, but it helped a lot of boys, and they did a lot of work. It was a good place to train men. We got retreat and reveille and had a formation for most of those ceremonies every day we was in winter camp. In the summer, we were up on Turkey Creek and built that Sibley Dam. That was a little different thing. We weren't quite so military there, but it was pretty much military just like the army. Maybe not quite as strict but just about. There was uniforms, and everything was pretty much like army life. It was a good place to train men and get them mobilized. All you had to do was issue them guns, and you'd have an army.

Did you serve in the military?

I was in World War II. I was discharged in Salt Lake City in 1945. Then I laid around Buffalo for a while, and I went to work for Bill Eaton's Dude Ranch. Dorothy [Dorothy Warriner Skiles] was the ranch nurse. I worked there three straight summers. She worked there one year before I was there. We married in 1948.

How did you get involved with the brand inspecting work?

I applied for it. Well, I was looking for a full-time job. I felt it was time to make a change, so I applied for the job. The Stock Growers, which I worked for, took over the first of July in 1961, and I went to work for them. Sometimes I wish that I hadn't because I had something going for myself down here when I had the shoe and saddle repair. I had a pretty good little business down there–really did. I bought it from Joe Sarantha. It was just a little bitsy–it was attached to the back porch–just a little old shop that wasn't as big as this room right here. I done leather working in the Army. I went through the field artillery school in Fort Sill in saddlery work. For part of my service there in Fort Bliss, I was troop saddler. There was four of us that did repair on tack outfits and saddles and things. At that time, the cavalry was still mounted. There was horses everywhere you looked. It was heartbreaking when they moved them out and moved in that anti-aircraft gunnery. It was heartbreaking to see the horses go and the stables filled up with machinery.

Well, I was brand inspector for 10 years. Then in 1971, Leo Wickham, who was my supervisor, he retired, and I inherited the boss's job for this district. At that time, it was Sheridan, Johnson, Campbell, Weston, and Crook. It was five counties–a big district at that time–for 15 years I was Supervisor of District No. 8.

What exactly does a brand inspector do?

He issues titles, changes titles, and inspects brands prior to the change of title for cattle that move out of the country here across state lines. It's a fairly new thing, but it changes ownership. That wasn't the law for a long time, but it did make change of ownership on cattle and sheep law. You need a change of ownership, and you needed a brand inspection, so we looked at the brands and transferred titles. The fall was our busy season when all these calves or steers were shipped to feed lots. Everything was inspected at a point of origin on the ranch. We inspected them and changed ownership to their new owners. They had to be inspected and a form issued before they could leave the county of origin. The State had always handled it prior to 1960, but the Stock Growers Association made petitions for that job, and the State hired them as an agent to see that that job was done.

We had an awful lot of good times, and I enjoyed the work. I like to work cattle. It was natural for me. There was camaraderie amongst brand inspectors. We had fun for a number of years. We'd have brand inspector's conventions. There was roughly 70 inspectors in the State, and they'd all be there. It was quite a party, I'll guarantee you.

Were you involved in any of the cattle mutilations that people felt were done by UFOs?

Yes, quite a bit. The sheriff and I and the game wardens and the highway patrol–we've investigated a lot of those reports. Yes, I was really involved in that. You don't hear about it anymore, but everybody was looking at the sky all the time. It wove that old yarn, but you had to investigate those things. Some of them would sure make you wonder how it happened, and others you could tell at a glance that it was poison or predators. They made more of it than they should have. People were excited and wanted to make the news. They had helicopters stalking down cows. If there was a cow poisoned someplace, why, it was sure to be a man from outer space that had killed it. As a general rule, you would find out that it was forage poisoning or something like that.

None that I saw that couldn't have been natural. One little incident that kind of dignifies that response that you get from people–I was in the sheriff's office when it was called in about this calf up here at the spring right up here at the foot of the mountain. There was a dead calf they suspected. There was quite a lot of heat, you know, this mutilation thing. Bo Turk and I jumped in the car and went up there. The calf was laying by this little spring, and he had a three-cornered cut in its shoulder. It was just as square as that paper. Well, this fellow that discovered it said you can tell it's been mutilated. He said, "That's a surgical tool there that's cut that." He was sure enough dead. We went back down to the highway, and there was tracks along the road there where the cattle had been. Coming back from there, every pickup that we saw had one of those square-angled iron bumpers on it. I know that's what hit the calf. He was going up on the highway, and that pickup hit it, and they probably didn't know they hit him. It was going fast and cut just like a knife. Well, I told that fellow that. Mad–he was the maddest fellow you ever saw. "You don't tell me that. That was mutilated by..." He was not going to have anything but a man from outer space had sat down there and put that hole in that calf. You run into that an awful lot.

We had fun with it because we had some down there out of Kaycee up on Red Fork on the Bar C Ranch that were supposedly knocked down by helicopters. They were in a row down a field like that. That says poison to me. Anyway, I had inspected the cows away from these calves, and there were about 800 calves in that pasture. If there had been a helicopter that come down close enough to knock a calf down, there wouldn't have been a fence left in that country. They would have stampeded those calves through every fence down there, so I made some decisions. They was coming in and going to water, which cattle do when they got poisoned, and they just fell over. I've seen that happen I don't know how many times–cattle in a row. After a rain, a lot of times little greenery will come up, and they will wolf it down. At a certain phase in a plant's life it will make it poison. Well, it was poison, but they weren't going to have it that way.

You were a horseback rider in a lot of the fairs and rodeos. You have been real involved with the rodeos.

Team roping–Jim Mader and I won the buckle here one time in the old-age roping.

Pony Express Trail Riders

Tell me about the Pony Express trail ride.

This is one we rode in Cheyenne. That was an experience brought to life here. I went down there in 1959. Three of us went. We promised when we got through with that if they had one in 25 years, we'd go again, and we did. It was the Chamber of Commerce thing. We have this seventy-fifth anniversary and then the hundredth anniversary for the City of Buffalo. The first year Carl Waugh and me and Joe Felix were the riders. The last time when we went, Joe was up here and wanted to go, but he got hurt in the early part of our getting ready and couldn't go as a rider, but Carl and I did. We were going clear to Cheyenne. Three days riding is all. We're on 10 miles and off 20. The

165

first year I think I rode 40 miles. It was Joe Felix–I could see Joe was tired, and I wasn't, so I said, "Joe, I would like to ride that thoroughbred horse of yours one time." Boy, he fell off, and I took it, and I made 40 miles for me that day. That's about as long as we'd ride. We'd move along. We'd trot and gallop. We didn't run full tilt, but we got over the country. We covered about 100 miles a day. Last time we had a trailer house. The first year I think we had bedrolls.

Tell me a little bit about the mountain trail ride. That's become sort of a local tradition.

Yes, indeed, it really has. It is a real traditional. I went on it the first year in 1964. I was on 22 of those without a break. It was a lot of fun. I made a lot of friends–a lot of them dentists and doctors and lawyers and a lot of Buffalo well-to-do people that go on that trail ride. There are some of these businessmen–it just absolutely kills them. One of our local men here–old Bill Kirven–god, he suffers terrible. That's the only time of the year that he rides. Old Ray Braten is tougher than a boot. He lays out those rides and sets the pace for them. He's famous for killing them off. I look forward to it and do enjoy it. The first ride, why, I got the buggy and the team ready. I pulled a freight wagon right along with the riders. We moved camp every day. We moved the mess tents–the whole works. It made quite a lot of work. All I did was take care of the team and drive that buggy full of a little whiskey and cold drinks. That made it kind of fun for me, and they paid me. I got to where they invited me, so I had a standing invitation.

❦❦❦❦❦

Lowell E. "Slats" Slayton
1923-2013
From interviews with Prisoner of War Survivors
In 1994, when 71 years old

Prisoner of War Survivor

You know, I don't imagine there's a whole lot of us prisoners of war left because we are starting to die off as we get older. Every month I get a prisoner of war magazine called *Prisoners of War of America*. It lists all of them, so we are decreasing in number.

I was a staff sergeant–tail gunner. I was what you call a first armor tail gunner on a B-17. When I entered the service, I was 18 years old. When I was shot down, I was 20. I enlisted in the Air Corps on October 8, 1942, and was discharged September 21, 1945, so I was in the service almost exactly three years. I spent 14 of those months in a prison camp. I think the only thing that really saved us guys more than anything was our youth.

That particular day, the Eighth Air Force was recalled, but the first wing of the first division, which I was in, didn't get the recall, so we headed into Germany pretty much unprotected. What happened to us that day–the Germans had ME 210s that were twin-engine bombers with rockets underneath their wings. They could stay out of firing range and lob the rockets into our formations. Well, unfortunately, one came right through our tail section behind my back, cut all the ailerons, and left a hole this big around, and we went into an immediate dive. It sounded like a freight train going through there when that rocket went through the tail. I couldn't figure out what was happening. Of course, it all happened so fast–just boom, boom–and it's over. We must have fallen 2,000 feet before our pilot managed to pull the plane out of the dive. We had a full bomb load on of twelve 500-pound demolitions. We hadn't even gotten anywhere near our target.

When I got hit in the tail, it hit my oxygen supply, so I'm unconscious in the tail. I had five pieces of shrapnel here and a little piece here, and then I had seven other pieces in this forearm, where my armor plating didn't protect me. I finally came to in the bomber's tail. I saw the escape hatch was off, so I crawled out on the tail and crawled up through the waist gunner. After we lost the two engines, the pilot decided he was going to ride it in and try to crash land the plane. He was trying to get the plane to go in between this big farmhouse and big oak tree to make a belly landing and hope for the best.

The pilot succeeded in landing, and he took off on the run, and I'm trying to crawl out of the plane. We always carried our GI shoes with us, and I wanted to get my GI shoes so I could put them on. So I'm just crawling along dragging my one leg and pulling myself by my arms. This German is just screaming at me like mad. I don't know what the hell he is saying, so I just keep on crawling, but I hear this old bolt go shut in his rifle. It wasn't hard to understand that, so I stopped and did my best to sit up and put my arms up in the air. He didn't shoot, and I stayed right there and didn't move any further. I remember we hit the ground that afternoon at 3:00.

I guess the hardest part of being a prisoner of war is not knowing when you're going to get out. The anxiety of how long you're going to be there was the hardest part. We had a secret BBC radio in camp. When D-Day came on the continent, we had the news by 10:00 a.m. on our secret radio. We were telling the guards that our guys had landed in Normandy, and they wouldn't believe us. We had the news faster than they did.

We did our own cooking. We'd get a Red Cross food parcel every week. Maybe once in a while we'd only get one every other week, but most of the time we got one every week. The Germans gave us some ersatz coffee, which was terrible coffee. They gave us kohlrabi and a little millet to make cereal out of in the mornings. They dragged these horses off the Russian front, and our guys would try to clean them up. They'd be full of maggots. We would cook this cabbage and horsemeat together. My food partner–if he saw a maggot, he couldn't eat anymore, so I'd get the rest of his soup. We'd just take the maggots out, throw them on the table, and keep on eating. They were always cooked anyway.

You kinda pooled your food and stuff. When Christmas came, the American Red Cross food parcel had turkey and plum pudding in it. They had to short one person in each barracks of a parcel because there wasn't enough to go around, so they asked for volunteers in each room. Nobody would volunteer in our room, so I did and took a Canadian parcel instead. Right after I volunteered, Sam Peer said, "I'll tell you what– why don't you and I split the parcels?" We wound up with the best setup of everybody. The Canadian parcels had a lot of soups which weren't in the American parcels.

Sam took a liking to me right away. See, there was only 16 bunks in a room, but there was 24 of us in the room, so the last eight guys that came into the room had to put their straw mattress out on the floor to sleep. They'd roll them up and put them under the bunks during the day so we'd have room to walk around in the room. Most guys didn't like anybody sitting on their bunk because it'd flatten the mattress straw so bad that you couldn't get really comfortable. They only gave us five bed slats on the bunks because guys had used the bed slats before to shore up tunnels when trying to escape. They only gave us enough slats so that we wouldn't fall through the bed. I invited Sam to come up and sit on my bunk with me if he wanted to, and he thought that was just great because nobody else had ever invited him to sit on their bunk.

A lot of guys got on each other's nerves a lot. I mean you're incarcerated like that, and you've got 24 guys in a room. We were confined to those barracks only at night. We could go out in the compound during the day. We just had room to walk around the entire compound. There was four compounds in each camp. You could visit anybody in any of the barracks. We had a commandant who couldn't understand English at all. He'd come in and say, "Heil, the Fuhrer," and we'd say, "The fewer the better." He liked us guys hailing the Fuhrer of his country.

We had to evacuate Stalag Lu-6 in Lithuania. Russians had made a spearhead below us all the way to the Baltic Sea, and the Germans only had one way of getting us out, and that was putting us on boats. I understand the U.S. Government was paying the Russians $50 per head for any of us they could liberate. Whether that was true or not, I don't know. Anyway, they put us in the hulls of these two fishing boats. There must have been, oh, gotta be better than 2,000 of us in this Stalag Lu-6. It was all British and American Air Force people. We were in a standing position in the hull of this thing for at least 36 hours. They let one person at a time up on deck to do his constitutional thing and passed a bucket around for everything else down there.

We finally got down in the Bay of Schwam, where they unloaded us and put us in these rail cars. I don't know how long we were in those cars, but we weren't in there overnight–just most of a day. It was approximately five miles into this camp. There's a German marine captain who is telling all the guards that we murdered all their wives and children. He told them, "We're going to run them into camp. If anyone falls out, bayonet him or sic the dogs on him," so they started running us. When we evacuated the other camp, we took all the Red Cross food and clothing with us. Russ Schliar, my food partner, is carrying four food parcels on his shoulders, and I'm carrying all the Red Cross clothing on my shoulders. Fortunately, when I was in the other prison camp, I would get out and run three to four miles every single morning around the inside warning wire of the camp. Russ and I were both in real good shape. We managed to run the whole five miles. We never faltered once or fell out of line. Unfortunately, as soon as we got to the camp, they took every bit of this Red Cross clothing and food away from us. You're so angry at this time that you just wanted to reach out and hit somebody so bad, but you have to restrain yourself. You didn't know what's going to happen to you.

I escaped on what was called the Black Hunger March. It started February 6, 1945, and I escaped the 16th of April. The rest of the column was finally liberated around May 8th. We had already walked over 400 miles when I escaped. It was cold. We had to sleep out in barns. They were walking us from the Russian front to the Allied front, trying to keep us away from the front lines. At first they told us we'd only be marching about a week or so. We weren't eating very well. We were very poorly fed after about a week out. German rations were very meager–very, very poor. If we got any water at all, we drank it.

February 6th to April 16th–it was a little over two months that we'd already walked over 400 miles when I finally got a real acute case of dysentery and was getting in really bad shape. I was passing blood. It's amazing how it saps your strength. I just made up my mind right then and there. It didn't take me long to make a decision. I said to my-self, "They're going to shoot me, or I'm going to get away. There's no sense of me staying and dying with dysentery." I knew I had to do something. Another kid, Ray Busiahn, found out–I never have figured out how he ever managed to know I was going to try to escape. He came up to me and said, "I hear you're going to try to get out." I said, "How did you know?" I can't even remember what kind of an answer he gave me, so he stayed with me. They put us in a barn that night, and we tried to figure every which way to get out of that barn, but there was no way because the only exits in the barn were well-guarded.

The next day there must have been at least 1,500 of us traveling in this column. I think we were under-guarded a little bit. There were guards here and another one up another 50 feet. They stopped for noon break, and our guard went over a ways to re-lieve himself and left his canteen sitting there by the side of the road. I just got the impulse. I grabbed his canteen and took off into that wooded area. I signaled Ray as I went back into the woods for at least a mile.

We were so tickled to find such a big wooded area. There was a lot of dead foliage and leaves in April. We just kind of buried ourselves in this stuff. All of a sudden, we could hear footsteps and dogs coming through. They had to have come within 50 yards of us. I was really, really scared at that time. My heart was in my mouth, but all of a sudden the noise got fainter and fainter. God, I think we lucked out! We didn't move from there at all until dark and did all of our traveling at night. We followed the moon and the stars. We heard the British Third Army wasn't too far from where we were. The second night out about 2:00 in the morning and just pitch black out, we decided, "Heck, let's not go around this village. Let's go right through it. All of a sudden we could hear footsteps coming toward us as we were going through the middle of this town. It so happened to be a German who was on the other side of the street. He couldn't see us, and we couldn't see him. He asked us in German where we were going. I thought, "Oh brother!" Right away, my buddy answered him in German. Then the German asked us something else, and Ray just answered, "Ya vol." [Yes, sir]. The German kept going his way, and I said to Ray, "What the hell did he ask us, and how did you answer him?" I didn't know Ray could speak German. His folks were born in Germany, and Ray spoke fluent German. We just took off for the hills and never went through a village again. We walked until morning and found a wooded area and dug in again. The minute there was any sign of life coming, we didn't make ourselves available.

We found a root cellar and stole some carrots. The third night we ran into five Russians who had escaped from another column. They had just finished eating and had a whole bunch of potatoes. Ray conversed with them in German to find out where they got the potatoes. They said not to worry about it. They filled an old milk pail half full of potatoes and boiled it up for us. We had some rock salt we shaved in there and ate those potatoes. It burned the living daylights out of the inside of my mouth! We were almost barbaric–just shoveling it in, you know. We couldn't eat fast enough. The fact that it was too hot didn't bother us one iota. We ate the whole half pail right then and there. So we stayed with the Russians that night.

The next morning they cooked some more potatoes for us before we got ready to hide. But first, I said, "I'm going out to the edge of the forest and take a look." I went out, and as far as I could see were American tanks–just a whole line of them. I bet there had to be a mile long of American tanks coming up this road. I went back and told Ray, "We aren't staying here. All I can see out there is American tanks." So we started down this road, and a couple of British guys–see, the British Third Army was using American tanks. These two Englishmen–limeys as we called them in those days–they just stuck their heads out of a tank and asked, "You guys POWs?" I don't know what they thought we were. We hadn't shaved, washed, or anything for three months almost. We said "yeah" and just kept walking. Finally, a truck came along and picked us up and took us into this little town of Celle, Germany. There they asked us, "You guys want to eat or be deloused?" We were so lousy with lice it was unbelievable. We said, "We have starved this long. For god's sake delouse us," so they stripped all our clothing off of us and deloused us with DDT. They gave us British clothing to wear and fed us. The British flew me to an American Station Hospital in England. I had dysentery, trench mouth, yellow jaundice, lice, malnutrition. They weighed me right away in England, but I'd been eating for three days and was up to 104 pounds by then. They figured I must have weighed no more than probably 97 pounds when I was actually liberated, so you can see how quickly this dysentery saps you. So that's the end of that part of that story.

❦❦❦❦

Guy L. "Leroy" Smith
1907-2003
From an interview with Patty Myers
In 1982, when 75 years old

The Overshoes

I remember one time I was going to go home Friday evening early in the spring. The days were getting pretty long. I had a little black horse. Somehow or other he sneaked to one side of me and got out and headed for home. I immediately took off after him to try to get in the lead of him and catch him. I remember going across the street which was more of a road then. They graveled those streets about 1922. I had on my overshoes, but they weren't buckled. I figured I could travel better without them, so I kicked them off and took off trying to get around this horse. I got up the river six or seven miles, and I hadn't got around the horse, but here was Mother coming in the buggy. I got a ride with her, otherwise it would have been a 17 mile walk.

The funny thing about those overshoes–later on when we got sheep, I came along there one time, and here were those overshoes still sitting out there in the greasewood where I had kicked them off. It was a number of years later, and they weren't in very good shape, but I was sure that was those were my overshoes.

❦❦❦❦

Eugene F. "Gene" Snider
1915-1981
From an interview with Patty Myers
In 1979, when 64 years old

Never Ask

Well, Dad [Horace Snider] was around 7 years old at the time of the Johnson County Invasion in 1892, but all through the years it was always a no-no to talk about that around the house. In those days, if somebody rode into your place or stopped to visit you, one of the first things I learned was never to ask where he came from or where he was going. That was entirely his business. He was always welcome to stay the night.

My dad would not talk about past history, and I grew up under the impression that the family was a bunch of outlaws, but in later years I've discovered that his dad, E.U. Snider, was quite an upstanding character and done quite a lot for Johnson County.

My dad just grew up in the streets as a hoodlum and more or less an outlaw, I guess. He cowboyed and worked around the country for a number of years. I don't even know the date when he married my mother. They moved to Colorado for several years. Then he came back to Midwest and worked there for several years at various jobs. I've heard him talk about hauling nitroglycerin with a team and buckboard and riding watching for claim jumpers, which was quite a thing in those days.

He homesteaded up east close to the mesa at the end of the horn. Later on, he bought a little ranch in 1920 on Crazy Woman by Greub. He more or less starved out there, so he went to work at Billy Creek, hauling coal for the Carter Oil Company. He stayed there at one phase or the other of that work until he died in 1954.

Dad, of course, grew up as a cowboy and worked horses. He just loved horses and could train them. He was very good at it. As long as he lived, he always had a horse around either to ride or for entertainment. He liked to work workhorses. What he done in the oilfield was just contract work before the trucks came in. I know he roped a coyote when he was past 60.

I can't remember a great deal about the ranch on Crazy Woman. I can remember it but nothing very good about it. It was too small to make a living on and too much of a nuisance to really keep. During the Depression my brother and I tried to. Dad gave it to my brother and I, and we had a little bunch of cattle. I finally just walked off. Well, we both did. I thought there was an easier way of making a living than trying to grub that sagebrush, and I went to work in the oilfields. My brother stayed another year or two and finally sold the cattle for $18 a head to the government, and they killed them and left them. That was something I could never understand. They just killed the sheep and cattle by the thousands. They would skin the sheep and take the hides.

I was in the CCC for a year. It was a hell of a good idea at the time. You can still see evidence of it in the mountains–campgrounds they built and timber they thinned. A lot of places they thinned is just now showing up where it's a beautiful stand. The road through Crazy Woman Canyon–I worked on it when I first went in. Then we went out to Idaho and then Jackson Hole and Nevada and finally wound up down at Guernsey. We built quite a park down there. The guys got $30 a month, and they had to send $25 of it home. If you got a better job, you could work up as high as $45 a month. Then you kept all over $25. You got your clothes furnished. You wore Army reject uniforms, but it didn't matter. You got all your food, and the food was fairly good. You lived in tents or barracks. The living conditions weren't good, but it was better than sleeping on the streets or some hobo jungle.

My brother had quite a thing going in the CCCs. He was in there about two years. He run the commissary and had a loan shark business going. See, you only got the $5 a month, so at the first of the month everybody was rich. Later on, they'd need cigarettes or stuff. Well, he would loan them money at about 25 percent interest, and he was right there to where he could collect it. He come out of there with enough to–well, he bought him a new car when he got out just on his loan shark business.

I would say it was active in the county from around 1930s. It was one of Roosevelt's first projects. They had Army officers control the camp as civilian bosses. If they had gone just a little farther and given them a little military training, the boys that were in there when the war broke out, they would have had quite a bunch. There were some mighty fine fellows in there. I was in with a bunch of old kids from Kentucky. They were the nicest old kids I was ever around in my life. It done a lot of good at the time.

To start with I went to school at Greub and then had a school at Billy Creek a couple of years. After the fifth grade on I went to school in Buffalo.

At one time, Billy Creek was a stagecoach or mail stop. There is still signs there and an old cellar. Later on, a fellow by the name of Thornley Smith raised turkeys and had his headquarters there. He ranged his turkeys all over the country. Turkey Smith they called him. I worked for him for about a year.

Billy Creek oilfield was just a typical oilfield at the time. In those days, the transportation wasn't what it is today, so they had to live at the location. The companies would just build houses for their personnel, office buildings, and usually a house for the superintendent. Then the working men–it was just up to them to do whatever they wanted to. They'd build their own shacks. They took their families. They had them all over the state. I've been to dozens of them. A lot of them were just what they called tent houses. They built a floor up 4 feet and then put a tent on it. Hell, it was cold.

The cookhouses fed just the working men. They deducted so much out of their pay for board and room. Whether you ate or not, why, you had to pay for it, but usually they fed very good. I mean food you couldn't get anyplace else. Midwest had a reputation of being one of the finest cafes in the country. They did serve the best of food. Things like lobster wasn't unusual in those days. It would have to be iced. You know, a lot of it could be flown in. There was a few years that they even let the public in.

Any wells that produced was on private property. The oil companies would come in and lease it before they drilled. Oh, the landowner would get a share or percent of it. You see, all that was ever hit there was gas, and it wasn't worth anything at that time. I think one fellow told me his royalty for one year was something like $30.

I remember the first gas well that boomed in–going by and seeing it. It was just the gas blowing up and rocks. You could hear it as far away as Buffalo. It blew for 10 days or so before they could get it capped. My dad was working there. He hauled the coal for the first well. They hit gas, so they had fuel after that. He built the pits and moved the rigs, and he freighted several rigs from Billy Creek to Buffalo and hauled them into the railroad by team and wagon. However, a lot of the rigs were built on site in those days. The bowl wheel or the band wheel and different parts of those rigs were made right on the job. The boilers and engines were about all that had to be freighted because the derricks were wooden, and they were either burnt when they were through with them or chopped down.

What always impressed me most was we had a team of horses Dad was working there, and it broke their eardrums. They were just stone deaf. We worked those horses for years after that. They would turn around and watch you all the time. There was no way you could scare them. I guess they would watch you so you would pick up lines and get ready, and then they would take off. They were a real good team, but they were stone deaf. I remember one time Dad took them over to the ranch. He was going to put up hay. In those days, you used these overshot stackers. He put them on a stacker. I was driving and came to the end. The teeth came out and came up when I pulled the cable out. Then it came up and dumped the hay. Well, when they come to the end, why, that was fine with them. They were clomp, clomping along. I drove that stacker half way across the field, hollering "whoa, whoa." I couldn't get them stopped. Dad finally ran out. He knew how to drive them, but, hell, I didn't know how to drive a deaf team. I was hollering "whoa" or "get up." They were just powerful old brutes.

He had a team of Percherons that he had from Clarence Gammon. They were a beautiful team. These horses, they weren't too satisfactory on the farm. He hooked this old team to a buck rake, and one horse over here and one over there. He got them all hitched up and got on the seat and said "get up." The old horses looked at one another and kind of shook their heads. They just demolished that buck rake–Dad hollering and beating on them. I laughed until I was sick over that.

The neighbors were Gammons and Baileys, and "Daddy" Burnett was over at the 41 Ranch and Hakerts up at Klondike. The ones that impressed me the most out there in those days were the old bachelors. Oh, there was quite a settlement of them. Speck Peters, of course, was one that everybody knew and can remember. On up a little ways further was an old boy by the name of Charlie Hamilton. He had a homestead and was there for years.

Another one was a fellow by the name of Mickey McClellan. Mickey made his living just riding the grub line. He'd walk for miles and carry the gossip, but he'd always make one meal a day in a different place. He'd range from about the Willow Glen Ranch to about the 41 Ranch. He'd walk every place. Mickey McClellan was real interesting to talk to. The old devil was in San Francisco during the earthquake and made a lot of money cleaning brick out there. They would take these bricks and clean them at so much a brick. I think that's the only money he ever made in his life. He left there and came to Wyoming. I don't know how he got to Buffalo. He took up a homestead there and lived there for years. Then he lived in a little old one-room cabin. There was just barely room for a bed and stove in there. The rest of this cabin was full of junk– harness piled up and tin cans. It had a dirt floor. It was just unbelievable that place. It caught fire one night and burned him pretty bad, so he sold the place and came to town. He had been all over the United States as a hobo and, evidently, came from a very wealthy family because I know one time two of his sisters came out to see him. They wrote and told him they was coming, and he wrote back and said he wouldn't be here–that he had to be back in the mountains and had a bunch of sheep. Hell, he never owned a sheep in his life. Anyway, he hid out, and his sisters came and got my brother and I to take them over to his place. When they saw how he lived, they were really upset. They thought he owned–evidently, he had been writing and telling them he was a big sheepman out there. Old Mickey was hiding up the creek there and was watching the whole thing. He lived that way for years. He'd work a little in the summertime and stack a little hay. I hauled his groceries for years. Cornmeal and bacon was all I knew of him ever buying. He died here a number of years back.

The old bachelors, they had quite a nest over there. Every once in a while, they would team up together. Oh, Speck, he was the ringleader of the whole works. Speck was real sharp. He run kind of a joint over there for a while. Of course, anybody that was in the county can remember hearing stories about him. All these old bachelors seemed to eke a living out one way or another–mostly by hook or crook. I used to go by and visit with them.

Frank Miller–well, I don't know how to peg him. He was evidently well-educated. He came to this country from Czechoslovakia and took up that homestead. He was a carpenter and a rig builder. He worked in the oilfields and always had high hopes of making quite a thing of his ranch out there. He got married during the Depression and had one kid. Then his wife quit him. After a few years here, well, she decided she would go to high school, and she came to town. That was after the kid was in high school too. She just came to high school with him. That was a mistake. He was out on the ranch, you know, grubbing sagebrush and was pretty happy. She got a little education, and she up and quit him and kind of rolled him for what money he had. Beeb Gammon and I were about the only two that weren't afraid of him, and he kind of liked us. He was never out of range in his house to where he couldn't grab a loaded rifle or pistol, and he was a dead shot. He built rifles. He must have had 30 or 40 rifles around that house.

One time, I went to see how the old devil was doing, and the door was locked from the inside. It had one of those chain locks. You could get it open only about 3 inches. I tried and hollered and yelled. I could kind of hear something in there. I just knew he was dead in there but couldn't guarantee it. I couldn't see in, so I went and got Beeb, and he said, "Oh, I'm not afraid of him. Hell, we'll go in there. He's harmless." I said, "Well, you just reach inside then and undo that chain, and we will look in." When his fingers would get in, he would just freeze–you know, no way. Finally, I said, "Well, I'll tell you. I'll rattle on the door, and you look in the kitchen window where you can look clear through the house. You crawl around the fence there and look through the window." "Oh," Beeb said, "Yeah, yeah." Pretty soon he came back and said, "You look through the window. I'm not going to get my damn head up there." By god, finally, we could hear Miller gasping in there, so one of us got enough courage to reach in and undo the chain. Miller was sitting there in a chair with a blanket and no heat in the cabin, and he was almost dead. He just hadn't fell over yet, you know. We built up a fire and thawed him out and got him to town to the doctor. He lived a couple of weeks in there. He could speak seven languages. He was a great believer in the Masonic Lodge, and he was a Shriner. His whole life was devoted to that Shrine. He told me one time he was going to leave his place to the Shrine Crippled Children's Hospital. "The next time I go to town I'm going to have my will made out." Well, he never quite got around to that, and the vultures got it instead of the crippled children.

The Masonic Lodge in Buffalo has quite a lot to do with area history. They have a vault down in the basement, and they have all of the old handwritten records there. I was looking up some information one time. They have the minutes of the meeting from the date the first group got together to establish the lodge all the way through to the present time. It was really interesting how serious those old fellows took the lodge. Of course, they was one of the main organizations of the time, not only here but all over the country.

They held their own trials within the lodge. If one brother gypped the other and didn't think it was fair or stole a cow from him, instead of going to court, they went through the lodge and held their trials. They would find them guilty or not guilty. One of the things I especially wanted to look up was the Masonic Lodge had quite a hand in the burial of George Wellman, who was shot during the Johnson County Cattle War. It was quite a to-do. They weren't going to let him be buried from a church. Even the preacher at the Episcopal Church had a shotgun under his vestments, and all the good brethren had a pistol under their apron. Anyway, they buried the old boy from here. I looked that up in the minutes of the meeting to see if anything come out, and it said "We met for the funeral of brother so-and-so and conducted funeral services at such and such a time." That's all the description they gave of that.

It hasn't been too many years ago that John Driskill was Master of the Lodge. It came up there was going to be the seventy-fifth anniversary of laying the cornerstone of the Episcopal Church. They thought it would be nice if a few of the brethren showed up and attended church that Sunday and give a talk and have a little celebration. They expected maybe 10 or 12 would show up. Not only did the lodge fill up, the church was full and out into the street. Every denomination in the country showed up which was more than I've ever seen. They just packed the place. I remember John Driskill saying he was never so proud that he was Master. He led them from the lodge to the church.

Grandmother Ramsbottom was a little different. I never knew too much about her. I guess she was around 18 when she came to the United States. She came from England. She would stay on the ranch for a year at a time, never leave, and was just as happy as a jaybird singing with her flowers. She corresponded with people all over the world. When shipping time came, she got her little go-away bag and packed up what she wanted and took a trip. She went to Omaha first. I think she got a free pass to Omaha with the cattle they shipped. When they got that cattle check, she evidently took her share. If the Old Man wanted to go, he was welcome to follow along. She'd travel for about a month and then come back and be just happy for another year. She died aboard ship on her way to England. She had been over there several times. When she took this trip, she took in the best shows, art, museums. If she wanted anything, oh, maybe she would go to town once or twice, but if she really wanted anything, she would call Old Fred Dillinger at the New York Store or Skipton and Flynn Store to put in orders. She had electric lights and running water. She was always very active in her mind. She didn't have much company and didn't want any.

I remember Edward "Daddy" Burnett when he was on the 41 Ranch. He was real tall and straight, just like a typical English lord. Oh, to my knowledge he was a wonderful person. Everybody spoke very well of him. He was goodhearted and good to his neighbors. He was a real shrewd stockman the way everybody talked. I know my wife's brother was working for him one time and said it was about 20 degrees below zero, and Mr. Burnett was dressed real light. Lawrence said he had on all the clothes he could get on–Scotch cap and overshoes and gloves–and he said, "Mr. Burnett, how can you stand to be dressed so light in this kind of weather? I've got on all the clothes I own." Mr. Burnett said, "Well, Lawrence, are you cold?" and he said, "Hell, yes, I'm cold." Mr. Burnett said, "Well, I am too." He figured it didn't do any good to put on a lot of clothes if you're going to be cold anyway.

I wish I had just listened to the stories that I have heard. I knew such characters, for instance, Old Johnny Greub out there. The Old Man, he used to love to visit. Old Johnny Greub–they run the Greub post office. We used to get our mail there. He used to love to visit with the kids. He was always laying on a cot in the living room. He had a strap to pull himself up because he had a broken back. I think he was bedridden for 17 years, and they finally operated on him. I know it was quite a joke that Mr. Hesse and Mr. Hays and a bunch of them talked him into going for this operation. He didn't think it would do any good, but, by gosh, he outlived all of the others. He was a wonderful old man. He knew the history, and he would tell me about hunting buffalo.

Another one I knew real well and visited with by the hour was Jack Ridley. Rattlesnake Jack, he could tell some wild tales, and he had lived quite a life. He was way back up Crazy Woman Canyon–homesteaded up there as far back up as you could get. He raised a large family. I never knew about his past. Of course, he wouldn't talk about it. Like I said before, I was always taught never to ask where you come from or where you were going. If a stranger rode in, why, if he wanted to volunteer information, fine. If he didn't, you kept your mouth shut.

Geraldine Lee Songer

1916-1986
From an interview with Patty Myers
In 1982, when 66 years old

Life in Sourdough Logging Camp

I was born in Oakdale, Nebraska, to Dora May Norred and William J. Lee on January 8, 1916. They parted. My father went into the Army when I was 11 months old. My mother remarried, and I lived with her and my stepfather in Glasgow, Montana. Then my mother died when I was 6 years old, and my stepfather, Carl Johnson, brought us out here–my sister, Maurine, and I–to Aunt Ruby and Uncle Harry Kershner. This was about in November 1922.

Carl came with us. It was close to Thanksgiving time because the neighbor ladies had made us each little cakes to bring along on the train. Maurine and I were altogether different. She had eaten hers, but I was always rather conservative, and I saved mine until I got out here to the ranch. I can still see those red plush seats on the train. They were scratchy and the cold. We were so tired. The old engine stopped and let us out in the middle of the night–no lights, no nothing, no station. We had to walk about half a mile over to Aunt Ruby and Uncle Harry's house through the snow. It wasn't very deep. It was strange for my sister and I because she was only 3 and I was 6. Carl–Daddy Johnson–brought us out here and left us with them, and he went on to start logging in the mountains. We lived with them until later on we went to the mountains with my stepfather to live with him up there. The main cook kind of took care of us, and we ran like little wild Indians.

There were the four partners up there. This logging operation and tie hack business expanded until they had, it seems to me, six or seven camps. I know they did have four at least because we went to school up at Camp 4.

After Joe Hall, Carl Johnson, Andy Hanson, and Bart Bartholomew, all became partners, sometime in that length of time, Joe married Hazel Ingersoll, and she was our teacher up there. They lived in Camp 3. They had the only radio that was in any of the camps at all. They had living quarters, and the schoolroom was attached to that. She had a piano. How they got it up there, I don't know, but she did have a piano. When there was going to be boxing broadcast over the radio, the men would come. They couldn't all fit into their small living quarters, so they would stand outside the window in the cold to listen to their radio–to listen to this boxer fight.

As nearly as I can remember, most of Camp 3 was clear way up above Sourdough. I think it was getting on up pretty close to Seven Brothers Lakes. There was another camp beyond that. Camp 1 was where the commissary was. This was where the men could buy their snuff and their hard candy. They kept boots and overshoes and blankets and shirts and things like that. Of course, the men, they'd send down when they wanted something from town, but they tried to keep a few things there. All the dry good supplies were kept for all the camps. This was the cooking supplies.

They could go and get anything they wanted. It was the same way at the New York Store. See, Daddy Johnson bought the things that the men wanted down at the New York Store. Now, whether it was charged to the tie camp or to the men individually, I don't know, but they had a good reputation. They always paid, and there was never any problem of them getting anything that they wanted. They got good service and good material.

My stepfather had purchased a Star car. It was a beautiful thing–great big and heavy. That's how we came to town. Of course, we children and my stepfather's wife, Mary, we didn't come to town very often. Anyone else who came down, they came down with the logging trucks. They had a few trucks.

Tie Hack Work at Sourdough

With the ties–the men would fell the trees. Then they'd take the peeler and peel the bark off. The peeler is a long instrument with kinda like a short narrow hoe thing on the end of it. Then they'd use a great big broadax and hack the sides of it. That's why it's called tie hack. Then they'd take a crosscut saw–two men on it– and saw it into lengths for railroad ties. They'd stack these all up at different places, and they'd dam up the water. In the spring when runoff came and that got real full, they'd have what they called the tie drive.

They had these great big grappling hooks, oh, 12 to 14 feet long. The men had heavy boots with calks in them. It was almost like watching dancers out there. In the middle of the creek they'd jump from one to the other. It was dangerous, but it was beautiful to watch. The cook wagon would go ahead about as far as they thought they'd drive the ties and have all the meals ready for them. They brought the lunch to them at noon, and they'd take turns coming in to eat. At night they had a good hot supper.

They had these big flumes that was made from boards–just green lumber sawed– and put on things that were kind of like a sawhorse–only it made a V-shaped flume. When they wanted the ties that were way up in the mountains, why, they'd turn the water in there and float the ties down the flume to where they were going to stack them for the tie drive. Of course, Maurine and I had been cautioned and cautioned that we were not to ever walk the flume. It was dangerous. That water came down very swiftly. But we did a couple of times. Why, we'd usually fall in and get wet, but we usually got dry before we got home.

The tie drive itself was down Sourdough into Clear Creek, then into Buffalo. Everyone, oh, they'd just gather when the tie drive was going to be. It was almost like when we're going to have a parade here. Everyone watched for the ties to come down. They loved it. It was quite a sight.

I don't know how they stopped them at night. I think maybe they just got them to a quiet place, and they would more or less float. When they got ready to go the next morning, why, they pushed them with these great big grappling hooks and get them started down again. Oh, sometimes it took a week. It would take a long time because there would be thousands of ties.

They just had the one bridge then. They had to be very careful because a time or two the ties got jammed up, and that would cause flooding, you know, so they had to be careful. Then they went on down around the creek, down the bend, and to the railroad siding because the railroad did come in here then, and they would load them.

In the winter, we were brought down to Buffalo and boarded with Mr. and Mrs. Fred Wildenberger and went to school here. In the summer, we stayed in the mountains with my stepfather in different logging camps. Then he married Mary Mikolitch Kostenbauer, so we lived with them.

I used to ride on the bobsled in the winter to go up to school–Maurine and I and Daddy Johnson. We all lived at Camp 1, and I'd ride on the bobsled to go up there. Then when school was out, I'd put on my skis. It was approximately three miles. That's why they called it Camp 3. I put on my skis, and it took me just about three minutes to come down that hill. Oh, I loved it. I wouldn't dare put on a pair of skis now. I don't know how I did then.

I did go to school in the mountains at Hunter Ranger Station and lived with Ethel and Ivan Morgareidge. Ethel taught me to knit and sew, how to make French seams, to take small stitches. She was a wonderful teacher. She sent away to Lifebuoy and got charts for us. We washed with Lifebuoy soap.

When Mr. and Mrs. Hall were up here and she was going to have her first child, we children didn't think anything about it. In fact, I don't even remember thinking it strange that she got larger. When it was time for the baby to be born, they couldn't get her to town. School was let out. She was in labor, and we could hear her cries. It seemed strange. We couldn't quite figure out what was going on. Then later on, why, she had this beautiful little baby girl. She'd bring her in a basket, and we went right on with school. There were several families. I believe at one time we probably had between 12 and 14 children. It would vary as some of the families moved or quit, but we always had an average with Mrs. Hall of nine. I know the grades went up to the eighth grade. The bigger boys were supposed to keep the fires going and the ashes taken out and the wood brought in and the water pail filled. It was really a nice time. I remember it fondly. She had me doing the reading or do the public speaking. I was very shy. If I had some poetry to say or something for a Christmas program, as we practiced, I was inclined to be a little pigeon-toed. The more nervous I got, the more my feet turned in. She had to correct that. She'd keep telling me to stand a certain way. I got over it, but when I got nervous, my toes would start turning in. She taught us so many, as I look back now, worthwhile things.

One time, Sundown Taffner–he's our chief of police now–he and his mother and family lived up there, and I took care of the children. I had them out for a walk one day, and we saw this lynx cat. He was stalking us as we walked along. I'll tell you, it didn't take me long–I had four or five little children that I had walking along with me–to get them back to the camp. I really was scared. I told the men, and they went out and killed it. It was a big cat they said–one of the biggest they had ever seen. The strange thing was the animals didn't seem to bother us. I suppose had we bothered them, then they would have. Even in the snow it was nothing to see either bear tracks or cougar tracks or lynx tracks on the way to school.

We were snowed in, but we never got depressed in the snow. Life was fun and easy. They had dances at South Fork Inn. I don't know how many–maybe at least once a month. All the tie hacks and their families and the lumber workers–we'd all pile on maybe four or five great big bobsleds with a whole bunch of blankets and hot water bottles and go down to South Fork Inn and have dances. Children were always welcome at all these dances. No one ever thought of leaving their children home or getting a babysitter. We went right along, and the children could get out there on the dance floor and dance too. There was quite a bit of social life in the camps. The different camps would get together. They always had bobsleds and plenty of horses. It was a good life.

Maurine and I had the same mother, but different fathers. As far as Carl, Daddy Johnson–I called him Daddy–I never ever had a feeling of resentment toward him or anger. He was really quiet. He didn't show affection. He never said, "I love you," and he didn't put his arms around us–either his daughter or me–but we were never ever treated any differently. He didn't do anything more for her than he did for me. We were treated the same exactly. We were fed and clothed. He wasn't a foreigner but of Swedish heritage, and his wife was Austrian. They had different ways. They didn't show affection, but we knew we were loved. We were secure and happy.

Oh, we ran through the mountains. We picked wild raspberries and strawberries. We chewed pitch gum. We climbed up on the highest rock we could find and lay and watch the clouds. It was really one of the happiest times of my life. I feel fortunate that I had a stepfather like Carl Johnson. I had such a good carefree childhood.

When I was going through some of my mother's things in her trunk, I found out that my name wasn't Johnson. I found out my name was Lee and who my father was and who my grandfather was, so I wrote to my grandfather, Benjamin J. Lee. My grandfather lived in Bassett, Nebraska. He wrote to my father, who, in turn, wrote to an attorney. My father hadn't known where I was all these many years. He said he tried to find me. Consequently, an attorney wrote to me.

The government, while he was in the Army, had taken a certain amount of money from his paycheck for me. They knew he had a child. This amounted to about $1,500. You figure 50 years ago that was quite a lot of money. So the attorney sent me the money to Carl Johnson. He took me to Worland and put me on the train. I went out to live with my father and his family in Oakdale, Nebraska. I was going out to my own father. I realized that Carl was not my own father. He was Maurine's father. Sometimes when we would get into an argument or something, she would say, "Well, it's my dad." The only feeling that I had was that I didn't have a father of my own, so I was quite excited to go out there.

During the time I was out there with my father, it was Prohibition, and he was a bootlegger. There were a lot of children, and I loved my stepmother dearly. Dad had– they called them beer cellars. It was the basement. He made home brew, and I had to wash a lot of beer bottles. Well, he was just a bootlegger. They'd come and sit and drink home brew, you know, and he used to get drunk. That's the only word you could say for it. This was really rather disappointing. He was pretty ornery. So I stayed there until I was about 15.

I had the opportunity to go on a trip with my stepmother's sister, Mrs. Montgomery. We went through Salt Lake City. When we came to the mountains up here, I asked if she wouldn't stop because I knew where Daddy Johnson's tie camp was. I wanted to see him because I was so homesick for the mountains and the hills–the life I'd known. I don't remember crying, but I was close to it, and I asked him, "Daddy, can't I stay here?" and he said, "Well, sure." He was very quiet-spoken.

My sister and I had to sleep in a tent, but it was pretty wonderful to be back again. I ran over and told my aunt that I was going to stay with Daddy Johnson, and I did. Then in July of that year, my cousin, Ruth Hanson, and the young man she was going with came up to the mountains. They wanted me to come back down and stay with Uncle Harry and the family, so I did. Away we went.

Then I met Clark Finley. In six weeks we was married. I met him in the last part of June in 1931. He was a rodeo bull and bareback rider. We went to Hardin, Montana, and his brother and sister, Bessie and Claude Finley, were our witnesses. I was 15, and he was 21. Of course, we did have to lie about my age and say I was 18. Nevertheless, we were married.

Well, we were married three years before Bonnie was born, which was a good thing. A girl of 15 isn't really ready. I didn't know how to cook or boil water without burning it. His poor dear mother tried to teach me. He loved homemade bread. First, he was out of work. He was sheepherding, but he quit herding sheep, and he went to washing dishes at the Capitol Hotel after he met me. It used to be Pap Myers' Hotel. There was the hotel and the rooms upstairs, and it had a restaurant there. We had a little room up there that we paid $5 a week for. It had a hot plate in it, and we had this old kind of oven that you could sit on gas burners. A kerosene stove–that was what it was. Anyway, after about a week of showing up at the Masonic Temple, day after day after day, they put him to work.

I decided I would bake some bread. Well, it set there for about three days. It never did rise, and I couldn't figure out what in the world was the matter. I hated to ask Grandma Finley, but finally I did. I asked her why that didn't rise, and she said, "Did you make it like I told you? Put a tablespoon of salt and about a half a cup of sugar?" I confessed, "No, I put in a tablespoon of sugar and a half a cup of salt!" Eventually, I learned how to cook after I got over the habit of reading romance magazines and waiting till the potatoes burned to turn them over. We survived.

It was the Depression. After the Masonic Hall was built and he was through working there, Grandma and Grandpa Finley gave us–they had two or three lots up on North Carrington Street. They helped us build a little–it must have been a 12 to 14 to 16 foot tar paper shack on the back of their lot. That was where we lived. It was just as warm and cozy as it could be. I remember I planted some sweet peas out there. Clark got work with the City.

After Clark was working for the City, we managed to buy a lot of our own. We bought our logs from Bill Shosten up on the mountains. We paid him maybe $2 or $3 a month–whatever we could. I think the logs for our house cost us probably $50, and we got a loan from Wyoming Loan and Trust. We had only to pay, I think, $5.87 a month as our home mortgage loan. We had a two-room log cabin. We had a bedroom and living room and dining room and kitchen all together. Bonnie and Don–we had a pull-out couch for them. When Dave came along, well, for a while we had his crib in our bedroom. Then Clark built two more beautiful rooms on, so we had more room for the children.

We had water outside–a hydrant. We were very fortunate. We had to carry it into the house. Then we got the water piped into the house and heated it in a copper wash boiler. For quite a few years I washed clothes on the board. Eventually, he got me a washing machine. In the meantime, when Bonnie and Don were very young, we moved the tar paper shack over onto our own lot.

Clark worked for the WPA. They had wood down back of the courthouse. They'd go down and saw that wood. They put it up in cords, and the County sold it. I can remember one time Mr. John Flint came up to our little shack. He had two of the loveliest wool blankets for us because he knew we were having a hard time of it. It got pretty cold even in a tar paper shack. They'd bring us some groceries and things. When they had a surplus, whatever there was of surplus, if it were oatmeal or flour or beans, we could go down and get those. They didn't cost anything because it was a matter of survival, but, you know, we never felt underprivileged. We were always glad that we had a home–a roof over our heads and something to eat. If we had a bit of bacon grease to put in it, we were lucky. We had beans and cornbread, and we were happy to have them.

When the war years came along, we had ration stamps. That's when I learned to drink my coffee black because we'd rather save sugar to make a cake or something like that. I learned to make cakes and cookies without eggs and very little sugar. We used honey because the children and Clark liked something sweet.

We always had a garden. We canned a lot of fruit and vegetables. We'd go out chokecherry hunting, picking, and made chokecherry syrup. Someone was always willing to share apples. We had apple butter. We didn't have butter, and our margarine we bought in a great big pound block. It was white like lard, and you had to put the color in yourself. It had a little packet of coloring, and you had to mix that all up with either a fork or your hand, then shape it and put it in the cooler. That was the way the margarine was then.

Everyone wanted to give their children better than what they had, but we never felt a lack of anything. After our first child, Bonnie, was born, it sounds almost unbelievable, but Clark gave me $5. I went down to Penney's and bought the prettiest little yellow housedress and a pair of tennis shoes, an under slip, and a pair of silk hose–all for $5. That was my outfit. If I went to church, I wore that. If I came to town, that's what I wore. I had one good outfit–all for $5. It's almost unbelievable.

After Clark and I were married, we used to walk down and watch the ball games. We walked everywhere. Once in a while we would drive down to Grandma and Grandpa Finley's on a Saturday night, but the way we got where we wanted to go was walking. That was our entertainment for the evening. We didn't have a radio. Clark liked to read, and I did too, so we made good use of the library. From the time that I could read and started to school, I have been a library patron. I can remember the different librarians, and how we were very, very quiet. Anyhow, we did read, and if we wanted to get out, we'd take a walk. We'd walk down to past where there was a footbridge where the other bridge is now. By the Buffalo Apartments, why, there was a footbridge. That was the swinging bridge. Oh, my, it bothered me every time I had to go across there.

I can remember when a blacksmith shop and stables were down where Greg Goddard's office is now. When Clark and I were married, there was a store where the Buffalo Chamber of Commerce is that was run by the Fenusz family. They had more of a delicatessen type of store and candies. Then on down the street were Adams and Young. They had a butcher in there.

I went to school with several ladies. One of them, her father was the butcher in there. If we'd go in, why, he would give us a hot dog to eat. When we'd go up the street, Marian Erhart's father had the tobacco shop. We'd go in there, and he would always give us a piece of candy. Of course, I wasn't supposed to walk that far with the girls because I lived clear up in the north end of town with Mr. and Mrs. Wildenberger. One time, oh, I wanted to see the inside of Florence Bartlett's house because they had an upstairs. I'm not sure whether I really did or whether I created it, but I had to go to the bathroom when I got close to her house, so she took me in, and I got to go up that beautiful curved winding stairway. I was always curious about things, you know.

I can remember when the bandshell was on the Courthouse lawn. Those beautiful big pine trees were not there. We'd go down and sit and watch and listen to the band. I don't know if Fred Kostenbauer had the little Model A. I think he did. Clark and I were in the rumble seat. This speaks for the morals of Buffalo. We were sitting there on the street, parked, listening to the band concert. Clark put his arm just barely around my shoulder. He didn't even put it around my waist. He didn't pull me over close to him– just laid his arm and hand over on my shoulder, and here come the police. He came down there, and he walked up to the car, and he said, "If you want to do that kind of stuff, you get off Main Street." We were so embarrassed we left.

At Christmas time, they always had a tree over there. The music club or someone– anyway a choir–they sang carols, and they handed out great big, to me it seems like, big-sized sacks of candy to every child that came. It was just a beautiful time with the snow. Everyone participated. It was part of growing up in Johnson County because there weren't that many things to do.

When the twins were a little over 2 years old, Clark and I were divorced. Later, I went to southern California while the two older boys, Don and Dave, were in the Navy. Then for health reasons after 10 years in southern California I came back to Buffalo for surgery and stayed with my daughter and her husband, Bonnie and Howard Turk. I had the surgery and then worked for Virginia Purdy out at the 28 Ranch. Then I met and married Roy Songer–Francis Leroy Songer. I don't know the exact year. I was 50. Then he died in 1967 suddenly of a heart attack about six weeks after we were married.

꠹꠹꠹꠹

Helen Broge Straight & Nelda Broge Straight
Helen 1930-2022 & Nelda 1932-2016
From an interview with Patty Myers
In 1995, when Helen was 65 years old & Nelda was 63

Two Sisters Marry Two Brothers

It was often difficult to determine in the recorded interview tape which sister responded to the question. Therefore, no name is given for some questions.

*I*nterviewer Patty Myers: *Nelda and Helen, I want to start by saying your name and your maiden name and where you were born and a little bit about your family.*

Nelda: Nelda Straight. I was born in Illinois–maiden name is Broge. It is a German name.

Helen: Helen Ling Broge Straight–born just across the county line in Illinois because our house burned down just before I was born, and I grew up in the next county.

How and when did the Broge family move to Buffalo, and how did you meet the Straight boys?

Helen: Nelda and I moved to Sheridan. I met Pete Straight through a mutual friend, and then he introduced Nelda and Lee Straight.

Was it a double wedding?
   Nelda: No, I got married in June, and Helen got married in October 1951.

Was it a long romance or a short romance?
   Helen: Hers was very short. Mine was not real long.
   Nelda: I met Lee in March and started going with him sometime in May and married him June 9th.

Were you out of high school and working women?
   Nelda: Yes, we worked both of us in Freeport, Illinois, at offices. We waited till I got to be 18 before we left. We always had a dream from the time I was 14 and Helen was about 16 of coming out here, so we started saving our money. We just headed out. We was going to go to Nevada, but outside of Dubuque, Iowa, we got on the wrong road and went down through Texas and Oklahoma and up through–we really took us far away.
   Helen: We hit every state we could. After we got started, we thought, "What the heck."

Was that when you moved to Sheridan?
   Well, we lived in Nevada first, but we couldn't get a job. It was just all gambling and stuff like that. We was running out of money, so we looked at our topo [map] and places to pick to live. We decided–well, Wyoming was going back towards home, and Sheridan was the heart of the cattle industry, so we thought, "We'll try there, and if we have to give up, then we'll be closer to home." It was a big enough town, so we thought we could find something. We figured we would get down to a certain amount of money, and then if we didn't have a job by then, we would have to go home.

Was the attraction the West or the cowboys of the West?
   We wanted to buy a ranch and had a little plan for a house and everything and thought the land was cheap out here. We could have bought a ranch for what we paid for a dumb car.

In the 1950s, women didn't very often go off adventuring by themselves.
   Especially us–we were so bashful and backward and dumb.

How did your folks feel about you taking off like that?
   Nelda: They never said anything. We got in touch with them after three weeks, I think, and they were worried stiff about us. One time, when we were in Texas, we got picked up by the sheriff. He thought we were runaways, so he called Dad, and he said, "Well, I didn't want them to go, but there wasn't much I could do about it." I was 18, and Helen was 20. The sheriff thought we were 14 year olds.

Did you have trouble finding jobs when you got to Sheridan?

Helen: We had just one traveler's check left, so we thought we would have to go home. Nelda got a job, and that kept us going until I got a job. We had a little apartment. Then things kept going until she got married. Then I was on my own.

How did you meet the Straight boys?

Helen: A mutual friend introduced me.

Were they living in Buffalo at that time?

Nelda: Sometimes we would drive down. They worked, and we would drive down just to bum around.

It was in the 1960s before you had the homestead, so what did you do in between?

Nelda: We went to Alaska right after we were married. Lee drove a truck up there, and I rode along. Then we came back and worked in mills and up in the lumber camps. Then he went to work for the County. That's where he heard about the homestead. He worked different jobs.

Helen: Pete worked mostly on lumber and some at Lisle LaNier's ranch. We worked for Jack Nelding for a year or two and once in a while construction but mostly lumber. He was at Buckingham Lumber Company for years.

Were they lumberjacks?

Helen: They did mostly skidding.

Did you live at the Sourdough camps?

Helen: Ours was Crazy Woman Canyon. We lived at Crazy Woman Canyon when we were first married until Jan was born. The day she was born, Pete got laid off. There was three or four cabins there and some barns. It is just about three miles this side of the pass. Pete's father had horses up there. He and his uncle, they had horses that they used for skidding.

Pete & Nelda Straight's Cabin – 1961

What about you and Lee, Nelda?

Nelda: We lived in those camps too. We lived in Sheep Mountain and then Crazy Woman. Then we lived over across on the Canyon Creek Camp, and we went to Sundance and worked in a mill down there for a while. We really moved a lot even after the kids were born until they kinda got in school. Then we kinda settled a bit. Wanda—that's my oldest girl–started in school in Buffalo. Then we moved to Kaycee for a year. Then we came back and stayed here around Buffalo after that. He worked different jobs–drove truck and did some cowboying–in the log camps and over at the mill.

You said that Lee had heard about homesteading when he worked for the County.

Nelda: Garth Hulet was Lee's boss at the time, and he heard it somewhere. He told Lee about it. Garth filed back up in there, and Lee Moffett filed clear up there where that runaway truck runoff is. Bill Ross filed going down by the gun range. We filed on this, and he told Pete about it. Pete was sick at that time. He had a lung operation. So he asked Pete, and Pete said, "Sure," so then he filed another part. We filed on five acres to begin with. BLM thought everyone was going to file and buy it. Why, then they cut into two and a half acres. I don't know if they legally could have done that or not. I got a letter on that. I was looking in the safe the other day. It explained why they just gave us two and a half. I had never seen that letter before or don't remember.

Did the brothers get two and a half a piece? You had the five acres total where the two houses are sitting. Were you the only ones who put houses on them?

Nelda: They didn't think they could get water. They didn't think they could put a road up in there. Garth is up there. The right-of-way went right up through the middle of his. He didn't think there would be a good place to make a house, so he just kind of let his go back. I heard Bill Ross said he couldn't make a road. Most of them thought they couldn't get water up here, but I know Lee was a good witcher. He witched all our wells.

How many wells do you have?

Nelda: I've two up there, and she's got one. We shared this one at first. That's the first one we drilled. It is not a very good well. I mean it's got good water, but there is not much of it. We decided to have Mark Albright Drilling. He's the one that drilled the well up here or his company. Lee worked for them at the time, so they just let him bring the rig up and drill that one out there.

With the original demands for homesteading, you had to do some kind of land improvement.

We had to build at least an 18x24, and we put up a 24x24. We figured we could move that somewhere else if we didn't prove up on it. We put them on foundations, but you can still move them, you know, lift them up.

Did you have to pay money up front for the property?

Oh, yeah, about $150 I think it was. I think our filing fee was $15, and our lease money after they accepted our filing fee you had to pay another $135.

How long did you have to stay on it?

We had three years to prove up on it. You had to build a house, you had to have water, and you had to have a septic system of some kind. Well, we didn't really have water. We had a seismograph come and see if there was water. They just went down until they got water. We put an old handpump in there to say that we had water. The septic system had to be inspected. We had to send plans in for the house, plans in for the septic system, and all that stuff. A guy from Worland come out and inspected our septic system before we could cover it up.

How long did it take you to feel like you were permanent?

Nelda: Well, when we first moved up here, to be honest, I kept thinking, "I wonder if we are supposed to be up here." But it wasn't very long–maybe a year–maybe not even that long after we really got moved up here and started driving out the sagebrush and pushing the rocks out so we would have a yard.

Helen: When she moved up, she just had the outside walls. She didn't have any interior walls at all.

Nelda: We didn't have any doors or windows in. Then Mom came and visited, and she slept–she said, "I hope I don't snore with my mouth open, or I'll get a miller in it."

Helen: We built our house down at Buckingham–all the walls–and then just brought them up on a big truck and set them up.

Did you put up a prefab house?

Helen: Well, they weren't in, but the holes were there. It wasn't too long, and we had the windows in. We had all the interior walls same day.

Nelda: We moved up here two years before Helen did.

Helen: We didn't have electricity up here when Nelda and Lee moved up. They did most of theirs by hand.

Nelda: We hauled water from the cold spring down there for two years or a year and a half. I can remember hauling water from there.

Helen: I remember hauling water because our water froze up. Pete was down there getting water, and he fell in the creek at the cold springs. It was in the wintertime, and when he came back up here, he was just froze.

This was 1963?

Helen When we moved up–when we filed on it.

Nelda: We moved up in 1966.

You both had children by then?

Helen: All my kids –Janice, James, Charlotte, and Camille.

Nelda: I had two–Wanda and Jack. Then I had Michael in '68.

When did you start adding on to the houses?

Nelda: I would say 1969 because I don't think we had it when Mike was born in 1968. I got a picture of him when he was about 1 or 2 years old pounding nails, so 1969 to 1970, I would say.

Helen: They had rock in the bottom of their garage. Lee couldn't get it out, so he blasted it out and knocked some holes in the side of their house. It looked like they'd been shot with a shotgun.

Nelda: Had a couple of my windows broken, but Lee got it out–well, part of it. What he wanted to do was get down low enough so he could have a window in that upstairs bedroom instead of just have it blank there. It used to be so hot up there because there was not much ventilation.

Helen: When Pete first started, he wasn't much of a carpenter. He couldn't even read a yardstick. Ask him a measurement, and he would say, "Well, it's two marks past the half," but he learned.

Nelda: Lee always said he was the jack-of-all-trades and master-of-none, and he really was. He knew how to do just about everything. I mean he put the electricity in, and he was a well driller. He built the house. Just about everything there was to do, he did it.

Helen: It seemed like a mansion when we first moved up here. We actually had a bedroom for the kids–one for Jan and one for the boys. We were in the basement. We figured that was the only way of ever owning a home. We couldn't save enough to put a down payment on anything.

Nelda: Lee always said he always had a dream when he was hunting up there to having a home up there. It came true, but sometimes I think he wished it hadn't because all the work he got into, but it worked out fine.

彬彬彬彬彬

Barbara Gibson Stevens
1898-1991
From an interview with Patty Myers
In 1982, when 84 years old

Girl Scout Leader

I became involved with the Girl Scouts after I had been here not quite a year. It was really Girl Scouts before they were doing 4-H. They had a large group. I had never done any scouting work before, but it was just like anything that was in the teaching line because I had been a teacher. I got really involved in Girl Scouts, so you don't have much time for other things. My husband [Frank Stevens] said he never knew what he was going to eat in the evening or how many were going to be here because the scouts tried out for their food badges at my house, and I fed him all the meals, and they entertained their mothers here. I mean the folks that were working for their badges. Mrs. Max Waegele lived across on the corner then. She came over evenings and taught us first aid and homecare class. Mrs. Waegele was a good friend. She was a registered nurse, and while she did not work, she got so much pleasure out of helping the girls with their bed care and all their first aid for their badges. Some of the girls have let me know in later years how much that helped them.

They urged that we have uniforms, but they were dresses. We just ignored it. Our group wasn't as closely supervised as it was three or four years later, and by that time I didn't care for that supervision, so I no longer continued it. I just felt it was time for me to get out. When we went to the mountain, we had our girls wear jeans. I had a custom knickers suit and a dress, and I had boots–not jodhpurs–but similar to that. I didn't wear jeans because Frank didn't want me to.

The first year we had three different camps I supervised. It was at the Knebel cabin. We put tents up. There was another couple that had another cabin almost in the same yard, and they let us use that too. Phyllis Knebel was one of my Girl Scouts. Then we went to Lucasta Camp. I think they leased it. There was the big building, and there was a second cabin on that too. We always had a couple of tents. It was a well-organized camp. Mrs. Lillian Watt did the cooking. We organized the girls into groups. One day you were camp cleaner, and next day you were kitchen helper. We had enough girls for the number of days we were there.

We had arts and crafts. They worked on their various badges. We didn't do any cooking badges up there, but the housekeeping badge was all right to do. In a way, it was a quiet camp. They never were allowed to go out of sound of my scout whistle because I was responsible for some 30 girls, and you're thinking of their parents. Whether the girls liked it or not, they had to stay within the sound of my whistle.

I remember one evening when we took the Girl Scouts up there. We marched them all up there, and Marianne Rothwell said, "Oh, Mrs. Stevens, why did you change to a dress? You look so nice in your trousers, and you're perfectly welcome to wear them here." I said, "Not after we have been popping corn." I had put the pan down in my lap, and it was just all black." You take 30 children visiting to a home like the Rothwell home on the mountains, and you're a little bit concerned. Mrs. Rothwell said, "You know this place is all fenced, Mrs. Stevens. Now, you just don't worry about your children at all. Let them have the run of the place until it's picnic time." That was my first really relaxed time of the whole week. I remember it with so much pleasure because it was such a lovely thing for them to do. They brought so much out from town–candy and watermelons. We let the girls have some, and then we gave each of them a spoonful of milk of magnesia. Some of them weren't so happy about it, but we didn't have any sick children either. You had to watch that very closely. Roda Wall fixed a medicine chest and first aid kit for us. We didn't have any need for it.

Frank loaded everything in the truck–the bed rolls and all of that. Different ones took cars. Frank came up every day to see if we needed fresh meat, and many mothers sent up fresh vegetables from their garden. We planned our meals entirely before we left, so we knew just what we were going to have, so there we were until the cars came

191

for us.

I remember one evening–I believe it was when we were at Lucasta Camp–we made sandwiches. Each carried their own, and then we tramped up over the hills up back and all around. They enjoyed that so much. We had a forest ranger who came and talked to us. It was a lot of work, but it was lots of fun.

𒀭𒀭𒀭𒀭

Glenn D. "Jack" Sweem
1918-2001
From an interview with Patty Myers
In 1996, when 78 years old

World War II Pilot

My cousin who I was working with told me, "The Japs bombed Pearl Harbor today." I thought about it and decided, "Well, I'm gonna get in it," so the next Tuesday morning I went to Sheridan and volunteered. I left a month later–January 7, 1942–for the service. I always wanted to fly. I remember when I went into the recruiting office, why, I told them I was volunteering, and the officer said, "Fine, fine." He got the papers out, and I signed up. Then he asked me, "What branch you want go in?" and I said, "Air Corps, of course," and he says, "Well, what do you want to do?" and I told him, "Fly," so he asked, "How much college have you had?" and I said, "Two years." His reply was, "Not enough. It's four years' requirement to go into aviation cadets," so I told him, "Just tear the darn papers up. I'm not volunteering," but he said, "Oh, no. You're in now," so I asked him, "Well, how do I get to fly?" "Well, you can declare previous service, being as you're already in as private. You can take a supplementary college exam. If you pass that, then you can take a physical, and if you pass that and the mental test, you're an aviation cadet." So I went the hard way. I went through cadet school and graduated in May 13, 1943. Then I ended up in North Africa–B-17 crew. I flew out of North Africa and then moved to Italy and flew out of there.

I flew 52 missions. I was about half flak happy, I guess, at the time, so they sent me home, and I went into the training command. Well, if you ever rode over one of those targets, and they're shooting anti-aircraft at ya so thick that you can walk on it, why, after about 52 missions, you get pretty flighty–a nervous condition, ya know. You see that flak break out there in front, and then the next one is a little closer, and you wait for the third one, and it might be behind you, or it might be right ahead of you or off to the side. You can't maneuver because you fly straight and level when you're on a target run, so you're always watching that flak. You've always got a bunch of enemy fighters on ya. After a while, why, it makes you a little nervous, so they call it flak happy. It's combat fatigue.

Well, it might have been glamorous, but there's no foxholes up there, and our losses were tremendous–probably, three to one over ground troops or maybe five to one because I remember in our outfit we lost over 2,400 bombers in just the time I was over there. All of our losses were in enemy territory. It wasn't over friendly territory. We were penetrating the enemy territory all the time. We lost so many over the Alps, flying into Germany and Austria and the Balkans. Oilfields was the main source of fuel for the Axis. The targets we were bombing were ball-bearing and aircraft factories and tank factories. They were well-protected with anti-aircraft guns and fighter escorts. You were lucky if you made what we called a milk run–when you didn't get shot up with fighters and hit a target they weren't expecting us to hit and had very little flak. You know, you get so many wounded because of the anti-aircraft guns. See, the skin on those B-17s, was only .032 of an inch. You can just about stick your finger through it. You get so many wounded. Sometimes they were bleeding so badly you had to throw them out of the plane. We'd bail them out. We'd put a static line on them and bail them out over some inhabited place, hoping that somebody would pick them up and stop their bleeding because in rarefied air there was no way to stop bleeding. There's not enough oxygen to coagulate the blood. If they're gut shot or have an arm blown off or something like that, you can't do much for them up there except give a shoot of a little morphine. They were all taken prisoner of war. You hope that there's some compassion there. They'd put them in the hospital and maybe sew them up. Otherwise, if we tried to carry them home, why, they'd bleed to death.

In Africa it was 110 to 120 to 130 degrees temperature in the daytime, and water was scarce. Our water was hauled from the Atlas Mountains to the desert by the British in these wooden tank wagons. The water we got, why, it was just as green as grass, and it stunk. It had so much chlorine and algae we'd aerate it by pouring it back and forth between vessels to get some of the chlorine out of it. We were allowed a gallon of water a day, and at that temperature you drank that much before breakfast. It was for washing, drinking, your laundry, so we did our laundry in 110 octane gas. I was 32 days without a bath. We didn't have enough water to even shave. One of my waist gunners was quite a scrounger, and there was some Arab natives one time came by our base. He went out and visited with them and came home with an old pair of these hand clippers with some teeth broken out of it. We'd take those old clippers and clip our beards. Our oxygen masks fit around our face, but our beards let in the rarefied air, which caused red-outs. Also, with the water situation, we didn't have any water to take baths.

One time, we was coming back from a mission in Europe. A cloud front always laid across the coast of Africa. You either went over the top of it and tried to find a way through it to your base, or else you'd hedge hop over the Atlas Mountains, hoping you didn't hit a mountain with the fog and cloud cover. So this day, why, we was gonna go in under the front, and we was right down on the Mediterranean Sea. You could just about reach out and touch the water. We was just hedge hopping, and that water looked so darn good. We got back to our base, and we got in a command car, and we drove 80 miles to the Mediterranean Sea and took a bath. We didn't think about salt water. Man, we was undressed by the time the car stopped. We ran out into the water, soaped up, and the soap turned to rubber. We had to use sand to wash the soap out of our hair, but it sure felt good.

Our barracks were canvas tents and cots. You'd just parboil in the daytime. Then at night it cools down, and the scorpions and centipedes come out as soon as it gets dark and starts getting cold. They hunt a place to get warm. We was always getting air raids from Germans–red alerts as we called them–so we'd leave our flying boots set right there by our bunk. When the siren came on, we'd stick our feet in our boots and run for a foxhole. Well, this was a convenient place for these scorpions to get in, and we had about as many casualties from scorpions and centipedes as we did from enemy action. Some of those kids, their leg would swell up twice the normal size and turn black, and they'd be grounded for maybe two, three weeks, or a month. A lot of our groceries came in gallon cans, so we'd take these cans and put them under the legs of our cots and pour motor oil and gasoline in them so that the scorpions couldn't crawl up and get in bed. The centipedes, they weren't as poisonous as the scorpions, but you always had to watch for them too.

Well, I got tired of jumping up every hour or so and running for a foxhole. We had a bunch of Italian and German prisoners of war on our base, so one day, I got about a dozen of them prisoners out of the compound and brought them up there with shovels. I had them dig me a hole 16x16 and five foot deep. I put the tent over the top of the hole. That gave me a big foxhole. I figured if the enemy can hit that, why, I deserved to die. It didn't take long for everybody to start digging their tents in. The tent up on top would give ya about eight foot of head clearance at the edge. We'd go into these native towns that had been bombed and pick up tile and cement block and stone to build the walls and put tile on the floor. Believe it or not, we had to have stoves when we was in North Africa because at night it gets chilly, so we concocted stoves out of gas tanks and copper tubing from wrecked German and Italian planes. We could heat the tent warm enough where you could stand the night temperatures.

The Germans figured if they could keep us awake and harass us enough, why, we'd lose our efficiency, so they would maybe just send over a lone plane. We called them "Washing Machine Charlie." He'd come buzz over the area, and we didn't know whether there was gonna be a formation of bombers or only one, but they'd sound the red alert and turn on the siren, and we'd run out and jump in the foxhole. We'd sit there for maybe 30 minutes or an hour before they'd blow the all clear. We'd go back to bed, and pretty soon they'd blow again. Generally, on most of our missions we'd get out of bed at 2:30 or 3:00 in the morning and go to breakfast and our briefing. By that time, it'd be coming daylight, and we could take off. So from the Germans you'd get two or three interruptions in the night plus getting up at that time of morning, why, you lost a lot of sleep, and after a while it gets to ya. You're not as efficient as you would be if you had a full night's sleep.

Well, I came back to the states and went into the training command after I spent three months in the hospital at Fort George Wright in Washington. In that command I had Chinese and Mexican students, and that was an ordeal. That was worse than combat because you didn't speak their language. You had your student in a PT17 two-seater open cockpit plane. When you wanted to talk to your student, you talked to the tower, and the interpreter there would tell your student what you wanted. The student would then talk to the interpreter, and the interpreter would talk to you.

❦❦❦❦

John H. "Sundown" Taffner
1928-2013
From an interview with Shawn McIntyre
In 1991, when 63 years old

How I Came to Be Called "Sundown"

Interviewer Shawn McIntyre: Sundown, who were your first family members to move to Johnson County?

My great-grandfather came here in a covered wagon with my grandfather. My grandfather was only a small child when he came in, so they have been here a lot of years.

How did you get the name Sundown?

Well, I was raised on a ranch that my uncle, Dave Whaley, owned out northwest of town. One day, at the dinner table he says, "John,"–that's my real name–he says, "sundown you're out where decent people are. At sun up you are just getting up and around. You are really a lazy little bugger." The hired men, they picked up on that. From that day on, I was known as Ole Sundowner.

How was your home life as a kid?

Oh, I was raised, like I said earlier, mostly by my uncle who lived out on a ranch. I had a very good childhood I thought. I'd go out and spend at least the summers, and I'd go to school some out at Upper Johnson Creek School. I enjoyed very much being in the country and being able to do whatever I wanted to do.

Describe what sort of chores you had back then.

We used to have to milk the cows and clean the barns, dig dandelions out of the lawn, take care of the garden, and hoe the weeds. Of course, in those days you packed coal, and you packed some water. Kids had quite a few chores to do.

Describe a typical day for a police officer when you first started on the police force.

When I first started on the police force, there was only three of us working at that time, so it worked fairly well in hours, and we only had one day a week off. Things was pretty relaxed. Most of our problems came from local bars, so usually it was take care of the bars and the businesses. You didn't have much for traffic nor did you have much problem with the younger people. Children, they all weren't running around in automobiles. They were afoot, and they pretty well behaved. Toward the end of my retirement, I think a typical day would have been mostly patrolling in a vehicle. When I first started, we had one unmarked car. That one was all we had. We didn't have any lights. We did have a siren on it but no lights, no emblems or anything to signify that it was a police car. Of course, at the end of my career we had probably four police cruisers all marked with lights and emergency equipment. Most of our time at the end of my career was done investigating crimes and patrolling the town in vehicles–what they called preventive patrol.

What is the main change you have seen in Johnson County over your lifetime here?

Probably, the biggest change has been the influx of people. I've been here through three oil booms, and I was here when they put the Interstate system in. I think it was due to the Interstate system that started bringing more and more new people to this area. At one time, you could walk down the street and probably knew 85 to 90 percent of all the people in town. Now, you're lucky if you know a third of them.

🌿🌿🌿🌿🌿

Garvin C. Taylor
1917-1993
Interview with Patty Myers
In 1992, when 74 years old

Garvin Taylor–Storyteller

I knew that Butch Cassidy didn't die in South America because Smokey Rowan seen him in 1934 in Lander at the rodeo. Smokey knew him. Of course, my dad [Edward O. Taylor] had told me about him being here in 1915. He was always helpful to all those guys. They never harmed anybody back of the Wall–never done nothing to them except help them out when they was shorthanded or something. They'd never done any injury. It was a live and let live sort of a deal in them days.

Bill Stubbs, he was a brother of Jim, who bought the Blue Creek Ranch. He was going down the road in a wagon one day just down where I live, and he run into some of the Hat Ranch cowboys, and they was telling him the news about a posse was trailing Kid Curry with bloodhounds. "Oh," he said, "you are way behind times. He stole the

Edward O. Taylor

bloodhounds, and he's trailing the posse." That was back in 1893 or '94.

Jim Stubbs come there in 1889. That was up here at the old Billy Hill place that he sold to Billy Brock. He just had it a short time, and Butch Cassidy rode up there and give a kid 50¢ to come into the NH headquarters and tell him, "There's a man out here wants to see you." He went out, and it was Butch, and he told him, "Jim, I'm on the run, and I have to have some money, and I want to sell that place." "How much do you want?" "$1,500." "All right." He paid him for it, and Butch told him, "I'll get the deed to you," and he did. It took about a year. Rap Harold brought the deed over the next fall. He was around there from then on until he died in 1941 or 1942.

Rap Harold, the guy that brought the deed over, he told me and Bunny [Taylor] about it many a time. He said, "I rode up there, and this fella said, 'Well, get your horse and turn him loose in there. There's grain over there in the grainery, and there's hay in the haymow. Come on up. We'll have some supper. I'm Jim Stubbs.'" Rap said, "Well, I've got something for you." He wore a vest, and he pulled this deed out and handed it to him. He liked the country, and he stayed there. My dad kinda inherited Rap from Jim. Oh, he worked other places, but most of the time he was around Blue Creek. His real name was Lemon D. Harold. He was a half-breed Indian.

See, Butch was in a bind and on the run. He and Uncle Jim knew one another for years. Well, Butch was a hell of a cowboy, and he worked for different outfits, and they naturally knew one another. They was personal friends too. He knew Jim, and he wanted to sell the outfit, and Uncle Jim wanted it. He knew that he had that sold to Billy Brock, so he sold that other ranch to Billy Brock and moved over there to Blue Creek. It was a year to getting that deed, but that didn't bother them old-timers.

1889–it was in the fall of the year. There was a dance there at the NH, and Jim had went over to it. Butch rode up there and sent his kid in–told him, "Tell Jim Stubbs I want to see him." Well, Jim didn't know who wanted to see him, but he wandered out, and it was Butch Cassidy. Butch told him, "I'm on the run, and I've got to have some money," and he sold Uncle Jim the place.

I never will forget one time there was a guy come whittle-diggin' up there in a Model T Ford long about 1927–was hot on the trail of Butch Cassidy's buried wealth. Uncle Jim looked at him and said, "You're a little far north for that, fella. Why, when they made a strike, they went to Fanny Porter's whorehouse in San Antone."

Uncle Jim loaned them money a lot of times. They'd have to rob a bank to pay him. You know, he was a realist. It was chicken today and feathers tomorrow with those guys. You know, they'd get $7-8,000 apiece, but they'd retire to Fanny Porter's, and that money didn't last too long even in those days. Why save it? There was always another bank or train, you know. It was a lot faster than driving an old pokey cow along the road. They didn't steal cattle much. There was cow thieves that did some, but Cassidy and Curry and Lonabaugh–why, go steal an old slow moving cow when you could rob a train when they was bringing the money back?

Cassidy went to the pen in 1894 or '95. He was in there for 10 or 12 months, and they turned him loose. He left here about 1900–something like that–and went to South America–probably 1897 or '98–right at the turn of the century. Well, they was down there six or eight years, and there was a couple of guys got killed down there. This guy that they worked for as mine guards–he just identified them as Cassidy and Lonabaugh. The Pinkertons, they quit looking for them. They'd been identified. He didn't know who they was that was dead there, but he just said it was them.

Course, they come back. I think that was supposed to be in 1909 or '06. They come here in 1910, and Uncle Jim was gone. Then he come in 1915, and he was there. Them old-timers was live and let live. Well, Butch's dead. Let him stay dead. He'd never done them any injury.

If you was shorthanded or up against a bind, Butch'd pitch in and help you for whatever time it took to get you straightened out. They helped Uncle Jim a lot of times–all them guys. They was just good neighbors. They'd keep a fresh horse there. Whatever they needed they'd always see to it that they got it. They never bothered anybody. Why fiddle with some little old two-bit rancher when, there was trains running every day and banks? It was a lot easier to hit them than it was some poor SOB with a hundred head of cattle, you know.

Let me tell you about bootlegging during my time. There was a fella by the name of Jim Jones, who was a distiller. Prohibition was on, so they set up six or seven stills and made whiskey, and they had an instant market. Now, a lot of people would probably be ashamed of that, but it was desperation. It was the only way they could save themselves. The stock business and the farming business–the fall of 1919 cattle was worth $125 a head. In the spring of 1920, they wouldn't bring $20 a pair.

Bill Stubbs–the bank foreclosed and sold his stuff to Harlans–the old Flying Horseshoe brand and the cattle for $20 a head. Well, that was for cows with calf. The other stuff brought about $14. He never did recover from it

Then these guys, Bill Stubbs and Old Jim Jones, set up this bunch of stills. Jim was a distiller, and there was an instant market for it. You know, I've seen federals in carloads raiding our place, but the stills were seven or eight miles away–some of them further than that. There never was nothing in our cellar or the house or the barn.

Along in the fall of 1937, the Old Man and I was coming down Eagle Creek Canyon. He said, "You know, I hung a keg of whiskey up here in one of these trees." There was still leaves on the trees, but I spotted it, so I climbed up there with my saddle rope. This rope was still around it, you know–two loops–but it was about wore through. Well, I got a couple of half-hitches on it with my rope and lowered it to the ground, and there was probably seven gallons left in it. I guess it was full when he put it up there. Well, Dad broached the keg and pronounced it good. To me, it just put a knife in my back. I didn't think it was very good. I drank a little bootleg whiskey in my time and never did find any pleasure in it. I know I took one drink, and that was enough for me. That was 10 years after my dad quit bootlegging.

We lived back of the Hole-in-the-Wall up this side of Buffalo Creek, and the Old Man had an old what they called a Dodge Commercial. It would have been about a half-ton pickup now—an old four-cylinder thing. I remember we delivered 10 kegs of bootleg to Lee Hill out between Waltman and Arminto one night. Lee was a big-time bootlegger. He gave him $1,000 for it—pulled out a wad of bills and it didn't shrink it much—$100 a keg, $10 a gallon. Dunk [Duncan C.] McLellan at Arminto, he had a hotel and pool hall and gambling and bootleg joint. He'd buy a keg of whiskey from the Old Man every once in a while. It was local distribution. Them guys, they run whiskey in from Canada too, you know. That was a little on the dangerous side—roads not being much good in them days.

I knew all the old bootleggers—Lee Hill, Frank Converse, our vaunted sheriff, D.O. Howsley. There was quite a whiskey ring. They was taken to Cheyenne and tried there on conspiracy charges of avoiding the Volstead Act. They spent—Howsley told me this himself—they spent $200,000 clearing a little bootlegger by the name of Meeks. Well, it was the cheapest way out for them.

Dave Davidson—I knew him well. He had a 500-gallon still out there in one of those draws out on the Medicine Bow Road. I used to go out to his ranch. He showed it to me one time. He said he bought corn in Rawlins and Laramie and sugar here, thither, and yon and in Casper. This was down in a brushy draw. He had it pretty modern. He had kind of a gas heating stove. They didn't bring it to a boil. They would just get it to where it would steam, and it would come out of a coil and into a barrel of cold water. Then it would drip, and they would run that off. I know the theory of how it worked. I wouldn't have the slightest idea how to put one together. You'd buy corn, and you bought so much sugar at this store and that one where it was a little hard to trace. They didn't buy it all at one place because that would give them too much of a lead on you. You had to be a little careful with it.

I've seen the law in there—carloads of them. Of course, I didn't know nothing what they was doing. I was just a kid. A kid ain't interested in much of that stuff anyhow. If he knows about it, he might be, but if he don't know nothing, he ain't. That was kind of the way the outfit was kept out of the hands of the bankers.

The Blue Creek Ranch sold out to this Chuck, C.C. Willis. He bought the old main Blue Creek right there where Butch Cassidy had his homestead and stuff. He bought that. We had it a hundred years.

❦❦❦❦❦

Theodore D. "Bunny" Taylor

1919-2009
From an interview with Patty Myers
In 1992, when 73 years old

In His Time Everything Was Interesting

Interviewer Patty Myers: Tell me about the nickname "Bunny."

Oh lord! Well, my name is Theodore. That's why I have a nickname. I didn't have anything to do with it. Anyway, I come from a large family, and my oldest sister did all the babysitting. See, I was the ninth child, so when she nicknamed me Bunny, it stuck. That's where I got it.

Where did your parents settle?

They lived up Powder River here. Seven or eight miles is where they raised their family. They started having children in 1903, and the last one was born in 1926. In them 23 years, they had 10 kids. They had five boys and five girls. My father's name was Robert Taylor–nicknamed Bob. He came into Wyoming down by Lusk when he was 13 years old, and he never did leave. He came up to Powder River and lived his life there. My mom, she was 17 years younger than he was. She came with her dad and mother and a couple of older sisters. They came from Arizona and New Mexico. When they got to Chugwater, Wyoming, the horses was tired, and everybody was tired. They rented a little pasture, and they unloaded the cookstove and washed clothes, and they took the horseshoes off the horses and visited around.

The thing my mom tells about it was going over the pass and coming down at Chugwater. When they got here, they went to work for the NH Ranch. They sent my mom down here, and she stayed with John and Effie Nolan to go to school. That was the year of the Wilcox train robbery. Part of the robbers come to Kaycee, and they went to that house down there. They called Mr. John Nolan by his first name. They stayed in the house. He took the horses some place. There was three or four of them. They got up and cooked for them, and my mom carried them food. They stayed in the house all day. It was two or three days, why, Nolan come back with some horses. She said she remembers they had to have some real good horses. They said, "They don't have to be too gentle, but they really got to be good ones." At night they took off. When they left, they gave her a little gold ring. I don't know if they stole it or what. Anyway, I didn't even know they did anything–only they blew up the car. When my mom's first grand-daughter got old enough to come to school, she lived over there. Her parents lived at Mayoworth, and she was pretty lonesome. My mom thought it would be nice to give her something, so she gave her that little gold ring. Course, right away the kid lost it. After my mom was gone, there was a guy working here. He didn't have anyplace to stay, so he was going to stay in the south room up there. There is little cracks in the floor. He was sweeping it out, and he rolled that little ring out. "Bunny," he says, "here's the prettiest little gold ring. Would you have any idea who that belonged to?" I says, "Yeah, by god, I do. I'll tell you." I told him about it, and he gave it to me, and I put her away.

So what you are saying is that you know this story that connected the Hole-in-the-Wall gang to Kaycee at the time of the Wilcox train robbery.

Well, the thing of it is, see, I really don't know the guys that my mother carried the grub to, but I know they was involved in that. She said it was a couple of months before 'cause they said for her not to say anything. She says in them days children didn't ask questions. Anyway, it was a couple of months till they finally decided that's what they was. Course, I think Old John Nolan–the people that came knew him. They were drifters. They didn't belong here.

Did your dad take out a homestead up there?

Yeah, he did. It was quite a while later. I think 320 acres on the river there is what he got deeded. He was a cowboy, and his friend Old Billy Briscoe was too. At the time they came in, they was both kids in Nebraska. Course, they left home. There was quite a lot of horseracing there. They both was little guys, and they was riding them race-horses. There was a herd come through there, and it was supposed to come to that town, so the guys that brought it–some of them had to go back. They sold it, and the people that bought it was going to take it on toward Montana. They was shorthanded, so they hired them two kids. They come into Wyoming. About Lusk was where they was. Neither one of them ever left Wyoming after that. Billy Briscoe was on the Sweetwater most of his life, and my dad was on Powder River. In their time everything was interesting, you know. Briscoe–the morning after they hung Jim Averill and old Kate [Ella Watson] down there–he was one of the cowboys that come down the creek. My father was with the Smith brothers at the Hole-in-the-Wall when they shot Old Bob Smith. In their lifetime, everything was like that, you know. They had a lot of interesting things in their lives.

How did your mother [Cecil Ritter Taylor] manage after your dad died?

She still had a whole passel of kids. Oh, it was awful. It sure was. She was a hard-working woman. In them days, once in a while some of the girls did some laundry for somebody, but you didn't make any money at it. It was tough going. My father had a lot of friends–oh, trappers–and they'd bring meat and stuff. Our family was always real close. That's really all that mattered, you know.

Did your mother manage to hang onto the property?

Oh, no, lord, no. See, it was in February, so we was living in Kaycee 'cause all them girls had to go to school. There was a mortgage on the place. I don't know if it was delinquent, but we never ever went back there.

Did you go to the military from Kaycee?

After a roundup on the 8th of December, we had this car with a radio in it. Me and Kenny Jackson bought it together. We was drinking beer and listening, and the Japs bombed Pearl Harbor, by god. I think it was the 20th or the 21st we went to Sheridan and enlisted. There was quite a bunch of us. The two Parker boys and two Haines boys and Rex Yeigh and me. When we got up there, you had to go in the old post office building, and they got us all lined out. Old Dick Jarrard was pretty drunk. You had to sign your name, and he couldn't do 'er. That old boy said, "Well, you can't go." Rex, he went over and talked to the guy, and I wrote "Richard Jarrard" real good and sat back down. We got him in. They said, "You be at Kaycee, and we'll pick you up. We'll let you know." See, they would pick us up on the 7th of January. That's what they did. They put us on the bus. Old Warren Schlicht was driving the bus, and he knew us. They had to stop at the drug store in Midwest. We used to go over there, dancing all the time. See, we knew all of them girls over at Edgerton. We says to Old Orin, "Run us over to Edgerton." He says, "Oh, god, I can't do that." Of course, all the bars–there was about five bars–they was open. Anyway, we got scattered. Old Orin, he finally got us to Casper, and we had missed the bus out of there. They chewed him and scolded him. But they was rid of us for four years anyway. Well, we went to Fort Leavenworth, Kansas. When we left there, they split us. The bunch I went with was to Sheppard Field, Texas. There was about 10 of us guys they shipped down to southern England to a base down there. By golly, the second night we was there, why, a couple of old kids I had been with quite a lot, we found out where the pub was. Old Dick Jarrard was sitting in there. I said, "Hello, Dick," and he said, "Hi." He was a master sergeant and a chief armorer. I kept trying to talk to him, and he finally says, "Who the hell are you?" I says, "I'm Bunny Taylor." He says, "Who?" I says, "Bunny Taylor. Hell, I joined the Army with you." "Oh, Jesus Christ, yes," he says, "God, you've changed a lot." I said, "Well, so have you." He was the only one I seen that I knew all the time I was over there. I was chief armorer for a squadron. You work on guns and bombs and fuses. I was a master sergeant when I went overseas.

Was it especially hard for you to be in the military after you got separated from the Kaycee group?

No, it wasn't. See, we made $30 a month cowboying. When we went in there, it was $19 you got. You could get PX boots and get tobacco with it. No, it wasn't too tough for us. We never had a very high standard of living. It didn't crowd us much. I didn't gain a pound or lose a pound. I weighed about 138 pounds.

You didn't suffer from homesickness?

Oh, hell no, I hadn't been home, you know. No, it never bothered me much.

⚜⚜⚜⚜

Clara Buell Thompson
1899-1986
From an interview with Patty Myers
In 1983, when 84 years old

Jack & Betty 13 Months Apart

Interviewer Patty Myers: How did you meet your husband, Howard Thompson?

Oh, he came out here in 1919 after the war. He was running a grocery store in Illinois–he and his brother-in-law. When the war came along, Howard joined the Army. He saw a sign in downtown Chicago that said, " Join the ordnance and be in France in 30 days," so he joined the ordnance and spent the rest of the war in Maryland.

He came out to Buffalo on the train. He and his partner–a feller he met in the Army–came out. They met a woman on the train from Sheridan who told them if they got off the train in Sheridan and come to Buffalo, there was a fellow in Buffalo that was locating people on homesteads. That was Edwin Burritt. So they came to Buffalo, and Burritt brought them down here and located them on a homestead just where the bridge crosses South Fork. Howard's house was right there by where the bridge is. They built them a stone house out there. The two of them had the one cabin.

Where were you working?

Oh, I was probably working in the Telephone Store when I first met him. I used to work there and the bank. I think I must have known him first about 1920. We were married in February 1925.

Did you quit working after your marriage?

Yes. We ran the filling station over here for years and had a wholesale gas business. That's what we did. That's where the road went, you see, right through town. We had a truck and delivered up and down the river–below Sussex even. Usually, Howard had two or three men working for him. We never did run the ranch. We just had hired help. Howard didn't work on it himself. In fact, I don't think he was much of a farmer. He was a city boy from Chicago and didn't know much about ranching.

You had two children?

Yeah, Betty and Jack. They both still live here.

Tell me about your children.

You see, when the kids were just little, I had plenty to do because they were just 13 months apart. Jack was a premature baby. He demanded almost constant care. He weighed 3 ¾ pounds when he was born, and he went down to three and a half pounds. Dr. [W.J.] Knebel came down here when Jack was born, but he was born before the doctor got here. Dr. Knebel said that he might live a couple days, but he's still here. He's 60 years old now.

Sonny Sellars was just a little fella. His mother let him come over and see Jack. Sonny was about 3 years old. Jack was a terrible looking baby. Anyway, Sonny went home and said to his mother, "Mama, they have a baby over there that looks just like a monkey." Jack had hair all over his face. You see, the hair wears off before they are born, but Jack was six weeks premature.

You never want the care of a baby like that. You don't sleep. If it hadn't been for my folks, I don't know how I could have done it. I was lucky because my mother and father lived here, and my mother [Stella Buell] came down and stayed with me. We slept with Jack in between us to keep him warm at night. Then we kept hot water bottles packed around him in the daytime. Of course, Mother would go home to the ranch in the daytime. They said not to let him cry too much, so Dad [Ira Buell] would come down and just sit and hold him by the hour to keep him from crying. Dad was a county commissioner and wasn't very busy except for attending commissioner meetings in Buffalo about three days a month and looking at bridges and things. As long as Dad held him, Jack didn't cry too much. He was a 24-hour a day job.

I was so afraid that Betty would be premature because she and Jack was born just 13 months apart. I thought to myself, "How will I ever manage?" because Jack was still an awful lot of care yet, you see. We had to have a special milk for him. The doctor recommended it–some kind of thing we mixed with water.

❦❦❦❦

Thomas M. "Tom" Tisdale
1922-1992
From an interview with Patty Myers
In 1990, when 68 years old

Tales of the Johnson County Cattle War

Interviewer Patty Myers: Tom, what do you want to talk about this morning?

Let's see, when I was little, why, we lived at the extreme north end of Buffalo. It was about a mile from school. Dad [Martin "Mart" Tisdale] was sheriff. Behind the sheriff's office where the parking lot is for the cars now, the kids would play mumble peg and hopscotch and marbles–whatever kids do.

The WPA fellows got paid so much for splitting a cord of wood–people were broke. They would pile the wood up on the sidewalk and against City Hall. I think they got paid by the cord for splitting wood. So I'd go over and bedevil them for a little bit and talk to them. When there wasn't anything else to do, I'd go into the courthouse. After work at 5:00, why, it was usually the same group–A.L. Brock, Tommy Carr, Fred Pettit–seemed like there was some other old-timers that would get in there–and Dad. They just absolutely didn't discuss the Cattle War during working hours. When the rest of the office closed, then they would bring up the Cattle War.

I remember George Adams was always happening in with some story he'd heard about the Cattle War. As soon as he would leave, why, everyone would tell what he had heard and who had told him about it or what they had actually seen. Dad was just kind of a referee. He was only 5 years old at the time of the Cattle War, so he hadn't seen much. I would be around looking at the wanted posters and stuff and heard these stories so many times I couldn't help but digest some of them.

Bill Potts was a night marshal. He got paid some by the stores for going around checking their doors to be sure that the backdoors were closed. People were always going off and leaving the places unlocked, so that was part of his duty.

Bill was a little boy when Billy Deane, a deputy from Johnson County, was killed. They were shearing sheep right west of here about a half a mile. I remember him telling the story about Billy Deane going out and shooting at these outlaws as they came down the river. He started to shoot at them with his rifle, but the rifle jammed, so he jerked his pistol out and was shooting at these fellows, and the fellows just loped on off and didn't pay much attention to him. Later, these fellows came back up the creek. One of them slipped off and shot Billy. I just remember them telling stories–the things that had happened.

One of the stories–at the TA Ranch, why, the little fellows had awful poor guns. If they were going deer hunting, they would get close enough to the deer, but this long distance shooting at the Invaders wasn't part of it. Someplace I got a list of the guns that were taken away from the Invaders–Belgium hunting rifles and some pretty fancy big game guns for that period. So the little fellows weren't getting very close to the TA.

So they decided the guy they wanted to kill the worst was Billy Irvine. So those fellows were getting around down there, and they weren't too worried about getting shot because of the extreme distance. Irvine was out in the horse corral, checking the horses. Anyway, some horses had got shot. In Irvine's letters he tells about having to go out and destroy some of these horses. So Irvine was out in the horse corral. It had been snowing, and they were watching him with field glasses. Jack Flagg insists that Irvine had shot at him here at Kaycee. In 1886, when Irvine came to Buffalo, why, Flagg swore out a warrant for him and accused him of shooting. Irvine denied it in his letters and said that he was on the far side and that he didn't shoot at Flagg. That's as far as it went. Irvine got out of the charges in 1896.

Anyway, Flagg insisted on taking this buffalo gun and shooting at Irvine. Well, everybody was furious. They wanted Harmon Fraker to shoot at him because they didn't want to just be shooting for fun. They wanted to get Irvine. But Flagg prevailed. I guess he was a pretty strong-minded sort of person. So he shot at Irvine. Dad measured the distance. I think he said it was 525 yards. Flagg knocked the bootheel off of Irvine's boot and knocked him down.

Oddly enough, there were several people got shot with gun accidents. If they were all expert gunmen, it looked to me like there was a pretty high percentage of fellows were shot by gun accidents. I suspect that maybe Irvine had these people scared enough of him that they were afraid to say anything. Anyway, this is one of the stories that they would tell.

A story that I think is of interest–when Major Frank Wolcott came out to surrender, he demanded to know who he was surrendering to. Wolcott acted pretty cocky, and Colonel Fechet from Fort McKinney was being about as nice as he could be under the conditions. Major Wolcott was kind of talking down to the Colonel a little bit. Finally, Wolcott declared they would surrender to the United States Army but not that son-of-a bitch. He pointed to Sheriff Red Angus. Well, Wolcott had a double action pistol with ivory grips. When he said he would surrender to the United States Army, he threw the pistol to the ground. Lou Webb was supposed to have picked the pistol up. I've always tried to figure out what happened to that pistol. It's just little stories like that that I think nobody has ever brought up.

Like Omie and Bessie Smith going–when Jack Flagg came to the Smith Ranch and told them about what was happening at Kaycee, they all saddled up. They only had one horse apiece and headed for Kaycee. I don't remember exactly the number of fellows there was supposed to have been. Anyway, they headed for Kaycee and knew they were going to be afoot when they got back. So the two Smith girls–this is a story that came to me from the Moore family. Lee Moore was one of the fellows that was there, and his grandson told me this story. So the girls went up to Hesse's. They knew who was responsible for this deal at Kaycee, so they went up to Hesse's and stole the horse herd, and when the little fellows got back–see, they were getting ready to gather horses for a roundup. They had to get the horses in off the range, and these spring snows were causing them quite a bit of misery. You see, they needed to get these horses in and get them in pretty good shape–feed them oats and maybe in a month's time have them ready for a roundup. They all had one good horse with them, but they had to go start gathering horses and getting horses ready for the roundup. Anyway, when they got back, they knew they were going to be afoot, so they rode to the Invasion on Hesse's horses. When they got back, why, by that time, it was time to go to the Invasion so they were riding Hesse's horses.

Fred Pettit was supposed to have been an awful good cowboy. He was an Englishman. He was a top hand for Hesse. I don't know what he lived off of. He was a justice of the peace or whatever they called them when I was a kid. He was in all these discussions, and they weren't pulling any punches. Okay, this guy saw it this way, and this guy saw it this way, and they were on different sides of the fence. They weren't trying to narrow it down to what really did happen. I guess they all seemed pretty much in agreement that maybe this fellow come in and reported something. He had a tendency to maybe stretch the point a little, and so they would try and figure out which story was most likely to be closest to right. There would be some awful wild stories that were

206

obviously just made up. You know, time changes a lot of things. They would discount stories so fast that didn't make any sense at all. There wasn't any animosity among them.

Tommy Carr–at the time of the Hall cabin incident, he was working for the Bar C and Mike Shonsey. I guess his wife was cooking there, so he kind of got in the doghouse from something he said about when they tried to kill Nate Champion at the Hall cabin. He had to leave there at the time of the killing of George Wellman. The day or two before Wellman was killed, he was at the mouth of Dry Fork. There was quite a few fellows that stayed there at the mouth of Dry Fork. Now, I don't know who all worked there. Wilbur Robbins, I remember him telling me that his parents worked at the Bar C at the time the Hole-in-the-Wall outlaws were around there. I don't know who all did work there.

I know there had been some trouble at the TTT Ranch, and I know Grandfather Hard Winter Davis had quit them at the TTT. I'd heard a rumor that he gave them a speech before he quit them about he didn't want anybody's blood on him. But I never could ever tie that down. Elmer Brock told my brother-in-law, Frank Hinckley, that Grandfather gave them a sermon that would make a Baptist minister blanch. His understanding was they were coming in to protect their own property, and this death list and the people they were going to kill and everything–he didn't want anything to do with it. He lived the rest of his life with Billy Irvine, going around making snide remarks about Grandfather Davis being a coward.

I did a little further checking, and I found out that in the *Northwest Livestock Journal* in 1887, Lee Moore and Nick Ray accepted delivery of a large number of horses–like 125 horses–and they were taking them for the Ogallala Ranch. This would give the Ogallala Ranch a cavy. It seems like it was in the neighborhood of 800 head of horses. Can you imagine that many horses for roundup? But it was huge country they were in, and I guess they would use a lot of horses. So come to find out–this Nick Ray had worked for the Ogallala in Nebraska and then came to Wyoming working for the Ogallala. Some way or another, why, when Lee Moore went to work as kind of a wagon boss under Bill Irvine, working for the Ogallala, which belonged to a fellow named Paxton, why, Moore and Nick Ray got to be pretty good friends. I've got some old tally books and stuff of Irvine's. Nick Ray worked for the outfit for quite a long period of time and was a trusted employee. I got this story from Lee Moore, who is now dead. They pulled out on a roundup wagon–it was to be at certain places on certain days, rain or shine. They were supposed to meet certain schedules, and other wagons would meet them. It was pretty well figured, and there wasn't an awful lot of room for any slack time.

Lee Moore was running this wagon, and they got out on the roundup. Nick Ray's horse stuck a leg in a hole and turned over with him, and they thought he had punctured a lung and broke a collar bone. Ray was really hurting, and they were scared to move him. Well, they made some short circles of cattle and didn't move the bed wagon. They couldn't go off and leave Ray. He didn't seem to get any better, so they loaded him on the bed wagon and took him into the Ogallala. Of course, messing up the schedule of the roundup sure didn't appeal to Billy Irvine very much. He was furious, and he declared Nick Ray was a whiner and no good so-and-so and he didn't want to work anyway and they couldn't leave him there at the ranch. Of course, they run a roadhouse and charged people that came through. Anyhow, finally, to get Ray to the Ogallala to get him taken care of, Lee Moore had to agree that he would pay some horrible sum–like $2.00 a day–to board Ray there until he got well.

So then Lee Moore had to say he would pay this. Moore told Ray, "As soon as you get well enough to travel, take that black horse of mine out of the horse pasture and go up Powder River and look for Nate Champion. Explain to him the situation and tell him I sent you. I'm sure he will let you stay with him until you get healed up." So this is the way it was, and that's what he did.

According to Irvine, Nick Ray stole off of him in Nebraska and followed him to Wyoming and stole off of him here. I guess working for Irvine on Ogallala was stealing off of him. Nick Ray was a rep for him. I've got proof of that from the tally books. He must have been a pretty decent sort of cowboy, or they wouldn't have given him that responsibility.

I told you the story of Ross Gilbertson–about Champion telling my grandfather that when they came into the Hall cabin and told him to throw his hands up, he threw his right hand up and got his pistol with his left hand. Champion was left handed, which they didn't know. They were watching his right hand and couldn't see very good because there wasn't much for windows in this cabin. He was in this double bed with Ross Gilbertson. Gilbertson didn't throw his hands up. He just rolled as far away from Champion as he could get. Well, Champion felt that Gilbertson was in on leading them into the cabin and telling them what they were doing and where they would be. It sure wasn't any outlaw hold out.

There is a story about Hesse and Canton just barely getting away and getting ahead of these guys. They were trying to intercept them when they were going to Douglas. They raced their horses and just barely got away from them. They knew a shortcut and figured some way to get away from all the bad guys. Anyway, they weren't too popular.

By the grapevine, Canton had been trying to get money out of Hesse. He had come back from Alaska and needed money. The little guys' grapevine had got this word. So they take Dad–he was 13 years old–to Buffalo about 45 miles horseback. Anyway, this is the way I remember this story of Dad's. They get to Buffalo where the Stockman's Hotel was back then. That's where the stage stopped. When they get there, Dad and, I guess, these two cowboys–Webb and Gardner–were going to point Canton out. Dad was supposed to go up to Canton–he was supposed to have his pistol stuck back in the waistband of his trousers. Whatever Canton said, Dad was supposed to go up to him and ask, "Are you Frank Canton?" Then Dad was supposed to say, "Well, I'm the son of the man you murdered," and Dad was supposed to go for his gun.

Well, this is where Webb and Gardner come into it. Dad was more scared of Webb and Gardner than he was of Frank Canton. Anyway he got there, and the cattlemen's grapevine had got ahold of Canton. They turned Canton around and sent him back to Cheyenne. This is just one of the stories, and I don't have any reason to doubt it.

🌿🌿🌿🌿

Berlyn H. "Bo" Turk
1911-1990
From an interview with Patty Myers
In 1983, when 72 years old

Will There Be Shootin'?

Interviewer Patty Myers: I know your family has been in Johnson County a long time.

They came in the spring of 1915. My dad had been out here and spent some time and homesteaded in Nine Mile earlier. We came to Buffalo when I was probably about 4 years old. He went to work as a barber for Old Jack Mead and was night policeman.

Did your mom stay out on the homestead?

No, we didn't go out there until 1916. We went to Sussex that next spring, and my dad got a job with Hard Winter Davis. He was ranch foreman and worked at it for years. My mother and the kids lived on the homestead for about three years. I know somebody asked her how old she was one time, and she said, "Well, do I have to count that three years I lived on that homestead?" At that time, you had to plow 30 acres and put it into a small crop. We had a few stock, an old saddle mare, and a saddle horse. Kids grew up fast. We had to hunt rabbits. We had to carry water. Water was the big problem. The only neighbor we had was Clarence Eklund probably five miles away.

Do you remember Hard Winter Davis?

Oh, yes. Mother cooked for the Davises in the wintertime, and we went to school there. The next school I went to was at Sussex. We rode from the Davis place–they called it the Spectacle Ranch at that time. Henry Winter Davis, he was a typical Englishman–a very good man. My older brother was probably 12 or 13. He drove the horse for their carriage for them all the time. Dorothy and Madge Davis were top hands. They didn't ask anybody to ride their horse for them or saddle it. Frank was the youngest. They were all regular ranch people. That big house was across the river. They brought it across on the ice about 1918 up where it is today. When Mr. Davis died, the Bell Cattle Co. took over the ranch, and they never did finish it. Cy Blair came up in 1921 and was the cow foreman for the Bell Cattle Co. They loaned on cattle. I went to work for them in the spring of 1921. I was 11 years old and wrangled horses for roundup. At that time, he paid more than anybody in the country. I got $2 a day.

Did your family hang onto that homestead property?

No, Dad sold it to Ernest Vest, but he bought a ranch from Charlie Hoard. That's where the schoolhouse is on part of that property. He gave them seven acres for the Sussex School. The schoolhouse burnt at Sussex, so they built a new one. They appropriated some money and were to have two years of high school. When anybody asks me how much education did I have, I always say, "Well, I went until the schoolhouse burned!" At least twice we went to school in Buffalo in the early grades–1919 and '20. I had two years high school at Sussex.

Did your dad give up barbering?

No, he never did. The barber shop was adjacent to the saloon, and the freighters would come in. That was the only place where they could take a bath. They stayed open all night, so anytime they come in, they were presentable the next morning. Freighting was a big business. It was the only excitement that they had. My mother used to say that she would sit there and watch those people go out. They didn't want to leave Buffalo very bad. They'd get stuck out in the street, and they'd go out and holler and scream at the horses. Then they'd unhitch the horses and go back to the bar. Of course, the streets were all mud. It'd take four head of horses to pull an empty wagon down the street. They'd turn these freight outfits around in front of Buffalo City Hall. That was a wide spot. They'd get stuck turning around, and that would give them an excuse to stay in town another day. Everything [freight] came out of Buffalo. We'd come up from Sussex. There'd be a string of them–four or five wagons. One time, they told me to go down and get water from North Fork of Powder. They had a big coffeepot, and they said, "Just dip it in there." I came back and said, "It's muddy," and they said, "Just dip it in anyway." I had to get a big stick to dig the coffee grounds out that had settled in that mud, but that's the way they made it good.

When did you become a young man on your own? You were working by age 11.

My dad bought horses when I was probably about 14, and we shipped them East each spring. We broke horses all summer to ship the next year along in the 1920s. I just can't remember being around home much when I was a lad. I didn't live in Buffalo a great lot. I worked for the Cross H Ranch for Wiley Shoumaker. I thought that was better than going to school, I guess. I helped put that water line into Buffalo. They forgot to paint a bunch of that. I think it was 36 inch line that was supposed to be painted on the inside. So they looked us all over. Don Caywood and I were the smallest of all the hired men, so they put us to painting the inside of the pipe. We crawled through and painted the inside of it up to where they forgot to paint it. Don and I were pretty close there!

When did you meet Doris [Doris Dawson Turk]?

Well, we pretty much grew up together–probably around 1926 along in there. Her dad was Jim Dawson. They had land out on Dry Creek. I came trailing a bunch of horses from Meadow Creek where Linch is now to Buffalo to ship. We had about five carloads in this bunch of horses. We stayed all night at Gosney's. There was Earl Sutton and Leo Gosney had a horse outfit. We put these horses in there. They were going to town with a load of whiskey. They made whiskey and took it into dances. There was some big celebrations at Kaycee. Much to the disgust of my brothers and the other trailers, I rode in with them to sell this whiskey. That's when I first met her. It was a carnival and a dance. It was up over what was later the old Golden Rule Store. They had a dancehall up over there, and they had the carnival over in the park. Trailing took two days. We had fast horses and changed saddle horses.

When did you get married?

Well, it will be 52 years this 31st of August that I married Doris Dawson. We were married in Helena, Montana, in 1931. I was on a pipeline job in Helena, and she came up there. I followed that pipeline work and went to Sioux Falls, South Dakota, from there. Then we went into Iowa and to Missoura to help lay some pipe. Got tired of that, so we come back and went to work for Elmer Brock at the Brock Company. Then I went to work at the Veterans' Hospital in Sheridan and worked there five years. They advertised for a barber. When we were small kids, my parents were sticklers on the education. Because my dad was a barber, he'd make us practice shaving a jug and cutting each other's hair. The war broke out, and we did whatever had to be done at the hospital.

Sheriff Mart Tisdale - 1940

In 1929, I worked as the deputy sheriff and police in Kaycee for a year. That was my first law experience. Mart Tisdale was sheriff, and I worked under him. Talton Taylor was wanted for murder. Somebody told Tisdale he would be at a ranch, so I went up with him. I wondered all the way there if we're going into shootin', you know, but we walked into the ranch, and everybody was eating super. Had a long table, and there were people there. I thought we were gonna start shootin'! So we went through a porch and hung our coats up with everybody else's and sat down at the table. Tisdale sat across from Talton there. We ate supper, and when we got ready to go, Tisdale said, "Well, I guess we better go. Talton, you got your stuff all ready? You ready to go?" We walked out and got in the car. I got in the backseat. We got to Kaycee, and he dropped me off. They never mentioned anything about shooting. They talked about trapping and everything else. Taylor knew that if he ever went for a gun, Tisdale'd shoot him, so that's all

211

there was to it. I would never have known it was a sheriff and a prisoner. He didn't mention what he was picking him up for–didn't give him his Miranda rights. Then in 1945 in March, I went to work for the Sheridan Police Department. In 1948, I was Night Chief. In the spring of '51, I was Chief there until '56 when I went to Buffalo. Cy Blair got elected mayor and offered me what I thought was a better deal, so I went to Buffalo as Chief of Police. I was there for 10 years. Then I was elected Sheriff and was Sheriff for 10 years.

What were the feelings when the sheepmen and Basques started taking hold?

Well, I don't think there were any hard feelings. When the Depression hit and the drought and the pestilence, the dry farmer couldn't make it. The Basques were able to get money, and they bought up that land. That's how they got it. I don't know where they got the money. That's how they got their foothold. When I was a small lad, the Scotch had all the sheep. The Scots were the ones that brought all the sheep to Johnson County–the Scotch Outfit, the Youngs. Well, it was about 1919 and '20 they run out of feed, and they were all gonna bring them into Buffalo. They could bring feed in on the railroad. It started to rain up in the higher country. They took the wagon boxes and chained them together and made a floating bridge clear across Powder River at old Fort Reno, and something like 30,000 sheep they run through, but they lost them all before they got to Buffalo–wiped them out.

Entertainment?

We didn't have time. We worked in that hay all summer long putting it up and all

Old Time Hay Stacker

winter throwing it out to stock. The only picnic we had was when we went out to gather stock. You get a little tired of bivouacking by the time you get on top of the mountain with your stock. I went up on the mountains, pulling wagons or trailing herd, but I never spent any time on the mountains.

Tell me about the sporting houses in town.

I'll tell you a good story. Do you remember Gray Norval? He came to Buffalo when he was 16 and got a job with the Colorado Ditch Company. They were going to irrigate everything from the Bighorns to the Belle Fourche River. They built a reservoir. You can still see signs of it up there at Elgin Park. That's where he was working. They paid him, so he went down to cash his check. Everybody told him, "You can go up to Maggie Jesse's. She cashes checks." Old August Hettinger was the marshal and a forest ranger. He was the law. Anyway, Gray started up there about 2:00 in the afternoon, and Old August Hettinger asked him, "Boy, where are you goin'?" Gray said, "I'm goin' up to Maggie Jesse's and cash my check," and Hettinger told him, "No, you don't. You be a gentleman. You wait till dark and sneak up there!"

What about the gypsies who used to camp in Buffalo?

Well, the only story I know about the gypsies–the city council got a letter. They didn't call themselves gypsies, but they said there were 80 trailer houses that wanted to spend a week in the park to rest up and they had heard it was a friendly community. So the council told me, "Run them out," so I said, "Put it in writing," but they wouldn't put it in writing. When they put the parking meters in, they put two meters over in the park for the tourists. They'd open up those meters about once a month, and there'd be a few dimes–60¢. These gypsies–I met them and escorted them down into the park. When they left there, they put $25 in them meters. I've found that if you treat people right, they'll treat you right back. Oh, they piled up their junk, and it took a truck to haul it off. They bought tires and changed tires on their cars.

Do you remember any of the Indians that used to visit Buffalo?

Oh, yes, they used to have a fair–had them Indian dances. A lot of people knew the Indians–called them by name. They'd go out there and dance with the Indians. Get some moonshine in them and go out and dance all night with the Indians.

🌿🌿🌿🌿🌿

Louise Brown Turk
1921-2013
From a Johnson County Historical Society presentation
In 1987, when 92 years old

Family Life During the Great Depression

I was born in November 1921 just as the country was beginning to feel a letdown following the end of World War I. I kept hearing the grownups talking about something called a Depression. I wasn't sure what it was, but I knew it was something bad. Whatever it was, I was pretty sure we were safe from it until one night after my brother, Danny, was born, I overheard Mom and Dad [Daniel T. And Helen Skinner Brown] talking. Mom had given birth to three babies in two and a half years. James, Ruthie, and Danny had all happened so close together that none of them was paid for. James had died a few hours after he was born, so they also had the expense of a funeral. As young as I was, I recognized the worry in their voices.

We had to walk through Waugh Murphy's barnyard on our way to school, and sometimes we stopped to talk to Waugh and his hired man, a little Frenchman named Paul Lahitte. His English was so poor he may as well have spoken Chinese as far as I was concerned. We returned home from school one evening late in the fall and discovered Paul had moved into our bunkhouse. With winter coming on, Waugh no longer had work for him. Dad told Paul he could stay in our bunkhouse and work for his room and board. When spring came, he planted the garden and began taking care of it. He ended up spending the rest of his life with us and became as much a part of the family as if he were born into it. He shared the good times and the bad–the trials and the tribulations.

The Depression worsened steadily, and I suddenly realized we were the victims of it the same as millions of other people. The years 1933 and 1934 were terrible drought years in Wyoming. I can remember walking home from school in the afternoons, and the air was so filled with dust that the sun looked like a big orange-red ball in the western sky. I hated the way things looked with no blue sky or clouds and just that dirty air hanging over all of us.

I didn't realize until years later that sheep and cattle were dying of starvation. A lot of the livestock was in such poor condition they could not be shipped, and even if they could, there was no market for them. The government paid a token price for each animal–about $14 a head for the cattle and $2 each for sheep–and slaughtered them.

I remember very well a day in September of 1934 that my dad took all of our old ewes to be slaughtered under one of the government programs. The sheep were killed at a site on the Meike Ranch just a short distance from Powder River. According to an eyewitness, Jack Andrew, the sheep were killed by hitting them in the head with a small sledgehammer. I was filled with horror that anyone could wantonly slaughter all those sheep. I realize now that it was probably more humane than letting them starve.

Not all the sheep that were killed were starving, but with feed so scarce and no market at all for livestock, ranchers took part in the project just to realize a little money from the old cows and ewes they had. It meant they wouldn't have to winter them and could put the feed into the younger stock. The government condemned the meat from the slaughter and prohibited the distribution of any of it for food. Whenever a ewe in good condition was killed, the hindquarters were salvaged and hung in a big cottonwood tree by the kill site. However, when the government men left that night, they said that whatever happened to that meat after they were gone was none of their concern, so everyone, including my dad, helped themselves.

I don't really know what happened to the rest of my dad's sheep, but I guess he sold them to pay the overdue lease on the ranch. Without them we had no way of making a living because the ranch was too small to support itself without livestock to eat the hay and grain.

Dad had filed on a homestead on Four Mile before he met Mom, but he relinquished that filing and refiled on a homestead on the north side of the Pine Ridge six miles southeast of Sussex. He renewed the filing several times as provided by the Homestead Act. He either had to prove up on it or let it revert back to the government, so he decided to move to the homestead. We could live there rent free, and he hoped to get ranch work or a Works Project Administration job.

In February we began packing. How do you pack the accumulation of 19 years of marriage–the contents of a 10-room house moving into a 12x18 foot cabin? When we moved to the homestead, Paul faithfully came with us. Three adults, six kids, and an assortment of cats, dogs, chickens, one canary, cattle, and horses made the move.

Dad always said he wanted to live where he could see in all directions, and the site he picked for our homestead cabin certainly met those qualifications. Our little settlement crouched on a flattop hogback and a clearing in the sagebrush–sun baked in the summer, blasted by blizzards in fall, winter, and spring, and in the path of every wind that blew. But no one ever sneaked up on us. We could see for miles in every direction except the south where the Pine Ridge rose up a quarter of a mile away.

I'm not sure what kind of a deal Dad made for the cabin. He got it in the fall 1935 and moved it onto the homestead. Several neighborhood men helped him jack it up and put skids under it. They moved it from the Gibbs homestead to ours with tractors. Dad borrowed Cy Blair's ranch truck to move everything out to the homestead. He could get only within a quarter of a mile of the cabin with the truck because of an uncrossable draw, so everything was unloaded into a pile, then hauled to the cabin with a team and wagon. Mom and the younger kids unpacked and moved things into the cabin while Dad made several more trips to the ranch until he had everything moved and piled in the draw.

Meanwhile, my brother, Fred, and I were on horseback driving the cows. There were about 15 head–mostly milk stock–and a Durham bull. We arrived tired and hungry with the herd. There was no fence, so all we could do was turn them loose and hope they would stay. They did until they got rested up from the trek out there. From then on, Fred and I spent every day hunting them and bringing them back from wherever they strayed to. We fought them all that summer until Dad sold them in the fall because we didn't have any winter feed for them.

Our first night on the homestead was a memorable one. We had a borrowed sheep wagon that Marsh and Paul slept in. Mom and Dad slept on a three quarter-size bed in the cabin, and the rest of us made beds on the floor using every bit of available space.

Arranged around the walls of the cabin was a big iron cookstove, a dresser, Mom's Singer sewing machine, the bed, Dad's big rolltop desk, a bookcase converted to a dish cupboard, a homemade kitchen counter, and a homemade corner cabinet that held the water bucket and wash basin. A homemade dining table stood in the middle of the room. We had no chairs, so we used wooden apple crates to sit on. During the day, these were pushed under the table when not in use to give more floor space. At night they were stacked on top of the table so one of the smaller kids could sleep under the table.

This was a pretty drastic change from our two-story 10-room house, but we were young, and we soon adjusted to our primitive lifestyle. I suppose it must have been harder on Mom than it was for the rest of us, having everyone under foot and everything crammed into such a small space. One thing that was simplified was housekeeping. Once the bed was made and all the bedding folded or rolled and stacked on the bed, the bare wood floor was quickly swept and scrubbed. As soon as warmer weather came, Fred and I moved outdoors with our beds.

Water or the lack of it was a never-ending problem. When we first moved to the homestead, some little grassy-bottom potholes held clean rainwater and provided us with good drinking water. Dad had built a reservoir the year before in a draw east of the cabin. It filled with clean snow water during runoff, and we used this for drinking water too. When warmer weather came though, we found our water supply inhabited by a variety of water creatures, ranging from water dogs to the many-legged black beetles that were in the mud at the bottom. We finally managed to acquire several 60-gallon wood vinegar barrels from the Sussex Store and started hauling water from the American Ranch. Dad would load the empty barrels on the box wagon, hitch up the team, and make the long trip into civilization and back. It took all day to make the 16-mile round trip. The water always tasted slightly of vinegar. We soon learned not to waste one drop of water. In winter, we kept a water barrel in the cabin next to the big range to keep it from freezing. There was always a dishpan full of clean snow melting on the back of the stove. As the snow was converted to water, it was added to the barrel. We always strained it through a clean cloth because there was apt to be some foreign material, such as rabbit droppings or sage leaves in the snow.

As soon as we got settled at the homestead, we dug postholes and fenced the yard and garden. The ground was like cement, so it was hard physical labor. Using a crowbar and axe, we built a cellar which gave Mom some much-needed storage space for a lot of things including a number of eight-pound lard pails full of clean rendered mutton tallow. Dad complained about her insisting on moving all that tallow to the homestead, but it turned out later to be a godsend.

We planted a garden and carried the water from our reservoir. Every step of it was up hill. As the weather got hotter and drier, our enthusiasm for gardening grew cooler. Every day the sun blazed down without a sprinkle of rain, and every day the garden looked sorrier. Then as the prairie grass dried up, the rabbits moved in to eat what green stuff there was. We moved an old army cot out into garden, but the rabbits came right up and ate the vegetables under the cot with someone sleeping on it.

Dad sold the Durham bull and with that money bought a tent large enough for the army cot and a three quarter-sized bed to fit in. When fall came, he boarded up the sides of the tent, and we made a stove out of a metal barrel. As luck would have it, that turned out to be a really severe winter. Our barrel stove would be white-hot when we went to bed, but in an hour it would be stone cold. Fred and Danny slept on the bed, and Ruthie and I shared the cot. I think we would have frozen to death in bed if we hadn't been sleeping two to a bed. Worse than getting in bed at night was getting up in the morning. Looking back, I wonder how we ever survived.

There was no bank near the cabin where we could build a dugout, so the next sum-

216

mer, we dug a large hole away from the cabin and put a cellar-type roof on it to keep the snow off the steps and built a stairway down into it. Before winter came again we were snugly housed in our dugout.

In the early spring of 1937, Dad's bank in Buffalo contacted him and offered him a deal on a small band of old ewes that the Eychaner Ranch was selling. Dad agreed to their terms, and once more, we were in the sheep business. The timing couldn't have been worse. We got them in the early spring before they lambed, and it began to rain almost immediately. These ewes had wintered poorly, and being old ewes, I suppose, their teeth were bad, so they weren't faring too well on our short grass.

Our land was gumbo, which when wet sticks and clings in huge clumps to whatever it comes in contact with. I can still see those poor old ewes heavy with unborn lambs and weighed down with wet wool slogging solidly through the mud trying to find something to eat. Every little bit, one would collapse and lie there in the mud rolling her eyes in despair. No amount of urging would get one of them back on their feet again, and attempts to stand them up were futile. Their legs just simply would not hold them up. Most of the ones that went down never got up again, so we took a loss right off the bat. As it turned out, that was the last rain we had all summer. Then the grasshoppers moved in and ate what little grass hadn't already burned to a crisp. The leased range conditions continued to deteriorate, and we finally lost the sheep. By the time the bank foreclosed, we were all relieved to see them go. They had netted us absolutely no income and many hours of grief, not to mention the expense of a leased pasture at Midwest.

After we moved to the homestead, Dad and Paul had a few government jobs using our team of horses, but even those jobs were far and few between, so we had no income most of the time. We lived for the most part on beans and cottontail rabbits. About a quarter of a mile north of the cabin was a big flat bottom draw that was full of brush and had lots of banks where the rabbits seemed to really thrive and multiply. Fred and I hunted them with a .22 rifle until we ran out of shells and had no money to buy more. Then we took Marsh's muskrat traps and trapped the rabbits at their den. It must have been a good year for rabbits, and it was a good thing for my family that they were plentiful. The second year we were on the homestead Mom started a lot of tomato plants in the house but decided it would be a waste of time to set them out, so she gave them to Pete Meike. That fall he brought us two bushels of tomatoes ranging from green to ripe. He also brought us some of the biggest squash I ever saw.

Dad left on a temporary job and took what money he still had left from a WPA job and bought us a five-pound box of cheese and a slab of bacon. We feasted like kings for a while. Big chunks of squash baked with a strip of bacon was a tasty treat beyond imagining after the diet we had been on. The cheese and tomatoes were almost too good to be true. Later in the fall about the time our bonanza of food ran out, Islingers brought us several heads of cabbage from their garden, and a dry farmer from the Fifteen Mile area brought us 100 pounds of dry navy beans. After the cabbage was gone, we were back to beans and rabbit. We had run out of flour, so Mom could no longer bake bread. The government gave big bags of bran to anyone who wanted it for feed for milk cows. We no longer had the cows, but we still had two bags of bran. Mom mixed it with salt and water and fried it in patties in the mutton tallow she had brought from the ranch. The tallow was very stale but clean, so even though it wasn't tasty, it did add a necessary element to our diets.

Keeping the kids in school got to be our biggest problem. All they had for school lunches was rabbit and bran–dough gods as we called them–fried in mutton tallow. Our credit had been shut off at the Sussex Store because we owed the incredible amount of $80, so until something was paid on it, we couldn't buy anything. The kids came home every night, vowing they would not go back to school the next day because the other kids teased them about their lunches.

Mom kept the kids nicely dressed because she was a good seamstress and had plenty of material to work with. My aunt sent castoff dresses and coats that Mom ripped up and made over into dresses, shirts, pants, and coats. Shoes were the biggest problem. Not only were the kids hard on shoes, they were growing as well. Dad had a cobbler outfit complete with different-sized lasts, wax thread, and a big piece of sole leather. Fred became the family cobbler and with practice was quite expert at shoe repair. He patched and resoled the kid's shoes until there was just nothing left to work on. Finally, the day came when Mom was forced to keep the kids home from school, since they were the same as barefoot. She told the bus driver not to come for them anymore.

Of course, it was only a matter of days before the teacher notified the county superintendent that the Brown children had been withdrawn from school. She, in turn, passed the information to the proper authorities. The next thing we knew a man from the relief office arrived at the homestead. When he departed his briefcase held a completed questionnaire bearing all the information about the destitute Brown family. Dad had steadfastly refused to even consider relief. Having to ask for welfare was to him a shameful thing–an acknowledgment of failure to care for his family. His pride simply would not let him do it. However, when the decision was taken out of his hands, I think he must have been greatly relieved to know that his family would be taken care of. Mom must have felt as if a terrible burden had been lifted from her when we received the first month's check–$19. A week later sporting new shoes from Montgomery Ward, the kids were back in school.

Even with the relief check we lived mostly on beans. We bought flour, yeast, salt, and lard. Mom could bake bread for sandwiches for the kids' lunches, and they were able to have cheese and peanut butter, but we hadn't had potatoes in months, nor eggs since we arrived at the homestead. Our chickens had barely survived that first summer on the homestead, but with fall coming on we had no place to keep them and nothing to feed them, so we ate them.

Although we had some tough times on the homestead, we also had a lot of good times. The experience didn't hurt us a bit, and it gave us an appreciation of the necessities of life.

🌿🌿🌿🌿

Robert E. "Bob" Twing
1925-2024
From an interview with Nancy Tabb
In 2017, when 92 years old

Lots of Memories

I shouldn't tell this on myself. Anyway, I remember in high school where a certain teacher's room was. We had all signed up for her class, so we got there, and come to find out, we were way overbooked that first day. Well, I was one of the last ones to come into the classroom. Just as I walked through the door, somebody picked up an eraser off the blackboard and smacked me in the face with it. Well, what was my reaction? I picked it up, and just as I threw it, the teacher walked in the door, so I got sent to see Mr. Strother. I ended up taking World History instead of that class. But that class wound up at least every week having a 500 or 1,000 word essay all the way through that school year. I liked my World History class. I'm glad I got out of that other class.

I can remember an old Dodge that my dad had. Of course, at that time it wasn't old, but it must have been a late 1920s model. It had the side curtains with the plastic windows on it. Whenever you went anywhere, you always carried at least one spare tire besides the one that was on the car–sometimes two–because you were gonna have flat tires. The tires in those days weren't like nylon, you know, so it seemed like you was always changing tires.

My dad tells the story that he was going from the ranch there at Rock Creek over to the old ranch above Banner, and, at that time, there was just a two-track that ran on the west side of Lake DeSmet just out in the sagebrush. So he started down that sagebrush road, and here comes another farmer in a Model T. I mean it is just two tracks. Well, Dad moved–just got out of the tracks. The other fellow saw him, but he made the same move towards Dad. Dad kept moving over, but the fellow kept coming toward him, and the fellow ran into Dad out there in the sagebrush. Dad said the fellow had just bought this Model T, and with no top on it he was just standing up holding the steering wheel and hollering "whoa, whoa."

I'll tell you a little side story in that same area that just came to mind. There was a young couple that started ranching over in that area and built a house. I can't tell you just where, but it was on the west side of the lake. They had mail service once a week. It would come out, and this woman would walk up to the top of the ridge where the road was. Of course, in those days, it wasn't even a county road–just a two-track, I should say. She was with child, probably seven months so quite heavy. So she went up to get the mail. It was open range at that time, and they had brought in a bunch of steers from Texas–big longhorn steers. She started up there, and this one started following her and then took after her–no place to go and no trees to hide behind, you know. She gathered herself together the best she could and tried to run. Out of nowhere this cowboy came, roped this steer, and held it till she got away.

The only snakes we had around was the prairie rattlers. Of course, around Lake DeSmet they claim there was an old volcanic area with the red scoria–great place for snakes. When I was a kid growing up over on the east side of the lake, there was actually two hot air holes. You could go there anytime of the year, and there would be hot air. Of course, in the wintertime, those rattlesnakes would come back to those places and den up in those holes to be warm. When we used to drive cattle from the ranch around the south end of the lake to get over to the property, if we didn't get five or six snakes in the drive, it was a poor day. Sometimes we would get as many as 10. If cattle get on a rattlesnake and it starts hissing, the cattle will spread. I only had one cow that I can truthfully say was bit by a rattler.

Bob & Betty Twing

When I was in the service in 1943, Ernie West, a government trapper, went to those hot air holes up there. This is when they first came up with cyanide gas. He got some about the size of a pop can and took one of those and wired a blasting cap on it and dropped it down that hole and worked it down as far as he could. Then he covered it with dirt and exploded it. When I came back from the service, it was a couple of years before you even found a snake hole.

I was deputy sheriff for a while. You know, we was having some problems out in the country, so they deputized me. This was way back in time. There was a miniature Bonnie and Clyde–this fellow and a 16-year-old girl. I think he was 19. Anyway, they headed out from Nebraska. I think that they killed her mother and then stole her car. Then they killed two or three other people. I was called in on that. We got a call from the southern part of the state that they were coming this way. They called the sheriff out here, and he called me and told me, "You man the radio in the office while I'm gone." So I was there for not quite 48 hours. They caught them before they got up here because the next step was I was gonna have to set up a roadblock.

One Friday, we were haying a little early–a good 10 days earlier than usual. We had baled but didn't have enough hay to top the stack out to finish the pyramid, so all of the bales were out in the field. We were having the noon day meal, and as I recall, for some reason I had let the boys go to town that was helping me. We wasn't going to start anything until the next Monday. So we were having the noon meal. It was a little cloudy, but all of a sudden we had a terrific ball of lightning that hit pretty close. We got up and went out on the porch and looked, and this storm just came on west and boiled over us. It was a horrendous storm–no hail in it, just water. Actually, you couldn't see 30 feet in it. It was a cloud burst. It rained 4.3 inches of water in 45 minutes. Man, water was just everywhere across the fields!

It run down our well, so that wasn't good. The next day we got out and was looking around. Betty, my wife, said maybe we ought to bank up around that well because it was only about a foot high. I said it will never happen again. Well, the next day we were eating lunch, and the same thing happened. The same cloud came over the same way. It fell 3.4 inches that day in 40 minutes. It washed out culverts, fences, everything. All the hay meadows were covered with silt and branches and mud.

My neighbors over there–two of them were working on Johnson Creek and got caught in that flood. They climbed up a tree and stayed there until the water went down. I guess it was pretty scary with 6 or 8 feet of water under them. The next day they were out there cleaning up and got caught in practically the same tree and went through the same thing. I told them they are awful slow learners. We had seen big storms before but never one right after another particularly in the same exact area.

When I was in the service, one Sunday was open post. I was laying across my bunk, writing letters, and a fellow from across the hall came in and said, "Hey, Wyoming, how would you like to go meet some neat girls?" Best offer I had had all day. These guys had been down to the USO the night before and had met some girls. This one girl had invited them up to her house that evening. She told them, "Pick up a couple more boys if you can, and we will make it a foursome. We'll go to church Sunday night." That was something the colonel had told us. He said, "On Sunday if you are not in church, you will not be on the sidewalks of this town." You were either in the dorm or you were in church. Anyway, Sunday night, I caught the bus and headed out there to this girl's place. I was the first one there, so she told me, "Just go back on in the living room. There is a neighbor girl already here." So I walked in, and Betty was setting there all by herself. I walked in and stuck out my hand and said, "Hi, I'm Bob Twing," so she stood up and said, "I'm Betty Garner." That started a conversation that lasted 70 years. We were married 69 years.

When I wrote that blue book, *West of the Bozeman Trail*, it really sold well locally. I sold over 800 copies. The people that's read it have said that it is their heritage too. I wrote it for my kids basically. Then the neighborhood kids said, "Hey, that is our heritage. We helped you move cattle and all that, so it is our heritage too." A lot of them are in it, you know. I am working on some short stories now. We are looking at 40 stories, and I should finish number 37 the next day or so [*On the Banks of Sayles Creek* published in 2015]. You know, before Betty passed away in 2014, we had started writing this book–her and I–the blue book. She made it through that book but not the second book.

I hadn't been in church for about three years with me taking care of Betty. I didn't want to go off and leave her. So after she passed away, I started going back to church. I was in Sunday school class, and we had a visiting pastor at that time. This pastor put out a challenge, "Do you know what you have that the Lord can use?" A Sunday or two later, when I was in Sunday school class, something came up, and I had lived through that experience, so I shared that with the class. Some of the class came around afterwards and thanked me for sharing. The first book started with my granddaughter saying, "Grandpa, all these stories you have been writing for me are great." My daughter had kept them all, and we have got a book now. Who would have thought? So that is where my writing books really started. [Robert Twing published his third book, *Kicking Up Dust*, in 2018.]

彬彬彬彬彬

Mary Kilkenney Voiles
1895-1977
From a KBBS Radio program
In 1976, when 84 Years Old

The Reservoir Broke

Early Sunday morning about 3:00 a man came to our door and knocked. He didn't tarry. He just came to the door and knocked and said, "Get out and flee for your lives because Kearney Lake Reservoir has broken, and all that water is coming down Piney Creek." Well, Mother drug us kids out of bed and drug us out to a root cellar we had about a quarter of a mile from the house that was on a hill. Father rushed out to the barn and hooked up the team and went up a little ways to shut off an irrigation ditch that came down through our yard. Then he come back and threw in a little food and a few blankets and a can of water into the wagon. Just as he was crossing that irrigation ditch going to the hills where we were, he looked up and saw this wall of water coming. They said that it was about a 75 foot wall of water. Well, he just raced the horses to the hill. We just stood out there on the hill and watched that water.

Well, we probably watched that water coming, oh, for four or five hours. It was a huge wall of water. There was stock and rocks and trees–everything you can imagine coming down in that flood of water. You could look across Piney Creek and just barely see the top of the big old cottonwood trees there, so you know how deep that water was. Well, we watched the flood for a while, and the folks built a campfire and fixed us some breakfast. Of course, nobody had eaten breakfast. We were sitting out there around that campfire when a team and wagon drove up. It was George Buell and his family. They had come from the lake. They had been over there fishing. Of course, Sunday morning they thought they would just drive over and spend the day with us. Well, it was a pretty discouraging looking site when you looked at all that water because it was still rolling. From where they came from the Buells had known nothing about the flood.

🌿🌿🌿🌿

Gilbert L. "Gil" Walker
1925-2024
From an interview with Craig Cope
In 1991, when 66 years old

Life in the Bighorn Mountains

Interviewer Craig Cope: Gil, when did you come to Wyoming?

I came to Wyoming in July 1954 to go into the logging business after having logged in California and Oregon. We moved into Hyattville to log with the Coal Springs Lumber Company. At that time, Coal Springs Lumber Company was a partnership of the Seymour Brothers and Ray Hanson, my father-in-law. Ray had been in the logging business ever since he was a child–not too much education, but he was really an excellent logger that could make some money in the timber business.

How long did you spend on the Hyattville–Basin side of the mountain before you came over to Johnson County?

We were logging in the Hyattville area and up above Deer Haven Lodge from 1954 until 1969. At that time, Ray sold his sawmill, and I worked several years for Wyoming Sawmills and other loggers before I went to work for the Forest Service. We moved into Buffalo in 1972. I was dispatched on a project with the Buffalo District of the Forest Service as an equipment operator. We had a large backlog of slash disposal in the Caribou Mesa area, which amounted to, I think, around 1,500 acres. We moved into the Hunter Station work center house and lived there approximately one year until we purchased a home in Buffalo and moved downtown.

Did you do any work besides logging before you went to work for the Forest Service?

Yes. We had a ranch at Hyattville, which we bought in 1955. We were there for 10 years, raising cattle and sheep and still in the logging business. My family took care of the ranch, and in my spare time I helped out. That included a lot of fencing and irrigating. I did work on some oil rigs. When I came to Wyoming, I was looking for a different type of work than logging, but after working on the oil drilling units off and on for three or four years, it wasn't an occupation I really liked.

I understand you had a lodge east of Ten Sleep.

When we sold our ranch after 10 years, we went back to Oregon and leased a ranch with some cattle, but the weather was extremely costly for raising cattle there, and we discovered that Wyoming was by far the cheapest for trying to make any money in the livestock business. After we finished our lease in Oregon, we moved to Ten Sleep. We were logging again up above Meadowlark Resort. We started hauling out on the highway through Deer Haven Lodge. Before that, we had built a road from Hyattville. Hyattville Logging Road is being used yet. We built that road for approximately $5,000 with a small crew. We didn't put many culverts in. It was just a haul road for logging. It wasn't a high standard road by any means. That was probably 1960. We bought the Canyon Lodge, which was up in the canyon six miles east of Ten Sleep. It had eight motel units and a cafe which Arlene, my wife, gradually worked up to a very good clientele in the restaurant business. We built a 50-seating restaurant. She had smorgasbords every weekend and did quite well with the food end of things. It was quite marginal for trying to make any money, since it was out-of-town for tourists to stop. When they left the Black Hills or Buffalo, they were heading to Yellowstone Park. If you got a good tourist year and there was no place to stay in Buffalo, then sometimes you would get quite a few people. Usually, your tourist season started the 20th of June, and by August the 20th it was about over. We did guide hunters for 10 years and had an outfitting service. Arlene and I both guided and did quite well. At that time, out-of-staters could not hunt on the National Forest without a guide. We had out-of-state fellows that came back every year, and it was a way that we supplemented our income to make the payments.

Tell me about some of the old-timers that were working on the mountain.

Andy Hanson was still running a post and pole operation logging with horses. He started that mill after working for the tie outfits that were in there. That was probably in the 1930s and '40s. Andy told me that once there were five camps back in there and that they hand-hewed the ties and floated them down to Buffalo on Clear Creek. His operation was salvaging what was left. He used an old set of gin poles. He skidded with a horse and then loaded the logs up onto his truck with the horse using a single pulley. Then he would haul the logs over to his mill. He made a lot of house logs too. He wintered and stayed all year up in the Sourdough area. He had cabins set up and a corral. The people he employed stayed right in the camp. His sawmill set up right there above the righthand fork of Sourdough Creek. The sawdust pile would get close to the creek, so they would burn it every year. Andy finally left due to his health and moved downtown. His cabins were sold, and the land was reseeded and put back to natural as best we could at that time.

Tell me about work that you did in the District.

Well, one project that was always, I thought, top priority in the District that we worked on was trying to get the Crazy Woman Canyon back to where people could travel. The CCCs built that road in the 1930s using jackhammers and all types of older equipment. They had the surface in very good shape and the drainage. As the years went by, the Forest Service contracted or had a co-op agreement with the County to take care of that road. Due to changing of people that came to the District for some reason, there was some discrepancy in the way they were doing their work and the County was not allowed to do the work anymore. At that time, the forest was going through some money pains and didn't have any money to do maintenance on these types of roads, so Crazy Woman's road got in such terrible shape in the early 1970s that you could hardly get down through there with a touring car or a sedan. Clear through probably 1978, the road kept getting less and less attention. We got like $500 for the whole road system so got very little work done on it. Due to hailstorms and snow melt, the drainage got so it couldn't handle the water and made ruts in the road. Because it was identified on the State maps as a through road to Highway 16 from Old Highway 87, numerous people would try to go up there with their cars and drag the oil pans and ruin the bottoms of their cars. So, it was really a good project that they got completed around 1989.

The trails in the District require a lot of attention every year, and I was involved with them quite a bit. There has been a lot of money put into recreation trails these last few years. One thing that really was successful was when Craig Cope got the private individuals, like Paradise Guest Ranch, to do some of the maintenance in a co-op agreement on the trails that they use so heavily in the dude business. Jim Anderson, who is at Paradise now, has done an excellent job. Plus they pay quite a fee to use the trails, which a lot of people don't know.

𝒲𝒲𝒲𝒲𝒲

Roda McBride Wall
1897-1976
From a KBBS Radio program
In 1975, when 78 years old

Living at a Former Fort

K*BBS Radio Host: Roda has already begun her story. We start the conversation here.*

Well, I was very fond of going to school, and when the school burned, it was a very terrible thing. They soon rebuilt the grade school the following year. I don't recall just what month the school burned, but it was winter. I think it was after Christmas. All the pupils who were in that building had to be sent to school in various places in town. I was attending a white frame building.

Where did your grandfather come from?

He came from Nebraska, where he had been teaching. He came out here and was interviewed and saw the lay of the land and was delighted with it and took the job. Sam, my brother, was just a baby. Sam often told the joke on himself that he had come to Wyoming for his health. When people would ask, "What was the matter with you?" he'd say, "Well, I was 3 weeks old and had the colic."

Where did they live?

First, they lived on the east side of the creek down below the bridge. Papa bought a little ranch were Mrs. Janice Norval lives. I don't know when it was because it was before I was on the scene. However, that was where I was born.

When did you move to the house south of town?

Well, he moved there when I was 4 years old. He had lived down at the little ranch that he bought probably three years before that. Then we lived at the Soldiers' Home. There was a great number of houses for the people who were coming into the town and the military. It was no longer a post, and there was no longer soldiers up there. They had all these houses that were vacant, and the military gave civilians a right to move up there. I was too young to remember when we moved. My earliest recollections are living at the post. I remember quite a few things that happened after we moved. I don't remember anything prior to that. I don't know how many there were living up there. Mrs. Tisdale and her children lived next door to us on one side, and Jack Flagg's family lived on the other side, and the Alvin T. Clark family lived up there. There was a family by the name of Weir from down on Lower Powder River that lived up there, and there were several other families that I don't remember their name. They were nice two-story homes. They had a wonderful staircase to slide down. They had nice posts where we would land and play. They had a big woodshed at the back. It was really a delightful place to live. There were trees and places for gardens. There were big red barns behind each one of them for, I suppose, just the riding horses that the cavalry used. It was a cavalry post. We had great times playing in those barns. My first Christmas recollection is there. We were permitted to use those buildings. We had a good many group entertainments up at the dancehall besides dances. We all took food–sort of a potluck thing– and had a Christmas program. There was a beautifully decorated Christmas tree, and each family took their family gifts up there for their children. I don't remember anything of the dinner, nor do I remember anything of the entertainment. As any tiny child would be, I was interested in having Santa come. I was standing on a chair between my father and mother so I could see better, and when Santa came out, I said in a shrill, childish voice, "That's not Santa Claus. That's Jack Flagg."

How long was Fort McKinney active?

I don't remember how long the fort was active. After the cavalry were moved out–it was I don't know when–but they sent soldiers down to the TA Ranch during the Johnson County Invasion, so there were soldiers there in 1892.

Fort McKinney

Were you around during the Cattle War?

No, that was before my time. My father was here. He was a very friendly man. Each side would tell him their story, and they would want him to side with them. As a teacher, he always told them, "Now, I have your children in school. I have no opinions about the Invasion. I don't own a cow." He always said that the white-caps always walked down the east side of the street, the rustlers walked down the west side of the street, and he walked down the middle of the street. I don't remember any of those things except in our games at school we chose up the white-caps and the rustlers and played games. It carried over a long while.

Was there hostility among the school children?

Yes, there was some hostility among the children. It would creep in. I guess I walked down the middle. The churches, of course, they lost their attendance. People wouldn't go to the church that the other side went to. A number of years after it all happened, Mrs. Lydia Munkres and Mrs. Sibyl Mather were much distressed. They were sisters-in-law. They had big houses and loved to give parties. They hesitated to give a party, but, finally, as my mother told me, everyone in town was invited to a party. They didn't know how many would come, of course, but they prepared a great deal of food. In those days, when you had a party, you didn't just have tea and cookies. It wasn't a cocktail party. You had salads and sandwiches and two kinds of cake and two kinds of ice cream and all sorts of good things. When it came time to serve the food, Mother was in the kitchen helping them–they were both good friends of hers–and they were worried that they were going to run out of food. Toward the end of serving, why, Mrs. Mather drew her hand across her brow–it was a warm summer August afternoon– and she said, "Who would have ever known all the dern fools would come?" They said it was the occasion that the church attendance was much greater the following Sunday, and it was the thing that needed to be done to break the ice.

I understand in those days the young fellows had to work on the ranches and go to school part-time.

Well, many of the boys didn't get to come to school or perhaps had a few lessons at home. There were country schools where they went for a while, but it was nothing in advance education by any means. When Father came here, the two previous principals had been run out of town by these young men who were in school. They made life so miserable for the teachers that they left, and Father had the same problems with them. Of course, they were practically grown men, yet they were still in school. They walked over the fence and knocked the panel of fence down. Father didn't like that and told them that it had to stop. After he had issued this edict, why, at noon when they came back, he was watching to see whether they all came in the gates. There were plenty of gates on all four sides of the schoolyard, but one student who was tall as Father–my father was over 6 feet– walked over the fence and knocked down a panel. Father probably had had a little feeling that he might do that because he provided himself with a bench close by. He was right there. He grabbed the boy by the collar and put him across his knee and spanked him. It was the most humiliating thing that could happen to a young man. The boy didn't walk over the fence anymore. They grew fond of Father because he taught them to play games. Being raised on ranches, they never had boys to play with.

You mentioned that you were born where Mrs. Norval lives now.

Yes. Father had bought the ranch, but the only ranch house that was on it was over on a gumbo flat, and when it was wet, it was a terrible place to live, so Father built a log house where we lived on the ranch. It was in 1901 that we moved to the McBride Ranch. Then a couple of years later–we lived two years in the log house–he built the framework house that still stands there. The Cummings family were our nearest neighbors. They were there before we moved. Alice and then later Bessie were the children we played with most as youngsters. We had lots of fun together.

Didn't your dad go into politics?

Oh, yes, he was very much in politics. He was a member of the House of Representatives. He was also in the Senate. We were always going to political rallies all over the country. Of course, everybody went to the political rallies because they were someplace to go, and they wanted to hear what the men who were running the state had to say. They were a great source of fun. Everybody had to bring their children. There were no babysitters. My first memory of dancing was dancing with Congressman Mondell when he was running for office. He stayed at our house, and we went and listened to a speech and participated in the dance. When Father was in the Senate, we were entertained at Governor Carey's home, and I played with their daughter's lovely French dolls.

❦❦❦❦

Wilma Fowler Wallace

1939-Present
From an interview with Nancy Tabb
In 2022, when 83 years old

German POWs and Sugar Beets

I was born in Madison County, Arkansas, September 13, 1939. It was in my grandparents' house–not a hospital. My parents were Olen and Ruby McChristian Fowler. We came to Wyoming when I was two years old. I had one brother, Les Fowler. He was two years younger than me.

My dad worked for his uncle, Cline Fowler, who had a ranch down on Piney Creek. We lived there for a few years. Then my dad leased a ranch down below Clearmont and raised Hereford cattle and barley and oats and sugar beets.

We lived four miles toward Arvada. It was called Big Corrals. Dad leased it from John Rice, who was killed in a plane crash. When that happened, they put all these places up for sale. Dad wanted to buy it really bad, but it sold for $50,000, and he didn't have $50,000. He had good credit, but he didn't have $50,000. Dad was raised by his grandparents, and his grandfather told him, "Don't ever go in debt," so he was afraid to buy it. Later, Dad kicked himself his entire life for that.

I remember during World War II Dad had German prisoners work for him. He had the German prisoners to top sugar beets. There was a camp in Clearmont where the prisoners stayed at night. Dad would get them in the morning in his big old beet truck and take them back at night. You weren't supposed to feed the POWs. They brought their lunch, but most of the farmers' wives fed them. I remember that there was a guard with his gun, but what he did all day was sleep on the cot in the shade by the beet field.

Their camp was right where the Catholic Church is now. I don't think there was even a fence there. The prisoners weren't a threat. They were a real addition to the community because they played baseball. Some of them were artists and musicians. My aunt and uncle, Joe and Rose Fowler, also had prisoners. Aunt Rose wrote to a lot of them after they left. They were devastated when they went home to their country in Germany. Some of them eventually became United States citizens. You see, they were brought here as prisoners of war during World War II. When the war ended, they didn't want to go back. They were treated very well here.

Have you ever read the book, *World War II: POW Camps in Wyoming*? It's all about the German prisoners that were in Wyoming. It is awesome. It's just amazing and so special to me because a lot of it I remember.

Dad would harvest the beets about the end of October or the first part of November. Of course, back then–this was in the 1940s–there was no fancy machinery. Dad had a truck and a tractor. The POWs used a big type of knife–a machete. They went along and pulled the beet out of the ground by hand. Then they had to pick the greens up and whack them off with the machete. Dad had a machine that when the prisoners threw the beets down on the ground, it that would pick the beets up, and a chute would load them into a truck. The men worked down a furrow all bent over. It was backbreaking work.

A lot of beets would fall off of the truck, so one job that my brother and I had was we would have to run along and pick those beets up. We picked up the beets and loaded them into Dad's beet truck. Then Dad would take the beets to Clearmont and put them on a big scale. It was right where that big tower is on the road to Clearmont. Then they would load the beets onto the train. The train went to Sheridan. I don't know if they ended up going to Hardin, Montana, or Worland, Wyoming. There were factories at both of those places.

I'm not sure, but they must have planted beet seeds. The plant had to be thinned just like you would when you planted a carrot because if the plants were really thick, they wouldn't grow big. They have a terrible odor. It was disgusting.

Dad also had Mexican fellows who thinned the beets. Dad had houses on the farm that they lived in. I know he paid the Mexicans because I have cancelled checks.

Dad, he worked so hard. I remember that he would take his beet truck and go to Clearmont. He would get manure and load it by hand with a pitchfork. Then he'd take his truck to the farm and unload the manure on the beet field by hand to fertilize it. Of course, he irrigated.

I have scrapbooks of my family working beets. I also have some of the tickets for when the beets were shipped that were signed by Mae Huson, who was a longtime resident of Clearmont then and Buffalo.

❦❦❦❦

David J. "Dave" Watt
1888-1988
From a KBBS Radio program
In 1975, when 87 years old

The Watt Family & a Stagecoach Stop

The Watt family left Scotland and came to Canada. It took them six weeks by ship to come across. They worked their way west into Canada and came to Ottawa and Toronto, two rather small towns in those days, and they obtained some land some six or seven miles away from a smaller town. They got it through the Canadian government.

Cullen Watt, one of the older brothers in the family, came to Wyoming before my dad [Peter C. Watt] did. He left home when he was a rather young man. I've heard the name of Omaha mentioned where he got a job with freight outfits that was hauling freight into what was then Territorial Wyoming. They were herding ox, and he was the night herder. He came into Wyoming in the vicinity of Buffalo with a freight outfit.

My father came the latter part of 1884. He was the youngest boy of the family. He worked for his brother and eventually took up a homestead of 160 acres in the Clear Creek valley which is now a portion of the home place. Cullen had land east of Buffalo and also obtained land at a later date down on Piney Creek. The land that my father took up as a homestead he proved up on in his own name.

Mr. & Mrs. Peter Watt's Wedding

After my father had filed on his land, he built a log house consisting of two rooms. Later, they built another room or two onto it. He got the logs up above Story along the base of the mountains. He cut the timber, made his own shingles, hauled them down, and got his house pretty well built as time went by. In 1886, I think it was, he went to Canada and married Margaret McConnell. Soon after their marriage, they left Canada for Wyoming. They came on the Northern Pacific Railroad that came in from the vicinity of Minneapolis. They got off at a stopping place for the train on the Yellowstone River somewhere in the vicinity of Custer, Montana. They had two four-horse out-fits to haul their loot home from the train. When they left Custer, Montana, they were 10 days on the road.

They camped out at night. This was in February. They set up a tent, of course–had a little iron stove to burn wood for heat. It was mostly all Indians. They seldom ever seen a white man. One night, when there was a blizzard, they were camped close to where there was Indians. One of the Indians managed to point to a small log cabin or building. Finally, they got the idea that he meant that they could use that, so they moved some of their sleeping equipment into that building. It had just one small window with no glass in it and no door, but it did have kind of a roof over it and logs on the side, so it provided some shelter in the storm. But they come up with something that they didn't anticipate as the days went by. They had the grandest crop of lice that they ever imagined.

When they lived on the ranch, one day a large group of Indians came along and set up camp close by. My mother was there alone and was pretty well frightened. They had a ladder that they could get up into the attic and stored some stuff up there, so she took the cat and her son and herself up in the attic and stayed there. My father was working about two miles away from home. He seen the Indians coming, but it took him a while to get home. They were friendly and were all around the house, but they didn't come in. When my father got home, why, he had to give them some sugar and different things they wanted. They always wanted something to eat. The next day they moved on. That was one time that she really was frightened.

The closest woman neighbor was approximately 10 miles. From Ucross to what was in those days the M.T. Redmond Ranch–the Marton brothers now own it–she was the only woman in the valley. The rest of them were bachelors. The land was all taken up by single men. Near the Redmond place was her sister, Mrs. Cullen Watt [Eliza Jane McConnell Watt]. That's where I was born.

My mother's family lived in a small community known as Eden Mills in Canada. There were five girls and two boys. One girl was already here before my mother came. Then my mother came here, and as the years went by another daughter, Rufus Copps' mother [Mary Ann McConnell Copps], came. The two boys were here for a period of time. In fact, five sisters and their husbands are all out at Willow Grove Cemetery now.

When the Wyoming Railroad finally landed in Clearmont, the produce that was picked up at Gillette was then transferred to Clearmont. That meant that the mail came to Clearmont. At that time, the stagecoach was set up to haul mail from Clearmont to Buffalo. When J.G. Oliver had that contract, the halfway house, as they referred to it, was where they changed horses. It happened to be at the Watt ranch. We seen a good deal of the people who came and went on the stagecoach.

Mother furnished the meals for them most of the time. That was quite a problem. One stagecoach come in at 11:00, she had dinner for the rest of us at noon, and the other stagecoach came in before 1:00 It was kind of like running a restaurant–get one bunch out of the way in time for the next. Anyway, with the aid of the women folks, Mother had help. In those days, when you could hire help, they took care of them, but in due course of time they moved on their way.

There were even two babies born there. They really didn't have any choice. They came on the stage and was fortunate to get as far as our house. When a baby was born, they stayed longer in those days then they do nowadays. They were around there for about eight days.

Ed Lawrence was a bachelor. I remember one day Ed was on the stage. They changed horses at the ranch. He pulled in and got off, and he was dressed a little different than he generally was. My dad said to him, "Ed, where are you headed for? You're all dressed up." "Oh," he said, "I'm going back East. I got tired of baking pancakes and frying eggs for myself. I'm going to see if I can't get a helper." Well, it wasn't too long until he came back with his wife and son. She had a son perhaps 4 or 5 years old. That's Charlie Lawrence, who is my age.

Regarding the train that came by the place–after the CB&Q [Chicago, Burlington & Quincy Railroad] had their road built, there was talk of the road somewhere along the present railroad to south as far as Casper. Isaac B. Smith, who lived in Cedar Rapids, Iowa, and his associates got interested and purchased a lot of land along Clear Creek. They contracted to buy it and keep it or turn it back if they didn't want it all. Eventually, they started a railroad, and in February of 1913, they laid the first rails at Clearmont. They built a portion of the road so that it could be used. As they got up to Ucross, that was the end of the road for quite some time. The end of the road was at the

Watt Ranch for some 18 months before they got more road built.

During that period of time we had a good many people coming in and filing on homesteads. When they got off the train at Watt's Siding, there was nothing there but a siding and a boxcar they used to put freight in and a small house that the agent and his wife lived in. We got an overflow of people needing help. It certainly did keep us pretty busy. The railroad got into Buffalo eventually. It runs in my mind that Isaac B. Smith announced the arrival of the railroad in the Town of Buffalo about 1918. Some 20 years later they announced their last trip, as they went out of business.

During the time that the Wyoming Railway was in business, Charlie Fieldgrove was hauling school children into Buffalo. During one of the severe winters and pretty much in the spring of the year, the highways were just dirt roads, and they became almost impassable for automobiles or trucks. Fieldgrove got permission from the Wyoming Railway to put iron wheels on his school bus, and he hauled the children from the vicinity of Ucross to Buffalo on the railroad. By this time, there were more families on the creek. The amount of children was no one concrete number but generally 10 to 15. When Don [his son, Don Watt] first went to school and was hauled in, they had a man that was hauling the youngsters to school in a cut down Ford—no top, just a windshield. They sat out in the open, you might say. Of course, he only had five or six, seven at the most to haul. They did have a schoolhouse for a while down on what is the Marton place. Our youngsters never went to school there. They were hauled into town.

I didn't start to school until I was 7 years old due to the fact that there were no schools on Clear Creek closer to our place than the one in Buffalo. They did eventually have a school in the Jim Murray house. Jim was a bachelor man with a two-room house. He built a lean-to on the north side to store his produce in. They set that aside and had a wooden table and a few chairs and a little piece of blackboard. We had school there for five months. That was my first school. The next year they built a small schoolhouse. We used the new schoolhouse for two seven-month terms of school. The third year there was five of us moved away, and they wouldn't support a school for one student, so my folks brought me into Buffalo to go to school. I started in the fourth grade in Buffalo and continued until I graduated in the spring of 1910. During that period of time, I was roomed and boarded wherever they could get a spot for me. Otis Miller, Charlie Lawrence, Clarence Gammon, Francis Mulholland, Ella Williams, Rose Bodan were in my class. Did I name Frances Fowler? And myself.

They had a limited amount of sports in the local school here. During the period of time that I went to school, there was no football. We did play quite a little basketball, and, of course, they had races and jumping. We made pretty much our own entertainment. There was quite a few dances and parties at the different homes. Somebody had a skating rink here for a while. We skated on Clear Creek, but it never seemed to be a very good proposition because the creek would overflow, and it would be rough. The young folks did skate on it, but it wasn't very good. Sometimes the City flooded a spot that we could skate on a little bit.

I was married October 6, 1915. She [Hazel Woodside Watt] was 21, and I was 26. We lived with the folks for perhaps a year or so on the ranch. My dad bought the place in Buffalo previously built by W.C. Copps. That's the house that my folks lived in. I operated on the ranch after the folks moved off for some 43 years.

My wife's family–the Woodsides–came to Wyoming in covered wagons. I believe it was 1894. I think she was 4 years old when she came to Wyoming. Her dad drove one of the stagecoaches from Clearmont to Buffalo when the railroad got to Clearmont when the CB&Q went into business. It wasn't until 1913 that the Wyoming Railway took over, and he drove one of its first stage outfits. Later, he got contracts from Buffalo to Kaycee and served on that for quite a long time. Then he got one from Sheridan to Buffalo. That's when they moved to Sheridan.

I was on the school board 18 years. It was all lady teachers except the principal. Bess Muir and her sister came here. They were not married in those days, and both taught in the school system here. Eventually, Bess got married and resigned. Several years later, we had a vacancy in the same field as she taught. She made application for it, and it was unusual that the board would hire a married teacher. After they found out that we made a deal with her, they got up a petition that we shouldn't employ her because she was married. But the board thought enough of her ability that we did hire her, and she went on to teach for quite a few years after that.

First National Bank Parade Wagon

Something happened that I'd like to tell. During the local County Fair in the parade Charlie Fieldgrove was here with his horses and wagon and his wife. Whoever was running the Fair business invited Wilbur Holt, Sr., Margaret Bowman, Charlie Lawrence, Bubbie Lott, Karl Walters, and me to ride on this wagon. Well, we pulled up on North DeSmet and sat there for quite a while before the parade got under way. Of course, we talked about everything from A to Z. We were going over which was the oldest houses in Buffalo and who the people were that owned them and one thing and another, and Wilbur Holt said, "You won't believe this, but I'm going to tell you something about one of my experiences. When I was first married, I didn't have much money. I didn't have anyplace to take my wife. We just lived wherever we could get a spot. I heard of a house in southeast Buffalo that was for sale. It's the house across the alley from where Voiles lives. I hunted the man up that owned that house and approached him about if he wanted to rent it. No, he didn't want to rent it. He wanted to sell it. He was leaving town. He said, 'Nobody wants to buy the house, and I don't want to go away and leave it. You wouldn't be the son of that drug store man down the street–Holt?' I said, 'Yes, I am.' 'Well,' he said, 'you look like a pretty good kid. I'll tell you what I'll do. I want $500 cash, but I haven't been able to get it. You give me $15 and move in and give me $15 every three months until you've paid out the $500. Then it's your house.' I said, 'I just happen to have $15.' That's about all I did have. I gave him the $15. Now you can't even buy a doorknob on a house for that."

※※※※※

Hazel Woodside Watt
1894-1989
From an interview with Pat Phillips

A Glimpse at Hazel's Life

I was born September 23, 1894, on the Woodside farm 12 miles out of Edgar, Iowa. We lived there until April 1898 when my dad decided to come to Wyoming. He had been out West before around Douglas and Orin Junction, so we started west with a covered wagon, a team of horses, a span of mules, and our belongings.

One day while the men were out hunting, a cloudburst came down off of the hill. We were camped near the creek. Mom [Lois Vandel Woodside] and Dell got the harness and things up in the wagon and saved them. My dad always tied the horses and mules to the wagon at night. One night someone tried to steal the mules. Just as the man came up to the mules, one of them brayed and woke Dad [Bert Woodside], so he caught the man. We traveled on and came to Douglas. We was going to stay there, but there was an epidemic of scarlet fever, so we went on to Buffalo. We camped for two days down on Clear Creek near where the ballpark is now.

My dad sold his outfit and got work on the Jack Moore Ranch. Mom and I stayed at the Occidental Hotel. The hotel was managed by Tom and Etta Smith. Their daughter, Hazel, and I were great friends from then on. We were there when the big flood came. The hotel had water on the lower floor, and the chairs and the tables were swimming around.

Then my dad got a job working for J.G. Oliver. He drove the stage between Buffalo and Clearmont for four years. Then he bought the Kaycee stage line. It was an all-day trip. He would change teams at Billy Creek and at Ono, where he had a roadhouse. The passengers could get their meals there. He carried the mail by way of Greub, Mayoworth, and then to Kaycee. He went in all kinds of weather, and the roads were not good. He would leave Clearmont at midnight when the mail arrived by train and bring it to Buffalo. The stage from Buffalo would stop and change horses. He kept the Kaycee route for eight years and then bought out the Sheridan mail route and had that for a number of years.

In 1900, we built our house in Buffalo. I started school that year. The grade school building burned down, so the grades were held in different parts of town. I graduated with the class of 1913 in the fall. That fall I taught a three-month school term at Box Elder. Spring of 1914, I taught a term at Kaycee, and spring of 1915, I went to work for the telephone company.

Mr. & Mrs. David Watt's
Anniversary

I married David Watt at my home in Buffalo on October 6, 1915. We went to the World's Fair in San Francisco on our honeymoon–was gone about six weeks and came back to the Watt Ranch, where we lived until 1958.

Two children were born to us–Donald, born on our fourth wedding anniversary October 6, and Lois, born September 16, 1923. They rode the school bus to school. When the roads were bad and were impossible, they fixed a bus on wheels that could run up the railroad track. The railroad was built as far as Watt's Siding. Then a stage and later a bus brought them on to town.

In 1919, the Nine Mile country was opened for homesteaders. A great number came in then on the immigrant train as far as the siding. They would unload the train and stay at Watt's Siding until they could get into Buffalo and then to their claims. Some had their own cooking utensils, but many nights we would have 15 or 20 extra for meals.

🌿🌿🌿🌿🌿

Fay Lawrence Waugh
1927-2021
From an interview with Nancy Tabb
In 2017, when 90 years old

Fay & May–Riveters & Cadet Nurses

Interviewer Nancy Tabb: Tell me about yourself and your family.

I was born in 1927 out on the ranch. My mother and father was Frank Lawrence and Margaret Greub Lawrence. They both grew up around here on farms. Mother's family lived out on Piney Creek. She was one of 17 children, so that was a big family. Daddy lived out on Clear Creek. There was only four of them. His family was Ed and Bertha Lawrence. Grandma Greub was a Hepp before she was a Greub. He was Jacob Greub. Dad's family came from Wales. That's where the Lawrences came from.

When did those families come to this area?

Right around the turn of the century in the 1890s. Grandma Greub was born in New York. They came by stagecoach to Miles City, Montana. It took them six weeks to come from there to Buffalo. They had to keep throwing things off, and they'd get attacked by Indians, but for the most part, they were friendly Indians. She said the Indians did take a lot of their food stuff–like salt. Then for salt they used gunpowder to salt their things. They had a cousin out on Piney Creek, and he encouraged them to come. He went to Miles City, Montana, to meet them, so they came down by stagecoach. On Thanksgiving our big thing was to go out to Grandma Greub's for dinner. The winters then would get so bad that we would have to tunnel into the house. The snow would be way up on the windows. In the summer, we'd have picnics out along Piney Creek because that was the Greub ranch for all those years. I don't remember Grandma Lawrence nor Grandpa.

Tell me about your home where you grew up.

It is eight miles out on Upper French Creek. Daddy's father died and gave the ranch to him and his brother, Red [Clarence W. Lawrence]. Charlie was a half-brother, and he was mad because he didn't get a part, so Dad sold his share to Charlie. Then they went to California to live for a while, but he didn't like it there. One day he said to Mom, "If you want to go with me, you'd better get packed because I'm going back to Wyoming." She said, "Just like that?" and he said, "Just like that." So they came back. Dad had this money, so he bought this ranch out on French Creek. That is where May [Lawrence Dillinger] and I was born in 1927.

What did your dad do for a living?

He was a little bit of everything. He loved to buy and sell stuff. Daddy was one of these guys that sometimes he was a millionaire, and sometimes we'd didn't have a pot to pee in or a window to throw it out of.

Would you describe yourself as obedient or mischievous when you were a little child?

Well, we were obedient, but we were kind of mischievous too. We lived out on the ranch. It was during the Depression, and we didn't see people. We were scared to death when somebody came. We were kind of like a bunch of puppy dogs. We ducked and hid under the porch until we knew who they were or what they were. We played a lot of funny things too. Daddy had made us a teeter totter. He cut down a tree and put a silver plate on it. We'd go round and round or up and down. When the city kids would come to visit us, to be ornery we'd stick them in the middle and then swing them around and knock them down. We had a playhouse about a mile from us down at Wilbur Williams' place. They only had the one child, so he was part of us because he didn't have playmates. Birdie Williams gave us a chicken house, so we plastered that with pages out of a wallpaper book. We didn't really have anything in it, but if those

Twins Fay & May Lawrence with Ray & Jean

kids would come, we'd make 'em pay a penny to get to see it–just ornery things. They always come back, so they must have liked it. We had lots of big rocks, so we each claimed a rock, and we had lots of apple trees, so we climbed trees. For toys we'd get a block of wood or cut pictures out of the Montgomery Ward for people because we had no real toys at all, but we were happy because we didn't know any better. We spent hours playing let's pretend. We had one radio that you could hear sometimes. Our telephone was on the wall. When it rang two longs and a short, it was our number, so we got to answer if everybody else on the line didn't answer. There was a couple of people that spent all their time listening because that was their entertainment.

Do you remember any really hard winters on the ranch?

Yes, the year May and I were born was a very hard winter, but, of course, I don't remember that. That was one reason we got caught out there and was born on the ranch. Mother had gone to the doctor just to be told that she was pregnant, and then she never seen a doctor again. It started to snow, and she thought, "You know, I'd better gather up the turkey eggs." One thing they made some of their money was with turkeys, so she'd been down all day gathering the turkey eggs. She wasn't due until May, so she thought she had plenty of time to do that. So she was out gathering up the turkey eggs and started having some pains. She said to my dad, "You know, maybe you'd better go get the midwife. I'm not sure, but I think I'm going to have a party today," so he got on a horse and went over the hill. She called to town to her doctor, and her doctor had tick fever. He, said, "I'm going to have to find somebody else, Mrs. Lawrence. You'll have to have one of your sisters help you if I can't get a doctor for you." So that, of course, took a while. Mother was real nervous. She knew that things were moving pretty fast because she had to go up and down stairs to get ready for the birth cuz that's where she's going to have the baby. That's where the beds were. She called Birdie and said "Birdie, will you come up here. I think I'm going to have this baby before my husband gets back." "Oh," Birdie said, "Margie, I'll be right up," so she walked up there which was about a mile and a half. When she got there, Mother said, "Here, Birdie, look at this book. You'd better look at it because I know this is going to happen before..." Birdie gave the book a throw and says, "I'm too excited. I wouldn't know what to do." Birdie looked up and seen some lights coming down the road, so she left the house and ran down to open the gates. It was a doctor coming. While she was gone, I was born. I was on the bed when the doctor came in. He didn't even take off his coat. He got to taking care of her and said, "Mrs. Lawrence, you've got another baby in here." That was the first she had any idea. Here she was a month early–nothing prepared–so they put us in little shoeboxes on the oven door with cotton around it. That's how we came into the world.

Where did you go to school?

The first two years we rode two and a half miles horseback on an old white horse called Old Mary. We went over to the Johnson Creek School. We went everyday whether it was snow or rain or whatever. Mother dressed us in every kind of clothes you can think of, you know, and we'd go over the hill to school. We had one room. There was nine of us in that school of all ages. Mrs. Ethel Connor taught us. May and I had our own language, so we didn't talk very good. She had a hard time trying to get us to learn all kinds of things. Mother couldn't even understand us. May and I just jabbered back and forth. Ray was the only one who could understand us. He could figure us out.

Of course, none of us had any money. If somebody happened to get a penny, we'd go downtown from school and buy a piece of bubblegum. Well, the person who bought the bubblegum got to chew it first. Then we would take turns, and everybody got to chew the gum. We didn't think anything about it–didn't bother us at all.

Do you remember your grandparents talking about the Johnson County Cattle War when you were a young girl?

You know, they really didn't because they lived out on Piney Creek, but I'll tell you the truth about it. Grandma Greub had all these kids. When Mother was 6 years old, she had three siblings that was younger than her. Grandma Greub got up one morning, and the fire wasn't going, and she couldn't imagine what in the world was wrong, so she rang the bell. They had a bell if anything was wrong. She said, "Kids find your dad. Something is wrong." They found him out in the chicken house. He had committed suicide. He thought he was going to be sued on water rights. He went out there and left her with all those kids.

Did you attend church as a family when you were young?

Not as a young family cuz we only had one car, and we lived in the country. The only time we ever went to church was when we'd learned our little pieces out in country school, and they let us say it on Christmas Eve at the Congregational Church. Mother liked the Congregational Church because her mother, Grandma Greub, helped bring that church to Buffalo, so we always went to the Congregational Church for years when we moved in town.

Tell me some of your mother's or grandmother's favorite recipes that you remember.

Favorite recipes–not really. May and I did so much of the cooking because Mommy was busy making clothes for us. People and her sisters would give her hand-me-downs, and she would make clothes out of the sacks, so May and I, we really had to do a lot of the cooking. I loved the smells of ironing and making bread when you come home on the horse at night and you were tired and cold. I can still remember those smells.

Do you own any family heirlooms?

Well, I think the thing that we have that I love the best is the little sheep wagons. Carl's [her husband, Carl Waugh] dad made them, and he had absolutely no tools like we have. He made them all by hand. After Dad Waugh died, Carl decided when he wasn't able to work anymore, we would make sheep wagons together, so we did that. They're real precious. Uncle Billy made a lamp out of a willow tree. It was a real crooked one. He threaded the light cord up through it. It's up at the cabin. Mother had a violin. I'm not sure where she got the violin. I know where she got the piano. Both Grandma Greub and my dad knew she wanted a piano. They went to this sale. Grandpa was on one side of the auction, and my dad was farther away, and they was bidding against each other and didn't know it.

May & Fay Lawrence

When did you decide that you were going to be a nurse?

At first, I was going to be a secretary because when May and I was freshmen in high school, this guy from Chicago brought these millionaire sons out here. There was nine of them, so they asked if May and I would work up there that summer–cook breakfast and go on the pack trips with the boys to help take care of the things–so we did. Of course, this one kid–we got kind of friendly. You know how kids do. You hold hands and think you're in love. Anyway, he said, "Fay, when you grow up, why don't you be a secretary? I'm going to take my dad's place, and you can be my secretary and sit on my lap," so I thought I wanted to be a secretary. Oh boy, that sounded great! But the only thing I ever flunked in school was shorthand. For some reason, that was just completely blank to me, so I decided that wasn't so good. When the war came along and they needed nurses, both May and I decided to cuz we knew Dad didn't have the money to send us to college. We thought, "Gosh, that would be wonderful." Our principal told us that there was no sense trying that because we weren't smart enough. I think we decided to just show him we were smart enough, so we went on to be cadet nurses in 1945.

How old were you when you left home to be a cadet nurse?

I was 21 when I got married to Carl. That was a few years later, so 18. We had to go to Helena, Montana, for our pre-med stuff. We was there for six weeks. The day we finished there, the war ended. We could hardly get to the station for people kissing and hugging you. Everybody had gone crazy, and you didn't blame them.

We was only 15 years old when we talked them into letting us go to California to work in an airplane plant. We said we wanted to do something for the war. Dad did happen to have an aunt out there, so they did say we could go out if we'd live with the aunt. We got on a bus–never been on a bus before–and we went out there. On the way out there, we stopped in some town, and to go to the pot you had to put in a dime. We didn't have a dime, so we crawled under. Who knew you had to pay to go? When we got there, we didn't know what to do. We looked for a bus to take us up to Aunt Nell's and couldn't find one, so we hired a taxi. Well, when the taxi guy found out we was a couple of kids from Wyoming that didn't know anything, he asked, "Would you like to see the movie stars' homes?" Of course, we did, so he took us all around. He turned off his thing when we got there. It costs $2.46 cuz I put it in my book. Aunt Nell just had a fit. She asked, "How much did that cost you?" and we said, "Hardly anything."

We had each other, so we never really got scared. We didn't stay with Aunt Nell very long because she had boyfriends that came in. The people upstairs told us, "Why don't you come up and live with us?" They were Italians and were more fun. We just loved them. He'd take his car, and we'd go down to the beach. We got to go to the Palladium to dance a few times–the big bands, Harry James band. Anyhow, that turned out wonderful. They put us to work the next day we got there at Lockheed, making parts for airplanes. You'd change stations every so often so you didn't get bored. Some days our ride wouldn't show up, or the thing was on strike, so we'd thumb our way to work. In those days, you didn't think about those things. We worked there all summer.

What made you decide to come back to Buffalo?

One time, when I was in high school–I think I was a junior–we was at a high school dance, and these two guys came in. They were dressed in uniform. One was a beautiful Marine thing. I was sitting up on the side wall, since I was one of the people that never got to dance. I think they call us wallflowers. Anyhow, there was about six or eight of us sitting up there. These guys looked around, and this one guy came over and said, "Would you like to dance?" I said, "Me?" and he said, "Yes," so we danced one dance. That was all, and he left. They never danced another dance–just danced one dance and left. I thought he was pretty nice, but I didn't think much about him because we had to finish school. The only reason I knew who he was is he had dated my cousin. I knew the name–Carl Waugh. Anyhow, he went back to the service, and I finished high school. Then the first time May and I came home on furlough, it was raining cats and dogs. It was during Fair time, so they called off the Fair, and everybody ended up down at the Occidental Bar that night. I had a date with a kid I was going with from Kaycee. I'd been going with him a couple of years off and on when he came to town, so we went down there, and here was all these people, and everybody was pretty well loaded. So Carl said to me, "Would you go with me tonight?" and I said, "Well, I've got a date, but I think he's getting pretty drunk, so yes." May and I went back to Montana to do more training. The next time we were on furlough, we came home. Carl had just gotten out of four years of being a Marine, and he owned a cafe. Well, we went downtown, and they was having free coffee at the Capitol Hotel. It was the cafe he bought. Him and this other guy, Bill Ploesser, went in together. So we went in there and decided to have a free cup of coffee. He came over and sat down beside me and asked, "Would you have a date with me?" So all the time I was home on furlough for a few days, we went together. That was the beginning. Carl was pretty wild when he came out of the service after four years. My dad said, "Fay, that is not going to last. If you make your bed, don't think you can come home cuz you can't. You make your bed. You sleep in it." I thought, "Well, okay." I loved the guy. We were married 62 years.

Tell me about your wedding.

My wedding was the same day I graduated from nurse's training. May and I were supposed to have a double wedding, but in March while we were at the TB sanitation, Jim came up and said, "May, we're going to get married," so they ran off and got married. I stood up with her, and he had a cousin that stood up with him. After they got married, Carl and I decided we'd do something different. We talked it over and said we'd have it the same day I graduate because a lot of people will come up from Buffalo to see us graduate. I had all the girls I'd gone to training with for three years. So we had a tea in the afternoon, we had graduation, and at 7:00 we had a wedding and a reception. It was wonderful.

How many different places have you lived in Buffalo?

Oh, quite a few. You see, when we came into town when Carl and I was married, we lived at the bottom of High School Hill in one of those four apartments. They called them the Kinsey Apartments. We lived in one apartment, and Jackie and Bill Perry lived in the one right next to us. They had just gotten married, and she had just gotten out of school. She didn't know how to cook. One night, Carl said, "Fay, this couple is real good friends of mine. They spent an awful lot of money down at the cafe. Let's have them up for supper." That was my first supper, and I really worked all day long just doing everything. Forty-five minutes before it was time for them to come, Jackie called and said, "I'm sorry, Fay. We can't come. We have company come." Of course, I bawled and cried, and I thought, "Well, let's see, what am I going to do?" Here I had all this food, so I went over and knocked on Jackie's door and asked, "Jackie, what are you having for supper?" She said, "The only thing I know how to cook is soup, so we got soup," so I said, "Would you like to come to our house for supper? We'll have soup before the first course."

We went out on Dad's ranch at the end of the Horn after that. When we come back in, we lived over in the south part of town. We lived at the Soldiers' Home for four years. After that, we lived down by the Catholic Church in that big tall house down there on Lobban Avenue. When the wind would blow, it was so cold we had to sit with our feet up under us, so Carl says, "Fay, we're going buy a lot and build a house," and that's what we did in 1960. The house came by train to Clearmont–just the pieces. We bought an Eldor House is what it was called–$7,900. Carl and his dad built that. We lived there for a long time.

What did you like to do in Buffalo?

Well, I took up golfing, but Carl couldn't golf because he had an arm that gave him fits all the time. I did that for about eight years, but it wasn't fun without my partner. Carl was into a lot of American Legion stuff, so we went to a lot of the Legion stuff and loved to dance. We bought a trailer and loved that until Carl felt like he couldn't really drive it anymore in the big cities, so we gave that up. Praise the Lord, he knew what he couldn't do. I drove out on the roads, but when we got to the cities, I'd always have to turn it over to him. He had macular degeneration at the end, so it got kind of hard. And we loved our church.

What do you think is one of the most important inventions during your lifetime that made life easier?

When we was on the ranch, of course, it was a refrigerator with ice. We had an ice house. We'd bring the ice in and put it in the refrigerator. Our telephone was on the wall with the rings, and you'd have to call Central. My sister, Jeanie, worked there. She was a telephone girl. Our first television–we was at the Soldiers' Home then. It was so snowy. You could hardly see anything, but you'd sit there and look. Well, I was going to say we were so thrilled when we finally got a bathroom because we would take our baths in front of the cookstove. All of us, we'd take turns. We finally got a bathroom and could put the water in there and just pull the plug and let it go and could go to the toilet inside. When we'd go out to the outhouse, I don't ever remember a roll of toilet paper. We used the old catalog. Of course, the pages we liked the best was the slick, colored ones.

Tell me who were some of the older people in Buffalo that you looked up to when you were a young girl.

Well, Vivienne Hesse, she knew everybody's birthday in town. We always got a birthday card from her. I'll never forget I was riding down the street when we had the Idlewild Cafe. We had the Idlewild–big cafe–for 17 years. At times, we employed 35 people at the Idlewild. We was that big. That was one of our livelihoods. Anyhow, I was driving down the street. It was about Christmas time, and I'd made all these plates with candies and cookies, and Miss Vivienne pulled out in front of me like she so often did. I had to slam on my brakes and had all this stuff on my seat. I could have killed her! Horrible, just horrible driver. She would come from Sheridan, and if the moon was out, she'd leave her lights off. She never did marry. "The top of the morning to you." That was her thing.

Mrs. Brehl, she lived up above Seney's Drug. When us kids were on the ranch, she would pay us 50¢ to pick a gallon of chokecherries for her. Mr. Brehl would come out to the ranch and always brought us hard candy when we hardly ever seen candy, so we thought he was just wonderful too. I guess I liked the Seney boys because we kind of worked for them off and on. They would let May and I and Jeanie clean out the 5-gallon ice cream containers because we would work for them. They never paid us. That was our pay.

🌿🌿🌿🌿

Minnie M. West
1872-1953
From an interview with Margaret Hushbeck
In 1937, when 65 years old

Minnie Remembers

I arrived in Buffalo, Wyoming, October 31, 1886, at the age of 14 by way of the Missouri Valley and Elk Horn Railroad as far as Douglas. My mother, sister, and I rode in a Concord stage night and day over very rough roads. Fort Fetterman was the first stop out from Douglas. We made short stops at many stations along the way to change horses and drivers most of which I have forgotten. However, I do remember that two stops were Brown Springs and Antelope Springs. Upon coming to this country, I went to a ranch at the foot of the mountains west of where Story, Wyoming, is now to live.

Mules, horses, and oxen–better known in the West at that time as bulls–were used for freighting purposes. When I first came to this country, I called them "ox teams," but people laughed at me, and I soon could say "bull teams" as well as anyone.

I came to Buffalo in 1888 to attend school. The first schoolhouse in Buffalo was a one-room log building that stood where the Hersey Apartments are now. Later, school was moved to a brick building. The brick school was built two years before we came here. The schools were not graded at that time or for some time after. Church was held on Sundays with Rev. J.P. Sparrow as minister. The courthouse was a log building later replaced by a brick building which was built in 1884 and is still there. The log courthouse was sold to Dr. Watkins, I was told, when the new one was built.

Now, let me give you a glimpse of Buffalo long ago. On the corner where the light office now stands was the Carwile brothers' saloon. From there on to the bridge were the Ben Hertzman tailor shop, *The Echo* newspaper office, R.P. Hopkins' store where the Idlewild Cafe is now. Scattered in among these were several more saloons and the Hasbrouck store, where JCPenney now is. Over this was a hall in which entertainments were held–dances and plays. Much of the talent displayed here was unusual for such a small town.

On the east side of Main Street, Conrad had a general store, where the Creamery now stands. Also, on this side south of the creek were Speckbacker's meat market, Ray Pick's livery stable, Jacob Webber's shoe shop, Holt's drug store, C.P. Organ's hardware store–later owned by Munkres and Mather–Frank Eldred's horse and saddle shop, and Sam Lung's laundry. Two more saloons occupied places there–Joe Sharp's saloon where the Gamble Store is now and Jensen's just across the creek in the building now occupied by Swan and Pate. North of this was the Jones and French furniture store, Round's livery barn–afterwards owned and run by Mr. James K. Potts–and Steve Farwell's stationery store and Robert Foote's store where the Jack Meldrum's Texaco service station is. Both north and south sides could boast a millinery store. The United States Post Office has changed from one side to the other and one building to another so many times that it would be useless to follow its wanderings. There was a bank, several law offices, two or more blacksmith shops, a roller skating rink in an old building that stood on the corner of Main and Fort McKinney Streets where the new brick hardware store and lumber company is now. Buffalo's first greenhouse was owned and run by Herbert Saul on the property known since as the Ed Metcalf home.

The Congregational Church is in about the same place as it was then but has been rebuilt and enlarged. The Episcopalians met in the dining room of the Murray Hill Hotel now known as the Stockman's Hotel. The Catholic Church has been moved about a block from its old site and a new building erected.

Some of the early lodges in Buffalo were the Masons, the Knights of Pythias, and the Odd Fellows.

Buffalo did not have a water system as we now have when I first knew Buffalo. Water was 25¢ a barrel, and to attain this a flag was hung. Ed Hill drove the last water wagon in Buffalo.

The graveyard was first placed on top of the hill north of the Congregational Church in the east part of Buffalo south of Clear Creek. The bodies–all but one–were later moved to the present site of Willow Grove Cemetery. The one that was never moved was the body of Bill Booth, who was the first and only man, as far as I have heard, officially hanged in Buffalo. He was hanged for the murder of a man known as Dutch Jake, who lived southeast of town a little ways.

The winter of 1886 and 1887 broke up the large cattle industry. It was a very severe winter, and much of the land along the creeks had been taken up by new settlers who built fences. Many of the cattle drifted against these fences and died.

In the spring of 1887, land was bought from Ed B. Chaplin, and the fairgrounds was built. The first fair was held in September of that year, and Territorial Governor Thomas Moonlight attended the first fair at Buffalo.

Through legislative influence, Fort McKinney was abandoned in 1895.

Robert R. "Bob" Winingar
1925-2018
From a Hoofprints of the Past Museum presentation with Sandy Dixon*
In 2002, when 77 years old

Winingar Family History

Interviewer Sandy Dixon: I've always wondered where the name Winingar came from.

Winingars came to this country in 1722 and lived in Virginia and South Carolina. From there, they kind of started moving west. Ohio was the next place and on to Iowa. My granddad, John Wilson Winingar, was born in 1851 in Virginia. Grandmother was Martha Cowman. She was born 1855. There is no record that I know of where they were married. They apparently didn't stay too long at any one spot as they came west. I had uncles born in Ohio and Nebraska–also one in Kansas. From Kansas they came to Cheyenne.

My granddad was a carpenter in Cheyenne for quite a while. A guy named Phillips on Bear Creek hired him to come up to the Spang place. They came to the Ono area, which is three miles from this place where Phillips brought 1,500 head of horses with them. He sold horses to the Army at that time. They said if any one of the buyers wouldn't purchase by noon, they passed the jug around, and in the afternoon the same buyers bought the horses they wouldn't buy in the morning. That's when my granddad saw the Red Cliff Ranch up there, which he said was always going to be his home. So they moved my grandmother to Ono, which was a stage station on Steel Creek. Grandmother was postmistress there from 1889 to 1890 something. Then the post office moved to the ranch from Ono, but it was still called the Ono Post Office until it was abandoned in 1895.

Didn't the Winingars settle on Horse Creek?

Yeah, Horse Creek, which is about a mile and a half north from the original homestead. The Lazy XT brand was originally registered to my grandmother in 1886. My grandfather was a carpenter more than a cattleman. The kids–they kind of put us to cows. He built houses up and down Powder River–Cash's house, the big white house at the Willow Glen, and the house at Greub. He also built flumes and various bridges. I understand that if he was up at the ranch, rather than riding a horse down here to Kaycee when he was working, he'd walk back and forth. My uncle, Fred, was also a walker, but he trotted a lot. One time, my grandfather bet someone here in Kaycee that if that guy didn't ride his horse hard, Fred could beat him to Buffalo walking.

What were some of the ranches that were up in that area?

Ed Simmons had a homestead up on the end of the Horn, and Edgar Simmons had the one right on Steel Creek. McWilliams was cousins of my dad. Roe Brock had the Hammond place down there. Greubs were there then. Greubs were probably one of the original settlers in that country. Johnny Greub came up from Texas with a Texas trail herd and settled there. The Spangs were there. They was right below the Upper Willow Glen Ranch. When I was a kid, you could see an old foundation of a house. There was a tunnel dug from under the house to a draw maybe a quarter of a mile away. I often wondered why it was there.

My great-granddad, One-eyed Tex, lived up in there someplace.

There was a spring called Tex Springs south of the old lower Hammond place. I presume that it was Tex Shirk all right. I don't know if that Shirk Springs was named after his homestead was there.

Member of the Audience: When you go down Gammon Creek to North Fork, there is an old cabin part way down in there. My dad said it was the old Foster cabin.

Well, these two brothers–they cut pitch posts on the mountain and drug them down because at one time they had a fella up there cutting posts. They went up to take him groceries or something. About a 100 yards in front of the cabin there was a dead grizzly bear, and they knew something had happened. They looked in the cabin, and the cabin was tore up, and the grizzly bear had died. He had a butcher knife stuck in his ribs. The fella in the cabin, he was dead. With one door and no windows he shot the bear. That's when the fight started. Both of them lost. Apparently, all he had was a single-shot 12-gauge shotgun, and the barrel hit him in the head.

One time when I worked for Crow Gordon, I was staying in the cabin and working on the screen door. We had a little porch in front. There was some lawn chairs sitting on it, and something upset a lawn chair. I looked, and here come a black bear into the cabin. I didn't know whether to make it to the rear door or what. We had a little yellow Lhasa Apso dog. She was laying under my bed, growling, so I just yelled, and the bear run out of the cabin. I went to the door. It was moonlight, and he hadn't went very far from the cabin. I shot up in the air, and he left, so I went back to bed. About two seconds later, he was back on the porch. I yelled and screamed, and he run. I went to the door and was going to kill him this time, but I missed him. Anyway, he run away, and I never saw him again. The fella that was there after I was up there working for Crow–the bear was bothering him too. We had a 50-gallon drum up there for trash. The bear kind of tipped the oil drum up and had his head and front legs in it. The guy shot through the oil drum. He said he thought he hit the bear, and sure enough he had. My oldest son, Bobby, and I found it after we moved up there. He was out in the timber just a little ways dead.

Your dad played music.

My dad [Jesse Winingar] played the piano, yes. My granddad played the violin. Grandmother painted pictures. I'm not sure how many pictures Dad painted. There was a long while he painted, and then he quit. In later years after he kind of retired, he

Occidental Hotel
Pen & Ink Drawing by Jesse Winingar

started again. They were his better pictures, and he sold many of them. They are all over the country. He drew a lot of pen and ink sketches. Dad always said he went to that art school [Chicago Art Institute]. He said you had to draw a cup and a rose before he ever went there. He had the ability to draw before he went there.

When did your dad go to World War I?

Him and Henry McWilliams went to Sheridan to join the cavalry. They wasn't taking anybody, so they joined the Marine Corps and went to Paoli, Pennsylvania. They were still there when the war was over. That's where my dad met my mother [Adeline Winingar]. He came back home after the war, and then went back and married Mother, and she came west. She had never been west of Philadelphia and stayed here the rest of her life. Dad rode for Lou Webb at the Hat Ranch in the summertime at the cow camp, and Mother went with him. They had a big gray horse. Dad had ridden him a time or two. Whenever he fed him in the morning, he would always come to Mother. She wanted to try and ride him, so Dad said, "Okay." I guess she rode him day in and day out up there with not a bit of trouble. Charlie Brown came along one day and asked, "What the hell are you doing letting that woman ride that horse?" and Dad said, "They are getting along fine." Charlie said that the horse killed the last man. Apparently, he got along fine with Mother, but he couldn't stand to be around a man.

Tell us the story about Charlie Brown at the mailbox.

When they lived at the ranch was just before I was born. At the Greub Road down there we had a big mailbox because everybody got their mail, catalogs, and whatnot in this mailbox. It was on four posts. My granddad had built it. It was about 3 feet square. Apparently, one night, Charlie Brown came from Buffalo, going back to Webb's. He was a little, shall we say, under the weather. He got past the mailbox there aways, and he either fell off his horse and passed out or else got off and went to sleep. When he woke up the next morning, the sun was coming up, and the mailbox was between him and the sun. He thought it was a man standing there, and he emptied his six-shooter at the mailbox. All the folks' Christmas presents from Montgomery Ward was in there. Towels and dresses and shirts were full of holes. Mother wasn't too happy.

Did your folks go to Dance Hall Flats for the picnic?

Yeah. Fourth of July picnics everybody in the community gathered up there at the Hat Ranch at what they called Dance Hall Flats. I know my granddad would rather fish than eat. He would come over a day or two ahead of time and catch a lot of fish. That was the fish fry and the dance.

Tell us about when he caught Uncle Lee at the barn.

That's when he was first married to my mother. They came over to Sackett's, where Crow Gordon is now, and they had an old car of some kind. They came around the corner past where the barn is yet, and they see this wheat flying out the door. They stopped to see what it was. It was Lee Sackett. He was maybe about 4 or 5 years old, and they asked him, "What are you doing?" Lee said, "Oh, these SOBs around here don't think I do anything." I guess he was showing them he could work.

What about Johnny Craig?

He had originally worked down in Midwest when the oilfields first started up and made quite a bit of money for them days. He bought a tractor and a new wagon and put some machinery on, went to the Bighorns, and was going to make a fortune mining gold. From assessment holes and mines he had dug, him and a few with experience probably reached 1,000 feet into the ground but no gold. He had a cabin there on Doyle Creek. That was about the time the dude business started. Dad and Uncle Harry [Winingar] was going to have a dude ranch, so they was building that big cabin up there. They was going to take pack trips up to the cabin, stay a while, and come back. That was also during Prohibition. John had a still or two up there. Various people said my dad had one, but I think he was kind of the middleman. I don't think he had a still. From the kitchen into the big living room there was one door. We joked about it later. We always wondered why that door wouldn't open. Johnny Craig had a couple of stills but not right by that cabin—one down Doyle Creek and various places that I don't know nothing about—but I know that they made whiskey up there.

Wasn't Tex Raper up there during Prohibition?

He was young then. They had to go someplace, so they let Tex kind of take care of stuff because they figured if the revenuers caught him, they wouldn't do nothing to him because he was young. Somebody come by and told him, "Tex, the law is over there at Hazelton, and they are coming this way," so Tex left. That was in the winter. He walked from there to Ten Sleep, caught a ride to Worland, went to Casper, and then back up the Hole-in-the-Wall. I guess there wasn't a soul looking for him.

What about Scrap Iron?

We had quite a few horses they was corralling one time, and we had an old stud. He was a steel gray horse—pretty one called Scrap Iron. You could corral the horses—everyone but Scrap Iron. You couldn't get him into no corral. They tried and tried and come in for supper. They told Dad they just couldn't get him. Dad said, "Well, you ought to shot him," so the next day here come the horses. Dad said, "Where is Scrap Iron?" "We shot him," which they did.

When did you join the service?

I tried to when I was 16, and they wouldn't let me in. When I got to be 17, the folks signed for me, and I went into the Navy, which was in the later part of 1942. I went to boot camp in Farragut, Idaho, and from there to San Francisco. They put us on some kind of–Lion Six was the name of it. They took all of our Navy uniforms away from us and give us a rifle and pack and a helmet, and we wore a Marine uniform. They sent us down to the islands, and we operated radar is what our business was. Well, I got to griping. I joined the Navy, not the Marines. The enlistment I was in was from 17 to 21. When I turned 21, I reenlisted in the regular Navy. From then until I got out in 1949, I was on a ship all the time. When I went overseas the first time, I was on an old freighter–lift ship they called it–with Navy crews and Merchant Marine crews. The top speed of a lift ship was six knots at the best full out. There had been a Jap sub trailing for three days. Of course, we couldn't outrun a submerged Jap ship. About the next day, I was on watch on the gun deck up in front, and there was a merchant seaman with me. We were supposed to watch different directions, and he said, "Look out! Here it comes!" I said, "What?" A torpedo had disappeared from where we could see the water that close to the ship in front of us. Apparently, it was a sub, and he had one torpedo left because there was never another one. We was going as fast as we could. There was another–that's when I was in this half-way Marine outfit. We was operating the radar station. There was two of us on watch at all times. The radar would call out the signals and give you range and see where they was going, and there wasn't much going on at all. Theoretically, the world is supposed to be at war. At that time, we had been issued Thompson submachine guns. Nothing else to do, so we were cleaning our guns. Mine was laying on the table in front of me. This other guy was setting with the radar machine with his gun pointed at the door. Three Japs came in, and they didn't have any guns. I think they intended to surrender, but this guy just pulled the trigger on that submachine gun, and that was the end of that–about the end of me too. That was about the extent of my excitement.

Did you get married before you came home?

I came home first and then went back. Then we got married [Virginia Albidrez Winingar]. It was in Arizona. To this day, I don't know why I got out of the Navy. I was guaranteed four more years of duty at the closest station to my hometown. That would have been Sheridan. I should have done it, but I didn't.

*Supported in part by an award from the Wyoming State Historical Records Advisory Board through funding from the National Historical Publications and Records Commission (NHPRC), National Archives and Records Administration. Original recording provided by the Hoofprints of the Past Museum in Kaycee, Wyoming.

Belle Elgin Young
1898-1983
Talking to a Group of Students with Clare Johnson
In 1972, when 74 years old

Elgin Lime Kilns

I want to talk to you about things when I was a little girl. They started burning lime about the time I was born up until the time I was 12. Buffalo was a very small town. All freight had to be brought in by team and wagon–most of it from Rock River. That was before the train came to Clearmont.

While cement may have been manufactured and been in use in bigger places, there was none in Buffalo. All the mortar that was being used in the early days–or practically all of it–for the library and high school was made from lime mortar. There wasn't even paint. Most of the insides of the building were what we call whitewashed. It was just this same lime mixture thinned down to like paint would be today. It was white. You had no variety. Whether color could have been added to it or not, I don't know. It wasn't just Buffalo that used this lime. They came from all over the county and sometimes out of the county to get it.

Charlie Sisters was the first man to burn lime in this county. He had a home about, oh, four or five miles from Sisters Hill on Dry Canyon Creek. There was a beautiful spring there. He had two kilns right there and a nice home. I don't remember him. He must have taught my father [Walter Young] before I was old enough to remember any-thing about it. He taught my father all that he knew about burning lime. We were right at the foot of Sisters Hill.

We had two kilns up in this canyon at first. Later, we had kilns much closer to our house. There were two other families that tried this burning. They were over on the North Fork of Crazy Woman. To show you how tight the economics were–they were five miles further from town than we were, which made it a longer haul. Even that little distance they could hardly make a profit. Also, we had hordes of lodgepole pine grow-ing right close to the house and a very short haul. If we went up Sisters Hill, we could get all we wanted, and we got it free. You had to dry the trees. So we had that advan-tage–a closer haul and all the wood we could possibly burn at hand. It took lots of it because in an intense fire like that even a good lot burned rapidly. He used lodgepole pine hauled from around Elgin Park. We didn't have to pay stumpage for the dead trees, had better ground to log it off, and could get wood cheaper than our neighbors. They tried it and couldn't quite make it.

My guess is that Dad started about 1898. We had two kilns up in the canyon. We shot rock out of the cliffs, which was an awfully hard job, as there was no air compres-sor drills at that time, and we had to drill by hand.

Cannon's lumberyard north of the courthouse sold our lime for us on commission.

If I remember right, we got 45¢ a bushel, and the lumber company took 5¢. I suppose there was a pound in a bushel. We sold every bit of lime we had. It was all sold right away. There was quite a demand for it.

I was old enough to haul lime to the old high school on the hill and to the library. Frank Madison had the contract for the high school. The red sandstone was quarried on Dad's homestead and the white sandstone on Dry Kelly Creek.

In a letter from my brother he tells, "It was a long day to haul to Buffalo. I was old enough to make the trip. I think it took me at least 10 hours. Now, that's in and out by the time I got my dinner. Dad would never let us carry a lunch. He insisted that we have a hot meal, so we ate in a restaurant, which we enjoyed very much because people didn't get out a great deal in those days."

What some people do not understand is that the lime we burned was molten hot lime. When this lime was burned, it just looked like white froth. You only added water and sand. That was your mortar because there was no cement here. Lime took the place of cement. You put it in a big kettle if you were mixing a lot of it. Then you poured cold water on it. It just boiled and bubbled like a geyser. Then you added your sand just like any cement you wanted to use. We learned to be very careful not to get around that lime because you could get burned awful quick. I have no idea what made it do that because, of course, cement is cold. But that was boiling hot even after you added your sand and made your mortar. That's all there was to it. If you were mixing it to paint the inside of rooms, you simply mixed it with no sand at all, and it was just a steaming hot paint. It did rub off, but it had its advantages.

I was up at our old homestead a year ago. The building was there and the bathhouse. My father had built a bathhouse and put a bathtub in it. He wanted a long one so you could almost swim in it. We'd float in the bathtub, and as soon as we got out of it, he had a bath. Most of our buildings were made of stone put together with this mortar and were plastered inside and out. Of course, they were good and warm. We had a good stream of water coming down this canyon that flowed right past the house. He put a fireplace in the house and a big water tank in there. It was our task when we got home to fill that tank and start a fire in the fireplace. The walls of the buildings–the stable, the granary, and the bathhouse–are still standing as well as any mortar that was ever mixed, and there was never a bit of anything in them except the lime.

We quit in 1914–burned one kiln of lime, and that was all. That was because cement started coming in. It was much nicer to use than lime and probably cheaper. There was just no demand. When we first started burning lime, we burned kilns with a capacity of eight bushels. As the demand dropped off, it went down to three bushels.

You might like to know something about the kilns. They were a circular wall put together, of course, with lime. They were about 12 feet in diameter and circular like a silo except for the opening of the firebox. Inside the kiln it was 3½ feet of granite bricks. Three feet above that was where you put the wood in, so it would probably be

Lime Kiln at Sisters Hill

8 feet. To assure that it was level, there were big granite slabs laid across with airholes in between so that there would be a draft so the ashes would fall through. The walls of the kiln were about 2 feet thick and made of granite. An arch was built through the center. You see, the firebox run straight through, and this arch was built so that the lime wouldn't get down into the wall. The flame fell through the holes, but the rock never fell in. The lime never touched the coals. The firebox was about 3 feet high and 3 feet wide.

We brought the timber in on the wagon in long logs, and we sawed it about 6 or 8 feet. It was a two-man proposition once you got the lime in there. You filled that kiln so that it was rounded over like a bridge. You had to put a keystone in and get this out to get it just right, but that held out these bushels and bushels of rock. There was a barrier down about the fire level that held that up there. They put the rock to burn in from the top. An arch was built through the center.

The cliffs that you see out there at the edge of Sisters Hill are all limestone. They blasted that out and hauled it down in wagons. This pink limestone was lying on the flat ground. You could go out and dig it out of the flat ground and burn it. It was right there protruding–very available. You had to take a crowbar or something to get it out. Sometimes we'd burn that pink, but it was an inferior lime. You'd load that on a wagon or what we called a road devil. That was just a good deal like a sled only you could use it on rough ground and in dry weather.

It took about 72 hours to burn a kiln of lime. It was kept burning continuously for three days. It would be red hot. It was kept hot enough that you could see the flames sweltering up through this 12 feet or more of rock because on the level it would be 12 feet. Then it was heaped up so much as we could carry it off just about the shape of a rock that you put in the kiln to burn. Now, they really weren't rocks but just chunks. Among the prettiest sights I've ever seen is when they let the fire die down. That lime rock was almost clear and a beautiful rose or vermilion color. At night when it was dark, that was glowing.

The only trouble we ever had was that it burned my dad's mustache once. It burned part of it off, and he had to shave the rest. He felt very naked without it.

We had an old Englishman–Sam Perry had come here. I don't believe he ever worked for anyone but my dad when my dad was firing. He had a cabin up there in Elgin Park, and he would walk down when we were burning lime. He would take the night duty, and Dad and the boys would burn it in the daytime. Well, he was quite a recluse but a fine gentleman and a very well-educated man. He was the only babysitter we had. He came whenever the folks were in town. This was a very small community, and my dad was called for jury duty again and again, and Sam Perry would come down and stay with us.

❦❦❦❦

Hazel Myhre Zigweid
1912-1992
From an interview with Patty Myers
In 1982, when 70 years old

Johnson County Life

Interviewer Patty Myers: Let's talk about your life in Johnson County. Did you have chores at home when you were a kid?

We had to take care of the chickens, gather the eggs, go get the cows. As we got a little older, we had to help milk, of course. We were busy. Youngsters all had to carry in wood and coal and carry out ashes. This sort of thing, you know–we all had to do that. It was just expected of us.

Where did you get your water?

We had a well, yes. The first well had an old tripod and used a rope to pull up the bucket with the water. The well wasn't very deep. The water would stand a half hour or so, and there would be an oil scum on it. A little later, Dad dug another well farther down in the other direction, and we got much better water, and he put a pump in there.

Were you dry farmers?

Yes, definitely. No irrigating–it depended on rain and snow. Some years we had marvelous crops, and once in a while we got hailed on, and some years it got too dry. Our food was very plain. On the dry farm we had no way of watering a garden. Mother would always put one in. Sometimes we would get some garden out of it, and sometimes we wouldn't. If I remember right, we grew mostly wheat. Kaycee had a flour mill, and we'd take our wheat in and get the winter's flour.

Dad never did work out for anyone. We just got by with the wheat crop and a few cattle. I think Dad had 640 acres. He got the 320, and then they had the additional. A lot of that was grazing land. I suspect he had, oh, maybe a 100 acres in grain.

What did you to for entertainment?

Oh, we made our own fun–played with our cousins. Of course, we always did a lot of riding or went just walking–hightailed it all over the hills all day long and had an apple in our pocket.

Did you have trouble with rattlesnakes?

Not many. Although, you know, I can remember there was a school section east of our place. In the summertime, we'd run the cattle out there, and it was us kids' job to go get those cattle at milking time. I remember we would kill rattlesnakes with rocks– even our bridle reins. We'd take our bridles off and whack the snakes with it. Now, looking back, think how dangerous that was! I guess there were lots of rattlesnakes then, but we thought nothing of it.

Did you have a doctor?

We didn't know what a doctor was–really we didn't. If we had a cold, Mother gave us lots of lemonade. Mother didn't believe in aspirin–just mentholatum ointment or camphor oil–and she'd put mustard plaster on our chests and give us sage tea to drink– bitter awful stuff. Dad was not a drinking man, but he always had whiskey in the house for a hot toddy for bad colds. Of course, Mother would put about a teaspoon of whiskey in hot lemonade for we kids. You know, I don't think I ever saw a doctor until I started having my babies.

What did you have for transportation?

Well, we had horses and wagons. In the wintertime, we had a sled, of course, al-though we didn't often have enough snow to use it. When I was about 8 or 9, Dad got a little Ford with a box on the back. He put a spring seat from the wagon on back there for us to ride on. I got dumped out of it once. We had a little gulch to cross to get into our place. There were rocks in the bottom. He went across there one time, eased across, and he couldn't make it up, so he backed up and hit it and out tumbled kids.

How did you meet your husband?

He [Edward Zigweid] homesteaded out in the Antelope Basin. I was 11 years old, fell for him then, and never got over it. I was only a kid to him because we weren't married until I was 22. Of course, in those years we would have been married before that, but there wasn't any money. We dated four years before we got married–then got married on a shoestring.

We went to Antelope Basin to homestead when we were married. We were married just 10 months when Frances was born. She was 3 years old when we left the home-stead and moved out to the Ritter ranch. We just leased it for two years. Then we bought it. We kept the Basin place for pasture. I sold that about a year ago. I kept it all that time.

Did you raise a garden?

Oh, goodness, yes–great big garden. Of course, the first two years we were down there, we had to have summer hired help for the haying. The neighbors exchanged help to some extent. Oh, we had our meat and eggs and milk and garden. One day just for the fun of it, we averaged up our grocery bill. For the first two years it was $12 a month for coffee, sugar, the staples like that.

When we went there, we didn't have one thin dime. We had had a garden at my folks' the year before, and I did an awful lot of canning, and we had three great big open barrels full of pork we had put down–old-fashioned, sugar-cured, you know.

I have been so tired I just couldn't even sleep when I went to bed with six little kids. There was five years when I was never without diapers to wash. Frances was 5½ years old before we had anymore. Then we had three just bang, bang, bang.

So many times when we just had to have help, I worked out in the hayfield until the kids got old enough to do it. When Ed went out to irrigate, I'd go out to milk four or five cows. Cream was important. We sold cream. That paid our grocery bill for a long time. We had our own chickens. We sold eggs. We didn't have a great big bunch of chickens–oh, 50 or 60 just a small farm flock.

Was there a sense of community where you lived?

Yes, it held you together, that's right. Frances went away to nursing school in Alliance, Nebraska. The teacher there told us you could pick out the kids who had gone to rural school. They were always the best students. But I can't remember anything outstanding about our area. Things just went along day to day.

❦❦❦❦

We hope you enjoyed these unique stories
as much as we enjoyed sharing them with you.

Nancy, Dolly & Jonette

❦❦❦❦

Index

www.ingramcontent.com/pod-product-compliance
Lightning Source LLC
Chambersburg PA
CBHW082144120626
46553CB00010B/2754